FREEDOM'S
FURIES

Also by Timothy Sandefur

The Right to Earn a Living (2010)

The Conscience of the Constitution (2014)

The Permission Society (2016)

Cornerstone of Liberty:
Property Rights in 21st-Century America (with Christina Sandefur) (2016)

Frederick Douglass: Self-Made Man (2018)

The Ascent of Jacob Bronowski (2019)

Some Notes on the Silence (2022)

TIMOTHY SANDEFUR

FREEDOM'S FURIES

How Isabel Paterson, Rose Wilder Lane, and Ayn Rand
Found Liberty in an Age of Darkness

LIBERTARIANISM
.ORG

Print ISBN: 978-1-952223-43-3
eBook ISBN: 978-1-952223-44-0

Cover design: Derek Thornton, Notch Design.
Cover images courtesy of the Ayn Rand Institute and the Herbert Hoover Presidential Library.

Library of Congress Cataloging-in-Publication Data

Sandefur, Timothy, author.
  Freedom's furies : how Isabel Paterson, Rose Wilder Lane, and Ayn
  Rand found liberty in an age of darkness / Timothy Sandefur.
        pages cm
  Washington : Cato Institute, [2022]
  Includes bibliographical references and index.
ISBN 9781952223433 (paperback) | ISBN 9781952223440 (ebook) 1. Libertarianism—United
States—History—20th century. 2. Paterson, Isabel—Political and social views. 3. Rand, Ayn—
Political and social views. 4. Lane, Rose Wilder, 1886-1968—Political and social views.
5. Libertarian literature. 6. Liberty—Philosophy.
  JC559.U5 .S26 2022
  320.51/2—dc23   2022029038

Printed in the United States of America.

CATO INSTITUTE
1000 Massachusetts Ave. NW
Washington, DC 20001
www.cato.org

To Jason, Scott, and Matt
parce qu'ils étaient eux-mêmes, parce que c'était moi

CONTENTS

▶ Introduction ◀

In May 1943, British Prime Minister Winston Churchill stood before a joint session of the U.S. Congress to say that the war against the Axis powers was likely to become more grueling in the days to come. Nevertheless, he insisted, the Allies would prevail "by singleness of purpose, by steadfastness of conduct, by tenacity and endurance."[1] As members of the audience headed home that night, they might have spied the dome of the newly dedicated Jefferson Memorial, its fresh white marble inscribed with the words, "I have sworn upon the altar of God eternal hostility to every form of tyranny over the mind of man." And they might have paused before the windows of a bookstore and seen inside three volumes on the theme of freedom, all written by remarkable American women: *The God of the Machine* by Isabel Paterson, *The Discovery of Freedom* by Rose Wilder Lane, and *The Fountainhead* by Ayn Rand.

Brilliant, independent, and wedded to principles that placed them firmly in the minority of American society, these writers would later be described by journalist William F. Buckley as the "three furies of modern libertarianism."[2] And it was true; although other important books on freedom were published at that time by such writers as Albert Jay Nock, Garet Garrett, and F. A. Hayek, these women—at times friends, at other times fiercely estranged—were at the forefront of what became the libertarian movement as we know it today.

They had much in common: idealistic, eloquent, childless career women, devoted to literature and ideas and opposed to what they saw as the rise of tyranny in the United States. Yet they also had striking differences. Lane and

Paterson were westerners by birth, products of the 19th-century American frontier, with only the most meager formal schooling. Rand was a college-educated Russian immigrant. Lane was a world traveler who witnessed the Armenian genocide and the rise of fascism in Albania; personal friend to such prominent figures as Herbert Hoover and Dorothy Thompson, she chose to go "off the grid" and grow her own food rather than submit to the regimentation of the New Deal. She would do her best writing as the silent half of a partnership with her mother, Laura Ingalls Wilder, in a series of novels for children. Paterson was nostalgic, cynical, prone to fits of anger that eventually alienated most of her closest friends, but simultaneously the author of long, elegiac, evocative novels about love. Rand was solemn, rigidly principled, a generation younger than the other two, an atheist who harbored a deep sense of reverence and weighed every word she wrote so carefully that it took her an entire day to write a single letter.

Hovering over their lives were two overwhelming cultural influences. The first was a rebellion against so-called bourgeois values, which in the literary world took the form of a movement called the "Revolt from the Village." Its chief representative was Sinclair Lewis, whose best-selling naturalistic novel *Main Street* gave voice to his generation's frustration at the stifling conformity and ordinariness of small-town America. The second influence was the New Deal, the drastic change of American society presided over by the 12-year presidency of Franklin Delano Roosevelt. The "furies" would do their best to provide an intellectual resistance to this trend—in which they saw parallels with the conformity and dullness Lewis raged against. Their critique of the New Deal—rooted in principles of classical liberalism that dated back to the 18th-century Enlightenment and beyond—laid the intellectual groundwork for a revival of interest in economic and personal liberty that is today typically called libertarianism. But their work was not backward-looking. They saw themselves as resolutely modern. And it was not primarily about politics or economics. Instead, they sought to advance a principled case for individualism as a moral and cultural phenomenon—a value they thought precious and rare, and that they saw as threatened both by the stifling traditionalism that Lewis's literature satirized and by the collectivist trends of fascism and communism around the world and in America.

The word "furies" is perhaps more apt than Buckley realized. According to Greek myth, the Furies (or Erinyes) were spirits who pursued and punished people who committed great crimes, including treason and the breaking of oaths. In his *Oresteia* trilogy, the playwright Aeschylus depicted the Furies hunting down Orestes, son of Agamemnon and Clytemnestra, who murdered his mother for having killed his father. The cycle of revenge continues until at last Athena—goddess of reason—intercedes. From now on, she declares, crimes must be punished according to law, through a fair trial at which the prosecutor and the defendant will each have the chance to persuade the jury. The triumph of rational persuasion is symbolized by a name change: Athena dubs the Furies the "Eumenides," which means "the Gracious Ones."

Through an era of economic catastrophe and worldwide war, Paterson, Lane, and Rand resorted to persuasion in support of the principles of freedom and the rule of law that they hoped would secure forever the American dream they so loved. There certainly is a grace in that.

▰

No book could hope to encompass the full range of these three writers' work or their relationships to one another. Instead, this volume is meant as a portrait of a brief time in the lives of three outstanding American intellectuals. Fortunately, each has been the subject of superb biographies. This book could not have been written without the painstaking scholarship of Paterson's biographer Stephen Cox (author of *The Woman and the Dynamo: Isabel Paterson and the Idea of America*), or Lane's biographer William Holtz, whose *The Ghost in the Little House* initiated controversy when it detailed the extraordinary degree to which Lane was involved in composing her mother's *Little House* novels. I have also drawn much support from Christine Woodside's fine *Libertarians on the Prairie*. Ayn Rand's legacy is also a locus of debate, not only between admirers and detractors but even among her followers, whose differences are reflected in their attitudes toward different biographies. Anne Heller's *Ayn Rand and the World She Made* has been my primary support, but I have also relied on other published sources and drawn my own conclusions. Another invaluable source has been Brian Doherty's *Radicals for Capitalism*, outstanding for balancing complex stories about fascinating, sometimes difficult personalities with an explanation of the often complicated ideas they advanced.

My discussion of the economic and political aspects of the New Deal draws consciously on the free-market tradition of which Paterson, Lane, and Rand are such an important part. The reason is not only because I find it the most persuasive account of that era, but also because viewing the New Deal from the opposite perspective, as many writers have done, results in a distorted view of the work of all three women. It is not possible, for example, to understand why Lane viewed the Agricultural Adjustment Act as an assault on the rights of farmers if one overlooks the way it prolonged the Depression and worsened the plight of the poor. One cannot fully appreciate Rand's novel *The Fountainhead* without understanding why she viewed compromising politicians such as Wendell Willkie as inept defenders of capitalism. Unfortunately, although a powerfully argued and deeply researched free-market critique of the New Deal now exists, mainstream historians continue to disregard much of it. In learning about this subject, I am indebted to my wife, Christina Sandefur, on whose knowledge of Depression-era history and economics I have constantly drawn.

I first became interested in Rose Wilder Lane in 1996, during a trip through South Dakota with my parents, thanks especially to my mother, Julie Sandefur, a lifelong *Little House on the Prairie* fan. I am grateful also for the assistance of Scott Beienburg, Stephen Cox, Stephen Eide, Robert Hessen, Matt Kelly, Shoshana Milgram Knapp, Paul Matzko, Joanne Platt, Craig White of the Herbert Hoover Presidential Library, Christine Woodside, Jenniffer Woodson, and Jeff Britting of the Ayn Rand Institute. I am especially indebted to Eleanor O'Connor of the Cato Institute for her assistance. Any errors herein are, of course, entirely my own. This book was made possible by a grant from the Prometheus Foundation, and I am grateful to Craig Biddle, Annie Vinther Sanz, and Carl Barney for their help.

If America should now turn back, submit again to slavery,
it would be a betrayal so base, the human race might better perish.

—Isabel Paterson

This country isn't finished; it is still here and it will survive. . . .
Our great asset is intangible, it is in the minds and reactions of millions.

—Rose Wilder Lane

Mankind will never destroy itself. . . .
Nor should it think of itself as destroyed.

—Ayn Rand

Isabel Paterson, known to readers as "I.M.P.,"
was among the nation's most important literary journalists
and first among equals of the "Three Furies."

1

The Bookworm

One Sunday in September 1924, subscribers to the *New York Herald Tribune* were treated to a brand-new feature: a weekend books section full of bestseller lists, reviews, and commentary by some of the nation's leading intellectuals. Among the other items was an inconspicuous gossip column devoted to the publishing industry. Titled "Turns with a Bookworm," it began almost shyly: "A debut is so embarrassing." The unnamed author, who called herself simply "I.M.P.," affected "a casual air," then reported on a few forthcoming titles and chatted about Joseph Conrad and Henry James before signing off with "That will be all for to-day, thank you."[1] It was a mild introduction for a woman who would become one of the most influential thinkers of her age.

The initials were those of 38-year-old Isabel Mary Paterson, author of short stories and two little-read novels, who had been recruited to the *Herald Tribune* just a few years before by its literary editor, Burton Rascoe. Then only 30, Rascoe was a self-made man from Oklahoma, who started as a paperboy, then joined the writing staff of the *Chicago Tribune* while still in college, before moving to New York in 1922. That was the year he first met Paterson, at a lunch where he immediately took "a violent dislike" to her on account of her abrasive manner. "Nearly every time I opened my mouth to express an opinion," he recalled, "Mrs. Paterson flatly and emphatically expressed a contrary opinion, in a way to imply that I was a little better than an idiot."[2]

That meeting had been set up by Paterson's agent, who was trying to sell some of her stories. Rascoe was not interested. But he was looking to hire a secretary and was surprised when Paterson appeared at his office a few days after their lunch, saying she wanted the job. The dark-haired, nearsighted Paterson was smart, diligent, and willing to work for whatever Rascoe offered.[3] So he agreed, and he rapidly came to admire her intellectual independence and extraordinary breadth of knowledge. They remained friends forever after.

Being friends with Paterson was no easy accomplishment. Described by William F. Buckley as "intolerably impolite, impossibly arrogant, [and] obstinately vindictive," Paterson was brusque and intimidating, with a literary knowledge that ranged from medieval philosophy to the intricacies of monetary policy.[4] Most of that knowledge was self-acquired. Born on a forested island on the Canadian side of Lake Huron on January 22, 1886, she had only two years of formal education before leaving school at the age of 11. Her father was an alcoholic ne'er-do-well who squandered what little money he earned, and her mother was a long-suffering, hard-working woman whom Paterson loved dearly. When the family's house was destroyed by a forest fire, they moved to Michigan, later to Utah, then to the Northwest Territories of Canada. In short, Paterson was a product of the American frontier, with vivid memories of witnessing Sioux and Blackfoot ceremonies, living in log houses, watching covered wagons on the plains, and viewing the long fingers of railroad tracks as they reached farther and farther west. Her childhood left a permanent mark on her, one that lasted throughout her decades living and working in Manhattan, during which she delighted in correcting minor details about prairie life that eastern novelists got wrong.

Few details are known about her early years. Around the age of 18, she took a job in Calgary as secretary to Richard Bedford Bennett, a railroad executive who later became prime minister of Canada. In 1910, she married a man named Kenneth Paterson, but the marriage lasted only a few weeks before the couple separated. According to her biographer, Stephen Cox, Paterson kept details of the marriage to herself "with impenetrable secrecy."[5] He likely suffered from tuberculosis, and the exact date of his death is unknown. Despite their breakup, they never officially divorced, and Paterson kept his name, referring to herself as "Mrs." for the rest of her life.

Months after her marriage failed, she moved to Spokane, Washington, where she was hired by the editor of a newspaper called the *Inland Herald*. Soon she was composing editorials and short stories, first for the *Herald*, and, when it failed, for the *Vancouver World*. That paper gave her a column titled "What Every Woman Knows," which she signed I.M.P., the initials she would make famous. Her closest friends called her Pat.

In 1912, she moved to New York, where she got a job writing for the *New York American*, and a few years later for *Hearst's Magazine*. She also wrote two semiautobiographical novels, *The Shadow Riders* and *The Magpie's Nest*, which were published in 1916 and 1917, respectively. Both were love stories featuring plucky heroines from the Pacific Northwest who pursue independence in an optimistic land of opportunity and enterprise, and both received respectable reviews, including some modest praise from the nation's foremost book critic, H. L. Mencken. But neither was a great success. Around that time, Paterson moved to San Francisco, but how long she stayed or what she did while there is unknown.

She was living there when the United States entered World War I—an incident that brought an end to the era of opportunity and progress that historian Walter Lord later called "the Confident Years, the Buoyant Years, the Spirited Years."[6] And it seems likely that Paterson was horrified by the wave of ultranationalism and repression that the war ushered in, especially by the military draft. Twenty years later, in the run-up to World War II, she would denounce conscription as the greatest of all political evils, and the definitive act of a tyrant. It embodied the premise that the individual belongs to the state; that his life— and, inevitably, all his other rights—exist solely at the discretion of government officials. Because the public remained severely divided over American involvement in the war, the Wilson administration drafted some 2.8 million men to serve, and a decade afterward, the Supreme Court would make the philosophical implications of conscription clear when it held in *Buck v. Bell* that if government could conscript men into the army, it could also sterilize "unfit" women against their will.[7] No individual rights, it seemed, were sacred against the power of the government.

Along with compulsory servitude, the federal government also adopted other measures to regiment the American populace as part of what sociologist Robert Nisbet later called the country's first experiment with totalitarianism.[8] The Lever Food and Fuel Control Act imposed an extensive rationing regime that controlled distribution of wheat, rye, sugar, meat, and other commodities.[9] The Espionage Act and the Sedition Act made it a crime to protest against the draft or to use "disloyal, profane, scurrilous, or abusive language about the form of the Government of the United States." Federal and state officials enforced these laws by arresting more than 150,000 Americans, including writers, speakers, political leaders, and ordinary citizens who opposed compulsory military service or the nation's participation in the war.[10] The Supreme Court upheld these prosecutions on the grounds that criticizing the draft was akin to shouting "fire" in a crowded theater.[11] These and other Wilson administration policies, wrote Nisbet, created an "atmosphere of outright terror in the lives of a considerable minority of Americans."[12]

On the battlefield, the Great War seemed to mark a shift in the history of the world. Humanity had never witnessed violence on such a scale—killing some 20 million people in unprecedented ways, such as submarine warfare, gas attacks, and aerial bombardment—all accompanied by a new willingness on the part of governments to transgress traditional limits of law and decency. The horror was so immense, observes author Geoff Dyer, that it transformed perceptions of the past: "Life in the decade and a half preceding 1914 has come to be viewed inevitably and unavoidably through the optic of the war that followed it," he writes, and indeed a powerful nostalgia gripped those who survived the war—a haunting sense that some ineffable and beautiful thing about the world was now so utterly transformed that it could never even be adequately described to anyone too young to remember it.[13] The degree to which this affected Paterson can only be inferred, since her exact experiences during World War I are unknown, but she later remembered being so appalled that she had "a nervous breakdown. . . . I thought I really would die, only not soon enough."[14] She would forever after nurture a sense that the country she had known and loved had vanished.

Thus, although she loathed to admit it, Paterson was a member of what literary scholars call the Lost Generation—that group of writers born between 1880 and 1900 who were "lost" beneath the tides of industrial transformation and the so-called war to end all wars. The writing of Lost Generation authors is characterized by alienation, disillusionment, a retreat from noble-sounding sentimentalism, and a preference for colloquial and skeptical language instead of the rhetoric of social improvement common in the Victorian era.[15] Paterson detested the phrase "Lost Generation," sometimes expressing the wish that its members would stay lost,[16] and the term is, indeed, misleadingly romantic in tone. Far from being lost, that generation was enormously creative and energetic. Yet the term holds some validity, for the cultural and economic changes of their youth did create America's first "generation gap" and led to a radical shift away from the optimism and moral confidence that had characterized the turn-of-the-century decades.[17]

Paterson was as much a part of the Lost Generation as one could be without becoming a Paris expatriate, as many of her contemporaries did. Her later novels are pervaded by an atmosphere of melancholy bewilderment at the disappearance of the bright age of cheerful resilience she remembered from childhood. "What a country this used to be," she would often say.[18] Born the same year that the Statue of Liberty was dedicated, she could never forget the astonishing industrial and scientific progress she had personally witnessed— such as seeing her first light bulb at the age of 16. (She had left it on all night because she was afraid to touch it.[19]) Only a year after that, the Wright brothers flew the first airplane at Kitty Hawk. It was a time when technology was bursting through the boundaries of time and space—and people seemed to take it almost as a matter of course that all the old barriers could now be crossed. "Nobody here got much excited about the invention of the airplane at the time," she remembered, not because people didn't care, but because their attitude had been "of course people could fly. . . . In this country at that time any one could do anything; the sky was no limit."[20] Paterson herself joined in the spectacle: in 1912, while working as a reporter, she rode along with pioneer aviator Harry Bingham Brown to set what was then a world altitude record of 5,000 feet. Aviation was "a lot more fun in the early days, when you sat on a six-inch strip of matchboard and held onto a wire strut, and looked down past your toes at nothing but the earth," she wrote years later. That was why, instead of "Lost Generation," she preferred to call it the "Airplane Generation."[21]

Yet within a short span of years, that opportunity and boldness disappeared like a dream—"sunk without a trace," as she put it in her autobiographical novel *If It Prove Fair Weather*. In that book, her alter ego, the melancholy, slightly bewildered main character, Emmy, observes that she feels like an Indian waiting for the buffalo to return, not realizing that they are already extinct. Emmy quotes to herself some lines by T. S. Eliot: "But where is the penny world I bought, / To eat with Pipit behind the screen?"[22] Paterson herself would live the final three decades of her life haunted by that sense of a lost world—one in which the virtues and beauties she had taken for granted were swept away by a vulgar and uninspiring new conception of modernity.

▰▲▰

By 1920, Paterson was living in Connecticut, working as a secretary to the sculptor Gutzon Borglum, famous today for carving Mount Rushmore. She left Borglum's studio two years later but cherished her memories of the opinionated, iconoclastic artist, whose personality, like his work, was immense, bold, and vehemently American. Borglum had been recruited five years before to create a monument to the Confederate army generals on the side of Stone Mountain in Georgia. A decade of tedious and bitter infighting with the Stone Mountain Memorial Association ensued. "Sketches and models leaned up against one wall," Paterson wrote in her column a few years later, "and every while or two he would drop whatever else he was doing and dash down to Washington to get a bill passed in favor of the Memorial, or to Atlanta to rally the home guard."[23] At last, the sculptor became so fed up with the political bickering and meddling with his work that he hacked his plaster miniatures to bits and threw them from the top of the mountain.[24] A sheriff's posse chased him out of the state for destroying what the association claimed was its property. (The work was completed by another artist.) It was a characteristic gesture for Borglum, who was rumored to have also melted down the life-size figures of angels he had sculpted for a New York cathedral, after church officials complained that they looked too feminine.[25]

Paterson admired Borglum's dramatic defiance and his rigid commitment to his artistic vision. Long afterward, she would fondly recount stories of her time with him. The experience left her certain that "there is such a thing as genius," and also that she herself "did not possess it."[26] Why she left his studio is not known, but in 1922, she embarked on a career at the *New York Tribune*, which a year later merged with a competitor to become the *Herald Tribune*. After the merger, the new owners promptly fired Burton Rascoe, the man who had just hired her, but his successor offered her a weekly column in the new books supplement. She would write it every week for the next quarter century.

The *Herald Tribune*, or "the *Trib*" as loyal readers called it, was destined to become one of the great newspapers in the United States. Elegantly designed, meticulously edited, and intelligently written, it was considered "the newspaperman's newspaper," and that sophistication was an important part of "Turns with a Bookworm."[27] Although it appeared in a weekly books section, "Turns" was not a book review column, but a literary news bulletin that Paterson wrote in a gossipy yet sophisticated style that combined personal squibs about writers, news about the publishing industry, and her own opinions on literature and current events. She used the editorial "we" instead of calling herself "I," and interspersed her comments with ellipses that gave the column a spontaneous, lighthearted quality even when she wrote indignantly on matters of principle. Its layout sometimes gave the sensation of reading a news wire, and Paterson often quoted from publicity materials that publishers sent her. One column, from July 7, 1934, exemplifies the form:

> The best new book on the Virgin Queen is Milton Waldman's *England's Elizabeth*; but here is still another, J. E. Neale's *Queen Elizabeth*, which has solid merit. . . . Yes, there is too such a place as Humptulips. . . . We've been there. . . . You might prefer Snoqualmie, Kitsumcallum, or Supzzum.[28]

That particular column went on to discuss a new play by Edward Hope, a novel called *You Can't Be Served*, a box of chocolates that an author had sent to Paterson, and her views about the gold standard.

Paterson's boss at the *Trib* was an Alabama-born literary scholar named Irita Van Doren, who took over as editor of the book section at the age of 35 and remained in that post for four decades. Van Doren's politics were "radically opposed" to Paterson's, and their relationship was sometimes rocky during the quarter century they worked together.[29] Yet Van Doren let Paterson be herself and never tried to censor her.

Paterson's extraordinary breadth of reading and busy schedule of book parties and literary luncheons made her a brilliant raconteur who could incorporate into her columns everything from Shakespearean allusions to personal reflections on the Talmud. She celebrated the poetry of Elinor Wylie and the comic novels of P. G. Wodehouse, denounced the psychoanalytic theories of Sigmund Freud and the modernist prose of Gertrude Stein (which she likened to "chopped alfalfa"[30]), and conversed in print with every novelist from Sinclair Lewis to Margaret Mitchell. Eventually, her column became a must-read for literary Manhattan. Paterson, wrote one author in 1937, "probably has more to say than any other critic in New York today as to which book shall be popular and which shall be passed by."[31]

She lived in Manhattan's Hell's Kitchen neighborhood, then a gang-infested working-class area, until she moved to Connecticut in 1934. She despised movies, enjoyed cooking, relished boat rides, and kept company with a cat named Brainless while she wrote, typically late at night, when the city had settled down. With her wide reading and no-nonsense air, she could be intimidating and at times downright misanthropic. She was the "Goddess of Common Sense," wrote critic Basil Davenport, who thought she "contemplate[d] the world with a mild impatience that people can make such a stupid mess of things."[32] But others did not find her impatience mild. One colleague said she had a wit "so searing that no rubber plant ever grows again in a room through which she has trod."[33] Another remembered how her sharp witticisms sometimes alienated fellow writers. "Screwing up her antic, monkey's face, strangely beautiful because of the intelligence of her lively eyes, she would let go her shafts, each tip poisoned."[34] Still another recalled first meeting her while she was on the phone: "She was facing me with steel-grey eyes, sharp, penetrating, vital. I thought she looked a bit austere. She was addressing the telephone in a most pained and pointed manner. She was saying, 'Why in God's name don't you give me the number I asked for?'"[35]

Regularly described with terms like "acidulous," "caustic," and "waspish," she was sometimes ferociously stubborn, even when she was obviously and confirmably wrong—a habit that worsened as she grew older.[36] Rose Wilder Lane once told Ayn Rand about an argument she'd had with Paterson over whether rosebushes could grow in the shade beneath trees. Paterson insisted they could not. The pair were then sitting together on Lane's patio, beside a maple under which a rosebush had flourished for years. But even when Lane pointed this out, Paterson angrily maintained that it was impossible. It was, Lane concluded, a case of "an irresistible force meeting the immovable rosebush-under-the-tree."[37]

▰▲▰

When "Turns" first appeared, Paterson could not have known that a new and perilous age was on the horizon. The United States, under the leadership of President Calvin Coolidge, was a prosperous nation of 114 million people, with a rapidly expanding economy that would grow by more than 40 percent during the decade. The end of World War I had brought an era of seeming prosperity. Politicians and economists began to speak of a "New Economic Era," in which the old principles of economics simply did not apply. A technological revolution was bringing automobiles, telephones, and radios within the reach of ordinary Americans and enabling young people to escape the small towns of their birth. The 1920s were the first time in which more Americans lived off farms than on them. The advent of machinery and drastic improvements in the standard of living were freeing many Americans who, had they lived a century earlier, would have been occupied trying to eke out a living, to instead seek lives of complexity, sophistication, and profundity. The result was an upheaval of traditional values—and, for many, the embrace of ideologies that filled the space once occupied by religion.

The ideas of Karl Marx, Charles Darwin, Sigmund Freud, and Friedrich Nietzsche were spurring a rebellion against society's prevailing values among both intellectuals and idealistic college students who were repelled by what seemed to them the vulgar and shallow culture of Middle America, with its sexual repression, jingoism, censorship, Christian Fundamentalism, prohibition of alcohol (which became federal law in 1920), and what would later be termed "consumerism." The Jazz Age was producing an artistic transformation that spurned the Victorian styles of previous decades and expressed the dreams and fears of a new, youthful era. It was, Paterson later wrote, a time when young midwesterners "yearned for 'distinction' and identified it largely with exotic adventure." They railed against what they called "puritanism"—"a handy though vague enemy"—and disavowed the moral and aesthetic standards of their elders for little reason other than that they were old. "Anything that had been accepted yesterday must be rejected today; nothing could be enjoyed for its own sake."[38] This clash between urban and rural, between traditional simplicity and the dangerous, even antisocial possibilities of the new age, became one of the definitive themes of Isabel Paterson's life. It was the fight over "Victorian" society—or what came to be pejoratively termed "bourgeois" values—and it reached literary circles in the form of a movement that critic Carl Van Doren—husband of Paterson's boss Irita—called the Revolt from the Village.[39]

The first stirring of that revolt came in 1915, when Edgar Lee Masters published *Spoon River Anthology*, a collection of poems profiling and satirizing the characters of a fictional small town. The book proved so influential that Paterson likened it to the archangel Gabriel; it "waked the Middle West" with its trumpet.[40] Earlier writers such as Mark Twain and O. Henry had viewed the American small town with nostalgia and a good-natured indulgence toward its residents' foibles, but Masters's book imagined it in darker terms, as populated by alcoholics, bankrupts, religious hypocrites, and the ghosts of lynching victims.

Four years later, it would inspire Sherwood Anderson to publish *Winesburg, Ohio*, a book of stories featuring the bizarre and neurotic characters of another midwestern village—characters Anderson called "grotesques." The powerful critic H. L. Mencken raved about Anderson's book, calling it "so vivid, so full of insight, so shiningly life-like and glowing," that "nothing quite like it has ever been done in America."[41] It was a massive success.

But the most important Village Rebel was Sinclair Lewis, whose novel *Main Street* became a blockbuster in 1920. Born in 1885 in Sauk Centre, Minnesota (population 1,695), Lewis started out with plans to become a Christian missionary but abandoned his faith while at Oberlin College and transferred to Yale, where he took up creative writing. He published almost a novel a year after 1912, but it was *Main Street* that brought him national fame. A penetrating exercise in naturalism and satire, it drew a damning picture of the dull, anti-intellectual atmosphere that young writers of the day sought to escape. Mencken called it a "masterpiece" that expressed "the essential tragedy of American life," and Paterson—who first met Lewis in 1914 when he was working for a New York publisher and politely rejected her novel *The Magpie's Nest*—agreed.[42] *Main Street*, she said, was the book whereby "American letters became competently autonomous, competently self-critical and superior to the opinion of Europe, regardful only of American standards."[43] Sinclair Lewis "*is* America," she thought. "He is uniquely, completely, representatively American."[44]

Set in a Minnesota town called Gopher Prairie, *Main Street* tells the story of housewife Carol Kennicott, who vaguely longs for a life of significance above the dismal engagements her neighbors consider worthwhile. After graduating from college, she marries a doctor named Will, viewing his work as important and hoping it will bring her a degree of social standing and sophistication. But her ennui only grows, and her husband and friends begin to regard her restiveness with suspicion. "Why can't you take folks as they are?" Will demands. "What you want is a nice sweet cow of a woman," she shoots back, "who will enjoy having your dear friends talk about the weather and spit on the floor!"[45] Carol comes to call the mundanity of life in Gopher Prairie—with its petty gossiping and ostracism—the "village virus."

Repulsed at the feeling that she is "being ironed into glossy medioc-rity," she tries to rebel in various ways but learns that there is really no way out.[46] "In a passionate escape there must be not only a place from which to flee but a place to which to flee," writes Lewis—but Carol has nowhere to go, either literally or spiritually.[47] When a bookish young tailor named Erik arrives in town, she finds herself drawn to him, and he to her. She feels foolish being attracted to a man so much her junior, but she cannot help it. "If it were some one more resolute than Erik, a fighter, an artist with bearded surly lips," she tells herself. "[But] they're only in books. Is that the real tragedy, that I never shall know tragedy . . .? No one big enough or pitiful enough to sacrifice for."[48] She loves Erik's poetic soul and urges him to escape Gopher Prairie. "Go!" she cries, parodying the famous words of Horace Greeley: "Young man, go East and grow up with the revolution!"[49] Erik does leave, but soon abandons his dream of becoming an artist and ends up living in obscurity.

Meanwhile, Carol endures the "village virus" until she can stand it no lon-ger. Telling her husband "I have a right to my own life," she packs her things and leaves for Washington, DC.[50] There she finds happiness and liberation—until Will arrives and persuades her to return to Minnesota. At first hopeful that things in Gopher Prairie will be different from what they were before she left, Carol swiftly discovers that nothing has changed, and she no longer has the strength to fight. Resigned to a life of quiet desperation, she stares out the window at the "silent fields to the west," knowing that "a hundred generations of Carols will aspire and go down in tragedy devoid of palls and solemn chant-ing, the humdrum inevitable tragedy of struggle against inertia."[51] In the end, the drabness so perfectly symbolized by the town's Main Street swallows her up entirely.

Not since *Uncle Tom's Cabin* had a novel hit American readers with such force.[52] Much of Lewis's appeal lay in his astonishing skill at caricature and at reproducing the idiomatic speech of ordinary people. Loaded with perfectly chosen detail, his sentences were honed to such precision that they ridiculed while maintaining a seamless illusion of straight-faced objectivity. At its best,

Lewis's narrative voice disappeared entirely, allowing his targets to fall on their own faces, in passages such as that in which Carol, in anger, "shot up out of bed, turned her back on [her husband], fished a lone and petrified chocolate out of her glove-box in the top right-hand drawer of the bureau, gnawed at it, found that it had cocoanut filling, said 'Damn!' wished that she had not said it, so that she might be superior to his colloquialism, and hurled the chocolate into the wastebasket, where it made an evil and mocking clatter among the debris of torn linen collars and toothpaste box."[53] The effect of such photographic specificity was to capture banality like a specimen under a glass. As Paterson put it, Lewis's writing derived a "repellent force" from a certain "savagery, [a] furious Swiftian disgust at the meanness of humanity itself."[54]

Yet for all its bleakness, there was passionate conviction at the novel's heart, which exploded in a virtual tirade in Chapter 22. The passage begins by listing Carol's favorite writers—they include Edgar Lee Masters, Sherwood Anderson, and H. L. Mencken—and describing how they make her feel about life in Gopher Prairie. There are "only two traditions of the American small town," she concludes. According to one, "the American village remains the one sure abode of friendship, honesty, and clean sweet marriageable girls," and according to the other, the small town is a cartoon world where kindly, grizzled veterans sit playing checkers at the general store. Neither reflects the reality she knows, one in which the villagers think "not in hoss-swapping but in cheap motor cars, telephones, ready-made clothes, silos, alfalfa, kodaks, phonographs, leather-upholstered Morris chairs, bridge-prizes, oil-stocks, motion-pictures, land-deals, unread sets of Mark Twain, and a chaste version of national politics." Will might be content with such a life, but Carol, and "hundreds of thousands" of others—"particularly women and young men"—are not.

The more intelligent young people (and the fortunate widows!) flee to the cities with agility and, despite the fictional tradition, resolutely stay there, seldom returning even for holidays. The most protesting patriots of the towns leave them in old age, if they can afford it, and go to live in California or in the cities.

The reason, Carol insisted, is not a whiskered rusticity. It is nothing so amusing!

It is an unimaginatively standardized background, a sluggishness of speech and manners, a rigid ruling of the spirit by the desire to appear respectable. It is contentment . . . the contentment of the quiet dead, who are scornful of the living for their restless walking. It is negation canonized as the one positive virtue. It is the prohibition of happiness. It is slavery self-sought and self-defended. It is dullness made God.

A savorless people, gulping tasteless food, and sitting afterward, coatless and thoughtless, in rocking-chairs prickly with inane decorations, listening to mechanical music, saying mechanical things about the excellence of Ford automobiles, and viewing themselves as the greatest race in the world.[55]

Moments like this merit the conclusion of Lewis scholar Mark Schorer that *Main Street* "seemed to characterize most strikingly a new national mood of self-criticism and even of self-disgust."[56] The book's very title soon became a symbol, representing the militant folksiness—the aggressive populism and dull, nativist conformity—that seemed to dominate much of the cultural and political landscape, and that reached its most horrific manifestations in the Ku Klux Klan and fascism. A dozen years later, the vigilante groups that burned Depression-era shantytowns and chased away their inhabitants with baseball bats would be labeled "Main Streeters."[57]

Lewis described the "village virus" so effectively that Paterson, finding Gopher Prairie "too terrible to contemplate," was unable to finish reading it.[58] Yet *Main Street* was not just an indictment of American philistines. It also made a halting, almost desperate effort to comprehend the place of idealism in a world that often celebrates, even canonizes, the mediocre. Despite being an officious busybody, Carol is ultimately a sympathetic character. When her effort to organize a drama troupe fails because of the citizens' poor acting skills, she tries to rally them: "I wonder if you can understand the 'fun' of making a beautiful thing," she pleads, "the pride and satisfaction of it, and the holiness."[59] But the constant frustration of her dreams turns her into a nag and a bore. Serving on the town's library committee, she grows annoyed that people prefer romance novels to great literature, and gradually her thirst for a more sophisticated life drives her to a nasty contempt of her neighbors and petty criticisms of their innocent enjoyments.

This conflict between idealism and mediocrity was Lewis's primary literary motif. Two years after *Main Street*, he published the equally scathing *Babbitt*, which depicted an ordinary American businessman, George F. Babbitt, whose midlife crisis ushers him from a state of naive normality into militant and bigoted groupthink. Lacking any real convictions, he is sometimes vaguely aware that his life is "incredibly mechanical. Mechanical business—a brisk selling of badly built houses. Mechanical religion—a dry, hard church, shut off from the real life of the streets, inhumanly respectable as a top-hat. Mechanical golf and dinner-parties and bridge and conversation. . . . Mechanical friendships—back-slapping and jocular, never daring to essay the test of quietness."[60] Yet he lacks the strength of character to break out of the commonplace, and subsists on hand-me-down ideas absorbed uncritically from his neighbors. He lives so much in the opinions of others that he feels a bewildering loneliness when nobody else is around, and retreats into dreary tradition and slogans to shelter himself from the obligation of personal independence. Eventually this becomes a resentment toward people who express "a spirit of rebellion against niceness and solid-citizenship."[61]

When he encounters a liberal lawyer named Seneca Doane, who speaks to him in a friendly way, Babbitt instantly discards his old conservatism and begins expressing vague sympathies with Doane's views. When his wife leaves town for a few months, he starts chasing other women, which leads to gossip. When a labor strike leads some of the town's business leaders to organize a "Good Citizens' League," devoted to "a wholesome sameness of thought, dress, painting, morals, and vocabulary"—principles its members are willing to back up with violence—he initially refuses to join, citing his newfound liberalism. "I know what the League stands for!" he tells his wife. "It stands for the suppression of free speech and free thought and everything else."[62] But lacking any personal integrity, he cannot resist the pressure when his friends and wife urge him to join anyway. Having substituted mindless patriotism and vague mottoes about strength for any genuine beliefs, Babbitt does join—and swiftly becomes one of the League's most militant members.[63] Instead of fleeing the "village virus" like Carol Kennicott, he embraces it as a replacement for his absent self-esteem. Published the same year that Benito Mussolini became dictator of Italy, *Babbitt* presented one of the earliest and most penetrating insights into the nature of fascism's appeal.

In 1925, Lewis took a different path with *Arrowsmith*, which reached an even bleaker conclusion. That novel was meant to set aside some of the satire and portray Babbitt's opposite—the heroic innovator and individualist. Its title character, Dr. Martin Arrowsmith, travels to the Caribbean to cure an outbreak of disease. Committed to scientific integrity and the potential of medical research—then still in its infancy—Arrowsmith arranges an experiment to test a possible cure. The experiment requires him to temporarily withhold medicine from some of the sick, as a control population to evaluate the treatment's effectiveness. But given the severity of the epidemic, Arrowsmith is pressured to abandon this scheme and simply give the medicine to everyone immediately. He knows this may bring temporary relief but will ultimately doom his efforts to find a real cure. Yet in the end, he surrenders.

Upon his return home, he is celebrated as a hero for aiding the sick, but he privately knows he has betrayed his scientific principles in doing so. Unable to overcome his self-contempt, he flees New York—and the praise of those too dull to realize what success has cost him—to work alone at a secluded location in Vermont. He does not triumph over mediocrity; he merely escapes it. Unlike Carol Kennicott or George Babbitt, he does end with a kind of victory. Yet the novel does not contradict Lewis's overall conviction that idealism is doomed in the company of other people.

Together, Lewis's novels expressed the way modern mass culture penalized originality and integrity, and rewarded obedience and cravenness. At their most extreme, these pressures gave birth to political movements rooted in hypernostalgic myths about the "good old days" that motivated violent oppression. But even in more subtle manifestations, the "village virus" elevated uniformity over uniqueness and appealed to the lowest common denominator instead of truth or beauty.

Lewis won the Pulitzer Prize for *Arrowsmith*—and refused it, to protest the fact that the Pulitzer committee had not awarded it to *Main Street*. "We have a sneaking suspicion that Mr. Lewis was laying for the award, with the fixed intention of lamming it over the outfield fence," Paterson wrote in "Turns" when she heard the news.[64] But Lewis was just getting started. In 1927, he published the scandalous *Elmer Gantry*, which lampooned religion and defended the teaching of evolution in the wake of the Scopes trial—rendering him even more of a scandal and a celebrity. Three years later, he became the first American to win the Nobel Prize in Literature. This time, he accepted. Some of his friends regarded that as a terrible mistake. Fame and wealth, thought H. L. Mencken—who had been instrumental in persuading Lewis to reject the Pulitzer—would destroy his talent.[65]

Lewis himself seemed to agree. "This is the end of me," he told a friend. "I cannot live up to it."[66] And his career would indeed peter out in the 1930s, with each successive novel appearing less important in light of the Great Depression, the catastrophic world war, and his own insatiable alcoholism and womanizing. But during the 1920s, he was America's most important novelist. "A revolution had overtaken American life in manners and morals and all intellectual assumptions," writes Mark Schorer—and Lewis's novels "played a major part, probably *the* major literary part, in the transformation."[67]

Among the great conflicts of the 20th century was the clash between these values—industry, diligence, respect for social structure—and the spirit of romanticism, which saw such things as drab, enervating, and complacent. To many of the young people who made up the Lost Generation, capitalist

America was less a land of opportunity than a miasma of conformity and mediocrity. *Main Street* fired one of the most devastating shots against bourgeois culture, viewing it in part as the seedbed of fascism. But in the 1930s, both fascists and communists would condemn bourgeois society and seek a totalitarian overhaul of every aspect of culture, so as to devote their respective nations to allegedly "higher" goods. To them, America was a boring "land of shopkeepers" rendered effete by their taste for comfortable family life. To some extent, all three "furies" joined in the anxieties that motivated this anti-bourgeois attitude. Yet they—especially Paterson—also recognized that bourgeois culture represented something rare and precious: the peaceful pursuit of individual happiness, free of the commands of political authorities. Each of the writers resolved this tension in different ways. Ayn Rand sought to romanticize bourgeois values—depicting industrialists and architects as heroes in the vein of Hugo or Ibsen. Lane emphasized that modern city dwellers should count their blessings and reflect on the victories of their forebears, who lived not so long ago. Paterson, less optimistic, demanded respect for the ordinary life—while remaining convinced that the modern age had doomed the culture she cherished.

The thirties, however, would witness a reaction against the intellectual and sexual freedoms of the 1920s, and a kind of social conservatism, often wrapped in folksiness and an appeal to team spirit. The Depression led many to believe that the libertinism of the twenties had been a kind of youthful self-indulgence, which could no longer be tolerated in the new, more mature age. Condemnation of the selfish attitudes and "social irresponsibility" of the twenties thus became a regular feature of social criticism. Just as the economy had supposedly matured from a frontier age into an era of bureaucratic redistribution, so American society was said to have grown up and put away childish things—especially its longing for greater personal freedoms.

Thus the Revolt from the Village represented a conflict between two worldviews: on the one hand, the communitarian, Victorian, "bourgeois" sense of respectability, conformity, and resilience—and on the other, a kind of romanticism: a rebellious passion for authenticity, significance, and freedom from traditional social limitations, especially focused on secularism and sexual liberation. To traditionalists, the Rebels appeared juvenile, dangerously revolutionary, suicidally radical. To the Rebels—who "emerged from the farms," in the words of critic Alfred Kazin, "with a fierce desire to assert their freedom"—the elders appeared dull, mundane, inhibited, and phony.[68] Both were right to some degree.[69]

Lewis succeeded because his novels so perfectly captured the vulgarity of small-town life. But within two decades, the Depression and World War II would force Americans to confront the fact that some of the bourgeois principles the Rebels had scorned—ordinary virtues of decorum and austerity—had merit. They were, after all, legacies of the 19th-century pioneers, who had endured enormous hardships, triumphed against overwhelming odds, and had important lessons to teach their children. When Lewis won the Nobel, Paterson remarked that the awards committee had been "unconsciously moved" by their own biases against the 19th-century inheritance. Lewis's satires, she thought, were "peculiarly flattering to the European legend of European cultural superiority."[70] And she predicted that American writers would soon have second thoughts—and rediscover the virtues of the American heartland.

For one thing, the Rebels themselves seemed to her just as censorious as the Victorians they scorned. For all their talk of the need for authenticity and significance, they often seemed merely prejudiced against wholesomeness—an attitude no less bigoted than that of the Babbitts. Many Middle Americans were happy with their small-town lives, and in her view, it did them little good to be ridiculed by literary intellectuals and told that their lives would mean nothing unless they made some grand gesture of self-assertion. "The old small town was illiterate, gossipy, petty and busy," Paterson admitted in her 1934 novel, *The Golden Vanity*, yet at the same time, its residents were "very decent people" who were content with "a neat house in the suburbs, with shrubbery and two cars and three children." There was nothing wrong with that, and cutting-edge intellectuals who "nagged" them "into believing they've got to drink too much and change partners" and rebel against society

Sinclair Lewis in 1930. The Nobel Prize–winning author of *Main Street* was the primary spokesman for the literary movement known as the Revolt from the Village. In 1936, Ayn Rand called him her favorite writer.

in order to live a genuine life were not evangelists of modernity—they were just busybodies of another sort, who failed to recognize that "respectability [and] the domestic virtues are genuine accomplishments."[71]

This idea—that the mundane lives of the people Lewis ridiculed were admirable in their own way—would prove crucial to Paterson's own writing. Suspicious of romanticism, she was wary toward the Village Rebels. She was no Babbitt herself; on the contrary, she thought capitalist culture was far richer and more radical than the Rebels—or indeed, nearly any of the writers of her lifetime—appreciated. But in a capitalist society, the great undertakings that make for superlative novels were not found on battlefields or the high seas, as in ages past, but in the office buildings of businesses—with architects, engineers, and geniuses of finance. Their "pure creative work" represented a new kind of heroism. It was regrettable that authors had not yet learned how to make fiction out of such material. That was partly due to practical difficulty—"how is one to dramatize a man figuring the overhead of a factory, or drawing the plan of a skyscraper?" Paterson wondered—but it also represented an intellectual bias. Writers such as Lewis or Sherwood Anderson did not really understand modern enterprise, she thought, and that led them to assume "that the business man doesn't know either, and that when success is attained, it is an empty mockery." In short, the kind of virtues that made for industrial progress had "not been assimilated by the novelist," and that meant writers either confined their depictions of heroism to historical fiction or wrote about characters who feel alienated, bored, or depressed at the state of modern life. Their work lacked "the heroic element, the celebration of the individual," and featured characters who, instead of doing things, had things done to them. The Village Rebels seemed to think that "in some respects life is not hard enough now." The result was a literature in which "the joy of life finds little expression."[72]

Next to Lewis, the leader of the Rebels was H. L. Mencken, the iconoclastic journalist who had risen from a Baltimore newspaper reporter to become coeditor of *The Smart Set*—the nation's most influential magazine of ideas and culture—and then of the even more prominent *American Mercury*, the premiere issue of which appeared the same year that Paterson launched "Turns with a Bookworm." Six years older than Paterson, Mencken spent his early career defying Fundamentalism and censorship. His reporting on the 1925 Scopes "monkey" trial made him a legend, and a year later he was arrested in Boston by officials who banned the *Mercury* for publishing an "indecent" short story. Mencken slashed the reputations of crusading do-gooders, denounced the "buncombe" of despotic democracy, and attacked the sacred cows of Victorian culture with an inimitable prose style that was at once worldly, abstract, cheerful, and snide. And he championed literary modernism, building the reputations of Lewis, Theodore Dreiser, and F. Scott Fitzgerald along the way. Scorning puritanism, he translated Friedrich Nietzsche, coined the term "booboisie" for the backwoods ignoramuses who ran American communities, and hailed *Main Street* as the crucial indictment of them and their "100% Americanism." These things made Mencken, in his own words, "the symbol and to some extent the leader" of "the revolt of postwar youth against the Old American certainties."[73]

Paterson admired Mencken's writing and shared his scorn for puritanical laws against prostitution and alcohol, but she could not join him in rejecting democracy in general. He and the writers he championed "made the rural Middle West synonymous with drab and gloomy immorality," she wrote. But "having met numerous Middle Westerners, we have always doubted if this was a well-balanced presentation of the case."[74] Mencken typically phrased his contempt in jocular tones—when asked why, if he despised it so much, he chose to remain in the United States, he answered "why do men go to zoos?"[75]—but he seems to have genuinely embraced an aristocratic politics in which the "superior" would rule the inferior. He believed, he said, in "liberty up to the extreme limits of the feasible and tolerable," but he also thought that "liberty and democracy are eternal enemies" and that freedom could only be preserved if government were entrusted to a "superbly efficient ruling caste."[76]

He based this view in part on the philosophy of Nietzsche, about whom he published the first American book in 1913. Nietzsche, who had died only

13 years before, had disparaged liberalism and "dialectic"—meaning the whole process of reasoning, debate, and discussion—and preferred instead a hierarchical society based on "aristocratic virtues," a view he ascribed to the ancient Greeks. Nietzsche thought Christianity had crippled mankind by overthrowing these virtues and substituting a morality rooted in a perverse celebration of the poor and ignorant, and hatred for the resilient and skillful. Beneath that morality lay a psychological phenomenon he called ressentiment. Deeper than mere jealousy, ressentiment meant a feeling of impotent rage on the part of weak and fearful people, which manifests itself in a desire for vengeance against the brave and strong—or, as Mencken put it, "the ambition of a common man to get his hand upon the collar of his superiors, or, failing that, to get his thumb into their eyes."[77] In Mencken's view, this was the secret motivation behind many "democratic" schemes to censor provocative writers, pry into people's sex lives, or ensure "fairness" by expropriating the earnings of the successful in order to subsidize the unsuccessful.

Paterson showed little interest in Nietzsche, and although she shared Mencken's disdain for the small-mindedness of the stereotypical village, she also found his tendency to rail against the common man's cherished beliefs excessive. He tended toward "sheer abuse," she declared, which "is always rather dull."[78] In fact, she thought Mencken and his admirers could be motivated by weakness and resentment just as often as their opponents were, and in their religious and literary opinions they were as much "a flock of lemmings" as the Fundamentalists.[79] In 1926, when Mencken published a list of Middle American stereotypes that he hoped future satirists would target, Paterson suavely replied that she hoped "one of them will depict a typical contributor to the *American Mercury*, for they all write in the same tone, style and mood. . . . It is the most rapid standardization process we ever saw in our life. . . . He must turn them out of a mold, like Edam cheeses."[80] As for Mencken's hostility toward democracy, it was often amusing, and always masterfully articulated, but Paterson thought the limited constitutional government created by the American Founders was superior to the reactionary politics Mencken professed. "Mencken yearns frequently and loudly for an aristocracy," she wrote. "How does he know he wouldn't have been cast as a lackey in such a social scheme? He doesn't know it. But it never even occurs to him as a possibility."[81]

▼▲◄

Those seeking to purge themselves of the "village virus" often found their escape in one variety or another of socialism. Although socialist theories have been around for millennia, and Americans experimented with various socialist schemes throughout the 19th century, the 1920s generation found the possibility of a socialist future attractive in ways their parents had not. American Progressives, following European intellectual trends, became persuaded that the principles of individualism had been superseded by new discoveries in social science. They swept aside such 18th-century notions as natural rights or the economic laws of supply and demand as mere superstitions, and argued that government's role was not merely to facilitate the pursuit of happiness by free individuals, but instead to use power to shape individuals in accordance with the irresistible historical forces of progress.[82] John Dewey, one of Progressivism's philosophical gurus, later said his contemporaries had come to believe that "the new science and new forces of productivity" demonstrated a dramatic truth: "the ends [of liberalism] can now be achieved *only* by reversal of the means to which early liberalism was committed." In other words, liberty must give way to "organized social planning."[83] Thus even those Progressives who did not become literal socialists, including Dewey, Louis Brandeis, and Jane Addams, began arguing for the replacement of self-reliance with (in Addams's words) a creed of "brotherhood, sacrifice, the subordination of individual and trade interests to the good of the working-class."[84]

Socialism had become a significant trend in America in the 1880s with the runaway success of Edward Bellamy's utopian novel *Looking Backward*, which projected a future world in which greed was eradicated and the state took responsibility for everyone. Indignant that governments seemed so often to serve the interests of the rich—especially the owners of railroads and banks—rustic farmers and idealistic youths alike were drawn to socialism's rhetoric of equality. Socialism also appealed to Christian morality, which taught that selfishness was wrong and that each person owes duties of charity toward all others. Walt Disney, born in Illinois in 1901, recalled how his father, Elias, was attracted to Christian socialism, even subscribing to the newspaper *Appeal to Reason*, whose editor, Eugene Debs, ran for president on the Socialist Party ticket. As an aspiring artist, Walt learned drawing by copying the paper's editorial cartoons.[85] But by the 1920s, socialism had lost its populist edge and become increasingly a movement of intellectuals, particularly writers, whose books Paterson would critique in her column.

She rejected socialism for the same reason that she dissented from Mencken's anti-democratic arrogance: "Those who imagine such a state would be an improvement on our present political system had better begin to imagine the bare possibility that they won't be running the communistic show."[86] A socialist state was far more likely to fall into the hands of the politically adept than the morally worthy. Nor was it plausible to think that people could be persuaded to produce wealth that would be enjoyed by others. Human beings were essentially, and inescapably, individualistic beings; they were not ants or bees, and could not be expected to subordinate their personal interests and desires to the needs of the collective, without some drastic change in their nature. Efforts to bring about such a change would incur tremendous suffering. Nor was such a change desirable, given that innovation and creativity are best spurred through the freedom to compete, not regimentation and uniformity.

As a classical liberal, Paterson adhered to the political and economic principles first articulated during the 18th-century Enlightenment. In economics, that meant the work of scholars such as Adam Smith, who overthrew the doctrines of mercantilism by arguing that wealth consists not of currency on hand but of the resources one possesses or can obtain by trade. Smith concluded that economic policies should focus on letting individuals produce and exchange as they see fit, to satisfy their own needs and wants, rather than controlling trade in order to strengthen society in the abstract or to protect existing industries from competition. Taxes, tariffs, coercive monopolies, and other government interventions into the marketplace tend to raise prices, Smith argued, and to deprive consumers of goods and services they need, while rewarding the politically well-connected rather than the impoverished.

In politics, classical liberalism meant the ideas of John Locke, who endorsed the individual's moral right to control his own life, free of interference by others or by the state, and the American Founding Fathers, who designed the Constitution to limit government power and maximize individual freedom. Paterson did not think socialism looked like a path to the modern future. On the contrary, it was a reactionary withdrawal from the advances made by the classical liberals and a regression to the superstitious, anti-individualist thinking of pre-Enlightenment days. "The economics of Adam Smith says that men will get along better the less they are tied and robbed by political officials," she wrote. "The 'economics' of Marxism is the bilious headache of a man who sat too many hours, days, weeks, months, and years in a public reading room until he mistook himself for Moses and the Absolute in one, and thought the state would wither away and the Red Sea roll back just because he said so."[87]

But to many Americans, socialism's economic dogmas were not its primary appeal. Socialists portrayed themselves as advocates of modernity, whose ideas were the next step in rational cultural progress. As part of their emphasis on class solidarity, they opposed social and legal distinctions based on race and sex, and envisioned a society in which women could enter the workforce free of the "Cult of True Womanhood," which held that women should remain in the home and raise the next generation of responsible citizens. "Socialism," Lida Parce Robinson proclaimed in the *Socialist Woman* magazine in 1908, "is feminism!"[88] And just as the Communist Party would attract many black intellectuals in the generation that followed by organizing opposition to segregation, so socialism made many converts in the early 20th century thanks to its secularism, feminism, and color blindness, all of which flew in the face of the puritanical and hierarchical strictures of the Victorian era.[89] They called the social transformation which they dreamed of "the end of bourgeois morality."

Some intellectuals, particularly admirers of the English political philosopher Herbert Spencer, thought individualism and socialist collectivism could be reconciled in light of biological evolution. Although some historians today characterize him as an advocate of laissez faire, Spencer actually argued that private ownership of land was morally untenable—and that evolution was moving humanity toward a more perfect state of collectivization.[90] Highly popular in the United States, Spencer inspired a generation of Americans to embrace what one scholar calls a "distinctive" form of socialism that promised "a path from the chaotic capitalist present to a humane and orderly socialist future"—and that would fulfill, not supersede, individualism.[91] This would be a future in which big business was harnessed and small business liberated—in which workers would sacrifice for one another, yet at the same time be free to stand on their own two feet.

Among the most extreme exemplars of this awkward blend of independence and collectivism was the California-based adventure novelist Jack London. A brash and bellicose man, London's tales of the Alaskan gold rush and vivid stories such as *White Fang* appealed to countless readers thanks to their weird mixture of Darwinian ruthlessness, Marxist revolution, and Nietzschean triumph. He embraced socialism, yet his socialism was of a distinctly "radical chic" variety,[92] and he was far more interested in rebelling against what he called "orthodox bourgeois ethics" and "the sonorous platitudes of the bourgeois politicians" than in creating a collectivist utopia of government-managed paternalism.[93] In short, London knew what he was against: he opposed the sexually repressive customs of conventional society, the dogmatism and prejudice of religion, and the petty and ordinary quality of Middle American life. But it was less clear what he was for.

He was not alone. As the leading scholar of his political views observes, "If Jack London seemed muddled and inconsistent in theory and practice, so did the entire American socialist movement."[94] Intellectual leaders of the Progressive Era celebrated enterprising innovators—and especially sought to liberate the individuality of women—but at the same time, wanted to eliminate selfishness and competition, and to impose traditional middle-class values by law through such measures as exclusionary zoning, Prohibition, and the banning of divorce.[95]

London (who in the 1910s secretly bought many of his plot ideas from the then-unknown Sinclair Lewis[96]) appealed to readers who sympathized with the Revolt from the Village, and saw some glimmer of an alternative in stories that depicted muscular confrontation with nature. Isabel Paterson did not think highly of him—"there will always be a demand from men for boy's books," she sneered[97]—but she grasped his unusual individualistic creed: "It wasn't [real] socialism," she thought, but "the tag end of Herbert Spencer's philosophy, which was the American gospel during the last half of the nineteenth century, and vanished almost instantaneously in 1914," when war broke out in Europe.[98] That had been just two years before London died in Oakland, of a mixture of alcoholism and kidney disease.

In 1925, a novel about London—or, more accurately, a fictionalized biography, with London's name changed to avoid legal trouble—landed on Paterson's desk at the *Trib*. Written by a Missouri journalist named Rose Wilder Lane, the book was probably sent to Paterson by its publisher. It only merited passing notice in "Turns": "We might become indiscreetly vocal," Paterson wrote, "if we were to peruse Rose Wilder Lane's *He Was a Man*. . . . It's about a literary genius who riz from obscurity to dazzling fame." But brief as it was, being mentioned in Paterson's column was a step up for the 40-year-old Lane, who was just on the cusp of a career that would make her one of the most prominent writers of the era.

Lane did not learn of Paterson's reference to her for several months. That was because she was halfway around the world at the time—in Albania, a country she had fallen in love with a few years before and was trying to make her permanent home. When she wrote to thank Paterson for mentioning the book, she included a facetious invitation to visit, which Paterson answered in her column. "She doesn't really know us," declared I.M.P., "or she would never have given that invitation. We might accept it at any moment. That's the way we—well, it's the way we landed in a whole lot of trouble, at different times in our life. Somebody said to us casually, 'Why not jump off the kitchen roof?' or some such thing, and we jumped."[99] Lane answered again in another letter, explaining that she had first visited Albania in 1921 and had become so "fascinated by the turbulent little mountain principality" that she decided she wanted to stay. Repeating this in "Turns," Paterson wryly added that Lane could only be attracted to Albania "because she was born in Dakota."[100]

Lane's exchange with Paterson was the beginning of a friendship that lasted more than two decades. They would be years of fear and frustration, of poverty and war, and what sometimes appeared to them to be literally the end of the world. Through it all, they tried to articulate—even if only to preserve for some future generation—the ideals and principles they held dear. They shared thoughts in long, late-night telephone calls, overnight visits at each other's homes, and a correspondence that must have been voluminous. Long-winded and anecdotal, Lane's letters sometimes stretched to a dozen pages, and Paterson's were equally long, snapped out on her typewriter, full of typos, witty literary allusions, and long quotations from books. Sadly, they appear to have destroyed their letters when their friendship dissolved, under the weight of personal squabbles and advancing age, leaving little on which to reconstruct their conversations today except for Lane's diaries and Paterson's frequent quotations in "Turns." But all of that was in the far distance in 1925. For now, they were content with lives of literature and adventure.

Rose Wilder Lane, a world-famous journalist and author. Her most lasting contribution to American literature would be the *Little House* series of novels that she secretly coauthored with her mother, Laura Ingalls Wilder.

2

The Wandering Jew

Paterson's mention of Rose Wilder Lane's book marked a coming of age in the career of an ambitious and iconoclastic young writer. The only daughter of an obscure family that she would later make famous, Lane had been working as a journalist for nearly a decade already, and recognition by one of the East Coast's leading critics would help transform her into one of the most popular and best-paid novelists in the country.

Born the same year as Paterson, on December 5, 1886, to Almanzo Wilder and his wife Laura Ingalls Wilder, Rose would ultimately be responsible—perhaps more than any other American author—for romanticizing the image of 19th-century farm life. But the truth was, she hated it. While growing up in South Dakota and Missouri, she had despised its dreary and endless chores and the suffocating small-mindedness of the people around her. As soon as her writing earned her enough money to escape, she fled. And when dwindling finances forced her to return home, she wrestled with the tension she found in the demands of liberty and responsibility, and which she articulated so well when she defined freedom as "the slavery of self-discipline."[1]

In fact, at the time Paterson mentioned her in "Turns," Lane was as far as she could get from her hometown of Mansfield, Missouri. She was in Albania, working on plans to move permanently to the Balkans. After having fallen in love with Albania's exotic, otherworldly landscape, she had published a travelogue called *The Peaks of Shala* in 1923, and, three years later, bought a house near Tirana. She hoped to live there with some literary friends and experience life as it "must have been before cities and machines and office-desks brought dull skins and eyes, joy-rides, padded shoulders, and crippling collars."[2] It had been a long journey, one driven by what she called "the restlessness of ambition, with its sense of missing, on a farm, all the adventures and rewards that one dimly feels are elsewhere."[3]

She had good reason to flee the prairie. Among her earliest childhood memories was the exotic sound of the word "diphtheria," which she learned in 1888, when both of her parents suffered from that deadly illness. Although still not fully recovered, her father tried to get back to work—"man-like," Lane wrote, he "would not listen to reason and stay in bed"[4]—and suffered a stroke, or perhaps contracted polio, which left him with permanent nerve damage. Diligent and laconic, Almanzo Wilder labored constantly on the farm. So did his wife, who in spare moments told Rose stories about her own childhood and parents, Charles and Caroline Ingalls, who had suffered through the locust swarms, prairie fires, and harsh winters that marked the era of westward expansion.

Almanzo and Laura Wilder bounced from place to place frequently in their daughter's early years, before settling in De Smet, South Dakota, in the fall of 1892. There they enrolled her in school, but her education was interrupted only a year later, when the family moved to Mansfield. There, she entered school again, but was swiftly disappointed by the fact that she already knew more—at least in her opinion—than some of the teachers. She certainly was a bookworm, devouring everything from Herbert Spencer and Thomas Gray to Tom Paine, who became one of her favorites. A smart daydreamer, she felt isolated and disappointed by her fellow students. "If only such men as the Spartans lived in these days," she wrote in a school notebook in 1900, "life would be worth living."[5]

Three years later, when she was 16, she traveled to Crowley, Louisiana, to live for a year with an aunt and complete high school. The trip gave her a small taste of the larger world; there were fancy carriages, restaurants, and radical new political ideas. Her aunt was a politically modern woman, and shared with her the ideas of Edward Bellamy's *Looking Backward* and Eugene Debs's presidential campaign. Socialism seemed to offer a viable alternative to a society dominated by powerful eastern industrial interests and meddlesome Victorian moralizing. It remained with Lane long afterward, and she later claimed that she became "a convinced, though not a practicing, communist."[6] This may have been an exaggeration—she was always prone to exaggeration—but there is no reason to doubt that she remained enamored of socialism for at least two decades. Long afterward, she looked back on her youthful experiences when she reviewed a memoir by the disillusioned former communist Ralph Chaplin: "The boy went to school and church; but he found outside them, and by chance, his only stimulus to thinking, and the only appeal to youth's desire to improve the world. This was Marxian socialism. . . . You will remember this book as if you had lived it; and, in a sense, everyone has."[7]

Lane's relationship with her family has become the focus of much research, thanks to her collaboration with her mother on the *Little House on the Prairie* series of children's novels. As with many such relationships, however, the connection between mother and daughter was complicated—sometimes affectionate, sometimes resentful, and too personal to be fully understood by any later historian. Lane tended to be extremely sensitive and suffered bouts of what she described as suicidal depression. Whether the coldness of which she accused her parents actually existed or was an impression distorted by her own psyche is therefore a question that can never be resolved, particularly since only she, and not her parents, kept a diary. For example, we cannot judge from this distance whether her mother really did manipulate her with passive-aggressive tactics, extracting what she wanted by playing the role of martyr, as both Rose and her friends claimed—or whether Rose merely perceived that through the lens of her own self-inflicted guilt. Nor can we judge the exact basis for Lane's feeling that her mother "made me so miserable when I was a child that I've never got over it," as she wrote in her journal.[8] In any event, Lane wrote in 1927 that her early life had been one of "no affection, poverty, inferiority," and she seems to have spent much of her adulthood alternately trying to escape the scenes of her youth or diving back into them, in search of emotional sustenance.[9]

Lane was a member of the Lost Generation, and her experience manifested the social trends that affected many women of her age. Among other things, disputes between her and her mother reveal the tension brought on by experiences—and expectations—of personal privacy and autonomy, which were largely new phenomena during the transition from village life to the modern era. This was the tension that brought on the Revolt from the Village, and it appeared time and again in Lane's life, particularly in her rebellion against what she saw as her mother's excessive fear of public opinion. In 1933, when Lane was 47 and living on her parents' farm with her friend Catherine Brody, she raged in her diary about her mother trying to dissuade Brody from riding in a car with a man. "The talk about him is getting *thick*," said her mother. "Good God," Lane cried. "Why should we give a damn?"[10] Months later, she recorded another such incident: her mother refused to accept an invitation to a party out of fear that everybody would read about it in the local newspaper. "[Brody] and I said we didn't care what such people thought. [Brody] asked why she cared. 'You aren't dependent upon them for anything.' My mother said, 'Well I do care! I have to care, I have to live among 'em. I'm not going uptown Saturdays.'"[11] Exasperating incidents like these must have reinforced the feeling of suffocation that Sinclair Lewis had portrayed in *Main Street*.

▰▲▰

Something within her always dreamed of traveling. Putting her own youthful feelings into the words of one of her fictional characters, Lane recalled years later how she had longed to "start down that road and walk and walk and keep on walking and never come back."[12] When, at the age of five, her grandmother told her the Christian legend of the "Wandering Jew"—who supposedly taunted the crucified Jesus and was cursed for it by being compelled to roam the world for eternity—Lane replied that she wished she could be cursed the same way. The Wandering Jew became a personal symbol for her, and she spent most of the rest of her life either traveling, or wallowing in torment about being forced to stay still.

After graduating from high school, she returned to Mansfield, pestered a friend to teach her Morse code, and then left again—first for Kansas City and then Indiana—to earn a living as a telegraph operator. It was probably there that she met Claire Gillette Lane, a reporter for the *San Francisco Call*, with whom she fell in love. She moved to San Francisco to be with him in 1908, and they were married a year later. Not much is known about Gillette, as he was called, except for the fictionalized version of him that appears in Rose's 1919 novel, *Diverging Roads*. In that book, written in the wake of their divorce, he is portrayed as an irresponsible schemer, constantly chasing easy fortunes. But it seems more likely that although the couple participated in some dubious business ventures, he was a sober man who had difficulty understanding his wife's sometimes dramatic swings between a desire for a traditional family and a longing for bohemian adventure. "When Gillette came along," she later wrote in a journal, "I wanted him because (1) I wanted sex, (2) I took him at his own stated value, as representing success and money and the high cultural level of newspaper work."[13] This second role, he evidently did not fulfill. He was not—as one might assume from *Diverging Roads*—opposed to his wife having a career, and he appears to have genuinely loved her. But whatever the reason, Rose came to view life as his companion as incompatible with her sense of self.

The couple traveled, making money at various hustles, including on one occasion squeezing a railroad company for $1,000 after Gillette suffered a minor injury on a train. Rose suffered a miscarriage in 1909 and was forced to undergo a painful operation that left her unable to bear children and left a permanent psychological scar that she struggled to conceal. "I wasn't physically normal between 1909 and 1911," she later said, "nor mentally normal till 1914."[14] But many years afterward, she still looked back with grief on the loss of her only child. "It isn't true, what people say, that you will ever forget," she confided to a friend who suffered a similar misfortune. "But in time you do learn that unhappiness and loss are part of living."[15]

After a few years, the couple returned to California, where they shifted between San Francisco, Sacramento, and San Jose, doing a variety of jobs. Rose began writing for newspapers and working as a real estate agent while Gillette continued getting freelance work in promotional advertising. In January 1915, a friend got her a job on the *San Francisco Bulletin*, writing pieces for a page devoted to women's interests. This began her career as Rose Wilder Lane, the name she would keep even after her divorce became final three years later. Some of the articles she wrote on the foibles of men might suggest some of the frustrations she felt in her marriage—"If [men] had the smallest bit of logic in their entire make-up, three minutes of reflection would show them how absolutely illogical they are"[16]—although it's more likely she was simply composing jocular copy to fill space and make money. In any event, she found life as a homemaker dreary. Marriage left her "as unhappy as anyone can possibly be."[17]

She fell into one of the seasons of depression that periodically plagued her, and attempted suicide by dousing a rag with chloroform and falling asleep with it over her face. She awoke later with only a headache. Yet she found the experience transformative. She decided that she *did* love life, after all—what had made her miserable was the collapse of a dream of domesticity that she had never really believed in to begin with. Reflecting on the incident in 1926, she wrote of her realization that "human beings lose their way to happiness because they look for it where it is not."[18] What she had craved at that time was not actually oblivion, but a self-directed life in which she would be free to pursue the values that mattered to her, as opposed to meeting standards dictated by others. "The joy of freedom," she realized, gave charm even to the smallest incidents—whereas without that freedom, nothing could seem truly special. "To go where one wants to go, when one wants to, without consulting any other person's needs or plans. . . . That one may have companionship or solitude as one's mood dictates; in a word, to have nobody in one's life but one's self—that is both peace and exhilaration."[19] This yearning for independence was every bit as much a credo of feminism as Virginia Woolf's expression, years later, of the need for a woman writer to have "a room of her own."[20]

In the end, the Lanes' divorce seems to have had less to do with Gillette than with Rose's delayed discovery of the nature of her own personality. She had never lived by herself—having gone directly from her parents' home to life with Gillette—and had never tried to establish her own path.

Now she decided to make that attempt. "We had tasted independence," she later explained, describing her generation of women. "Our independence had taught us the delight of a selfish life. We had learned, as our mothers in their fathers' and husbands' families had never learned, the use of the personal pronoun, first person, *singular*. . . . We were happy with our work and our freedom. We thought we would be even happier, married. We were not. So we went back to the happiness we had known before we were married. It was as simple as that."[21]

By the time her divorce was finalized, Lane's work had impressed her editor at the *Bulletin*, Fremont Older, who became a mentor and encouraged her literary ambitions. With his assistance, she wrote a short biography of the daredevil pilot Art Smith, and two years later, a more in-depth one of Henry Ford, whom she met when he visited San Francisco's Panama-Pacific International Exposition in 1915. Both were written in a style now called "literary journalism," which features manufactured quotes and dramatizations of facts, but remains true to the actual events.[22] She would use the same technique when collaborating with her mother in the 1930s.

The success of the Smith and Ford biographies led her to take on other, similar projects, including books on Charlie Chaplin, Herbert Hoover, and Jack London. The Hoover biography resulted in a lifelong friendship with the man destined to become president. But the Chaplin and London books got her into trouble.

Lane wrote *Charlie Chaplin's Own Story* in the first person in Chaplin's voice, without the movie star's authorization. When he learned about this, he threatened to sue, and demanded that the publisher withdraw it. Lane pleaded with him to let the book go forward: "It is in the interest of both of us to have the book published," she wrote the actor. Going to court would be like "the two men who fought over a nut and brought the matter to a judge who ate the nut and divided the shell."[23] Chaplin did not relent—but for reasons that remain unknown, the book remains available today, complete with its false assertion that it is an autobiography.

The contretemps over Jack London was worse. A familiar figure in the San Francisco Bay area before his death in 1916 at the age of 40, London had become a literary sensation in 1903 with *Call of the Wild*, his Darwinist novel about a dog who fights his way to leadership of a team of sled dogs, and later of a pack of wolves. A series of similarly hypermasculine books followed, which ultimately made him one of the most popular writers in the world. After his death, his widow, Charmian, decided to write a biography of her husband, but when she learned that *Sunset* magazine had commissioned Lane to write one, she agreed to cooperate. She liked Lane—calling her "interesting and brainy"[24]—and did not object to the fictitious elements Lane inserted in the *Sunset* articles when they appeared in 1917–1918. But she changed her mind when she saw how the magazine was advertising the completed series. In part, she seems to have feared that the reprinting of Lane's serial in book form would harm sales of her own book. But she also had grown uncomfortable about the way Lane was romanticizing London's life.[25] When her objections succeeded in barring publication, Lane began reworking her manuscript into a novel, instead. That project would take six years.

In the meantime, she began working on *The Making of Herbert Hoover*. Hoover was then contemplating a run for president, to capitalize on the fame he had earned through his work as administrator of the Wilson administration's relief efforts for post–World War I Europe. A self-made man born to an Iowa blacksmith, Hoover had put himself through college at Stanford and become a successful mining engineer. After working for mining concerns in Australia and China, he decided when war broke out to organize charity efforts to send food and supplies to Belgium. He proved so successful that when the United States entered the war, Wilson asked him to run the U.S. Food Administration, which oversaw not only the distribution of relief to European allies but also the rationing of food in the United States. His management skills earned him a following among Progressives, whose ideology emphasized technocratic government planning, as opposed to the decentralized and seemingly uncoordinated outcomes of the free market. "Progressive reformers," writes Hoover scholar Joan Hoff Wilson, sought to organize the economy into economic units, overseen by government, to ensure that they "would work efficiently together in the public interest through a sense of community and social responsibility."[26] The "Great Engineer" from Stanford appeared to be the perfect champion for such a project.

Hoover never considered himself especially ideological, viewing himself instead as a scientific efficiency expert. But that very fact allowed both Democrats and Republicans to imagine him one of their own—a disinterested outsider, or in Lane's words, "a hard-headed and hard-boiled business man, with an international point of view and a large stock in practical humanitarian ideas."[27] Courted by both parties and celebrated for his competence, Hoover was ideally positioned for a White House run, and a celebratory biography would serve his candidacy well.

As with her works on Chaplin, Ford, and London, Lane wrote *The Making of Herbert Hoover* in a novelistic style that invented dialogue and incidents in order to convey an overall impression. There is little to recommend it today, and Hoover himself thought little of it. Even Lane called it "a cheap bit of work," of which she was "not particularly proud," but her heroic characterization of her subject does suggest the tone of her own political views at the time.[28] In her telling, Hoover came off as an industrialist, charitable on an individual level but ruthless in his willingness to cut expenses and risk the wrath of labor unions to achieve his goals—the perfect man for "a materialistic age, a pragmatic age."[29] She portrayed Hoover as the opposite of an ideologue—a scion of pioneer stock whose "love of living" was rooted in "that stern sense of moral duty that is the American religion. The value of life was not enjoyment, but accomplishment; it lay not in the emotional or spiritual values, but in the concrete task completed."[30]

Lane saw Hoover not as a deep thinker but as a pragmatist and "organizer," qualities she characterized as legacies of the American frontier experience.[31] "The basis of American morality is a practical attitude toward concrete facts," she wrote. "God came with the pioneers to a new continent," teaching the American people that "morality is the best policy" and that "the individualism of pioneer America" can transform "the primitive communism in which human society began" into an abundant and well-structured life.[32] This was the paradoxical Progressive vision of the technocratic, expertly organized economy: one that would rein in the alleged waste and selfishness of capitalism without descending into the stagnant poverty of the communist state. This program tended toward socialism, but without its emphasis on class warfare—indeed, with an express hostility to broad abstract theories—and with some respect for the need for economic incentives as well as a rhetoric of individual self-reliance. Whether or not such a middle ground was tenable would be a subject of controversy for the rest of the century.

▰▲◤

It is possible that Lane met Isabel Paterson during the years she lived in San Francisco, socializing with avant-garde writers and intellectuals. Paterson had moved to the city in late 1917 and remained there for perhaps three years. There is no evidence of their meeting, however; had one occurred, Lane would almost certainly have mentioned it. What is clear is that Lane kept busy writing; alongside her biographies, she wrote scores of articles for newspapers and magazines, including everything from Hollywood gossip and descriptions of the building of Hetch Hetchy Dam to her novel, *Diverging Roads*, which appeared first as a serial in *Sunset* and then as a book in 1919.

That novel—the title of which borrows from Robert Frost's 1916 poem "The Road Not Taken" and also puns cleverly on "Lane"—is a competently written, if not particularly memorable, feminist coming-of-age tale, with more than a hint of the Revolt from the Village theme. Its main character, Helen, is bored and alienated by small-town life. She is ineptly pursued by Paul, a kind but dull local man, before she is swept away by the attentions of Bert, a boosterish, modern, unreliable hustler with schemes of big fortune. They marry, but he soon begins to vanish for long stretches of time, returning occasionally with money obtained in mysterious ways. Finally, he disappears again, taking with him money that Helen has been forced to earn during his latest absence, and Helen eventually learns that he is running from the law, wanted for writing bad checks.

With Bert gone, Helen must earn her own way. She becomes a real estate agent, struggling to be treated as an equal by the men she works with. She finds that she is proud of her work, but despises the chauvinism of her male associates. "She was a good salesman," she thinks to herself. "This was the only thing she had saved from the wreckage. At least she would succeed in this. She would make money; she would clear Bert's name, which was hers; she would buy a little house and make it beautiful. . . . But she was a woman. They did not let her forget it."[33] After providing for herself by long, hard work, she chances to run into Paul. It turns out he still loves her. He begs her to divorce Bert and marry him instead. Then he stops himself. "I never thought that I could talk like this to a woman who hadn't any right to listen to me."

"Hush! Of course I have a right to listen to you," she answers. "I have every right to do as I please with myself."[34] She begins divorce proceedings against Bert and in the meantime gets a job as a newspaper writer. But when Paul learns of this, he is startled. "Why do you want an income?" he asks. "I can take care of you. . . . And when it comes to something to do—you're going to have me on your hands, you know!"[35]

Intriguingly, Lane changed the ending of the story at this point. In the magazine version, *Diverging Roads* ended with Helen accepting Paul's proposal.[36] But Lane added five chapters to the end of the book version—in which Helen realizes that although Paul is willing to indulge her interest in writing, he does not actually take her work seriously. "All right, run along and play in San Francisco," Paul tells her with a patronizing laugh. "Only I warn you, I'm not going to be called Mr. Helen Davies!"[37] Eventually, she grasps that a marriage with Paul will not work. "He doesn't love you," she tells herself. "He doesn't want you. It's someone else he wants—the girl you used to be."[38] Realizing that her feelings for him, too, are more nostalgia than genuine love, she changes her mind about marriage and chooses a writing career, instead. "It hurts to—to let go of anything beautiful," she tells a friend as she prepares to leave California for work as a reporter in Asia. "But something will come to take its place, something different, of course, but better. The future's always better than we can possibly think it will be."[39]

Diverging Roads ends on this wistful note—and with Helen's conviction that although freedom is sometimes a hard path, it is better than the dreary conformity and subjection that conventional marriage offers women. The novel was not a manifesto of liberation from male dominance, although it did comment repeatedly on sexism. Instead, it was a story of self-discovery. As literary scholar Julia Ehrhardt argues, Lane's depiction of a woman "who seeks happiness and self-fulfillment not through a romantic relationship but through satisfying work" was a "conception of middle-class selfhood that was quite radical at the time."[40] Helen finds a source of pride in her career; that leaves plenty of room in her life for relationships with others, but those relationships are not the source of her identity.

Lane had rushed to finish *Diverging Roads* in an effort to pay the bills after she quit her job at the *Bulletin* in solidarity with her editor Fremont Older, who resigned from the paper over a political dispute. She followed that novel with work as a ghostwriter for the traveling journalist Frederick O'Brien. After secretly writing O'Brien's *White Shadows in the South Seas*—which proved remarkably successful[41]—she ghostwrote several other travelogues for journalist Lowell Thomas. But she quickly spent the income from these projects and sought a new job with the Red Cross Publicity Bureau, which was then sending journalists to Europe to document the heroic efforts of volunteers to alleviate the suffering World War I had caused. After a series of delays, she reached Paris in the spring of 1920. And it was there, in December, that she met and fell in love with a beautiful and ambitious 27-year-old writer named Dorothy Thompson.

Daughter of a New York minister, Thompson had channeled her own spiritual drives into social causes by working for the women's suffrage movement as a writer and lecturer, and later for the National Social Unit Organization, a network of social workers and community organizers. Charming, vivacious, and smart, she was a skilled writer, and by 1920 she was ready to embark on a career that would make her one of the world's most celebrated journalists. Like Lane, she had come to Europe to write for the Red Cross, but she also hoped to visit Russia, to see for herself the communist experiment with which she was deeply intrigued. On her way to France, she had stayed briefly in Britain and scored a coup by interviewing leaders of the Irish Sinn Féin rebellion. That impressed the International News Service so much that it commissioned her to visit Austria.[42] Stopping in Paris, she encountered Lane—and was at first nonplussed by the older woman and the "sob stuff" she was writing.[43] But after a while she began to see Lane—already a well-established journalist—as something of a mentor. They stayed up late at night, talking about literature, philosophy, and travel. For her part, Lane adored the younger woman, calling her "a song, a poem, a flame in the sunlight." Thompson in return called her "Roses."[44]

They took a three-day hiking tour through the Loire Valley that became one of Lane's most cherished memories. It is impossible to determine now whether their relationship was sexual; although Thompson herself was bisexual and had a number of affairs with women, the evidence as to Lane's sexuality is unclear.[45] After about 1930, her deepest relationships were invariably with women, whom she regarded as more serious and rational than men, and she lived on emotionally intimate terms with several women throughout her life, particularly the writers Catherine Brody and Helen "Troub" Boylston, whom she met shortly after her encounter with Thompson. Her feelings for Thompson were certainly strong. Yet Lane's biographer William Holtz concludes that she "loved Dorothy like a younger sister."[46] Whatever the details, they remained close—notwithstanding some angry interruptions resulting from Thompson's idiosyncratic political views—until Thompson died in 1961. "Every woman has love affairs," Lane told her once. "It's the rarely fortunate one who has a sincere friend—I mean a *friend*."[47]

When summer came, Thompson departed for Vienna and Lane for Warsaw. Writing constantly, not only articles about what she witnessed but also stories, letters, and journal entries, Lane had a brief romance with a literary agent named Arthur Griggs, and another, longer one with a reporter named Guy Moyston, whom she had first met in San Francisco. Along the way, she encountered Boylston, nicknamed "Troub," short for "troubles," because she was prone to accidents. Boylston was also a writer and a trained nurse who, like Lane, was working for the Red Cross and would later publish a series of successful novels. They met on a train due to a mix-up in their sleeping arrangements and became almost lifelong companions.

After wide-ranging journeys and countless news dispatches, Lane decided to visit the Balkans in 1921. It would change her life forever. She devoured its picturesque landscape, savored long walks through its treacherous mountain passes, and delighted in its ancient folkways and vibrant ethnic costumes. This first, brief visit to Albania was followed by another the following year, when she stayed for a month and a half, working on *The Peaks of Shala*.

Albania cast a spell over Lane for many reasons. Foremost was the feeling of liberation from the burdens of both her family duties and society's expectations for a woman of her age. "No dusting, for there was no furniture; no making of beds, for there were no beds; no curtains to keep fresh, for there were no windows."[48] Indeed, her enchantment with Albania was largely a function of her disillusionment with America—a feeling she shared with other writers of the Lost Generation. When a reporter asked her about her fascination with the country, she replied that she loved it because "American women are the biggest slaves on earth and these Moslem women are perhaps the freest." In Europe and much of the United States, women could not own property or pursue a career, but "thanks to the peculiar organization of Moslem society," women could have both families and careers, because they oversaw the whole family unit, which was "organized somewhat like an American business," with the woman of the household being the "manager at the head."[49] Lane professed to be "essentially fond of simple folk," and told Paterson that she loved the fact that Albania retained its "medieval feudalism," with its people untainted by the cheap, acquisitive, tactlessness of America and Europe.[50]

Of course, this was pure romanticism. Rural Albania was hardly a place to live the bohemian literary life, and Lane had no real chance of finding a feminist haven among what she called "these simple communist people."[51] The conflict between the actual Albania and her idealized version becomes obvious in one passage in *The Peaks of Shala* in which Lane and her friends witness an older woman protesting against the confiscation of her home by tribal leaders. The tribesmen insist on taking it from her because now that her husband is dead, she lives alone and has no need for so large a house. But the woman complains that she built it herself and that it is wrong for them to seize it. "With my own hands I laid the roof upon it," she cries. "It is my house. I will not give up my house." She pleads all day, insisting that it is immoral for others to take what she has made, but the chiefs shrug off her complaints, calling her "insane" and "foolish." Lane intervenes to argue on her behalf, but the men pay little heed. "Houses belong to the tribe," one tells her. After a day of entreaty and demands, the frustrated woman is sent away without justice.

Lane makes no further comment on this episode—on the contrary, she depicts it in the tones of comic farce.[52] Yet the incident was an important step in developing her political views, and she returned to it often in her later writings. In 1943, she cited the episode as proof that communism is a primitive superstition that rests on the false assumption that wealth can be created by authoritarianism, instead of by the choices of independent people. "I tried for hours to convince [the tribesmen] that a [person] can own a house," she remembered. "My plea for the woman astounded them, but upon reflection they produced most of the sound arguments for communism: economic equality, economic security, and social order. . . . They were unable to imagine that any security, order or justice could exist among men who were not controlled by some intangible Authority, which could not permit an individual to own a house."[53] Three decades after that, she would tell a friend that she had gone to Europe "accepting all the socialist assumptions," but that "seeing Europe shocked and dislodged most of them."[54]

Such reflections were far in the future in 1922. At the time, she bemoaned what she saw as the inevitable coming of modern civilization to Albania's wild, fairy-tale landscape: "I felt a regret, purely romantic, perhaps, at the inevitable disappearance of this last surviving remnant of the Aryan primitive communism in which our forefathers lived," she wrote in *The Peaks of Shala*. "I am a conservative, even a reactionary."[55] And she never lost her love for this mental idyll of Albania. She even took it upon herself to "adopt" an Albanian teenager named Rexh Meta, the first of a half dozen young people she took under her wing. Meta helped rescue her from certain death when she contracted pneumonia during her first visit, and she sent him a stipend for the rest of her life, which enabled him to marry and complete his education at Cambridge University.[56]

▰

After a brief trip back to Paris, where she stayed for several months writing magazine articles and completing the Albania manuscript, she returned to Tirana, this time accompanied by a friend named Peggy Marquis. They stayed for a month and a half of exploration and adventure (at one point being trapped in the crossfire of an armed uprising) and often fended off proposals from local tribesmen, including—or so Lane claimed—one who later became king of Albania. She began to plan on living there permanently.

In August 1922, after a brief return to France to recuperate from malaria, Lane journeyed to Armenia with Marquis to cover the efforts of Near East Relief, a new charity organization chartered by the U.S. government to bring aid to war-ravaged Transcaucasia. At the time of her arrival, Armenia was still smoldering from battles, first with the Turks and then the Soviet Union. Although the word "genocide" would not be employed for another two decades, the Armenian genocide was then underway—one of the first episodes in the series of calamities that would make the 20th century the bloodiest in human history. Deportations, concentration camps, mass starvation, and massacres took between 800,000 and 1.5 million Armenian lives before Turkish rule gave way to Soviet communism in 1923.

The Bolsheviks were then in the process of forming the new Union of Soviet Socialist Republics. They had initially supported Turkish efforts to conquer Armenia, but then made a deal to take most of the country for themselves, while allowing the Turks to claim a portion. Vladimir Lenin and Joseph Stalin then began annexing the Balkan nations into the USSR, the official organization of which was announced only four months after Lane's arrival. Armenia was made part of the Transcaucasian Socialist Federative Soviet Republic, as was Stalin's native Georgia. But although called "federative," this absorption into the Soviet Union was not accompanied by any meaningful local autonomy; Armenia was ruled from Moscow, through party functionaries who proceeded to seize whatever private property remained in the war-torn region.[58]

Lane witnessed this firsthand, and what she saw shocked her intensely. "It was in Armenia that I learned fear," she told a friend.[58] There were mass graves, piles of skeletons of people slaughtered by the Turks, refugees living in teepees fashioned from cornstalks, an orphanage housing 30,000 children whose parents had been slaughtered. And there was the ignorance and tyranny of the invading Bolsheviks, who proclaimed themselves the liberators of these people, while brutalizing them and expropriating their food. "It was a situation to wring sympathy from the hardest heart," she wrote after interviewing farmers whose crops were confiscated by Soviet authorities. When she asked communist officials about it, they put her off with bureaucratic double-talk. "We intend to redistribute it to the neediest," said one. "We will see that they are the most needy by making them work for it. We have paid grain as wages to the builders of the Echmiadzin irrigation canal; we are paying grain to the workers on the Arpa-chai canal." In other words, the new government would enslave the people by seizing their belongings and selling them back in exchange for labor.[59] The Soviets also confiscated the property of the Armenian Church, and one local bishop told Lane in mournful tones that he believed his nation was destined for destruction. "'There is no hope for Armenia,' he said suddenly. 'We lie between Russia and Turkey. Russia will conquer, yes, but what will be our fate while she does it? It is our lands that will be devastated again, our people who will be killed, when Russia advances to Constantinople. We are doomed.'"[60]

From Armenia, Lane and Marquis traveled to Georgia, where they witnessed the process of "Sovietization" in the wake of that country's conquest by Lenin's forces. As in Armenia, this was managed primarily by Stalin and the local secret police, whose leader, Lavrenti Beria, later took charge of the NKVD, precursor to the KGB. In Moscow, Lenin announced the "New Economic Policy," a brief thawing of socialist control that allowed a slight degree of economic growth, and Lane observed its positive effects in a village outside Tiflis (now Tbilisi), where she paused for a teatime interview with a farmer and his wife. The home was tidy, carefully whitewashed, and lovingly decorated with icons and embroideries. They had no electricity, no plumbing, and little sanitation, but the farmers had produced enough to make it through the year. "There was not a poor man in the town. No Communist could have desired better proof of Communism's practical worth than the prosperous well-being of those villagers." Yet as he shared his tea with Lane, the farmer expressed his hostility to Soviet rule. "He did not like it. 'No! No!' His complaint was government interference with village affairs. He protested against the growing bureaucracy that was taking too many men from productive work. 'It is too big,' he said. 'Too big. And at the top, too small. It will not work.'"

The villagers practiced traditional, communitarian sharing—the farmland was held in common, and about every decade, they gathered to redistribute the land as circumstances warranted—yet they preserved a rough ethos of independence and common sense, manifested in this farmer's pride in his clean, whitewashed home. Soviet control would destroy it all, he predicted. Recalling this interview 13 years later, Lane wondered "whether that ancestral home, that village, have yet been wiped from the soil of Russia to make way for a communal farm. . . . Do my host and his wife eat, perhaps, in a communal dining hall and sleep in communal barracks?" In fact, only months after her visit, Soviet troops put down an armed uprising in Georgia, executing more than 12,000 people and initiating a wave of oppression that only worsened after Lenin's death in 1924.

As Lane remembered it, this encounter in Tiflis was when "the first doubt pierced" her "Communist faith." She began asking herself questions about political philosophy and economics. Communism promised that the state would organize society to enrich the poor, but was that actually possible? "In practical fact, the State, the Government, cannot exist," she explained a decade later.[61] It is only an abstraction—a name for political coercion of individuals and control over what they produce. Stripped of euphemisms such as "the common good," collectivism simply meant domination and regimentation by the state. As Moscow accumulated more bureaucrats, the system would impose greater and greater burdens on Georgian farmers, disregarding their rights and replacing their folkways with expropriation and compulsory labor.

▰

After leaving Georgia, Lane and Marquis headed for Turkey, Egypt, and Iraq. But Lane was already worn out, and after a grueling trek through the desert to reach Baghdad, she decided she had had enough. In October 1923, she returned to Paris and, after a month of recuperation, boarded a ship for America. On board, she met a 45-year-old journalist and novelist from Illinois named Garet Garrett. Now working as a correspondent for the *Saturday Evening Post*, Garrett helped Lane answer the questions about political philosophy that were now stirring in her mind. They talked at length during the Atlantic crossing, and he likely shared his ideas about free markets, the untenability of socialism, and the national character of the American people. She later recalled being exhausted not only by the "human misery" of Armenia, Georgia, Egypt, and British Iraq, and by the "revolting snobbery" of Western colonial officials, but also by the "killing toil and ignorance and humility" and "so-called 'spirituality' born of hopelessness and starvation" that she had witnessed among the local inhabitants.[62] Generations of political oppression, she suspected, had warped the cultures of such societies so that the people flattered and feared their rulers instead of seeking personal independence.

Garrett was then writing articles on similar themes for American readers, warning against what he saw as a dangerous influx of immigrants from European countries where the mores of free government were unknown.

Saturday Evening Post journalist Garet Garrett likely spurred Rose Wilder Lane to reflect on the influence of the pioneer experience on American culture.

The American character had been formed by the pioneer experience, he argued, which taught Americans to prize personal independence and self-direction. By the dawn of the 20th century, they had come to believe that the world was theirs for the making—an attitude that contrasted with the fatalism and resignation that Lane later called "Old World thinking." The basis of Old World thinking, she said, was an assumption that the universe is static, and that social order or economic prosperity can only come from the command of some lawmaking "Authority" rather than from the independent choices of free individuals. That authoritarian "delusion" doomed the peoples of other nations to an endless cycle of tyranny, followed by rebellion, followed by another tyranny—whereas free people looked for ways to solve their own problems. Garrett feared the cultural consequences of immigration from the Old World to the United States—writing in 1924 that "there had been no proletariat in this country" before "the tide of migrating humanity began to rise."[63] That was not a view Lane shared—on the contrary, she cherished the idea of America as a refuge for the world's oppressed—but her conversations with Garrett likely spurred her to focus on the nature of distinctively American cultural attitudes and their relationship to political liberty.

Recently separated from his wife, Garrett may also have been romantically interested in Lane, but at the time she thought him "self-conscious and conventional."[64] In any event, she was in the midst of a complicated long-term relationship with Guy Moyston, whom she had known since 1915 and with whom she spent much time in London in 1921 before traveling to the Balkans. Lane and Moyston exchanged passionate letters while making their separate ways across postwar Europe, but now that Lane was on her way home to her parents' Missouri farm to recover from her European experiences and complete several writing projects—including the Jack London book—her feelings started to change. When Moyston teased her about the quaintness of farm life, she exploded at him. "You just try it once," she snapped. "With the well frozen, I mean the bucket frozen in it, and the floors dirty with muddy feet and dogs and wood-dirt and ashes-dust . . . and the swill having to be cooked for the hogs, and a sick lamb in the corner, and—well, you just try it once."⁶⁵ Moyston and Lane's relationship lingered off and on until 1928, when Lane finally allowed it to dissolve. "Being constantly with any other person, even you, is incompatible with other things I want," she told him when he suggested marrying. "I DON'T WANT TO BE CLUTCHED."⁶⁶

Shortly after her return to Missouri, Lane wrote "Autumn," a short story that, according to scholar Julia Ehrhardt, indicates the "personal rebirth," or at least self-examination, that Lane was experiencing.⁶⁷ It concerns a writer named Evie who arrives home after traveling through Europe. Now her town's most famous resident, she is feted and taken to visit the townspeople who praise her elaborately. But when her sister, Rose, tries to reintroduce her to her former fiancé, the reunion fails. Evie realizes that she has outgrown the village of her youth and would never be happy as a wife. Far from lamenting this, however, she relishes the way her former small-town attitudes have given way to a "wilder sense of freedom." The author must have savored the pun.

▰

Lane meant to stay in Missouri only briefly, to earn some money and to arrange for her permanent move to Albania. But she ended up remaining at her parents' Rocky Ridge Farm for more than two years, writing scores of magazine articles and stories and completing the Jack London manuscript, now retitled *He Was a Man*.

Because it started as a biography, *He Was a Man* has never been recognized for what it really is: a semiautobiographical novel that blends Lane's own life with that of Jack London and is sometimes more candid than even *Diverging Roads* had been. In fact, it is partly a Village Rebel story, and partly what communist intellectuals would later call a "proletarian novel." That was their term for what they hoped would become a new literary form for the working class—one that would create the cultural conditions for revolution by combining a realistic portrayal of worker life with a dramatization of socialist ideology.⁶⁸ *He Was a Man* straddles these categories by showing how the main character's (in reality, Lane's) rebellion against the stifling dullness of the village attracts him to socialism. In it, London—renamed Gordon Blake—shares Lane's own longing to escape from the small town, and in that search takes up socialism as a cause that gives him personal meaning. "The restlessness which was Gordon Blake's is mine," Lane later told a friend. They shared "the common unease and discontent of Americans which makes us the greatest builders, the greatest destroyers, most incessant movers, always seeking and never satisfied."[69]

Her kinship with her character is clear from the start, which depicts Blake's impoverished childhood on a farm during the depression of 1893. Blake longs "to go far away, to get away from everything he knew and was so tired of knowing" and find "strange dangers to encounter and conquer," but adventure seems a long way off.[70] He feels that the rich and powerful are to blame for his lack of opportunity. But when he expresses resentment toward Wall Street millionaires, his father corrects him. "Them millionaires started poor's anybody, 'n' what they got they got by developin' the country," he tells Blake. "We ain't grateful enough to them millionaires that built up the railroads. They worked hard a-doin' it; they worked hard 'n' saved their money, 'n' I say, if they got rich, their riches was comin' to 'em."[71] Blake is not so sure. "How had the millionaires got a start[?]'" he asks—and why has he been denied a similar opportunity? "All he wanted was the chance."[72]

Blake storms into the office of the Southern Pacific Railroad in search of employment and gets a job shoveling coal. But the work is hard, and when he learns that the company fired another man to make room for him, and that his predecessor committed suicide in despair, he quits. He joins "Coxey's Army," the nation's first protest march on Washington, DC, in which some 10,000 demonstrators, led by an Ohio politician named Jacob Coxey, descended on the nation's capital in May 1894—a protest the real London did in fact join. Blake and his fellow protestors travel across the country, hijacking railroads and frightening the residents of small towns along the way. For Blake, the whole thing feels like "a long picnic," and he revels in the rebellious talk of his companions:

What was the use of a Constitution if Wall Street bossed the Country? But could Wall Street boss the country, if laboring men would stick together? A man had a right to his job. Then did a man have a right to own a factory, and shut it down, and throw men out of their jobs . . . ? The thing that was wrong was private property. Take their money away from 'em, damn 'em! Divide it up, share 'n' share alike. The country was rich enough for everybody; only trouble was, a few folks had everythin', 'n' the rest nothin'. . . . Take all the land in the United States 'n' divide it up, every man his own farm. Then there would be plenty for everybody.[73]

Blake is a haphazard socialist, however. He hardly even understands the doctrine and gets lost when his friends try to explain. For him, socialism is less a political theory than a channel for the nebulous grudges he feels toward the "the stupidities of middle-class American society."[74] He feels himself a "lonely and superior being," and projects his bitterness into an amorphous concept he labels capitalism, which he envisions as "some obscure thing that held him, that kept him down," or a "monster" responsible for everything bad in life.[75] Above all, capitalism represents sexual repression—whereas socialism represents a vitalist "will to power," that promises to vindicate his masculinity and his racial superiority.

Growing bored, Blake quits Coxey's Army before it reaches Washington and takes to the road as a solitary tramp.[76] He eventually decides to get an education and returns to California to enroll in school. There he reads *Looking Backward* and the *Appeal to Reason*. Still unclear about socialist economics, he asks some comrades how, in the coming utopia, people will be persuaded to work for the benefit of others instead of their own profit. They give conflicting answers: "the co-operative commonwealth" will "make a new humanity," they tell him, "but, after all, there was no altruism in Socialism; it rested on the eternal basis of human nature, which was selfishness. All men would profit by a fair distribution of the fruits of labor."[77] Still confused, Blake puts it out of his mind. "There must be something worth while in Socialism," he concludes, "to hold such men."[78]

In his rejection of bourgeois respectability and yearning for a more meaningful life, Blake is a Village Rebel, yet he feels tension between socialism and his own need for self-fulfillment, even feeling guilty for writing stories about the misery of workers, because that seems like a form of exploitation. He grows cynical about the possibility of mankind ever sharing wealth for the benefit of the poor, and he becomes frustrated and bored with his household, which seems to be descending into the *Main Street*-style respectability he despises. He quarrels with his wife over having to fix the lawnmower and attend dinner parties with friends. And although she tries to balance his needs as a writer with those of their growing family, Blake decides he cannot satisfy both. During one argument, she hurls at him the same words Gillette had once used against Lane during one of their arguments: "Why can't you be *human*?"[79] In the end, they divorce, and Blake moves to a farm with an alluring intellectual woman who fulfills him sexually, is "pliant to all his moods, answering all his desires," and makes him feel "his mastery over it all."[80]

He Was a Man makes clear that while Lane was skeptical about socialist economics, she was attracted to those elements of socialism that rejected the "bourgeois" morality of small-town America. Yet paradoxically enough, she also seems to have shared London's support for some of the Progressive Era's moralizing legislation, particularly the prohibition of alcohol. The real Jack London's struggles with drink were widely known during his lifetime, and in his book *John Barleycorn*, he argued that allowing liquor to be openly sold was like leaving a well uncovered for children to fall into. Letting people decide for themselves whether to drink was a relic of "what future ages will call the dark ages," he thought. "The only rational thing for the twentieth-century folk to do is to cover up the well."[81] In 1911, London endorsed female suffrage specifically because he hoped women would vote to ban alcohol nationwide.[82]

Ten years later, in a remarkable letter to *Harper's*, Lane appeared to endorse Prohibition on similar grounds. It represented a step away from barbarism, she thought, because "the foundation of civilization" lay in "the herd's control of the individual." Prohibiting alcohol was no more objectionable than banning murder:

> The essential difference between the taboo of the savage and the law
> of the civilized is that the one is based on individualism and the other

on social welfare. The measure of civilization's progress is the loss of individual liberty. In civilization natural impulses have been so curbed and restrained that they are atrophied; we no longer wish to be naked, to eat raw meat, to beat our wives; we are even reaching the point where considerable numbers of us take no pleasure in deciding differences of opinion with war-clubs. We have so long accepted prohibition of our individualistic impulses that we have ceased to have them. Has that been a loss, or a gain? I suppose it is impossible to say. . . . The individual's right to unquestioned personal exercise of the qualities of courage and self-control passed from him when murder was prohibited. . . . Yet we accept prohibition of murder, and compulsory education, without question, because in these matters—as in innumerable others—we have so long surrendered individual liberty that we no longer think of it in connection with them.[83]

As with her fictional doppelgänger, Lane's rebellion against the village of her childhood was intense, and it drove her in the direction of socialism, particularly for its promise of secularism and feminism. But for Lane, as for London, socialism somehow failed to satisfy the need for personal fulfillment. What remained in the end was the sense of alienation and restlessness that Lane and London shared. "It was because [London] loved life too much that he abused it," she wrote in a notebook. "He told himself that he did not care for life in order to protect himself from the pain of knowing that he would die. And he had a sense of somehow not having begun right—of a crooked start that made it impossible ever to get four-square with life, facts, himself—an inaccuracy at the beginning that made it impossible ever to reach the right answer."[84]

▰▲▰

Reviews of *He Was a Man* were mixed. The prominent editor Floyd Dell called it a work of "truth" and "beauty," and described Lane as "that rarest of all things, a realist and a romanticist both at once."[85] But critic Lawrence

Stallings was closer to the truth when he called it a failure, due largely to the fact that by making it a novel instead of a biography, Lane made it impossible to quote London's actual publications as proof of Blake's skills as a writer. "Consequently, we have a novel of a man who, the author assures us, was a great literary genius without being privileged to inspect one paragraph of his writing. We must take her word for it that Gordon Blake was a genius."[86]

Lane was herself ultimately unhappy with the book,[87] but it and her magazine stories—which she gathered into two more novels, *Cindy: An Ozark Romance* and *Hill-Billy*—were, along with her stock market investments, generating enough income that she could make plans for a permanent move to Albania with Troub Boylston. In the spring of 1926, the couple left Missouri for Paris, where they stayed for a few months studying Italian, Russian, and other languages, and enjoyed a reunion with Dorothy Thompson, who had just married a writer named Joseph Bard. Lane was uneasy about the marriage. She thought Thompson depended too much on Bard's approval, thus subduing her own personality and potentially stifling her own promising career as a writer. Lane held her tongue, but her fears proved prescient.

That fall, she and Boylston decided to pack up and drive from Paris to Albania—more than 2,000 miles—in a Model T they nicknamed Zenobia. They arrived in September. "What *is* Albania to me, really?" Lane asked herself in one of her long, introspective diary entries. "I can lose my life here, bit by bit, as I have always lost it."[88] She dreamed of completing some great literary work but found it impossible to concentrate, given the distractions of her new home and the need to produce magazine fiction to pay the bills. "I can't take myself seriously as a 'creative artist,'" she wrote to Guy Moyston. "If I can't— and I can't—be Shakespeare or Goethe, I'd rather raise good cabbages."[89]

At times, she relished the placidity of the Albanian countryside and the seeming simplicity of its people. She told Dorothy Thompson that Albania had "the most delicious spring you've ever tasted, and everything grows in a sort of glow of enjoyment."[90] She experienced a calm that enabled her to forget all her cares. "Why do we *want* so desperately?" she asked Thompson in another letter. "There's an equilibrium in us, if we'll let it be. . . . We suffer because we fight so, because we *want* so passionately, and so passionately in opposition to life and death and time and eternity." But Albania was anything but an idyll. Trapped between fascist Italy and communist Russia, it was on the verge of civil war, and its people knew immense suffering. Lane's panacea was only made possible by the income from her fiction and Troub's investment accounts. Still, the blissful times in her garden, or talking with charming Albanian villagers, free of family responsibilities and thousands of miles from her parents' farm, persuaded her that she was "specially created (by some incredible freak of the stars) for the Moslem woman's life."[91]

In truth, Lane never seriously considered adopting Islam, but her familiarity with it—and affection for it—would become the most lasting legacy of her time in Albania. It would also make her virtually unique in the history of classical liberalism, for few libertarian intellectuals have ever tried as she did to reconcile Islam with the human rights tradition of classical liberal political philosophy.[92] She was drawn, in part, by the extraordinary generosity she witnessed in postwar Albania.[93] Even in the depths of the Armenian genocide, she told a friend, "every household was a source of food and shelter and friendliness." She added, in a note remarkable for a former Red Cross employee, "No Red Cross ever did a finer job than the unorganized Moslem faith did then."[94] But along with its emphasis on charity, Islam offered what Lane considered a critical insight into political freedom.

Lane saw Islam as an essentially anti-authoritarian faith, rooted in the same principles of human equality and self-responsibility that were expressed in the American Declaration of Independence. Mohammed's basic teaching, she wrote in her 1943 manifesto *The Discovery of Freedom*, was that "there is no superior *kind* of man; men are humanly equal." This meant that "each individual must recognize his direct relation to God, his self-controlling, personal responsibility"[95]—a proposition incompatible with the hierarchy of an established priesthood or the imposition of religion by state authority. And the beneficial consequences of this equality, she thought, were demonstrated by the fact that during the Middle Ages, while Christian Europe was mired in clericalism, ignorance, and darkness, the Muslim world was developing "modern science—mathematics, astronomy, navigation, modern medicine and surgery, scientific agriculture."[96] Classical Islam had been free of the religious bigotry, sectarian warfare, and political oppression that marked medieval Christendom.[97] Most of all, she believed, Islam taught the principle of the "brotherhood of man," on which Muslims erected a culture that she called a "pure anarchy of freedom"—meaning that instead of relying on compulsion by the state, each person took responsibility for his own actions, and individual behavior was governed by persuasion and social pressure, not government coercion.[98]

But Lane's dream of an Albanian refuge was doomed. The serenity she had found during her first visits seemed to wither away as the decade neared its close. The country was struggling to retain its autonomy, and its monarch, King Zog, was growing desperate for some way to stave off Italian domination while resisting the efforts of domestic communists to draw closer to the Soviet Union. Only Italian money could fund anti-communist work, Zog thought, but that brought with it the influence of Mussolini's government. "You were right in a prophecy you once made," Lane told Dorothy Thompson in January 1928. "Albania, you said, would become *Main Street*. No, not quite like that, not *Main Street*—the *Via Mussolini*. My Albania's sunk."[99]

Lane decided she could not stay. Along with the increasing trend toward *Main Street*-style chauvinism, and the real risk of Italian annexation, was the fact that she was running out of money. Her books and articles brought a substantial income, as had her considerable stock market investments, but she spent rapidly, both on her own household and in regular stipends that she sent to her parents and Rexh Meta. Then a telegram arrived from her mother. What it said remains unknown, but it must have been important, for Lane made up her mind to return to Missouri immediately.

Albania had not given her the opportunity she had hoped for to create a lasting work of literature. There were too many distractions, and the need to pay bills drew her toward writing lucrative but forgettable magazine pieces. Yet despite her frustration, her career was blossoming. She won prestigious awards for short stories in 1922 and 1927, and her skill at twist endings and spooky tales was improving. There were hints of better work to come. Her 1927 story "Yarbwoman," for instance, featured a series of mysterious deaths that come about when people wear a pair of boots; it is later discovered that a snake's poisoned tooth is embedded in the sole. It was a tale that had been handed down through the family from her grandfather, Charles Ingalls.[100] Its success led her to consider turning other family legends into salable properties. In one notebook, she wrote that she might try "a series of pioneer stories, featuring the woman."[101] As Lane scholar Christine Woodside observes, this note is the earliest hint of what would become one of the most influential partnerships in American literature—between Rose Wilder Lane and Laura Ingalls Wilder.[102]

▰▲◣

Wilder had been writing a regular column for her hometown newspaper for more than a decade by then, sometimes recycling material from her daughter's letters from Europe. She had also published articles in *McCall's* and *Country Gentleman*. In each case, Laura had furnished the material and Rose had rewritten it in a style that magazines would print. Before her latest trip to Albania, Rose and her mother evidently discussed writing a memoir of Laura's childhood on the western plains, and together they drafted a letter to Laura's elderly aunt asking for some memories of the olden days. "It would be wonderful for the family to have such a record," Laura wrote. "I think too that Rose could make some stories from such a record, for publication."[103]

But that project would not come to fruition for some years. In the meantime, Lane returned to her parents' Rocky Ridge Farm and completed scores of short stories for *Country Gentleman*, *Ladies' Home Journal*, *Harper's*, and other magazines. She oversaw construction of a new house—complete with plumbing and electricity—which she paid for as a gift to her parents. It proved far more expensive than anticipated, but she could afford it, thanks in part to her heavy investments in the stock market, which was booming along impressively. Still, supervising construction took time away from writing.

So did her extensive reading. Inspired by her experiences in eastern Europe and the Middle East, Lane had begun studying books of history and political philosophy in an effort to understand what it was that made the United States so different from the rest of the world. As she thought it over, she became increasingly convinced that her former Village Rebel rejection of middle-class values had been premature—perhaps even immature. In a remarkable letter to Dorothy Thompson in August 1928, she expressed a more benevolent attitude toward the land of her birth than she had ever felt before. However much there was to dislike about the country, she thought, its culture contained a dynamism radically different from other societies— something intellectuals failed to appreciate in their haste to sneer at it. "We don't like America—*I* don't like it—because of its lack of form," she wrote. But she was coming to see that formlessness—or, in other words, its social and economic fluidity—as actually a great blessing: "It's exactly stability which America discards. . . . Is it possible for a civilization to *be* wholly dynamic? Wholly a vibration, a becoming, a force existing in itself, without direction, without an object for its verb? A civilization always *becoming*, never *being*, never never having the stability, the *form*, which is the beginning of death?"[104] She was beginning to think that America's vibrancy—its lack of the social hierarchy and cultural refinements Europeans considered essential—was just what made it unique and precious.

She was also beginning to suspect that the Village Rebels who had made *Main Street* a bestseller had misunderstood America all along—in fact, they had "never been able to bear" America, precisely because they failed to appreciate this dynamism. That was why they scorned the commonplace pleasures of ordinary people. However valid their reasons for mutiny against the village, their rebellion had mutated into a destructive hostility toward the simple beauties of existence. "My protest is really against this habit of the intellectuals, of discarding the essentially *human* attributes as beneath their own high level of intelligence," Lane wrote. That attitude was "the cushioned comfort of the withdrawal from human realities. . . . The end of most of our 'intellectuals' is sterility because of this narrowing, this withdrawal. Because of this snobbish refusal to admit common origins, common meanings, the essential identity beneath the whole sordid magnificent comedy-tragedy of humanity."[105]

It was a startling letter, particularly given that Lane sent it to Thompson only a month after learning that the younger woman had become engaged to marry the author of *Main Street* himself, Sinclair Lewis. The couple had met in Berlin a year before, and Thompson—whose first marriage had not yet been dissolved—swiftly fell in love with him. In fact, Lewis proposed to Thompson at a party she gave to celebrate the finalization of her divorce. Lane knew all too well that Thompson's first marriage had been miserable— her husband, Joseph Bard, was a philanderer who resented his wife for what he saw as her bossiness—and now Lane feared that Thompson was making another rash engagement. She wrote her friend a long, carefully worded letter urging her not to remarry, and to preserve her independence instead. She did not know Lewis at all, but she feared that Thompson would "submerge and deny [her] own qualities" and that "the person you are and may be" would "get lost completely."[106] Lane decided not to send the letter, however, and dispatched a different, more restrained note instead, one that only hinted at her concerns before concluding, "be happy, my dear."[107] Yet her first impulse had been right: Thompson's marriage to the alcoholic, emotionally distant Lewis would prove disastrous.

Twenty years later, Lane would declare that Lewis had "derailed American fiction" with *Main Street*, and that "all the successful American writers since then have gone to smash in the same ditch."[108] That novel, she thought, "mark[ed] the time when American fiction writers turned away" from the individualistic, freedom-loving tradition of such authors as Mark Twain, Edith Wharton, and Willa Cather, and became contemptuous of American life. Lewis "substituted satire for their comedy, a thin cynicism for their optimism, caricature for their sympathy, a snobbish, faintly disguised detachment for the uniquely American sense of human kinship."[109] By then, Lane had come to prefer the science fiction of Ray Bradbury and Robert Heinlein.

But at the dawn of the 1930s, her reappraisal of the Revolt from the Village had just started. It began with her recognition of a profound dichotomy between

the essentially static and authoritarian worldview she called Old World thinking, and the dynamic and individualistic ethos of America. In the years to
come, that contrast would find expression in her novels *Old Home Town* and
Free Land, and in the *Little House* series. As early as 1928, Isabel Paterson had
predicted that "the next great literary movement" in the United States would be
a "back to the small town" movement—because there was "a lot to be said for
the small town life" that *Main Street* and its admirers despised.[110] In the decade
that followed, Lane was one of the foremost writers who took that path, transforming her earlier rebellion into nostalgia for a past of stalwart virtue.

It was just when she was at the cusp of this insight that everything came
crashing down. On October 29, 1929, Lane was listening to the radio with
Troub Boylston when the news broadcaster announced the collapse on Wall
Street that was to inaugurate the Great Depression. Market declines had
already occurred in the spring and summer, and October saw investors increasingly selling their stocks. Then in the last week of the month, stocks fell again.
On "Black Tuesday," traders dumped more than 16 million shares in a selloff
that saw the Dow Jones Industrial Average plummet 23 percent in two days.
Lane, who had not only invested much of her own savings in the market
but had also persuaded her parents to join her, sensed the full scale of the
disaster. Turning to Troub with a pale, panicked look, she said simply, "This
is the end."[111]

Herbert Hoover became president eight years after Rose Wilder Lane's
biography *The Making of Herbert Hoover* was published.
The two became friends, and Lane tried to get him to publicize
Paterson's book *The God of the Machine*.

3

The Great Engineer

The economic downturn over the summer and autumn of 1929 was driven partly by the Federal Reserve's efforts to reduce the nation's money supply after having spent the previous decade expanding it. Since at least 1920, the government had followed an inflationary policy that encouraged inefficient long-term investments—what economists call "malinvestment"—both in the United States and abroad.[1] That policy was motivated in part by a desire to "stabilize" prices, a myopic notion that failed to distinguish between price decreases caused by cheaper production—which were beneficial—and those due to monetary manipulation, which could have unpredictable and possibly dangerous consequences. Yet the effort to stabilize prices, and particularly to prevent decreases in wages, was supported by the newly elected president, Herbert Hoover.

Renowned for his skill in government administration, Hoover was nothing like the champion of laissez faire that popular myth would later imagine. On the contrary, he was—as Lane described him in her 1920 book—a technocrat who thought bureaucratic experts could direct investment, improve business, and alleviate shortages. He prided himself on being "the Great Engineer," and while serving as secretary of commerce between 1921 and 1928, he proved an aggressive proponent of engineering the nation's economy. He sometimes irritated cabinet colleagues by insinuating himself into matters that fell within their purview, and even took over entire bureaus from the Departments of the Treasury and the Interior.[2] Yet his understanding of economics was riddled with fallacies.

Among the most significant was his belief that high wages caused prosperity. That conviction may have had its roots in his own experience growing up in poverty on a farm, where he imbibed the idea that—as he told Garet Garrett in 1928—"if prices are high, they mean comfort and automobiles; if prices are low, they mean increasing debt and privation."[3] That is not true, because wages are a cost of production, so policies aimed at increasing them cause scarcities, just as rules increasing the costs of raw materials do. High prices make consumers worse off, and as Adam Smith explained, "Consumption is the sole end and purpose of all production," so that "the interest of the producer ought to be attended to only so far as it may be necessary for promoting that of the consumer."[4]

Disregarding this advice, Hoover focused his attention on improving the lot of businesses instead of customers. Thus, when he became president, he sought to prevent precisely the wage reductions that would have ensured a rapid recovery. By keeping labor costs up, his policies deterred investment, limited business expansion, made it more expensive to hire people, drove many firms out of business, and prevented workers from finding new jobs where their skills were in greater demand.

Of course, the 1929 collapse was far from the first economic panic in American history. Major downturns had occurred throughout the 19th century and even as recently as 1920, caused, like the 1929 crash, by inflation sparked by excessive lending, which led to malinvestment. Those previous collapses had been painful, but each had corrected itself after a brief spike in unemployment and a fall in prices, which allowed businesses and workers to respond to changed conditions by finding new jobs or channeling capital into different, more profitable avenues of production. The worst of the previous depressions, the Panic of 1893—during which scores of companies had failed and unemployment shot up to 20 percent—remained in public memory for almost half a century as the severest economic crisis the nation had yet endured. It had inspired Coxey's Army—the march on Washington that Jack London and Lane's fictional Gordon Blake had briefly joined. In the summer of 1894, Coxey's followers arrived after a series of violent standoffs (on at least one occasion hijacking a locomotive) and set up camp outside Washington, DC, where the protest swelled to 1,000, perhaps more, before being dispersed by federal troops.[5] President Grover Cleveland had rejected Coxey's demands and refused to adopt an inflationary policy of government spending. So had his successor, William McKinley. As a consequence, the economy righted itself and returned on a sounder foundation after malinvestment petered out into more efficient allocations of resources.

But in 1929, Hoover was unwilling to let this normal economic process occur. Instead, insisting that labor is "not a commodity," he claimed that temporary unemployment "would deepen the depression by suddenly reducing purchasing power," and implemented plans to restrict economic productivity in order to raise prices and thereby "stabilize" industry.[6]

In his insistence on maintaining high wages, Hoover was not alone. As historian Arthur Schlesinger Jr. observes, many prominent business leaders and economists had come to believe that "high output, low prices, and high wages must be the new objectives."[7] That these three goals are incompatible was proved in the decades that followed. But Hoover's prioritization of high wages led his administration into schemes for stimulating *consumption*—encouraging consumers to spend, or even forcing them to do so, to prevent businesses from failing. One flaw in this approach was that it subsidized ventures that had no actual market demand, thereby diverting capital away from possible innovations that consumers actually wanted. Another flaw was that discouraging savings increases the risk of loss to consumers and deters them from making prudent financial choices. A third problem was that viewing prosperity as synonymous with high incomes for companies instead of the standard of living consumers experience made government beholden to the interests of politically influential business owners, thereby lending credence to the accusation that the government was serving the interests of industrial giants at the expense of the working class. "Who went on Federal relief first?" Isabel Paterson wrote years later. "It was the non-productive rich who first went on the dole."[8]

Scorning what he called the "arbitrary and dog-eat-dog attitude" of the free market, Hoover asked business owners to promise not to cut wages or halt construction.[9] They agreed, essentially forming a nationwide cartel devoted to

Laura Ingalls Wilder's childhood experiences formed the basis
of the *Little House* series of novels. A firm opponent of the New Deal,
Wilder believed Americans needed to remember the steadfast virtues
of pioneer days.

continuing the inflationary climb in spite of the crumbling market. The idea, as economic historian Amity Shlaes puts it, was that companies should "take the hit in profits instead of employment."[10] But keeping wages stable while profits fell, or continuing to build after demand collapsed, deprived businesses of the ability to streamline operations to suit new circumstances, and it sometimes drove them into bankruptcy, rendering all their workers jobless. Companies had survived previous downturns by reducing wages, but Hoover's refusal to allow this, wrote one economist in 1934, "caused many firms to discharge workers rather than appear as slackers by cutting wages, although they might have been able to continue operations if they had made such reductions."[11]

The Great Engineer's faith in government planning was shared by politicians of both parties, who were convinced that state and federal experts, free of the profit motive—and, in bureaucracies, freed even from accountability to voters—could dispassionately organize the system of production and exchange to avoid the alleged "waste" and "inefficiency" of the free market. Administrators would ensure that goods and services were provided in the right amounts and distributed in the right ways to the right people. The disastrous consequences that followed in the 1930s proved that it is impossible to obtain the knowledge necessary to determine the "right" amounts of production or the "right" recipients of it—and that government efforts to do so will be exploited by private interests in ways that violate individual freedom and worsen the economy.

Yet despite his support for government planning, Hoover considered himself an individualist. In fact, he had published a book in 1922 titled *American Individualism* in which he tried to combine these contradictory ideas. Writing that "we have long since abandoned the laissez faire of the 18th Century" and "the 'capitalism' of Adam Smith," in favor of "social and economic justice," he nevertheless insisted that he did *not* mean for politicians to control the economy.[12] Government should clamp down on "selfish impulses" and impose "restrictions on the strong and dominant," he thought, in order to achieve "a fair division of the product"—yet individuals must still have "liberty and stimulation to achievement."[13] He seemed to think that individualism could be promoted by empowering bureaucrats to first give each person "the chance and stimulation for the development of the best with which he has been endowed," and then to determine when that person's success had become excessive, whereupon they would "restrict" the individual accordingly, to ensure that he embraced a "vision of service . . . to the nation, and service to the world itself."[14]

In short, Hoover's version of individualism inherently assumed that government power was all-encompassing, and that the state could decide how much freedom each person needed and parcel it out accordingly. Little wonder that Isabel Paterson called his books "dreary nothings—no ideas, few facts, no form, no writing."[15] She preferred the classical version of individualism—the belief that each person has a right to pursue happiness without the government's interference or "assistance"—which had built the American frontier. To the argument that "liberty" meant some kind of positive direction or personal fulfillment with which the state could assist, Paterson replied, "Bosh. Liberty is an absence of restraint. And nothing else whatever. It is not a means, but an end."[16] True individualists do not ask the government to provide them with opportunities, she thought, or to hinder their competitors. They ask only to be left alone to put their skills to work and do their best, either to succeed or try again.

◢▲◣

In the wake of the stock market crash, however, Paterson was feeling like a failure herself. Her investments had been wiped out, totaling perhaps as much as $30,000. She found it hard to believe that only a year and a half earlier, she had been traveling Europe, taking a break from writing a novel, and seeing the sights with an old friend named Nat Roberts. Together they had visited Shakespeare's home, the Ardennes Forest, and the Cluny Museum. She had met the writer Ford Madox Ford, a long-time collaborator of one of her favorite novelists, Joseph Conrad, and he had asked her advice on the manuscript of a book he was struggling with. Her encouragement meant so much to him that he dedicated the finished work to her, calling her *"cher confrère"* and "my fairy godmother."[17] But now, that life seemed irrevocably lost.

It may also have been on that trip that an incident occurred that she was fond of relating afterward. Finding herself at an elegant dinner party where the conversation turned to H. G. Wells, then at the height of his celebrity, she shocked the people at her table by venturing that Wells—an eccentric socialist and advocate of "free love"—was a fool. Stammering with embarrassment, one gentleman tried to persuade her to moderate her opinion, but Paterson insisted. At last, the lady sitting beside Paterson introduced herself as Odette Keun, Wells's wife, and coolly explained that she considered her husband a genius. For a while, the shortsighted Paterson squinted at the woman through her glasses, before at last declaring, "I still say H. G. Wells is a fool."[18]

During their time in Europe, Paterson and Roberts seem to have fallen in love. But there were complications: Roberts was engaged to marry another woman and he was suffering from a terminal illness.[19] He had a stroke not long after Paterson returned home, and while recovering, he wrote to say that he planned to come to America to be with her. She considered returning to Europe to be with him—but at some point, both Roberts's fiancée and his ex-wife intervened. Not long afterward, Roberts died. "A complicated story," Paterson told a friend. "This isn't what you think, it probably isn't even what I think."[20] Whatever it was, it inspired Paterson's 1933 novel, the surprise best-seller *Never Ask the End*.

A largely plotless tale about two close friends, Marta and Pauline, who visit Paris in the company of an expatriate American businessman named Russ, the book consists almost entirely of the dialogue and internal thoughts of the characters, and especially of flashbacks and ruminations by Marta, a stand-in for Paterson herself. We gradually learn that Marta had once married a man named Keith, who had previously been Pauline's boyfriend. There are no hard feelings between the two women, though, because the marriage turned out badly and ended in divorce. Pauline's own marriage had also failed; her alcoholic husband died and left her with two children. Now both women find themselves attracted to Russ, but Marta—partly out of guilt over the incident with Keith—decides to stand back and allow Pauline to spend time with him. When, however, a business engagement delays Russ's arrival in London for so long that Pauline is forced to return to America alone, Marta and Russ are left together, and a brief romance ensues.

The novel's charm lies in long passages of reflection and reminiscence by the three characters, and it particularly struck a chord with readers who, like Paterson, had experienced the head-spinning changes of the previous half century and now stood at the brink of the decade-long Great Depression. "We've come so far," thinks Marta, who was born on the frontier in the 1880s and is a member of the "Airplane Generation."[21] "It's no wonder we're tired. Starting in a prairie schooner and covering the last lap by aeroplane. There and back. Americans are adaptable. . . . To experience all the stages of civilization in one lifetime, from the nomad to the machine age, demands the utmost."[22] Marta is astonished to think of how the world has transformed before her eyes. "She could remember reading of the Wrights' first flight. So she could also remember before that. It left one gasping, to think of belonging to both ages—to have seen the world swing out in space, and nothing to steer by but one far-off nameless star."[23]

Paterson is particularly eloquent in long passages discussing how drastically the lives of women have changed, and the ambiguous position in which modernity has left them. When Marta ponders her teenage years, she recalls the "enormous release of energy" that came with the first waves of feminism, "and also that secret grief, that sense of guilt, as of an undischarged obligation, springing from the inherited moral sentiment of family solidarity."[24] Many of her contemporaries, she reflects, came to regret choosing a career and independence over a family, but then again, "how could one not *try*?" Her own generation had been "an army of girls, without banners, in mutiny," who left their homes and the "child-bearing and drudgery and dependence" that had so long been women's destiny. Some people "tell us now it was a delusion, that we went to a more precarious dependence," but Marta knows better: "They don't know what it used to be like for women. And anyhow, it worked for us. We had our adventure."[25] The costs of independence may have been severe—but it was worth the price. Such passages must have resonated with women like Rose Wilder Lane, who had escaped the farm and traveled the world, only to be drawn back by a sense of family obligation. (In fact, Lane herself was given a cameo in the novel, appearing as the character Donna, an eccentric singer who grew up on the Dakota prairie and became a globe-trotting career woman.)

Never Ask the End was essentially Paterson's own spin on the Revolt from the Village. Marta has fled her own village, at least temporarily, for the sophistication and culture of Europe. But where Sinclair Lewis had seen the small town as insufferably dreary, Paterson's verdict was more measured. In some ways, she shared Lewis's revulsion at the conformity of village puritanism, and *Never Ask the End* even contains a Babbitt-like character named Ernest, a blowhard who pries incessantly into the other characters' private affairs. Marta is disgusted to learn that Ernest, a landlord, once evicted a tenant because he saw her on the porch kissing a man.[26] She cannot help but imagine herself in the woman's position. "You have to worry about the rent and wash the dishes and get the children to school and rush to work in the morning," she thinks, "and soon you'll be old and tired and all the moonlight and the roses will be gone to waste, and if you lean out the window, pick a flower, wish on a star—there is Ernest peering obscenely through the curtain—*yah, I saw you!*"[27] She makes fun of Ernest behind his back, but she also sees in him a malevolent force—a hatred for joy itself.

Paterson was not content to condemn all of Middle America as a bunch of nosy Ernests, however. She thought there was much good in the small town, too. "They tell us now it was puritanical in our time," Marta says, but in reality, "it was tough and wild. . . . Nobody could understand who didn't live through it, because every imaginable contradiction was true."[28] The nation she had known as a child had been full of kind people, bold inventors and breathtaking opportunities. Even in the villages, people had led unfathomably complicated lives. What was disappearing in the modern era, she thought, was not the puritanism of the Victorian age, but its idealism; not its ugliness and prudery, but its naive longing for the beautiful and true. *Never Ask the End* finishes on this foreboding note when Russ suggests that Marta accompany him on a side trip to Italy. She refuses. "With those blackshirts infesting it—I couldn't breathe." When Russ offers that Mussolini may be harsh, but he has restored the Italian economy and prevented communist revolution, Marta "flare[s] up" in indignation.

> She did genuinely hate regimentation and suppression; she hated it too much to be coherent. "We've had ours," she exclaimed, "we oughtn't to go back on ourselves." Americans, she meant. They had been free. It wasn't a joke; their freedom had been bought with a great price, and was worth it. She was grateful to all those valiant minds who had wrought and endured for her. Now those who had profited by it were going to destroy it, so no one else should ever have it. They didn't know what they were doing—but they ought to know!

Mussolini is just a "pop-eyed ham actor," she continues. "Every Babbitt in America fancies himself in the same part." Finished with her tirade, she blushes. "Of all inappropriate occasions for such an outburst. . . . A Fourth of July firecracker."[29]

In the book's final pages, Marta visits the Cluny Museum, while she awaits her ship back to America. She sits staring at broken, timeworn fragments of medieval statues buried in tall grass. "It is the material substance that is ghostly," she thinks. "It wears out, dissolves with time." All that is left behind are the doomed efforts of the past to bequeath to the future the ineffable qualities of lost ages. "What we desire is communication. . . . Perhaps, [in] some other [dimension], we achieve it, by a persistence to which even granite must yield."[30]

Free of the intense melancholy that would hover over Paterson's later novels, *Never Ask the End* is an alluring, elegiac book, and it sold remarkably well, considering its avant-garde prose style. Sinclair Lewis praised it as "important . . . completely different from any novel I have ever read."[31] Fanny Butcher called it "really intelligent" in the *Chicago Tribune*,[32] and the *Philadelphia Inquirer*'s Emily Clark deemed it "intensely American

. . . a fresh and beautiful and touching record of a notable period, and of the human reactions to that period."[33] Probably the review that meant the most to Paterson was written by her literary idol, the novelist Ellen Glasgow, who said the book contained "the whole approach to modern life, with its eagerness, its lightness, its disenchantment, its feeling for the moment as it passes."[34] Although Paterson was delighted by the praise, she was a little concerned about being labeled a sophisticate. "I wish everyone wouldn't go around telling everyone else '*You* wouldn't understand; it's too highbrow for you,'" she told Burton Rascoe. "Do they positively want to ruin my sales?"[35]

▰▲◣

From her office at the *Herald Tribune*, Paterson watched in bewilderment as the Hoover administration struggled to deal with the Depression. It seemed to her that since the crash had resulted from bad investment choices spurred by the government's monetary policies, there was no point in postponing the inevitable liquidation; the country should "cut the losses, and go on."[36] However much Hoover might want to stave off the pain, it would eventually come anyway, and delaying it only made things worse. Government was not capable of performing "any economic function beyond maintaining sound money and taking a chance with tariffs," Paterson wrote in "Turns." "Beyond that, government and business can be entwined only in the same way as Laocoön and the python, or which ever breed of snake it was. It doesn't do either of them any good and it's very hard to untangle them again."[37]

Yet instead of letting the market resolve unemployment by reducing labor costs, Hoover insisted that wages remain artificially high—thereby pricing many workers out of potential jobs. He then dramatically increased government spending to put people to work on public works projects. Such efforts are a common nostrum in times of economic crisis, but in reality, they are economically wasteful and counterproductive because they divert resources from more efficient uses into ventures that have no market demand, and shift work-ers away from self-supporting private payrolls and onto government projects funded by tax dollars. "If a man were paid to pick up pebbles on the beach and throw them into the ocean," Paterson later wrote, "it would be just the same as if he were in a 'government job,' or on the dole."[38] Public works, especially grandiose ones, offer an illusion of prosperity because they are visible, but they displace the more in-demand projects, with the result that consumers are actually worse off.

Still, such projects at least have the virtue of leaving *some* tangible improve-ment that might benefit someone. Hoover's next three responses to the crisis were less justifiable. Fixated as always on maintaining "stable" prices, he insti-tuted a price control program for agricultural goods, restricted immigration to prevent competition for jobs, and, in June 1930, agreed to the infamous Smoot-Hawley Tariff.

The administration's agriculture policies aimed not to increase the supply of affordable food for a nation in economic crisis, but the opposite: to keep food prices artificially high by destroying or exporting existing stock. This was a subject on which Hoover had experience, having worked during World War I to stabilize food prices, which he achieved in part by sending American produce to Europe as part of the humanitarian relief efforts Lane had reported on in Armenia and Georgia. At that time, Lane had written admiringly of the "skillful maneuvering" by which he "kept up the price of wheat and held down the price of flour"—efforts, she said, that benefited "every farmer who plowed a field."[39] Of course, that was true, but they only did so by taking wealth from struggling families who had to pay more for food.

In June 1929, months before the Depression began, Hoover had cre-ated the Federal Farm Board to lend money to farmers in exchange for their promise to keep produce off the market, and to organize growers into a cartel that would hold out for higher prices. These efforts failed because the board's willingness to buy wheat from farmers only encouraged them to plant more, and when at last the board had spent $300 million and accumulated 85 million bushels of the stuff, it shipped those surpluses to Europe to keep them away from American consumers.[40] That had calamitous consequences for Europeans struggling to pay off World War I debts. The board also urged cotton and wool producers to destroy their products to keep prices up, and, as it had with wheat, the board bought enormous quantities to stockpile away from the market. "If they'd dump the wheat and cotton," Paterson told Rascoe, and just "go through the inevitable bankruptcy which is now being prolonged," the economic pain would be swiftly resolved, "as a major operation is best for appendicitis."[41] By maintaining high prices and preventing economic readjustment, the administration was simply prolonging the trouble.

Restrictions on immigration had similar effects. Five years before the market crash, Congress had curtailed the flow of people into the country, and in March 1929, Hoover issued a presidential proclamation reducing immigration quotas still further.[42] By dampening competition for jobs, these restrictions increased the price of labor, which benefited those fortunate enough to already be employed, but only at the expense of those who were seeking jobs, as well as consumers, who, again, were forced to pay more for goods and services. And because these policies deterred hiring and kept unemployment high, they also lowered the incentive for employees to innovate or improve performance.

International trade restrictions also hurt consumers. By excluding competition from foreign imports, tariffs allow domestic producers to raise prices and reduce innovation and quality. That increases the cost of living, and because other countries often retaliate by adopting their own import restrictions, tariffs typically destroy the export markets of domestic manufacturers and farmers. When the Smoot-Hawley Tariff—one of the harshest constraints on foreign trade ever proposed—was sent to Hoover for his signature, economists from both parties urged him to veto it, warning that it would worsen the already high cost of living and ruin export markets for American businesses.[43] Yet Hoover was committed to these policies by his belief in keeping up the income of existing firms. The consequences were the economic equivalent of pouring gas on a fire.[44]

By the time of his first State of the Union address in December 1929, Hoover could proudly report on his swift response to what was then still only an economic slump. Although the economy was sending every possible signal that it needed to readjust—to shift employment and investment into different channels—the Great Engineer boasted that he had hastened to prevent this, and to ensure that "the fundamental businesses of the country shall continue as usual, that wages and therefore consuming power shall not be reduced, and that a special effort shall be made to expand construction work in order to assist in equalizing other deficits in employment."[45]

He was proud, too, that his efforts to prevent price decreases had been "voluntary," meaning they came about through government subsidies and agreements between industry leaders instead of outright compulsion. But tariffs were hardly "voluntary," and the subsidies were paid for with taxes. Cartel behavior by companies was no less economically harmful just because it was brought about through bureaucratically approved arrangements instead of outright coercion. In reality, Hoover often obtained "voluntary" agreements through intense pressure and threats to retaliate against businesses that said no. Yet he preferred to view his interventions as cooperative efforts by citizens to pull together, rather than as the creation of a command-and-control economy. He cherished the notion—which was not actually true—that his regulations of food distribution during World War I had succeeded through "voluntary conservation" instead of compulsory rationing.[46] His rhetoric of voluntarism must have sounded to Paterson and Lane like one of Sinclair Lewis's windbag characters pontificating about community spirit while stifling individual enterprise. Yet it may have soothed public anxieties at a time when prominent politicians and economists were calling for the outright seizure of industry and conscription of labor.

In fact, the Depression era was marked by what historian Ira Katznelson calls "a climate of universal fear," spurred not only by the domestic economic situation, but by dangers abroad.[47] In eastern Europe, the Soviet revolution had been succeeded by "war communism" and later by the Bolsheviks' first "Five-Year Plan," which included the confiscation of farms, the wholesale expropriation of crops, and, eventually, the intentional starvation of some 7 million people. In Italy, Mussolini's fascist government—hailed by many respectable statesmen, including Winston Churchill, as an ally in the fight against communism—instituted a police state, conquered northern Africa, and adopted an economic scheme of state-supported industrial cartels called Corporatism. Meanwhile, National Socialism was growing in Germany, where the government's legitimacy was teetering thanks to the Depression's effects. Liberal democracy seemed to be in retreat worldwide. Two years before Hoover's election, the prominent political scientist William Yandell Elliott had expressed the view that nationalism, tariffs, restrictions on immigration, oppression of minority groups, and other phenomena showed "that the age of democratic liberalism is dead and done for."[48] Literary critic Irving Babbitt simultaneously warned that if trends continued, "we may esteem ourselves fortunate if we get the American equivalent of a Mussolini; he may be needed to save us from the equivalent of a Lenin."[49]

But while leading intellectuals in Europe and America were openly admiring the bracing firmness that fascism or communism seemed to promise, Paterson doubted that socialist revolution would come to America any time soon.[50] Although worried about the short-term prospects, she thought the nation would right itself eventually. Whenever she felt "blue," she told Burton Rascoe, she just reminded herself there was little she or other citizens could do except "try to watch out if [the government is] going to begin inflating the currency."[51] And indeed, prominent economists and industrialists soon began saying that the worst was over. The downturn would reverse by the end of 1931.

Of course, it did not. Spending on investment continued to fall, while spending for immediate consumption rose. That meant that even as consumers saw only relatively minor changes at their department stores, businesses were suffering from a lack of capital, and employers found it increasingly difficult to make payroll at the above-market wages they had pledged to maintain. Some were forced to reduce pay in secret to avoid bankruptcy. Those that did so openly faced violent, even deadly protests by workers.[52]

Yet keeping wages constant meant companies had to choose between spending capital or borrowing from the government.[53] Such borrowing could only be financed with money taken from taxpayers who were already short of funds. Spending capital, however, meant hastening bankruptcy. Thus the "tragic year" of 1931 would see unemployment double, and landlords, particularly banks, confronted with the choice of either foreclosing on property—a politically unpalatable move that the government discouraged—or simply collapsing when tenants missed mortgage payments. Bank runs became one of the emblems of the age. And in December 1930, even the Bank of the United States was deemed insolvent—the largest bank collapse in the nation's history.

▰▲◣

Lane watched the crisis with fascination from her home in Missouri. "This period of 'depression' is as interesting as a war," she wrote in her diary. "I am sorry I have not kept a record of it from the first."[54] Her stock market investments had teetered on the brink for a while, but it gradually became clear that they were doomed. Her income from writing also dried up, as magazines began publishing stories they had stockpiled during previous years instead of commissioning new work. With the financial crisis, her dreams of returning to Albania faded away for good. Feeling "blue as the devil," she resorted once more to ghostwriting to pay the bills. It was something "no writer of my reputation" ever did, but she needed the money.[55] She longed to devote her time to some serious project, something she could believe in. "Money has nothing to do with it," she told a friend. "The job of writing has suddenly taken on a new aspect, a moral aspect, to me."[56] But she had no idea what such a project would look like.

The opportunity soon arrived. In May 1930, her mother handed her part of a handwritten manuscript of a memoir of her childhood, which she called *Pioneer Girl*. At first, Lane did not take the project too seriously. It was just a family chronicle, she thought, or perhaps a children's book, and she confessed that she knew "nothing whatever of the juvenile field."[57] Also, Laura Ingalls Wilder had little writing experience and was reluctant to let her daughter edit her work. But the manuscript contained good material, and Lane thought she might be able to draw on it for a series of magazine articles that could later be assembled into a book, as she had done with *Diverging Roads*, *Hill-Billy*, and *Cindy*. To test that notion, Lane typed up the manuscript and sent it to her agent in New York. Several weeks later, the answer came: it had potential, but was not ready for publication.

Written in the first person and in an accessible, if amateurish style, *Pioneer Girl* covered Wilder's life growing up on the frontier between 1869 and 1888. It was filled with fascinating details told from memory, and included all the incidents that would later become the most famous of the *Little House* series, such as the locust swarms that devastated farmers during the 1870s, and the "Hard Winter" of 1880–1881. Yet it lacked structure and came off as rambling; it was also too long to appeal to many readers. Lane thought it would have to be revised into a novel, but Wilder disapproved. In fact, she disapproved of fiction generally, which she considered a waste of time and often downright immoral. Four years later, when her daughter's book *Let the Hurricane Roar* became a bestseller, Wilder replied to one congratulatory letter with the prim remark that she had "nothing particular to say" about it. "It is of course fiction with incident and anecdotes gathered here and there and some purely imaginary. But you know what fiction writing is."[58]

Nevertheless, during the hot summer days of 1930, Lane began laboriously reworking her mother's manuscript. First, she shifted the story into the third person, simplified its language, and removed scenes that were inappropriate for children, to produce what she called "juvenile *Pioneer Girl*" or *When Grandma Was a Little Girl*. Then she laid this aside with the idea that she might later make a more adult book out of the same original material. Yet it was the "juvenile" version that she and her mother eventually molded into the first *Little House* novel. That fall, Lane traveled to New York to visit her agent in hopes of generating interest in her magazine stories and her mother's *Pioneer Girl* manuscript.

While she was there, news broke that Sinclair Lewis had been awarded the Nobel Prize. He and Dorothy Thompson, who had recently purchased a 300-acre farm in Vermont, would be traveling to Sweden to accept the award, and knowing that Lane was looking for a place to stay, Thompson suggested that she housesit for them and care for their five-month-old son, Michael. It was a luxurious home with a maid and a chauffeur, and Lane promptly accepted. But although she spent the winter writing and visiting publishers, none were interested in her mother's book. "They said if the same material were used as a basis for a fiction serial they'd take it," Lane reported home.[59] In January, Knopf said it might publish the juvenile version, but only if it were shortened. Lane, however, had not told her mother that she had prepared this juvenile version, and when she wrote to Wilder to explain and to say that they would have to immediately start editing the manuscript she had secretly prepared, Wilder was shocked. But she had little choice. She laid aside her distaste for fiction and began work. When Lewis and Thompson returned from Europe in March, Lane—after a farewell dinner with them and H. L. Mencken—headed home to Missouri to help.

By now, she had begun to think that her mother's memoir might be the basis for the serious literary project she had dreamed of pursuing. "I must stay in America and write American stuff," she wrote in her diary. "Sometimes I can almost *feel* this."[60] Soon she devised a plan. She would help her mother turn *Pioneer Girl* into autobiographical children's stories, but would simultaneously fashion her own adult novel based on the travails of her mother's parents, Charles and Caroline Ingalls. That would be hard work, given that she was already writing a series of stories for *Good Housekeeping* alongside her ghostwriting projects, and it was made harder by the fact that Wilder often balked at her alterations. "There can be no genuine pleasure in generosity to my mother who resents it and does not trouble to conceal resentment," Lane wrote in her diary.[61] Still, the manuscript for the first Laura Ingalls Wilder novel was completed by June. Calling it *Little Girl in the Big Woods*, Lane mailed it to the publishers with only her mother's name on it.

The publishers were thrilled and scheduled it for release in the spring of 1932. Retitled *Little House in the Big Woods*, it became an instant success. It was named a Junior Literary Guild selection, which guaranteed wide sales, and was praised in the *New York Times* and elsewhere, ensuring that it would sell better than anything Lane wrote herself. The book had not been intended as the first of a series, but given its success, Wilder almost immediately began work on a second manuscript, this one aimed at a younger audience and based on her husband's childhood. She called it *Farmer Boy*.

▼▲◥

By that time, the Hoover administration's efforts to micromanage the economy had become so complicated as to contradict themselves in several ways. On the one hand, the federal government urged farmers to reduce planting to prevent a fall in prices; on the other hand, it funded efforts to reclaim flooded land and open it for tillage, which resulted in *more* crops. It was expanding the money supply through massive lending and spending, while also decreasing it through taxation and tariffs, leading to a monetary chaos so severe that economists still debate whether 1931 should be characterized as a period of inflation or deflation. In some communities, the actual supply of currency dwindled to the point that locals resorted to barter instead of cash, or printed scrip to replace absent dollars.[62] On the whole, deflation is preferable to inflation, since it comes to a natural stopping point at the actual amount of currency in circulation and increases the consumer's capacity to buy, whereas inflation destroys the value of money, obliterates savings, renders planning impossible, and leads to irreparable economic catastrophe. Yet in 1931–1932, deflationary tactics also discouraged short-term lending, demoralizing wage earners whose debt burdens increased while their opportunities to borrow narrowed. Their dollars were theoretically worth more, but business failures left fewer places to spend them.

That demoralization was exacerbated by Hoover's reluctance to give direct government aid to the unemployed. He thought that was a job for private charities. Much of his lasting reputation as a "do nothing" president is likely traceable to this inconsistency: although he was actively working to subsidize businesses and banks, he hesitated to spend taxpayer money on unemployment relief. There was an economic rationale for this—subsidizing unemployment delays economic corrections by dissuading workers from seeking jobs where their skills are in demand—but that rationale had already been rendered moot by Hoover's insistence on maintaining high wage rates and pressuring businesses to keep workers on the payroll. In short, his enthusiasm for corporate welfare combined with his opposition to aiding the poor looked like hypocrisy and coldness. The president, said New York congressman Fiorello LaGuardia, was "forever estopped" from attacking "unemployment insurance by calling it a dole," since he supported "a millionaire's dole" and "a subsidy for broken bankers."[63] Such inconsistency, however, was the administration's trademark.

Of all the era's economic superstitions, none was more dangerous and persistent than the idea that economic competition was inefficient and destructive, and that businesses should band together—or be forced to band together—to compete "fairly," with fairness defined by the government. That idea embodied a premise, promoted by Progressives in the decades before the crash, that competition wasted resources because there was no "need" for, say, two railroads between the same two cities when there might be just one. According to this notion, the second railroad was a waste, because if expert government planners were put in charge, the materials and labor it consumed could be spent on other, more worthwhile uses. The fallacy in that argument is that government planners cannot know what the "needs" of the public are or will become in the future. Nor can industry leaders. Only the process of competition can determine it—a process that generates innovation and low prices by maintaining pressure on companies to improve and satisfy consumers with new and better products and services, while reducing costs so as to maintain a competitive edge. "Ruinous" competition is merely a dysphemism for what economist Joseph Schumpeter called "creative destruction"—that is, the dynamic process whereby firms that satisfy customers prosper and those that do not go under, whereupon their employees find new jobs in the more profitable industry.[64] Because political leaders can never anticipate consumer demand, they cannot prescribe the kinds of competition that are "fair." And because such prescriptions are most likely to be written by the largest *existing* companies—that have the ear of political authorities—they have the effect of barring newcomers from the market, which worsens scarcity and raises prices.

Paterson saw through such fallacies early. In her 1916 novel *The Shadow-Riders*, she had made the point in a passage in which two Canadian characters argue over international tariffs. "Our manufacturers can't afford to compete with the factories of the United States," says one. "We *need* competition," the other replies. "Our manufacturers haven't the enterprise to make as good [products]," and only free competition will change that.[65] Nevertheless, Progressives had enjoyed the opportunity to impose "fair competition" requirements and other restrictions during World War I, when government control over distribution reached unprecedented levels. Between 1917 and 1919, agencies such as the War Industries Board and Hoover's U.S. Food Administration appeared to vindicate Progressive beliefs in government planning. A decade later, many—including Hoover himself—pointed to that precedent, arguing that the Depression was analogous to a world war and should be dealt with in the same way.[66]

That was the basis for the idea that General Electric's president Gerard Swope proposed in September 1931. He recommended that the federal government create a system of industrial cartels under which all companies of more than 50 employees would be assigned to a trade association vested with authority to dictate the types and amounts of goods and services businesses could provide, and how much they could charge.[67] This would prevent "destructive" competition, by giving companies the power to prohibit their competitors from reducing prices or introducing new or improved products, which would "stabilize" the economy and ensure full employment. "Industry is not primarily for profit but rather for service," Swope declared. "One cannot loudly call for more stability in business and get it on a purely voluntary basis."[68] Although hardly the only such proposal—it mimicked the corporatism already being implemented in Italy and Germany—the Swope Plan gained the most attention and would later form the blueprint for the National Industrial Recovery Act. But at the time, Hoover labeled it "fascism" and rejected it as "merely a remaking of Mussolini's 'corporate state.'"[69]

Many similar schemes were offered by prominent intellectuals, including historian Charles Beard, who proposed "A Five-Year Plan for America" on the Soviet model,[70] and *New Republic* editor George Soule, whose 1932 book *A Planned Society* proposed political control over the entire economy. These writers, said one of Soule's colleagues, "were impatient for the coming of the Revolution; they talked of it, dreamed of it."[71] And they were not alone. That same year, novelist Theodore Dreiser published *Tragic America*, which he had originally planned to call *A New Deal for America*. It advocated the overthrow of capitalism and the replacement of the Constitution with a government that would control industry in the style of the Soviet Union, where he thought communism was "functioning admirably."[72]

Paterson learned of Dreiser's manuscript before publication, and she expressed her skepticism in characteristically wry fashion, in a "Turns" column devoted to the difficulties she was encountering while moving into her new Manhattan apartment. "Can Mr. Dreiser arrange a social and economic order in which nobody will ever have to move?" she asked. "And don't tell us how much better they do things in Russia. . . . Russia, from all we can gather, is exactly like our apartment at the present moment. They've taken down the old brick oven to install a modern range, and the range hasn't come yet, so they're all sleeping on the floor and subsisting on hand-outs from the neighbors."[73]

Dreiser probably changed his title because *A New Deal* had already been taken by economist Stuart Chase, whose book of that name also appeared in 1932. Chase—who considered it "a pity" that "the road" to socialist revolution in America was "temporarily closed"—looked forward to the day when the government would seize all industry and "solv[e] at a single stroke unemployment and inadequate standards of living."[74] It would do this, he said, by compelling all individuals to "work for the community." The government should forbid high interest rates, stock market speculation, the manufacturing of "useless" products, the creation of new clothing styles, businesses "rushing blindly to compete," and other "ways of making money"—and it should do so "by firing squad if necessary."[75] The 44-year-old Chase was inspired by the "new religion" of "Red Revolution," which he found "dramatic, idealistic, and, in the long run, constructive."[76] "Why," he asked, "should the Russians have all the fun of remaking a world?"[77]

Paterson was friendly with Chase, and although she thought his call for government control over the economy was "all wet," she treated his book mildly in her column.[78] She had a hard time taking revolutionary talk seriously. "What this country is trying to do is go home," she wrote in "Turns." "There ain't not going to be no revolution; and we are not going Communist. . . . We are just going crazy, but that is only temporary." Americans "cannot bear regimentation," which was why in times of crisis "our inevitable tendency is toward sheer confusion."[79] That was in any event preferable to the dictatorship Chase and others advocated. Rose Wilder Lane, too, considered the threat of communism overblown. Communists were "hardly a chemist's trace in our population," she thought, and their doctrines were not popular among the working classes. "In reality there's no more communism among these masses of unemployed than there is in your living room."[80]

But although they rolled their eyes at utopian schemes, both women feared the damage that might be inflicted by what Paterson called "highbrow reformers." They were "useful in opposition only, as a dissenting minority," she wrote in "Turns," but once in power, they could prove dangerous.[81] Self-proclaimed whiz kids like Chase—many of whom had never shouldered the burden of running a small business, let alone a national economy—were bad enough. But more ambitious magnates such as Gerard Swope were a real threat. "Mere amateurs could never have made such a stupendous, unparalleled mess" as the nation was now experiencing, Paterson later said. "That took experts."[82]

As 1932 began, Hoover's attention shifted. His tax increases and efforts to inflate the currency had left consumers with less expendable income and investors with fewer viable opportunities. The economy was stagnating, and his vaunted public works projects were either economically unfeasible or pointless for those who lacked the skills to work on them. He finally agreed to provide direct aid to the poor, boosting welfare spending to more than $300 million in 1932, 10 times what it had been in 1929.[83] But startled at the immense debt into which his spending had plunged the country, he also adopted draconian tax increases, encompassing everything from sales taxes on staple goods to a confiscatory tax on inheritances. The consequence was to strangle investment and penalize consumers who had too little in their pockets already.

Meanwhile, states began running out of money for public works projects and began halting them just as private industry had already stopped building—whereupon the administration sought to spur construction through drastic new spending increases. Much of this new money failed to reach Americans, however, because banks—terrified that another round of risky loans would lead to default and worsen their depositors' already shaky confidence—kept much of the money in their vaults instead.[84] Thus the actual amount of cash in circulation fell despite the federal floodgates being opened. The administration responded to this by establishing the Reconstruction Finance Corporation (RFC), a federal slush fund with power to hand out more than $3 billion with little official oversight—indeed, its operations were actually kept secret for its first several months, and when the secrecy was lifted, it became clear that officials had funneled taxpayer money to businesses in which they had personal interests. But even after these improprieties became known, the RFC's leaders continued to spend in accordance with political goals, benefitting members of Congress whose influence was considered important.[85]

Paterson thought Hoover's efforts to prop up industry and prevent unemployment were only delaying the inevitable, and salutary, economic restructuring. "Even if it makes us a crusted Tory," she wrote in "Turns," "we believe that no matter how far people have gone in the wrong direction, the best thing to do is to go back and start right again."[86] Government planning, let alone talk of revolutionary utopias, only made things worse. Allegedly ingenious planners like Chase and Swope had "got the political machinery dangerously entangled with the economic system, disrupting both; and they are now demanding that the government should save them from what they've done to it."[87] The wisest course was to let national "bankruptcy" take place swiftly, and start afresh.

She knew she would be accused of insensitivity for expressing these views: "We shall be asked indignantly, would you rather have people starve than have the Federal government extend or change its nature[?]"—but "the answer is the same as if they asked us, would you rather remain thirsty or carry water in a sieve[?]"[88] The idea that bureaucrats could plan the economy was premised on "assuming that engineers never would be unscrupulous—in short, that they aren't human"—and also on the misconception that the economy was a single, static thing, instead of a dynamic, ever-changing process.[89] Economics was always a matter of tradeoffs, not cure-alls. "By accepting change as one of the factors, it is possible to keep conditions tolerable and even agreeable; but insistence on finality, on nice blue-printed 'planning' insures only one result, and that is despotism tempered by imbecility."[90] In short, efforts at central planning risked empowering the politically influential to force their own desires on others. That was why America's Founders gave government no role in managing the economy to begin with. Paterson continued to "cling to the old-fashioned, Jeffersonian idea that an important part of government consists in letting people alone."[91] The Constitution's "unique feature," she thought, was that it represented "for the first time a purely political government"—meaning one that did not choose winners or losers in industry. The Founding Fathers had hoped "to keep economics as well as religion out of it."[92] But that constitutional order was now under threat.

Historian Charles Beard pronounced American "rugged individualism"
a myth in 1932. His two-volume *Rise of American Civilization*, coauthored
with his wife, Mary Beard, drew a response from Rose Wilder Lane
in the form of her novel *Free Land* and, later, her nonfiction
The Discovery of Freedom.

▰

Bad as the economic situation was, it was the Depression's social consequences that shocked Paterson and Lane most. Persistent unemployment, bank failures, and monetary chaos seemed to generate a crisis mentality that sent cultural shock waves across the nation. Historian Arthur Schlesinger later described a "contagion of fear"[93] and a "fog of despair"[94] that seemed to hover over the country, and the sensation was obvious to everyone. In "the bad old days just before the war," Paterson wrote, there had always been a feeling "that was rather picturesque and gay," but now, the optimism and independence she associated with the Airplane Generation seemed to be waning, replaced with a new sense of resignation and cynicism toward the very idea that America was a land of opportunity.[95] "Everyone was emotionally affected," recalled one teacher who lost his job around this time. "We developed a fear of the future which was very difficult to overcome . . . this constant dread: everything would be cut out from under you."[96] For some, this encouraged a spirit of angry entitlement and law breaking. When gangsters Bonnie Parker and Clyde Barrow went on a bank-robbing spree, some treated them as folk heroes. Two years later, John Dillinger was regarded as a Robin Hood figure for holding up banks and giving money to the poor.[97] But for most, the prevailing atmosphere was one of surrender. One bartender recalled that "the dominant thing was this helpless despair and submission. There was anger and rebellion among a few but, by and large, that quiet desperation."[98]

Lane was repelled by such attitudes. "I don't believe this terror of the future is justified by the facts," she wrote. "The more I see of public temper in this depression, the more I'm reluctantly concluding that this country's simply yellow. Our people are behaving like arrant cowards. And it's absurd."[99] But the sense of despondency was real. *The Nation* called 1931 a year "of suffering, bitterness, and increasing disillusionment."[100] That February, filmmaker Pare Lorentz wrote in *Scribner's*: "America is no longer the land of opportunity for a young man of honor and decency. The man who starts at the bottom of the corporation to work his way up is a fool. . . . The traditions of the founders of

America belong with the folk myths."[101] In December, the *New York Times* printed a lachrymose story about a couple who gave up seeking employment and retreated to an abandoned cabin in the Catskills to die of starvation.[102] The cultural malaise, recalled author Zora Neale Hurston, "was like a rotting fog hovering over the land. It was as if from a vigorous youth, the United States had arrived overnight at a decaying old age. It was a case of don't try anything. . . . No more individuals at all. . . . Nothing to do but hate bosses and work toward the day when [workers] could do away with their hated oppressors."[103]

In January 1932, tens of thousands of the unemployed, led by a Catholic priest named James Cox, departed from Pennsylvania for a march on Washington. Dubbed "Cox's Army" in an echo of Coxey's Army of 1894, it was far larger than its predecessor. In fact, it grew to such a size that Cox founded his own political party, the Jobless Party, which demanded still more spending on public works projects. It disbanded that autumn, and Cox endorsed New York governor Franklin Roosevelt for president, but by that time, an even larger crowd of protestors, dubbed the "Bonus Army," had arrived in the nation's capital. It consisted of some 15,000 World War I veterans and their families, who wanted the government to pay them bonuses it had promised them for their service. Those were not due until 1945, but given the circumstances, they wanted the money immediately. Ten thousand of them camped on a site on the Anacostia River across from the capital until late July, when Hoover—perhaps recalling that a similar march on Rome a decade earlier had overthrown the Italian government and installed Mussolini as dictator—ordered the army to disperse them. Things went badly. Shocking scenes of violence followed that left two Bonus marchers dead. It was an ugly blow to Hoover's reelection chances and to the national mood.

As often happens in hard times, some Americans began steeling their spirits by looking back on the challenges their ancestors had overcome. During that year's presidential campaign, both Hoover and his challenger, Franklin Roosevelt, invoked the "pioneer spirit" in their speeches, and writers and scholars emphasized how those who had tamed the West a half century earlier did so through self-reliance and the willingness to help their neighbors, virtues their grandchildren should embrace in the Depression.[104] Historian James Truslow Adams's newly published book *The Epic of America* introduced the phrase "American dream"—which he defined as "the hope of a better and freer life, a life in which a man might think as he would and develop as he willed."[105] Yet at the same time, other prominent intellectuals were beginning to deride the principles of personal independence that served as the basis of that dream. Individualism, they argued, was a lie.[106]

Foremost among them was Columbia University historian Charles Beard, whose 1913 volume *An Economic Interpretation of the Constitution of the United States* had become a central text of the Progressive movement. It argued that the United States was not founded as a land of opportunity, but was created by a group of wealthy elites who intended to protect their economic privileges against the lower classes. In 1931, Beard followed that up with an essay that would become equally essential to New Deal ideology. Titled "The Myth of Rugged American Individualism," it derided the "logomachy" of American self-reliance and argued that the nation's economic success had actually been a product of government subsidies and political favoritism. After a list of purported examples, Beard concluded that the idea of economic freedom had always been a fraud, concocted by plutocrats to fool workers into conquering the frontier on their behalf. And now that the frontier was closed, that doctrine had "become a danger to society." In "cold truth," Beard declared, the "individualist creed" was "principally responsible for the distress in which Western civilization finds itself."[107]

Many intellectuals and organizations agreed. *Business Week* announced that year that individualism "no longer works,"[108] and even the Federal Council of Churches, the nation's umbrella organization of Protestant denominations, denounced capitalism as "primeval selfishness" and insisted on a new, collectivist society as an expression of the Gospel. But Rose Wilder Lane and her mother disagreed. They thought the American ideal of individualism was a noble cause, and although imperfectly realized, even its approximation had created a society in which people enjoyed unprecedented opportunity to pursue happiness in freedom and peace. Now, as they refashioned the *Pioneer Girl* manuscript, it seemed all the more important to vindicate this principle.

By October 1932, Lane had adapted portions of the manuscript into a short novel she called *Courage*. It was intended as "a reply to pessimists," she said, and when it appeared in two installments in the *Saturday Evening Post*, it was a hit.[109] As with "juvenile *Pioneer Girl*," she appears to have worked on *Courage* without telling her mother, and may have felt no need to, since they had never discussed collaborating on *adult* stories. Instead, the plan was that her mother would write juvenile novels about her childhood, while Lane would write novels for grownups about her grandparents starting out on the Dakota prairie in the 1870s.

Drawing on what became two of the most famous incidents in the *Little House* canon, Lane depicted the newlywed Ingallses struggling against swarms of locusts and the terrible winter of 1880–1881. And although the resulting story was sometimes sentimental and flat by comparison with the books that were to come, it contains moments of genuine depth and inventiveness— particularly in its focus on the travails of frontier women. Its best feature, in fact, is a long segment in which Caroline must fend for herself when Charles leaves for a seasonal job on the railroad. Alone in their cabin with the baby, she suffers terrifying nightmares of Charles being killed in an accident. "She had not told Charles how she feared trains. When she slept, she saw the monstrous, inhuman things of steam and iron, swiftly coming, roaring, panting, staring with the headlights like eyes; things that seemed alive, but were not alive."[110]

The winter stretches on interminably, with only occasional visits from distant neighbors to relieve the isolation. During one ferocious blizzard, Caroline manages to free some cattle who get trapped in the ice, and takes one cow home to the barn for herself, only to come face-to-face with a wolf. She scares it away with a shovel and hides in the cabin with a pistol as the wolf pack returns to scratch at the door. Finally, she hears a person lost in the snow outside, and, not knowing whether it might be an outlaw, must decide whether to let him in. Finally, she does. It turns out to be Charles, returned from the

East. "Caroline was never able to say, even in her own thoughts, what she knew when she first came out of the dugout after the October blizzard. . . . She was aware of human dignity. She felt that she was alive, and that God was with life. She thought: 'The gates of hell shall not prevail against me.'"[111] Lane's characters are sometimes cloying in their stiff-upper-lip attitude, but in the passages featuring Caroline's struggles, she reached beyond *Pioneer Girl* and depicted the strength of character that survival on the prairie truly demanded of people.

Resilience, in fact, struck Lane as the quintessential human quality. "Man *is* revolt, unacceptance," she wrote in her diary a year later. "That's his apartness from all the life on earth."[112] While other animals live at the mercy of the elements, only human beings find ways to endure and surmount their circumstances. Just before sending the story to the *Post*, she found the perfect way to express this idea. One evening in the midst of conversation, her mother sighed, "Oh, well, let the hurricane roar." It was a line from an old hymn, she explained, one that reassured listeners: "We will weather the blast and will land at last / Safe on the evergreen shore."[113] Lane loved the phrase and changed the title of her novella from *Courage* to *Let the Hurricane Roar*.[114]

▰▲▰

In retrospect, it seems surprising that as late as the spring of 1932, Herbert Hoover had good reason to hope for reelection. Not until June did it become clear that Franklin Roosevelt would be his opponent. And when the nomination came, Hoover welcomed it, thinking that of possible Democratic rivals, Roosevelt was the one least likely to beat him.[115]

But Roosevelt was an ingenious politician, whose strengths turned out to be the perfect counterpoint to Hoover's weaknesses. Where Hoover was thin-skinned, uncharismatic, and wonkish, Roosevelt was cheerful, resolute, and optimistic. Hoover was reluctant to speak to the press and disliked crowds; Roosevelt managed the media with élan and loved applause. Hoover appeared focused on protecting big business from collapse; Roosevelt spoke of the need to help the poor. Yet Roosevelt was also skilled at enabling people to hear what they wanted to hear. Far more interested in popularity than in any political creed, he was entirely willing to switch messages to suit his audience. And his boundless energy and sense of humor seemed to lift everyone in the room.[116]

Hoover was also handicapped by the fact that he had alienated many Republicans and allowed much of his party's infrastructure to lapse. Its publicity operation had actually closed down in 1929, and his campaign's finances ran so low that cabinet members were sometimes forced to pay for radio advertisements out of their own pockets.[117] Another hindrance was Hoover's willingness to enforce Prohibition. In the dozen years since federal law had banned alcoholic beverages, the popularity of the idea had waned, and by 1932, political leaders knew it was a failure. Yet they lacked the courage to oppose it publicly, given the bitter tenaciousness of committed "drys," especially in rural districts. In 1928, Democratic presidential nominee Al Smith had openly favored repeal, only to lose convincingly to Hoover, who called Prohibition "a great social and economic experiment, noble in motive and far reaching in purpose."[118] Avowed opposition to it still seemed risky.

Hoover was not actually a Prohibition enthusiast, yet he signed the Increased Penalties Act of 1929 and was unwilling to endorse repeal three years later. His evasiveness on the issue led one observer to remark that the president "wouldn't commit himself to the time of day from a hatful of watches," and when the Republicans formulated their platform at their 1932 convention, he supported a confusing and vague provision that called for a referendum on the issue.[119] Reporting from the convention, H. L. Mencken thought the delegates wanted to endorse repeal, but were forced to "quibble and compromise," because "such is the word that comes from Washington." As a result, Hoover "blunders through the air like a doormat, and half of him lands inside and half outside."[120] Even when the president finally expressed a willingness to consider repeal, his running mate, Charles Curtis, gave an enthusiastic speech defending the alcohol ban.

Yet Roosevelt was also unwilling to alienate dry Democrats. At the party's convention in Chicago, he maintained a careful ambivalence while delegates advanced an explicit anti-Prohibition platform. Only after it passed did he declare his support for repeal. "That is what the crowd had come for," wrote Mencken, "that and nothing else. Beer in our time. Beer tomorrow. Beer this afternoon. Beer right now. . . . [Roosevelt] looked very thirsty himself."[121] Once started, anti-Prohibition momentum proved a powerful factor in the election, and Hoover's reluctance to endorse it even when its popularity became obvious was yet another hindrance to his campaign.

Meanwhile, Roosevelt wisely focused on the economic issues voters cared most about, while remaining vague about his specific plans, in hopes of winning votes from disaffected Republicans. In Roosevelt's mouth, the phrase "new deal"—eagerly used by socialist ideologues months before—became a loose appellation for a menu of schemes to be specified at a later date. He could be remarkably cynical in his manipulation of language. At a campaign stop in Sioux City, when advisers could not agree whether to endorse tariffs or oppose them, he instructed speechwriters to merge the two contradictory positions, which they managed to do.[122] He went on to criticize his opponent for spending "too much money" and giving government "too many functions." Hoover, he said, "has piled bureau on bureau, commission on commission, and has failed to anticipate the dire needs and the reduced earning power of the people."[123] Two years before, he had denounced the president's "doctrine of regulation and legislation by 'master minds,' in whose judgment and will all the people may gladly and quietly acquiesce," because that would "bring about government by oligarchy masquerading as democracy," and transfer "practically all authority and control" from state governments to Washington, DC.[124] Now on the campaign trail, he again portrayed himself as a small-government candidate, promising a huge audience in Pittsburgh that he would "reduce the cost of the current Federal Government operations by 25 percent" and balance the budget, even if that required a moratorium on spending and "a complete realignment of the unprecedented bureaucracy that has assembled in Washington in the past four years."[125] He condemned Hoover's "novel, radical, and unorthodox economic theories," and denounced the president for "taxing to the limit of the people's power to pay and for deficit spending—

all of which had put the government in an "impossible economic condition." Taxes were a "brake on any return to normal business activity," he said; their effects were "reflected in idle factories, tax-sold farms, and hence in the hordes of the hungry people, tramping the streets and seeking jobs in vain." Hoover's "extravagant government spending" was also imposing a "burden on farm and industrial activity."[126]

These are startling words, in light of Roosevelt's later policies; Marriner Eccles, who served in Roosevelt's administration for a decade, later remarked that anyone who reread the speeches of the 1932 campaign would think that "Roosevelt and Hoover speak each other's lines," and during the next campaign, Roosevelt's financial adviser James P. Warburg would publish a book asking "whether we agree with Governor Roosevelt, who in 1930 condemned" the attempt to establish "a bureaucratic dictatorship of 'master minds' in Washington"—or with "President Roosevelt, who in 1935 recommends it."[127] But candidate Roosevelt had no difficulty occupying contradictory positions. Even his closest associates acknowledged that although extremely intelligent, and undeniably pledged to the vaguely worded values of Progressivism, he had little knowledge of economics and few commitments to political principles.

Perhaps most revealing of all was an April 1932 speech in which he invoked a phrase originally used 60 years earlier by sociologist William Graham Sumner. "It is said that Napoleon lost the battle of Waterloo because he forgot his infantry," Roosevelt said. "The present administration in Washington provides a close parallel. It has either forgotten or it does not want to remember the infantry of our economic army . . . the forgotten man at the bottom of the economic pyramid."[128] Astute observers such as Isabel Paterson recognized this as a demagogic trick. Sumner had used the phrase "forgotten man" to refer not to recipients of government aid, but to the hard-working taxpayers who were forced to *pay* for that aid—laborers whose earnings are taxed to subsidize programs motivated by politicians' compassion. The actual "forgotten man," Paterson reminded readers, was "the productive man," who was made the "fall guy" when politicians redistribute wealth.[129] Sumner had been writing "in favor of honesty, decency, and minding your own business."[130] Now Roosevelt was appropriating the term to refer to those who received the money confiscated from Sumner's forgotten man. In other words, the forgotten man was being forgotten all over again.

Roosevelt's rhetoric seemed like an omen: the new administration would pursue a statist political agenda regardless of its true impact on America's productive citizens. Even some leading Democrats were maddened by his speeches. His old rival, Al Smith—who, unlike Roosevelt, had worked his way up from poverty—threatened to "take off my coat and fight to the end" against any candidate who "persists in any demagogic appeal to the masses of the working people of this country to destroy themselves by setting class against class."[131] But Roosevelt was not ideologically devoted to class warfare. He simply loved campaigning and craved the approval of crowds. He was happy to leave the details to others. Meanwhile, Hoover and Prohibition seemed like intolerable evils. Paterson hardly bought Roosevelt's small-government rhetoric, but she voted for him anyway, as did H. L. Mencken and Ayn Rand, primarily because of his pledge to end the alcohol ban.[132] Countless other fed-up voters did the same, and that November's election was a landslide repudiation of Herbert Hoover. What Americans would get instead remained to be seen.

Part Two

The Forgotten Man

H. L. Mencken, among the nation's most influential journalists in the 1920s, saw his popularity wane with the advent of the New Deal. In 1933, he retired from the *American Mercury*, the magazine he had founded. He inspired the character of Austin Heller in *The Fountainhead*.

4

The Dictator

On March 4, 1933, Franklin Roosevelt stood before a cheering crowd in the chilly air of the nation's capital and told Americans that the Great Depression was a catastrophe on the scale of the Great War, and that his administration would respond accordingly. He had two immediate priorities: to "put people to work" through "direct recruiting by the Government itself" and to redistribute land to "those best fitted" to own it. That would be accomplished partly by the forbidding of foreclosures, partly by price controls that would "raise the values of agricultural products," and partly by "national planning for and supervision of all forms of transportation and of communications." And although he planned to "recommend" these proposals to Congress, he was also prepared, "in the event that the Congress shall fail to take one of these two courses," to demand "broad Executive power to wage a war against the emergency, as great as the power that would be given to me if we were in fact invaded by a foreign foe." The American people were looking for "discipline and direction under leadership," he said, and he would see that they got it.[1]

Roosevelt recognized that his authoritarian rhetoric might scare some people, but such fears only amounted to "nameless, unreasoning, unjustified terror," which Americans should disregard. It was time for the nation to face the facts of a new age, one in which the "unscrupulous money changers," with their "outworn tradition" and lust for "mere monetary profit," had been driven from power and replaced by leaders who recognized "the falsity of material wealth" and understood that every person's "true destiny" lay in serving their "fellow men."

To anyone accustomed to the idiom of communist or fascist revolution, such language was alarming. There seemed to be much more to fear than merely fear itself, and not just in the United States. "By 1933," writes Ira Katznelson, "the European map of democracies no longer included Russia, Germany, Italy, Portugal, Austria, Poland, Yugoslavia, Bulgaria, Romania, Hungary, Latvia, or Estonia. With the exception of Britain, Scandinavia, and (still) France, all of interwar Europe turned authoritarian, dictatorial, or fascist."[2] Stalin was overseeing the genocide of millions in Ukraine and elsewhere. Mussolini (who in a March 1933 book review praised Roosevelt's campaign manifesto *Looking Forward* as "reminiscent of the ways and means by which Fascism has awakened the Italian people"[3]) was entering his second decade as ruler of Italy. In Germany, the Nazi Party had made Adolf Hitler chancellor. Only days before Roosevelt's inauguration, the burning of the Reichstag in Berlin gave the Nazis the pretext for issuing a decree that suspended civil liberties and ushered in a nationwide wave of oppression.

Political violence was even becoming commonplace in the United States. Riots erupted over housing shortages in Chicago in February 1931, after which Communist Party leaders organized a funeral procession for two members killed in the melee; 50,000 people attended.[4] A year later, the party organized a 3,000-person march on Ford's River Rouge plant in Michigan, which ended in violent clashes with police, who killed four.[5] Just a month before his inauguration, Roosevelt himself barely survived an assassination attempt that claimed the life of Chicago's mayor. The gunman went to the electric chair ranting, "I will kill all president and king, and all capitalist."[6]

Equally alarming was the fact that much of what the new president proposed to do exceeded the boundaries imposed by the Constitution. That document gave the national government no power to centrally organize the country's economy, to nullify private contracts, to eliminate the gold standard, or to seize property to manipulate prices. And although it did allow Congress to regulate interstate business, that did not entitle the federal government to supersede the authority of states, which held primary responsibility for setting the rules of trade. Only a dozen years earlier, there had been such widespread consensus about this that the prohibition of alcohol had necessitated a consti-tutional amendment. But the Roosevelt administration's supporters would take a different route: fashioning drastic new interpretations of the nation's highest law that would enable officials in Washington to control virtually every eco-nomic transaction in the country *without* amending the Constitution. Indeed, Roosevelt labeled the Constitution a relic of "the horse-and-buggy age,"[7] which had been "superseded entirely by what has happened and been learned in the meantime."[8] One of his advisers, Rexford Tugwell, agreed, confessing years later that the New Deal had been unconstitutional, and expressing regret that instead of admitting this, the White House had employed "tortured inter-pretations" of the Constitution to pretend otherwise.[9]

Fearful Americans cannot have been reassured by the February edito-rial in *Barron's* that advocated "a mild species of dictatorship," or by Walter Lippmann's advice to the new president that same month—"You have no alternative but to assume dictatorial powers"—or by the *New York Times* reporter who proclaimed in May that Americans had given Roosevelt "the authority of a dictator" as "a free gift, a sort of unanimous power of attorney. . . . America today literally asks for orders."[10] Publisher William Randolph Hearst—who admired Mussolini and Hitler so much that he gave them columns in his newspapers—financed a propaganda film called *Gabriel over the White House*, which premiered days after the inauguration and depicted the new president being guided by heaven to declare martial law, unilaterally cure the Depression, execute criminals, and end all war.[11] Even the Nazi Party celebrated Roosevelt's commitment to all-encompassing power with a story in its newspaper lauding what it called "Roosevelt's Dictatorial Recovery Measures."[12] In her diary, Rose Wilder Lane was succinct: "In inau-gural speech Roosevelt stated willingness to assume dictatorial powers."[13]

Isabel Paterson did not think Americans actually wanted orders, or a planned economy, or any of the massive transformations being proposed by the ideologues now gravitating toward the White House, soon to be labeled the Brain Trust. "What everyone yearns for," she wrote in "Turns with a Book-worm" a day after Roosevelt was sworn in, "is to return to private property,

Author Sherwood Anderson helped initiate the Revolt from the Village with his book *Winesburg, Ohio*. Rose Wilder Lane despised the book, and she responded to it in her 1935 novel, *Old Home Town*.

to get out from under the heavy load of taxes and too much government."[14] But the president had different ideas. He was surrounding himself with what historian Gary Dean Best calls "a plethora of 'crank' economists" eager to give government greater power to control the citizenry.[15] Paterson regarded them as "young men who went to college on an allowance, and then came out in nice white collars to jobs on politely radical magazines supported by kind wealthy ladies." Their political ideal, naturally enough, was "a mother's boy economic program with a kind maternal government taking care of everybody out of an inexhaustible income drawn from mysterious sources."[16]

Worse, they appeared ignorant of basic economics. Roosevelt himself had told the Democratic convention that "economic laws are not made by nature" but "by human beings," which struck Paterson as the equivalent of suggesting that the laws of mathematics or physics are manmade.[17] Economics was not a matter of mere convention or agreement, but a set of natural phenomena governed by inescapable principles relating to production and consumption. They could no more be altered by an act of political will than could the laws of thermodynamics.

Shortly after Roosevelt took office, Paterson encapsulated her opposition to the Hoover and Roosevelt administrations with a satirical "Turns" column that predicted what future economic textbooks would look like. They would begin by recommending war as a source of prosperity, she wrote, and would brush off concerns about the costs on the grounds that "you can do it all on loans, and, in fact, everybody will make a nice profit out of the commissions on the bonds." Business owners would be assured that they would profit by selling war materials, and that the stock market would rise. If debts started to come due, then the government could simply "'refinance' them with new bonds, and new profits out of new commissions. This is called the New Economic Era." Then when borrowers failed to repay, "the fact can be obscured for a little while longer by calling interest 'debt service' and non-payment of debts 'stabilization of the currency.' Bad debts must be called 'frozen assets' and 'credit' means new loans that cannot possibly be paid." When at last political leaders could find no new ways to evade the past-due notices, "there is then nothing to do but add noughts to infinity on the credit side of the ledger, call for a dictator and inaugurate a rain of paper [money] like the ticker tape hurled out of the Wall Street windows on a parade day. Announce that democracy will not work in a crisis, and grab whatever any individual has left. And [then] you have a lovely economics in which nothing ever need be paid, and if you think you have any rights you'll give everybody a big laugh."[18] The next decade would prove her prescient indeed.

◢◤

Although Lane and Paterson had corresponded since at least 1925, it is impossible to be sure when they first met in person. It seems most likely, however, that they did so in the spring of 1932, when Lane's friend Catherine Brody— then living with Lane and her parents on the farm in Mansfield—published a Depression-themed novel called *Nobody Starves* (the title was Lane's idea) and appeared at an event in New York City to promote it. Paterson attended, and Lane probably did, too.[19] They found they had much in common. Both born on the frontier in the waning days of the pioneer era, they had both put marriage behind them in favor of literary lives. They shared a passion for gardening, philosophy, literature, and, of course, politics.

Yet there was always to be a tension beneath the surface of their friendship. Lane may have felt a certain jealousy for Paterson's independence; tied as she was to her parents, she seems to have resented the way she had sacrificed her own bohemian lifestyle out of a sense of family obligation, which Paterson had not. For her part, Paterson was sometimes exasperated at Lane's eclectic philosophical beliefs, which seemed peculiar and contradictory. She seems also to have been suspicious of Lane's former communist ties, viewing them as proof of lasting moral and intellectual defects. In 1940, when another ex-communist named Freda Utley published a memoir admitting that the Soviet Union was not the worker's paradise she had once thought it was, Paterson declared in "Turns" that she had little sympathy for disillusioned former communists, because communism's basic flaws had been so "perfectly understood by rational persons for centuries" that anyone's belief in it "indicates incapacity to understand any question relating to politics or economics." Even after such people "have formally renounced Communism," therefore, their ideas "will seldom or never have any tangible basis."[20] Fifteen years later, when Lane and Paterson's friendship came to an angry end, Paterson would throw Lane's youthful affinity for socialism back in her face. But in 1933, the two were drawn together by their shock at the scale of Roosevelt's plans for revolutionizing America.

It was not just a matter of his economic ignorance. The administration's unprecedented expansion of authority represented a more fundamental shift in the entire ethos of American society: a retreat from a culture defined by self-reliant individualism toward a collectivist mentality steeped in malaise and envy. Individualism had been at the heart of American society since the Declaration of Independence recognized every person's right to pursue happiness. But it had been nebulously formulated, and its practical implementation was riddled with hypocrisy, given that the nation, among other things, practiced slavery. In fact, proslavery writers had openly inveighed against individualism, complaining—in the words of Virginia's George Fitzhugh—that there was "too much *individuality* in modern times."[21] Yet individualism gradually came to be seen as a sine qua non of American freedom and expanded to encompass formerly excluded groups. Benjamin Franklin's autobiography became a virtual guidebook for the entrepreneur, and Ralph Waldo Emerson's and Henry David Thoreau's essays celebrated the spiritual autonomy of the individual conscience—while in the South, Andrew Jackson's followers emphasized the common (white) man's freedom to compete against the moneyed interests of the East Coast. With slavery's abolition and the granting of voting rights to women, America had—albeit with glaring exceptions—rededicated itself to the proposition that every person has the right to make the important choices in his own life. And American culture celebrated those who made the most of themselves. The former slave Frederick Douglass toured the country lecturing about the "self-made" businessmen, scientists, and scholars who had "ascended high" after having "built their own ladder[s]."[22] Industrialists and financiers such as Andrew Carnegie, A. P. Giannini, Thomas Edison, and the Wright brothers were honored for having risen by their merits, without special privileges or government assistance.

As members of the Airplane Generation, Lane and Paterson had known firsthand the individualism and buoyancy of turn-of-the-century America—a nation that, whatever its failures, rejoiced in the ideas of opportunity, innovation, enterprise, big characters, stalwart farmers, and self-made men. They had known hardship, but they had also seen people bear up with a spirit that viewed self-reliance as both a goal and a reward. Yet that resilience now seemed to be withering away, replaced with a political culture that viewed people as inherently dependent; perpetual victims not of temporary emergencies but of unremitting cultural and social forces, against which only the state could protect them, at the price of their autonomy.

For all his faults, Hoover had treated the Depression as a temporary condition and celebrated "rugged individualism"—a phrase he coined. But now, political leaders spoke openly about the arrival of a new age in which personal initiative had no place, and individual enterprise was obsolete. Roosevelt declared on the campaign trail that "the day in which individualism was made the great watchword of American life" had ceased. A new era had begun, he said, in which the "mere builder" or "creator" was "likely to be a danger."[23] Harold Laski—a British socialist whom New Dealers treated as a guru—published *Democracy in Crisis*, arguing that "the primary assumptions of individualism" were now "obsolete."[24] Howard Williams, national organizer of the Farmer-Labor Party, told followers that individualism was a relic of the "horse-and-buggy age," which should be replaced with "a nationally planned economy."[25] An editorial in the *Kansas City Star* observed that "a social revolution is under way," and that the idea that "America not only was the land of opportunity and unrestricted individualism, but the haven of the oppressed from all lands" was vanishing. The idea of the individual "going it alone" would "no longer" be "tolerated," it concluded.[26] "Government," wrote reporter Jonathan Norton Leonard, "is plotting a more determined attack on the individual than it has ever plotted before."[27] A writer in *The Nation* agreed: "Individualism is at the crossroads," he observed, "and a very dangerous crossing it is."[28]

Some American intellectuals, not prepared to jettison individualism entirely, sought to change the word's meaning instead. Rather than referring to the individual's right to live his own life, Progressives such as John Dewey argued that people only become individuals *through* society, and therefore that government should control the economic and social spheres of life so as to create individuality for them. A year after Roosevelt's inauguration, Dewey declared that liberalism had shifted from its classical form—which viewed each person as sovereign and assigned government the sole task of protecting that sovereignty—into a new, collectivist form, according to which government would assist in "the development of individuality" by providing for all of the "'cultural,' economic, legal, and political institutions as well as science and art" that people relied on when developing their personalities.[29] Rather than the state's existing to preserve individual autonomy, it now was the very source of a person's selfhood. Even Dorothy Thompson embraced this doctrine. "Government has a positive function," she declared; "above all," its role was to "equalize and generalize the chance" of citizens to "attain intellectual and spiritual satisfaction."[30]

It was this cultural transformation that would prompt Paterson, Lane, and later Ayn Rand to spearhead an effort to revive the philosophy of individualism. Alexis de Tocqueville had written of the "mores"—the habits of mind—that form an even deeper foundation for a political society than its laws do. During the 1930s and 1940s, all three women would argue that the spirit of self-reliance was the keystone of American mores—the essential element that allowed for political liberalism, economic growth, the flourishing of geniuses such as Edison and the Wright brothers, and the peaceful pursuit of happiness by millions of unknown citizens. It was in hopes of reinforcing those values that Lane had written *Let the Hurricane Roar* and that Rand would write *The Fountainhead*.

Yet all three women saw individualism not just as a vague cultural norm, but as a definite philosophical creed. In politics, it meant the right of each individual to live according to his values, without interference from others, and to enjoy the fruits of his wise choices and bear responsibility for bad ones. It meant the kinds of personal freedom Carol Kennicott longed for in *Main Street*—freedom of speech, sexual autonomy, the right to dissent—as well as economic liberty and private property rights. Freedom did not mean a person's access to resources necessary for self-improvement, as John Dewey and Herbert Hoover believed. Paterson, Lane, and Rand viewed that notion as self-contradictory because such access could only be provided by depriving other individuals of their freedom or their earnings. Between what Dewey called the classical form of liberalism and its New Deal version, Paterson and her colleagues chose classical liberalism.

They rejected the label "conservative"—Lane preferred the term "American revolutionist," and Ayn Rand would call herself a "radical for capitalism"—and embraced the principles of racial and sexual equality today associated with liberalism, alongside the laissez faire capitalism and private property rights typically ascribed to conservatism. They venerated American traditions and celebrated laborers, merchants, and industrialists who built bourgeois culture, while nevertheless seeking a groundbreaking new era of personal autonomy. In short, they defied the political labels of their time and devoted their careers to individualism in its many philosophical, economic, social, historical, and even artistic dimensions.

▗▀▙

Immediately following his inauguration, Roosevelt made good on his threat to use extraordinary power. The day after taking office, he ordered the country's banks closed pursuant to the 1917 Trading with the Enemy Act. That act only applied during wartime, however, so his order was legally invalid. He therefore called a special session of Congress to ratify his actions retrospectively. The purpose of the "bank holiday"—which aimed to stop bank runs by allowing financial institutions to remain in business while disregarding their legal obligation to return funds to depositors—was to "restore confidence" in the economy. But the confidence it restored was largely illusory; when banks reopened, most were just as insolvent as ever, and depositors in that pre-ATM age were forced to do without cash in the interim, causing further financial strains.[31]

Roosevelt's nationwide bank holiday was just the first of a series of presidential dictates that removed the country from the gold standard, voided government promises to pay in gold, and even banned private possession of gold on pain of criminal penalties. The purpose of these decrees, most of which were issued by executive order, thanks to the 1933 Emergency Banking Act—with which Congress handed the new president power and then walked away—was to block dollar-holders from escaping inflation. The gold standard had imposed a degree of financial discipline on the government because, pursuant to so-called gold clauses, people entitled to payment under government contracts could demand gold instead of paper dollars. That meant any effort by government to inflate the currency could be counteracted by the private decisions of individuals who insisted on gold instead of devalued cash. By forbidding possession of gold and announcing that the government would not honor its contractual gold clauses, Roosevelt took a major step toward making dollars worth whatever political officials claimed they were worth—severing the monetary system from any connection to productivity or private decisionmaking.

Hardly anything Roosevelt did outraged Isabel Paterson more than this prohibition on gold. In "Turns," she reacted to the president's orders with bitter and brilliant lectures on the meaning of money. Currency, she explained, is not a mere social construct, but a tangible representation of production. For government to manufacture money by fiat—to, essentially, engage in counterfeit—was a form of theft, because it diminished the value of dollars held by people who had earned them. And that was no accident. In fact, such cheating was the "prime object of inflation." Roosevelt's policies were intended to operate as a hidden tax, which would "wipe out the savings of the smallish people" who "have the deplorable habit of paying their debts," in order to transfer their wealth to the government.[32]

Confiscating gold meant punishing anybody who had escaped the ruinous policies of the previous 15 years with any savings intact—literally threatening to jail "unpatriotic widows and orphans who had tried to hold out a nickel"[33]— and all for "the higher purpose" of inspiring "confidence." That word had once meant "certainty or faith," but it was now taking on a more sinister meaning, as in *confidence game.* "When it is perfectly certain that you get stung no matter which way you turn, therefore you may as well gamble in the stock market because money will probably be no good anyhow in a couple of years," she concluded, "*confidence* manifestly has reached a new high for all time." In the end, Roosevelt's team of monetary manipulators were only "a gathering of amateur philologists" who used euphemisms to disguise their expropriations.[34]

When columnist Walter Lippmann wrote that debates about inflation and the gold standard gave him a "headache," Paterson shot back that if he found monetary policy hard to understand, he should "go home and take an aspirin," and leave the thinking to grownups. Lippman ridiculed the idea that the administration's gold measures were a form of theft, arguing that gold, "like an umbrella," is "the property of the man who holds it."[35] No, Paterson replied, "all gold in the U.S. Treasury belonged to whoever had gold certificates," and by nullifying those certificates, Roosevelt was forcing people to accept a risk of inflation that they had tried to avoid. Gold was indeed "like an umbrella in that the owners were keeping it for a rainy day and it was stolen, seized by main force." True, the government claimed it was giving people "just compensation" by paying them in Federal Reserve notes, but that was a "shyster plea" since the whole point was that the notes could *not* compensate gold owners for the risks that compulsory conversion to paper money imposed on them.[36]

Roosevelt's efforts to control gold prices and the value of the dollar soon proved counterproductive. He took to proclaiming how much gold was worth every morning while eating breakfast in bed, basing his dictates on "lucky numbers."[37] This threw markets into such chaos that even economist John Maynard Keynes—otherwise an enthusiast for government manipulation of the economy—published a letter in the *New York Times* begging him to stop.[38] Roosevelt eventually backed away from his most aggressive efforts to control monetary values by decree, but his administration retained the ban on gold possession, the nullification of gold clauses, and its elimination of the gold standard.

Along with bank holidays and monetary changes, Roosevelt's famous "first 100 days" witnessed the creation of myriad new agencies and mandates intended to "stabilize" prices and subordinate the economy to bureaucratic control. Lawmakers passed more than a dozen major statutes, including the Glass-Steagall Act, which gave government unprecedented authority to control the institutions with which Americans entrusted their savings; the Economy Act, which repealed retirement and medical benefits for veterans; and legislation establishing the Public Works Administration, the Civilian Conservation Corps, and other programs funneling hundreds of millions of dollars into poor relief or government-run construction. Because the Hatch Act—which forbids the president from using government funds for political purposes—would not be adopted for another seven years, these federal dollars were distributed to Roosevelt's allies in accordance with political patronage.

Two of the most extreme laws that made up this so-called First New Deal were the Agricultural Adjustment Act (AAA) and the National Industrial Recovery Act (NIRA). The AAA was designed to keep the prices of agricultural products artificially high by establishing a system of farming cartels—essentially doubling down on the Hoover administration's efforts to persuade farmers to reduce planting. The NIRA did the same for industry. Modeled on the Swope Plan and Italian corporatism, it deputized the nation's business leaders to impose "codes of fair competition" that kept prices up and penalized entrepreneurship that might "disrupt" or "destabilize" the economy.[39]

The AAA taxed food producers and handed the proceeds to growers who promised to reduce production. It also offered loans and other subsidies to farmers to grow less food. But because the act was adopted months after seasonal planting had begun, administration officials also began ordering the destruction of existing crops and the slaughtering of livestock—not for distribution to the hungry but for fertilizer, despite the fact that the Agriculture Department was simultaneously telling people that the nation was facing food shortages. Voters were shocked to learn in September 1933 that in an effort to raise pork prices, the government had paid farmers $50 million to slaughter 6 million pigs instead of bringing them to market, and that farmers had been told to destroy, or "plow under," their cotton and tobacco crops.[40]

These "price stabilization" efforts succeeded only by making every consumer worse off—making food more expensive and harder to get—but as economic historian Jim Powell observes, "That wasn't the concern of the Department of Agriculture."[41] Five years later, John Steinbeck captured the perversity of such waste in *The Grapes of Wrath*: "Carloads of oranges dumped on the ground. . . . And men with hoses squirt kerosene on the oranges. . . . A million people hungry, needing the fruit—and kerosene sprayed over the golden mountains. . . . Dump potatoes in the rivers and place guards along the banks to keep the hungry people from fishing them out. Slaughter the pigs and bury them, and let the putrescence drip down into the earth. There is a crime here that goes beyond denunciation."[42] A more lighthearted reflection on the AAA's irrationality was penned by Ogden Nash:

Fiddle de dee, my next-door neighbors
They are giggling at their labors.
First they plant the tiny seed,
Then they water, then they weed,
Then they hoe and prune and lop,
Then they raise a record crop,
Then they laugh their sides asunder,
And plow the whole caboodle under.[43]

The AAA's heaviest burden fell on black sharecroppers, because federal subsidies were paid to landowners not to till their ground, but sharecroppers tilled ground they did not own. Thus the AAA effectively paid their employers to fire and evict them.[44] The act was never popular—most voters opposed it, and even Brain Trust member Rexford Tugwell considered it a failure.

"Only the large [farmers], perhaps 20 percent," benefited from the subsidies, he wrote. "Farm wages were not rising with farmers' incomes."[45] In 1935, the Supreme Court would declare portions of the act invalid, but Congress reenacted slightly modified versions of many of the same rules shortly afterward.

Even aside from its economic consequences, the AAA dealt a blow to the morale of America's rural communities by undermining the individualist ethos on which farmers had long prided themselves. Author E. B. White, who had recently moved to a farm in Maine, testified to the sensation he experienced when he received his first shipment of fertilizer from the federal government: "To be honest I must report that at the time I got the lime I experienced a slight feeling of resentment—a feeling not strong enough to prevent my applying for my share in the booty, but still a recognizable sensation. I seemed to have lost a little of my grip on life." It was "a slight sense of being under obligation to somebody, and this, instead of arousing my gratitude, took the form of mild resentment—the characteristic attitude of a person who has had a favor done him whether he liked it or not." The government's "Eagerness to 'adjust' me" with its "friendly control" gave White the sensation that "some intangible substance" within his spirit "was leeching away." He supported Roosevelt and the New Deal, yet he could not ignore the fact that the fertilizer had been "paid for in part by thousands of young ladies many of whom are nursing personal want comparable to my want of lime." Not only was it unjust to take wealth from them, but the program was also dispiriting to recipients—and politically dangerous. "By placing such large numbers of people under obligation to their government," White feared, "there will develop a self-perpetuating party capable of supplying itself with a safe majority."[46]

An even more severe wound to the spirit of independence was dealt by the NIRA, the longest step America had yet taken toward centralized economic planning. That act established one agency called the National Recovery Administration to implement nationwide government control over businesses, and another called the Public Works Administration to oversee government construction projects. In an effort to reduce unemployment, these agencies encouraged businesses to hire the jobless simply as a form of charity. The idea was best articulated by actor Jimmy Durante, who starred in a government-made musical film in which he pleaded with business owners to "Give a Man a Job":

DURANTE. You look like a banker. Who drives your car?
RICH MAN. I drive it myself. Have a cigar.
DURANTE. Keep your cigar and hire a chauffeur, / and keep a good man from becoming a loafer.

For bankers to hire drivers when they are content to drive themselves is economically foolish, because it wastes capital on jobs for which there is no market demand—capital that could instead be invested in projects the public actually wants. Keeping unnecessary staff on a payroll as a form of pity actually delays economic recovery and prevents people from finding employment opportunities for which there is greater need—and in the long run, this raises prices for consumers and makes goods and services scarcer. Government hiring likewise burdens the economy, since these jobs must be paid for by taxes taken from the private sector. Simply put, this type of hiring is a method of disguising, not curing, unemployment.

Worse than this was the NIRA's establishment of a series of nationwide industrial cartels. Based on the notion that economic competition is wasteful, and that, in the words of one supporter, "the most destructive forces in the so-called capitalistic system" were the "individualists" who refused to "plan and work for the welfare of either their entire industry or for the general increase in purchasing power and well-being," the NIRA sought to stamp out business rivalry by giving existing companies the power to draft "codes of fair competition."[47] Once approved by the administration, these codes dictated what businesses could charge and what they could produce. The government called these mandates voluntary, but businesses that did not comply were denied public contracts and were subjected to punishment by the Federal Trade Commission. They were also denounced in the press, which encouraged the public to boycott them.

Although the act specified that the codes "shall not permit monopolies or monopolistic practices," this was pure double-talk, because like the AAA—which supporters also called voluntary—the NIRA employed a specious form of democracy to disguise its coercive elements. It empowered the largest businesses to create restrictions on selling that they alone could afford to obey, and which were enforced by the government, thereby excluding potential rivals.[48] "Our large competitors planned and drafted their particular codes," explained the officers of one small Wisconsin lumber company. "Naturally they fitted the Code regulations according to their business."[49] Yet because the act included a provision whereby businesses voted on these restrictions, they were characterized as "democratic," notwithstanding the fact that small firms were inevitably outvoted.[50]

Thus the NIRA effectively created a nationwide oligopoly that squelched small businesses and startups. In June 1933, the owner of an Ohio tire company complained that his business could have effectively competed against Goodyear and other major firms in his town, if the codes had not prevented it. "Since we have so little of this consumer publicity when compared with them, our only hope is in our ability to make as good or a better tire than they make and to sell it at a less[er] price," he wrote, but the codes made that illegal—meaning, in effect, that "the government deliberately raised our prices up towards the prices at which the big companies wanted to sell."[51] Other businessmen suffered worse fates. A Pennsylvania battery maker was incarcerated when he paid his workers—with their consent—less than the 40 cents per hour the code required. Jersey City laundryman Jacob Maged was sent to jail and fined $100 for charging 35 cents to press a suit rather than 40 cents as dictated by the codes.[52] Sam Markowitz and his wife Rose were jailed in Cleveland for cleaning suits for 5 cents less than the codes mandated.[53] "You tried to tell me when I could open my doors and when to lock them, what I could sell for and what I should pay in wages," the owner of a wallpaper store complained to Roosevelt. "As to my profits you didn't give a —, yet I must pay the taxes you insolently piled upon me."[54]

A few large businesses resisted the pressure to participate in the NIRA scheme. Henry Ford refused, likening the act to Soviet economic planning. He could afford to stick his neck out. But the administration brought severe pressure to bear on him, depriving his company of government contracts.

"We have got to eliminate the purchase of Ford cars," Roosevelt told a press conference, because Ford had not "gone along" with the code.[55] Ford's factories were actually obeying the code's requirements already, but that did not satisfy the president, who demanded that Ford personally *sign* the code to signal his approval. He issued an executive order declaring that the federal government would not purchase cars made by "any person who shall not have certified that he is complying."[56] Ford still held out, and the government eventually backed down. But smaller entrepreneurs such as Maged and the Markowitzes lacked the wherewithal for such defiance.

To administer the NIRA, Roosevelt chose Brigadier General Hugh Johnson, who had masterminded implementation of the military draft during World War I and now insisted on what he called the "organization of both Industry and Labor to the ultimate."[57] The bellicose Johnson openly admired Mussolini's fascist corporatism, and once in office, launched into bluster about the evils of competition.[58] "Those who are not with us are against us," he declared.[59] "The public simply cannot tolerate non-compliance with [the NIRA codes], and they certainly cannot by their patronage support the enemies of their interest." He nevertheless insisted that the codes were not coercive. They "involve no Government intervention in business except to aid business," he claimed. If a company failed to comply, the government would take away the blue eagle symbol that NIRA participants were supposed to display, and urge buyers to shop elsewhere. But, Johnson added, "Of course [this] is not a boycott."[60]

The most famous incident involving the NIRA codes was the case of the Schechters, a Brooklyn family that ran a kosher poultry business. Under the "Code of Fair Competition for the Live Poultry Industry of the Metropolitan Area in and about the City of New York," they were forbidden to engage in "destructive price cutting"—meaning charging less than the code mandated. They were also required to engage in "straight selling" in their wholesale business—meaning they were forced to sell all their chickens to retailers at the same amount, regardless of size or health. The reasoning behind this rule was that retailers would otherwise choose the highest-quality chickens, leaving wholesalers with scrawny birds that could only be sold for less. By barring retailers from selecting the best poultry, the code was supposed to benefit wholesalers, including the Schechters, by keeping prices for small birds artificially elevated.

The Schechters refused to participate, however, and federal prosecutors charged them with violating code requirements by letting retail customers and butchers decide which chickens to buy from them. Intending the case as a show trial to vindicate the NIRA, prosecutors ended up doing the opposite. They sought to prove that the Schechters were engaged in "destructive" competition—but ended up proving that no principled difference exits between that and other competition. When one government lawyer demanded to know: "The competition in the whole slaughterhouse business is very keen, is it not?" Martin Schechter replied, "Well, it is keen in every other business in the same way."[61]

After being convicted, fined thousands of dollars, and sentenced to three months in jail for selling what the court deemed "unfit" chickens (even though only one chicken was ever proved to be unfit) and for violating the rule against letting customers choose their own birds, the Schechters appealed to the Supreme Court. When federal lawyers tried to explain the NIRA's requirements to the justices, they had difficulty because members of the audience kept interrupting them with laughter.[62]

Isabel Paterson thought the idea of government control over the economy was foolish arrogance. To "scientifically" organize any market, the planners—or, more accurately, prophets—would have to know "absolutely all the factors of present and past out of which the future must proceed, and to anticipate inerrantly all the possible new discoveries which may be made." Lacking such omniscience, their efforts to organize society would only put it in a straightjacket, by prohibiting innovation.[63] In the process, they would encourage cronyism by using government power to serve private interests. Here and elsewhere, her critique of the New Deal anticipated the writings of economists such as Ludwig von Mises and F. A. Hayek—then still largely unknown in the United States—who a decade later would publish analyses showing that economic planning is literally impossible, because planners cannot obtain or use the necessary information.[64] Paterson put the point bluntly in a letter to a friend. "This bastard oligarchic half-state-socialism we're getting into," she wrote, "looks to me like nothing but an everlasting mess."[65]

It wasn't just that planning was unfeasible, or that it would encourage a dangerous and irreversible blending of public and private enterprise. Rather, she thought the New Deal's basic fallacy lay in ignoring the role individual personality traits play in generating productivity. Economic planners and alleged experts "never ask themselves" how wealth comes to exist in the first place. They just "take it as a fact of nature," and go about redistributing it. But Paterson thought wealth creators—whom she called "self-starters"—practice a specific set of virtues: thrift, industry, diligence, foresight, independence, all of which are comparatively rare in human history. Self-starters were the people who "manage to plow and sow and reap, to build and make . . . against the tempest, though all bureaucrats stand massed against them."[66] Critiquing a book by a socialist in December 1933, Paterson objected that the author

assumes as his set-up a self-existent "economy of plenty." There is no such thing. That potential plenty depends entirely upon a minority being allowed to function. We do not mean a class, but a certain type of mind. It exists in various degrees and forms—business men and farmers and foremen and housewives, the people who will always somehow get things done, get some practicable result from whatever material is at hand and whatever other people they must work with. They are self-starters. And they are seldom conspicuous. [They] are never college professors nor politicians. Neither do we mean inventors, intellectuals, artists or writers—the creative artist is naturally anti-social. The self-starters, of course, use what more original minds discover, and their particular function is to hold everything together. One can't always see how they do it. A business may be so admirably organized that it looks as if it would run itself, but if you take out one or two men who keep it running and put in some bureaucrat who knows all the graphs and charts the business will go to pieces. They don't do it by rule, but by nature. And in an effort to regulate everything those people may easily be eliminated. They have been very nearly exterminated in Russia. Bureaucracy smothers them.[67]

Intellectual leaders were not receptive to this critique. Charles Beard had just published "The Myth of Rugged American Individualism," and the prominent sociologist Robert MacIver identified "a definite shift in attitudes" in American culture away from individualism.[68] Republican congressman Fiorello LaGuardia agreed. "We can no longer talk of the individual or depend on 'rugged individualism,'" he told his colleagues. "The only semblance of individuality that is left is the affliction, the misery, and the poverty that surround the individual when he loses his place in the ranks of his industrial regiment."[69] By 1934, political scientist Francis Coker could confidently declare that "an actual individualist economy" had "ceased to exist in the large industrial countries."[70]

To Paterson, however, and later to Lane and Rand, such sentiments did not indicate a modern and innovative way of understanding society and economics. On the contrary, they seemed to herald a regression to a culture based on envy and mediocrity, one that penalized rebelliousness and rewarded monotony and conformity. In fact, it seemed like the dullness of *Main Street* was being made not into a god, but into a government agency. The Brain Trust, Paterson declared, was made up of "the typical bureaucratic stuffed shirts . . . dealers in catch-words and the makers of paper plans."[71] In their hostility to original thinking and boat rocking, the servants of Roosevelt's alphabet soup of bureaus were no different from the busybodies and blowhards of Sinclair Lewis's novels. That was not progress, but atavism.

Meanwhile those who resisted the New Deal learned that dissent was costly. Although strong opposition to the administration existed in some quarters, many people feared to speak out at the risk of losing their jobs, or worse. Mandatory unionization under new federal labor laws increased the likelihood of violence against holdouts and "scabs," which soon became commonplace. When the Southern Tenant Farmers' Union tried to oppose the Agriculture Department's effort to displace farmers from their land, local vigilantes descended on them.[72] Even prominent figures risked retaliation if they spoke against the administration. In 1935, Roosevelt's Senate ally Hugo Black began using his chairmanship of the Lobby Investigation Committee to engage in a series of humiliating and abusive investigations into New Deal opponents that set the precedent for the McCarthy hearings of the 1950s.[73] On one occasion, he subpoenaed every telegram Western Union delivered to the Capitol relating to a piece of legislation. A federal court later declared that he acted illegally, but that it had no power to stop him.[74] When a constituent sent the senator a letter complaining that he was "making mountains out of molehills," Black wrote to the district attorney in the man's hometown with instructions to investigate his background.[75] After Roosevelt placed Black on the Supreme Court in 1937, Sen. Sherman Minton took over the committee and continued to use investigations to intimidate New Deal opponents. He subpoenaed the publisher of a small magazine called *Rural Progress*, demanding to know why it showed insufficient support for Roosevelt. "Your magazine," he scolded, "has persistently attempted to persuade its readers that the pending wage-hour legislation should not become law. . . . The record fails to show . . . where you advocate any program of the administration."[76] When Minton learned that Rudy Vallee had donated $5,000 to *Rural Progress*, he tried to humiliate the singer by splashing that fact across the front pages.[77] Minton, too, would be rewarded with a Supreme Court seat.

In Louisiana, Governor Huey Long—who opposed Roosevelt only because he thought the New Deal did not go far enough—intimidated his opponents in shockingly extreme ways, even overseeing enactment of a special tax on newspapers that opposed him. Roosevelt, fearing Long's rivalry, sicced the Internal Revenue Service on him.[78] The president used similar tactics against other political enemies, including Ohio governor Martin Davey, newspaper publishers Moses Annenberg and William Randolph Hearst, former Democrats-turned-opponents John Raskob and Pierre DuPont, and retired treasury secretary Andrew Mellon, whom the administration subjected to a baseless trial for tax evasion that ended only when Mellon died.[79] "My father may have been the originator of the concept of employing the IRS as a weapon of political retribution," wrote Elliott Roosevelt years later.[80] The president also ordered the FBI to surveil several political enemies.[81]

More effective than outright attacks, however, was the administration's domination of the media. This control was particularly thorough when it came to the newest media technology: radio. Broadcasters' need for government permission to remain on the air made them uniquely vulnerable to arm-twisting. In 1933, Roosevelt's radio commissioner Harold Lafount told broadcasters it was their "patriotic duty" to deny advertising time to businesses that were "disposed to defy, ignore, or modify" the NIRA codes.[82] A year later, a new Federal Communications Act created the Federal Communications Commission—staffed entirely by Roosevelt appointees—with power over the licensing of radio stations. The act also shortened the renewal period for licenses to six-month increments. That meant the price of remaining on the air was to mute criticism of the White House. Henry Bellows, vice president of CBS, announced that "no broadcast would be permitted" over his network "that in any way was critical of any policy of the administration."[83] When in 1940, Louis Armstrong released a song poking fun at New Deal "make work" projects, which included such lyrics as "sleep while you work, while you rest, while you play, / Lean on your shovel to pass the time away. . . . / The WPA . . . / Can't get fired, so I'll take my rest," Columbia Records received a call from Washington and withdrew the record.[84]

Roosevelt treated print media differently, rarely banning criticism outright. As one historian notes, he was much more effective at "the *cooptation of the press*," and managed newspapers and magazines not through express censorship—at least, not until World War II began and an official Office of Censorship was opened—but through inappropriately cozy relationships with journalists, including hiring them to work directly or indirectly for the administration.[85] The administration circumvented the 1911 Publicity Act by putting hundreds of press relations experts on the payroll and using taxpayer money for campaigning.

In fact, the New Deal was so heavily invested in propaganda that some historians have described it as more of a publicity campaign than an economic program. In one penetrating analysis, scholar Wolfgang Schivelbusch observes that "the marches, parades, and issue campaigns; the rashes of legislation; the creation of ministries, special commissions, and mass organizations; as well as the introduction of public holidays," were mainly intended to convince people that the administration "had actually created the new reality," when it had not done so.[86] And one critical element of that unreal new reality was the eradication of individualism—or, more precisely, its transformation into a new sense of collective responsibility that its supporters called "community spirit."

Just as the administration paid Jimmy Durante to sing songs encouraging inefficient hiring practices, so it also organized massive advertising campaigns to engender this attitude of collectivism. In language that could have come from the mouth of George Babbitt himself, one administration spokesman told a Nashville audience in 1933 that "one of the most significant trends in public thought" was "the substitution of community interests for rugged individualism. The spirit of the man of Galilee is exemplified in the slogan of the [NIRA]: 'We do our part.'"[87] A Wisconsin newspaper agreed: "Community spirit is a manufactured product and is created by community activity and nothing else," it declared. "Merchants can do no better than to sponsor community activities, for community spirit can easily be converted into community loyalty and community buying."[88] And the Burlington, North Carolina, *Daily Times-News* ran a large front-page ad raving: "Community spirit is a simple definition of loyalty to mutual interest and cooperation. . . . It is teamwork—a pulling power uniting the strength of all."[89]

Beginning in 1934, the federal Better Housing Program aimed to "Modernize Main Street for Profit!" not only by financing renovations of business properties, but also by running a publicity drive that included parades, posters, and speeches.[90] One goal of this program was to disguise joblessness by hiring 750,000 unemployed workers to hand out flyers "selling Modernization to Main Street."[91] But the broader purpose of such boosterism was to instill a sense of collective responsibility for society's economic welfare, as opposed to the outmoded individualism of the free-market era—all while maintaining a carefully cultivated façade of voluntary participation.[92] That mask did slip, sometimes. When Hugh Johnson unveiled the NIRA's "blue eagle" campaign—which included posters, statues, buttons, and massive parades intended to bolster support for the codes of fair competition—he called it "a frank dependence on the power and the willingness of the American people to act together as one person in an hour of great danger."[93] But he later added that anyone who "won't go along with the code" deserved "a sock right on the nose."[94]

▼▲▼

One casualty of the new age was H. L. Mencken. Like Paterson, he had supported Roosevelt in 1932—even praising him as "shrewd, candid, and bold," in contrast to the "incompetent," "preposterous," and "stupid" Hoover.[95] But after the inauguration, he grew increasingly critical. The administration's economic programs struck him as merely ramped-up versions of Hoover's foolish measures. But as he attacked them in his articles, his readership began to wane. Subscriptions to the *American Mercury* fell off, and intellectuals pronounced Mencken passé. "The Depression threw the college boys and gals into the arms of Roosevelt," he later admitted.[96] At the annual Gridiron Club dinner in December 1934—an event at which reporters and the president traded good-natured barbs—Mencken was chosen on account of his hostility to Roosevelt to present remarks on behalf of the press. His comments included some clever but mild teasing. But when it came time for Roosevelt to reply, the president simply read a lengthy speech attacking the "stupidity, cowardice, and Philistinism of working newspapermen." When he was done, he explained that he had been quoting at length from one of Mencken's own columns. According to one story, Mencken turned to Maryland governor Albert Ritchie, sitting beside him, and grumbled, "I'll get the son of a bitch. . . . I'll throw his 1932 campaign pledge speech right back at him."[97] Indeed, over the coming months, Mencken's attacks on the administration became increasingly bitter. The president, he thought, was a "quack" and a "snake-oil vendor," whose scheme was to frighten the public with "a din of alarming blather about the collapse of capitalism, the ruin of the Republic, and the imminence of revolution," and then offer cures that were "almost wholly fraudulent and ineffective."[98]

But at 52, Mencken—who had just married a woman with terminal tuberculosis—had less energy for this crusade than he had for those of earlier days. A year before, he had retired from the *Mercury* to spend more time at home. He continued to write vigorously against the New Deal, but his departure was widely seen as the end of an era. The national mood had shifted so much that the entire Zeitgeist of the 1920s, and particularly its rebellions, now seemed outmoded. Few writers personified that bygone age more than Mencken. Scorn for small-town mores had been one of his trademarks. But Americans were beginning to move beyond the Revolt from the Village and were reevaluating the virtues of simplicity and self-reliance that they saw as part of American pioneer spirit. One indication of this changed attitude was Rose Wilder Lane's success with *Let the Hurricane Roar*.

Published in book form in February 1933, the novella was a hit with critics and readers. The *Kansas City Star* declared it "vivid" and "satisfying," and the *L.A. Times* predicted that it would reawaken "the fortitude and faith of our forefathers."[99] That had certainly been Lane's goal. "Every yelp of anguish or prophecy of disaster you hear today," she told reporters, "you might have heard in the early '70s, when [the book's heroine] Caroline was living through that winter in the dug-out. You might have heard them again in 1893 [the year of the previous depression]. But then and now the mass of the people—half of whom are women—is silent and busy."[100] A decade later, when Sinclair Lewis was asked to select representative examples of midwestern fiction for an anthology called *The Three Readers*, he chose *Hurricane*, citing it as proof that "the Midwestern mentality" was not so "uncomplex and insular" as one might have imagined from reading Lewis's own novels.[101]

Lane's joy over the book's success was muted by her mother's unenthusiastic reaction, however. Knowing that Wilder disapproved of fiction—she had even refused to read Lane's previous novels because of the sex scenes—Lane had not bothered to tell her about the book and was reluctant to even show her the advertisements. When at last a friend did so, Wilder was scornful. "Why do they place it in the Dakotas?" she groused. "The names aren't right." When Lane asked what she meant, Wilder replied, "Caroline and Charles. They don't belong in that place at that time. I don't know—it's all wrong." Her words, Lane told her diary, "effectively destroy[ed] the simple perfection of my pleasure."[102]

Nevertheless, *Hurricane*'s popularity suggested a new avenue for Lane's writing. She wrote in her journal that summer that she thought there was "room for a movement of American writers, loving the American scene. Many inarticulate common people do. Such feeling in our literature would express authentic feeling, and bring (if they could come) our writers home. A period of so-called 'healthy criticism' (Sinclair Lewis, etc.) is near its end. The romantic escape has been our only alternative. But as a people we are, I think, just a little bit more adult *now*."[103] Notwithstanding the Depression, she could "*feel* a vitality in America," and she wanted to articulate it.[104] She wanted "to do good work," she wrote, "and this is probably my last opportunity."[105]

By that time, she was already writing another series of stories aimed at giving voice to her "more adult" view of the "American scene." She seems to have been planning this project, which became her book *Old Home Town*, for several years, referring to it as early as 1928 in a letter to Dorothy Thompson, in which she mentioned the "imitation O. Henry" stories she was drafting.[106] These stories, which she began publishing in magazines four years later, were her best fiction writing and her greatest concentrated effort to express the ambivalence she felt about the virtues and stresses of small-town life. They were "O. Henry" stories in the sense that they fit a pattern established by the writer William Sydney Porter, whose tales, published under the pen name O. Henry, often featured surprise twist endings in a style a later generation would associate with *The Twilight Zone*. His 1904 book *Cabbages and Kings* had brought together several interconnected stories into what is known today as a "fix-up"—something that is not exactly a novel, but also not an anthology— and in 1919, Sherwood Anderson's *Winesburg, Ohio*, which helped inaugurate the Revolt from the Village movement, had taken a similar form. Now Lane would take her shot.

The transition from O. Henry to Sherwood Anderson revealed the cultural shift sparked by World War I and the Revolt movement. Although O. Henry's stories had often featured working-class characters beset by hardship, they were nevertheless suffused with a sense of benevolence that helped make him America's most popular short story writer during the brief decade before his death in 1910—the only rival to Jack London in popular taste. Populated by plucky young career women and tramps with hearts of gold, the stories seemed firm in the conviction of an ultimate rightness to the universe—a conviction that sometimes came off as shallow sentimentalism. O. Henry rarely delved into the personalities or hidden motives of his characters, and he made little effort at the kind of realism that would come to dominate American literature in the decades that followed. Yet his stories articulated what one scholar calls an "optimism about the eventual success of the American experiment, always implicit even when he described the inequities and injustices of the social system."[107]

In *Winesburg, Ohio*, by contrast, Anderson had tried to invert this style, deemphasizing plot and focusing on his characters' psychology. The result, wrote H. L. Mencken, was "brilliant" with "images of men and women who walk in all the colors of reality."[108] But Anderson's stories were also dark, even nihilistic in tone.[109] Anderson considered it "absurd" to think that fiction should "point to a moral, uplift the people, make better citizens, etc.," and sought to write fiction that would plumb the dismal secrets that he imagined lay within every person.[110]

Lane disliked *Winesburg, Ohio*; in fact, she despised Anderson personally, in part because he had satirized her in his 1925 bestseller *Dark Laughter*. The two had met in Paris in 1921, and Anderson apparently decided that she was a scatterbrained prude—or at least that was how he caricatured her in the novel, where she appears as the character Rose Frank. "He doesn't know what he's writing about," Lane replied when she saw it. "He is the naughty little boy trying to peep through the keyhole of a water closet and not seeing anything but his own imaginings."[111] But she found *Winesburg* repellent for another reason. The "grotesques" featured in his nightmarish vignettes were motivated by venal and morbid appetites, not genuine desires or values. The result was a panorama of a village inhabited by religious fanatics and freakish neurotics, none of whom Anderson tried to portray as worthy human beings with comprehensible desires or values. The fictional Winesburg "isn't like any small town I've ever known," Lane thought. "It doesn't touch anywhere any of my experience of life or of life in small towns, it's only a bad, sensual dream."[112] Most of all, he failed to grasp that "the center of every personality is a wanting; and the life is a pattern of this wanting in conflict with obstacles."[113]

Thus Lane composed *Old Home Town* as a reply to Anderson (after whom she named one character, in a backhanded homage), and, to a lesser extent, to Sinclair Lewis. Based on her own youth in Mansfield, Missouri, the book consists of eight O. Henry–style stories with twist endings narrated by a character named Ernestine Blake, who is indeed earnest,[114] and who relates her neighbors' struggles, dreams, victories, and defeats as she viewed them during her teenage years. Some of the stories are even darker than Anderson's; in "Hired Girl," for instance, social pressures force a man to marry a woman he does not love; when, years later, his wife dies of old age, he is free to marry his childhood sweetheart—only to have that opportunity cut off again when he is once more forced into an unhappy marriage, this time his household servant, Almantha. Knowing the truth of his unhappiness is too much for Almantha to bear, and she commits suicide by hanging herself in a well.

Other chapters, however, are more uplifting. "Country Jake," for instance, features a bumpkin who wins the love of a wealthy townswoman through entrepreneurialism and hard work—a story that, although set in the 1900s, comments slyly on the Depression. And others make a feminist statement. In "Immoral Woman," hard-working Ella Sims longs to add a pretty front parlor on her house, but her shiftless husband fails to raise the necessary funds, so she gets a job herself, making hats for the town's general store. Then she learns that her husband has bought so much on credit from the same store that the owner withholds her wages. Refusing to give up, she continues working for the storekeeper to pay off the debt and earn some capital for herself. When rumors begin to circulate that she is having an affair with a traveling salesman, she flouts convention by leaving her husband and moving away to start her own fashion business. The chapter ends in contemporary times, with Ernestine, now grown, encountering Mrs. Sims in Paris. "The magazines had begun to print articles about her," Ernestine thinks. "It was a good story, the career of Ella Maybry Sims, creator of the Mary-Marie (trade-mark) frocks. American women from Canada to Mexico were wearing those cleverly designed fadeless cottons. . . . The biographies of her briefly mentioned an early marriage, leaving the inference that Mrs. Sims is a widow, and they did not exaggerate her fortune; the truth is staggering enough."[115]

In one sense, *Old Home Town* is a Village Rebel book—the characters either prevail by defying popular opinion or obliterate themselves by succumbing to it—and it has therefore struck some critics as odd that before publication, Lane added a preface that retreated from the rebellious implications of the chapters within. "It was a hard, narrow, relentless life," she wrote of the stifling village atmosphere against which Ernestine and other characters revolt. But "now some of us seem to see, in our country's most recent experiences, an unexpected proof that our parents knew what they were talking about . . . that facts are seldom pleasant and must be faced; that the only freedom is to be found within the slavery of self-discipline; that everything must be paid for. . . . This may be an old-fashioned, middle-class, small-town point of view. All that can be said for it is that it created America."[116]

This did seem an odd reversal. Yet nothing in Lane's words was insincere. What appears to the young Ernestine as suffocating and obsolete morality also reflects the accumulated wisdom of her parents' hard lives. Some of her mother's strictures might seem puritanical and petty, but they also make good common sense in a world fraught with danger. Lane's recognition of this tension was not an abandonment of her youthful individualism, but a matured respect for the relationship between the need for freedom and the demands of self-discipline. The point of *Old Home Town* was to appreciate the "wanting" of its characters, and to come to terms with the bourgeois culture the Village Rebels had fled, without surrendering to the philistinism of Main Street.

That reconciliation is suggested by the final chapter, "Nice Old Lady," which climaxes in Ernestine's rapprochement with her mother. Now grown and living in Europe, Ernestine thinks back to the fight she had with her parents when she first told them of her intention to go to college. "You simply cannot go to the city alone," her mother insisted. "Your character would be ruined. Ruined."

> I was too deeply frightened to be at all sure that I didn't want to be taken care of. But grimly I stuck to it that some girls did take care of themselves, nowadays. . . . It was not true, I knew it was not true, but I had to say it. And dizzy with that liberating lie, intoxicated by freedom, I heard defiance ring out again. "I don't *care!*". . . I was going to business college. The truth is that I was terrified, but I was going.[117]

After this argument, however, Ernestine's mother supports her daughter's decision, telling a neighbor, "I'm thankful my daughter's got gumption. . . . She wasn't going to marry some boy here and stick in this little town all her days."[118]

The story reflects Lane's newfound understanding of her parents' generation and gratitude for the freedom they gave her. Fifteen years after *Main Street*, she had come to see the village of her childhood with more nuance: acknowledging its injustice and ignorance, but also its realism and integrity, particularly in light of the extraordinary changes that had occurred since 1920. As Lane's biographer, William Holtz, put it, *Old Home Town* reflects Lane's effort "to cosmopolitanize the strengths of the small-town ethos that she had, like her heroine Ernestine, earlier rejected."[119]

Most strikingly, the book was, like *Main Street*, a feminist work, which protested against the way being "cared for" or "protected" deprived women of opportunities to make the most of themselves. At the same time, it honored the mothers who served as points of stability and sanity in a threatening and unpredictable world, even if doing so meant abandoning their own ambitions. For Lane, the essential quality of a free person's character could be found in this difficult balance between moral severity and personal liberation. The wild adventurer who likened herself to the Wandering Jew—and who resisted to the hilt being told how to live her life—nevertheless came to admire the bourgeois virtues of diligence, thrift, and wholesomeness, particularly as embodied by the women of previous generations. "I know now that the best of my life was its hardship," she wrote in 1938. "Struggling out of poverty developed in us an invaluable strength. Having conquered so much, we know we are stronger than adversity."[120] That was the spirit Lane tried to articulate in *Old Home Town*. It is perhaps no surprise that Sinclair Lewis found the book "enchanting."[121]

Lane was not the only one reevaluating the bourgeois virtues in the mid-1930s. Dorothy Thompson had just returned to the United States, having being expelled from Germany because of her critical reporting on Adolf Hitler, and now she announced plans to write a book called *The End of Bourgeois Morality*. Lane encouraged her in a wistful letter that recalled how they had both once longed for such a moral transformation. Two decades earlier, the Soviet Revolution had seemed to initiate a new age, one that offered an escape from the stifling and petty atmosphere memorialized in *Main Street*. "Our excitement in those days was, really, quite a personal thing," she told her friend, "for it came at last as a confirmation in external reality of our own dreams which we'd cherished so passionately. . . . Remember how we said and felt, 'The sun is rising in Russia!'?" But it was "a long way from those days to these," and Lane found herself appreciating the values she had once derided. "I have been heard saying with vigor, here and there, 'What we need is *morals*.'"[122]

Isabel Paterson had a similar reaction when she heard of Thompson's book plans. "We doubt if bourgeoisie morality can end without the human race ending also," she wrote in "Turns," "for bourgeoisie morality is based on the fact that people must be able to depend upon one another to a measurable extent, for the sake of the children." It was "no use shuffling the responsibility off onto the state; the state also is based on the integrity and dependability of the individual in relation to other individuals."[123]

Thompson never wrote her book, but other writers and dramatists were also reevaluating—and finding merit in—the virtues of Middle America.[124] Novels such as *Spring Came on Forever* by Bess Streeter Aldrich and *Vein of Iron* by Paterson's friend Ellen Glasgow focused on the endurance and inner strength of ordinary people, as did films like *Cavalcade* and *Little Women*. Some intellectuals sneered at these works as "escapism," but Paterson defended them in her column. "It drives [intellectuals] mad to think anyone should for a moment escape from Grim Reality, which is their specialty," she wrote. She had even heard one "young radical" denounce *"Little Women* lately for its 'bourgeois morality.'"[125] But Paterson—who had predicted a "back to the small town" literary movement since before the Depression[126]—took a moment to offer "a good word for the bourgeoisie."

It might seem "treasonable" to say so, but it struck her as bizarre "that the middle classes were always excoriated for thinking solely in material terms," when the opposite was true: the real materialists were the "planners who have got us in their clutches and are cleaning out the middle class." Bureaucrats and social workers "say, for instance, that 'farming does not pay' and must be made to pay," but the point of farming had never been to pay. The point of farming had been to "provide a good farmer with a living"—that is, independence— which "is what he really wants—his own way of living."[127]

True, "the bourgeois temperament does value money, comfort and what- ever measure of security is obtainable in a hazardous world," but there was nothing dishonorable in that. "Mostly this middle way of life is dictated by a sense of order, a sense of responsibility, pleasure in material things and a sense of continuity, a thought for the future." These were "indispensable qualities in any society. . . . Why should they be despised?" By contrast, "the gamblers, the improvident, the reckless" all "expect to be fed, during the lean years, by the steady-going ants whom they profess to scorn."[128]

This reference to "ants" was an allusion to Aesop's fable about the irre- sponsible grasshopper who wastes the spring in frivolity while the diligent ants labor to prepare for winter. When the snows begin to fall, the grasshopper is forced to beg the ants for food and shelter. Eight months after Paterson's column appeared, Walt Disney would release his cartoon version of the story, in which the lazy grasshopper takes advantage of the hard-working ants' generosity while singing "The World Owes Me a Living." (The cartoon, declared the *Tampa Times*, was "strikingly applicable to present day conditions." It "has a moral, with very real application; but how many will discern it?"[129])

Paterson saw a particularly strong connection between bourgeois values and the lives of women, who often found themselves cast in the role of the grasshopper. "Rose Wilder Lane thinks that perhaps if men ran the world's affairs as women run their homes, the world would be altogether different and saner," she reported in "Turns" in May. "She is referring to the 'fantastic situation that all the great financial experts of the world, all the Treasury Departments, can't grasp the simple fact principle that everything [has] to be paid for.' In finance, of course this is sheer disaster."[130] That question—the place of women in this disturbing new era of financial irresponsibility—would form the background of Paterson's most significant novel, *The Golden Vanity*, published in November 1934.

Hailed by critics as "searing" and "scintillating," the theme of *The Golden Vanity* is the relentless and bewildering passage of time; in Paterson's words, the sensation of "age as a process of loss, authority slipping away."[131] Loosely modeled on Shakespeare's *King Lear*, it concerns three cousins—Gina, Geraldine, and Mysie—who live through the stock market crash and the ensuing crisis. All were born into poverty, like Paterson herself, and at the opening of the novel—during the high times of the late 1920s—they have risen out of it on different trajectories. But the plot—which, as in all of Paterson's novels, is practically nonexistent—is not really the novel's narrative center of gravity. That lies in Paterson's sensitive study of these and other characters.

Gina is a gold digger who loathes everything about being poor; she manages to marry Arthur, the charming but hapless heir of the rich Siddall family. Raised by his grandmother, a Victorian grand dame named Charlotte, Arthur's fortune is so vast that he sponsors a socialist magazine, merely for the prestige—just as in real life, the Fords and Rockefellers were subsidizing the communist art of Diego Rivera, and Vincent Astor and Frederick Vanderbilt Field were underwriting left-wing journals such as *Today* and the *New Masses*.[132] But for all her newfound wealth, Gina remains riddled with envy—and is particularly frustrated at the way society ladies condescend to her. "She had married the greatest catch, one of the richest men, in an enormously rich country, good fortune beyond her wildest dreams; and still she was shut out. . . . She had got nothing of what she had represented to her imagination."[133] She loses interest in Arthur, and after their son Benjamin dies of polio, she turns to another man for comfort. She becomes pregnant and, panicked at the thought of losing her wealthy husband, leads Arthur to believe the child is his so he won't divorce her.

Geraldine, by contrast, is a writer who barely manages to keep her family solvent after her husband loses everything in the stock market crash. But that and caring for the kids prove too stressful, and she suffers a breakdown. Advised by doctors to take a vacation, she travels to Cuba to recuperate, and while there begins an affair with a mobster—not because she loves him, but because she desperately misses the sensation of being cared for by an assertive man. But when he is shot in a gangland altercation, Geraldine rushes home and gives up flirting with the underworld to resume her ordinary life.

The third cousin, Mysie, is an actress who puts on a devil-may-care attitude to conceal her feeling that everything she loves in life is somehow slipping away. On a brief trip to the Pacific Northwest to visit the town where she grew up, she tries to find a park where she played as a child. She discovers that it was destroyed years ago, replaced by homes and offices. "She was gazing at an open square of naked and infertile sand, with not a stick nor a stone nor a blade of herbage on its arid surface. A new concrete pavement bounded it rectangularly, one city block in an extensive grid of dismal blocks, of which the others were meagerly built over with new bleak small buildings and gas stations."[134] She learns that developers blasted the hills flat and built upon it in the twenties.

"The grading must have cost enormous sums," she reflected. "And loaded the city with taxes. . . . Whoever was responsible, I hope they're dead broke. That's what the planners are going to do for us everywhere. I hope they rot in hell. A flat hell, that goes on forever and ever." They didn't care about anything but money. And the money had gone back on them. Men had built the city for pride; and those who came later had destroyed it for profit.[135]

The novel's most interesting character, however, is Charlotte Siddall, Arthur's rich grandmother, who clings to her Victorian background even as the younger generation forgets it ever existed. She, too, has been leveling an older city—in her case, New York—because she is an investor in the Siddall Building, now under construction on Fifth Avenue. She has more common sense than the other characters, because she knows that balance sheets and accounts receivable must mean something real, and that fortunes built only on paper are valueless in hard times. Yet society has changed around her so rapidly and thoroughly that in her confusion she neglects her investments. She finds herself, like Shakespeare's Lear, losing her grasp on a changing world, prey to the new era's economic delusions.

Thus she is stunned to learn that the Siddall Building is a white elephant—there is no market demand for the office space it will provide, and its construction is riddled with fraud. Her investment agent, Julius, has been hiding the fact that half of the bonds to finance it have gone unsold, and that the family is wasting its capital on the project. (This was Paterson's reference to both Rockefeller Center and the Empire State Building, both then under construction, which upon completion found it nearly impossible to find tenants. The Empire State Building was soon nicknamed "the Empty State Building," and Rockefeller Center resorted to federal subsidies to stay afloat.[136]) One of Julius's business associates, Sam, who stands in for the jester in *King Lear*, reveals what has happened to Charlotte's fortune. "Julius handed you thirty million dollars' worth of soft soap," he gloats. In fact, Julius and his friends have already started seeking government bailouts. "Now they're in favor of unredeemable paper currency because they think it will prevent any chance of another showdown; and it inflates their book values so they can make their ledgers balance—on paper. . . . These birds think they are going to save their incomes—by mortgaging their capital. It's all to be paid out of thin air. They'll find the air getting thinner and thinner. If you want to know what's happened to you, it's simply that they got you on a short circuit. . . . And you and Julius running a Communist magazine; now that's a fancy touch."[137] Floored, Charlotte takes a drive to visit a wealthy old friend, the only one of her own age still alive, in hopes that he can help. But she finds him confined to a wheelchair, senile, clutching old silver coins and muttering, "There isn't any more money."[138] She flees in terror to her home and dies that evening playing solitaire.

Although studded with Paterson's commentary on politics and economics, *The Golden Vanity* is not really a political novel, but a meditation on the bizarre feeling of the passing of an era. "Where did the time go?" one character asks. "Only a minute ago I was young. And now I'm thirty-eight. There didn't seem to be any in between."[139] It is a question all the characters ask themselves repeatedly—except the men, who are all schemers or blithe fools snatched from P. G. Wodehouse novels, and placed in an all-too-real world where their starched collars provide little protection against thieves and vultures. *The Golden Vanity* is essentially a comedy, notwithstanding its tragic strains. Yet it ends on a bittersweet note, with Mysie laughing even as she reflects: "We'll never touch our shore again. That landfall is lost forever."[140] That might well have served as Paterson's personal motto.

Ayn Rand in 1943, the year her novel *The Fountainhead* was published. A Russian immigrant, Rand became one of the most outspoken defenders of individualism in American history.

5

The Refugee

In 1935, the Roosevelt administration shifted away from the emergency mentality of its first years and began erecting a permanent regulatory welfare state. It marked a fundamental shift in American society. This so-called Second New Deal included passage of the Social Security Act and the National Labor Relations Act, and the creation of the Works Progress Administration (WPA), an entity that would oversee the federal government's many public works schemes. The WPA even encompassed the arts, with subdivisions devoted to unemployed authors (the Federal Writers' Project [FWP]) and to actors and playwrights (the Federal Theatre Project [FTP]).

These initiatives clashed with the nation's constitutional tradition of separating the state and private enterprise, and sparked a showdown over basic American values, particularly the principle of individualism that New Dealers had already been targeting for three years. In this new stage of the Roosevelt era, not only business and property owners, but also novelists, dramatists, poets, historians, painters, and film directors would struggle over what one scholar has called the New Deal's "adventure in cultural collectivism."[1]

Among the important players in this drama were the Communist Party and its many supporters in the literary community. The party had just adopted a new program called the Popular Front, which aimed to expand party influence and recruit important intellectuals by muting criticism of the New Deal, which communists had initially spurned as a form of fascism. Among the Popular Front's first steps was the creation of the League of American Writers, a group devoted to "helping to accelerate the destruction of capitalism and the establishment of a workers' government."[2] Another was to infiltrate the FWP, which offered party members an opportunity to pursue these goals while earning a government paycheck. Among the communists and "fellow travelers" who joined the FWP were Saul Bellow, Richard Wright, Studs Terkel, and Kenneth Rexroth. Although it later became unfashionable to acknowledge the extreme left-wing politics of the FWP, it was an accepted fact of life at the time. The conservative poet Conrad Aiken quit the project in protest after only a few months when his Marxist office mates—objecting to an essay he wrote that argued that the essence of American literature was its "profound individualism"—insisted on commissioning a second essay to present an anti-individualist counterpoint.[3]

The FWP's most successful initiative was publishing a series of guidebooks devoted to the history and culture of each state. But it also prepared thousands of other manuscripts, many of which were essentially make-work tasks, never intended for publication. Communist poet Norman Macleod, who returned home from Moscow out of enthusiasm for the FWP, was disappointed to be given inane tasks that took so little time to complete that his colleagues spent afternoons drinking beer.[4] Saul Bellow was assigned to draft biographies of Illinois writers that were simply filed away, and to compile a list of magazines held by nearby libraries.[5] The project attracted some writers of distinction— including Zora Neale Hurston, whose writings were deemed too radical for publication[6]—but more often it employed authors of middling talents who resorted to government aid because they lacked the skills to earn a living in the marketplace. FWP director Henry Alsberg even insisted that the project employ those he called "the mediocre" in order to avoid becoming an elite institution.[7]

One dream of communist writers at this time was to produce a literary pearl from the Depression's swirling sands, which they called the "proletarian novel." By articulating the revolutionary imperatives of class struggle and voicing the yearnings of the economically oppressed, the ideal proletarian novel would serve as the "*Uncle Tom's Cabin* of Capitalism."[8] Such a work, as author Edwin Seaver told the 1935 American Writers' Congress, would be concerned with "political orientation, with economic orientation, with the materialist dialectic," and "not style, not form, not plot, not even characters."[9]

Proletarian novels had been around in one form or another since at least the 1900s. Sherwood Anderson's 1917 *Marching Men* was a proletarian novel, as was Upton Sinclair's *The Jungle* in 1906. Lane's own *He Was a Man* was, to some degree, a proletarian novel, and in 1932, her friend Catherine Brody made her own effort with *Nobody Starves*. (Sinclair Lewis praised it as "the real proletarian literature that everyone has said was impossible," but critics said it fell short because it had a hero, which was contrary to communist doctrine.[10]) Perhaps the ultimate expression of the form was Seaver's own 1937 *Between the Hammer and the Anvil*, in which the main characters were actually named Mr. and Mrs. John Doe. In the end, only two successful proletarian novels emerged from the Depression: Steinbeck's *The Grapes of Wrath* in 1939 and Wright's *Native Son* a year later.

Isabel Paterson considered the whole enterprise pointless. "The theory of Communism and the necessities of fiction are incompatible," she wrote in "Turns." Socialism in all its varieties "affirms that the individual is of no consequence," and that "only what happens to 'the mass' is important," yet it was impossible to portray the mass without focusing on the choices of individuals. Communist novels also tended to be "grossly libelous of the poor," since they portrayed vice as a consequence of poverty, while also downplaying the significance of individual character. This meant the protagonists of such novels were almost invariably engaged in crime and wickedness. And because that was supposed to be capitalism's fault rather than their own, they invariably came off as unappealingly helpless: incapable of preventing themselves from doing wrong. "The left-wing novelists take away from the poor all claim to humanity," she concluded, and unjustly "deny all decency to the proletarian characters."[11] Communist literature set out to depict the poor as deprived, but instead showed them as depraved.

Even if a communist author succeeded at writing a truly proletarian novel, however, Paterson thought it would be so boring that no actual worker would want to read it. People suffering under the Depression were far more interested

Ivar Kreuger, the Swedish "Match King," whose death in 1932
precipitated a scandal that helped inspire Rand's play *Night of January 16th*.

in tales of adventure and romance. Indeed, Paterson wrote, "the only proletarians I know read Zane Grey."[12] The biggest novel of 1933 was *Anthony Adverse*, a 1,000-page historical romance set in the Napoleonic Wars. Yet the "sternly sociological critics" who professed to speak on behalf of the poor derided such books as "evidence of a bourgeois and escapist mentality." Such a "patronizing attitude," Paterson thought, was indistinguishable from the prudishness of Victorian era censors.[13] Like Carol Kennicott at the library in *Main Street*, left-wing idealists had become busybodies, contemptuous of the very people they claimed to champion.

▼▲◀

But it was actually Sinclair Lewis himself who would make the more lasting contribution to the era's protest literature. In the autumn of 1935, he published his half-satirical, half-polemic novel *It Can't Happen Here*, which envisioned the rise of fascism in America under the leadership of a demagogue called "Buzz" Windrip, whom Lewis modeled primarily on Louisiana senator Huey Long. In the story, Windrip defeats Roosevelt for the 1936 Democratic nomination and wins the general election, wrapping his tyrannical designs in the slogans of ordinary, small-town America. Once elected, he sacks his moderate deputies; establishes concentration camps; disenfranchises blacks, Jews, and atheists; imposes an Italian-style corporatist economy; and prohibits the employment of women. He also cracks down on the press, ultimately sending the novel's hero, a dissenting journalist named Doremus Jessup, to prison. The Windrip administration then collapses in a series of palace coups, and rebellions break out in the Midwest. Jessup escapes and flees to Canada, where he becomes a secret agent for an underground resistance movement and returns to the United States on secret missions to restore freedom. The novel ends on a note of hope for the dawn of a new age—someday.

Lewis's worries about fascism in America were likely inspired by his wife. In 1925, shortly after her first meeting with Lane in Paris, Dorothy Thompson had traveled to Berlin, where she became the first woman to lead a major American news bureau. There, she witnessed the rise of National Socialism, interviewed the führer himself, and published *I Saw Hitler!*, one of the earliest books to warn the world of the gravity of the Nazi threat. In her view, the National Socialist movement represented an insidiously exaggerated form of the belligerent banality Lewis had satirized in *Main Street* and *Babbitt*. Hitler was a man of "startling insignificance," she wrote, a "formless, almost faceless" creature, "inconsequent and voluble, ill-poised, insecure"; the "very prototype of the Little Man."[14] With his rhetoric of national greatness and the "spirit of the people," he seemed to be "the apotheosis" of all the "Babbitts and sub-Babbitts" in Germany.[15] Indeed, he was so dully hostile to culture and modernity that Thompson had not at first believed that he could become a dictator. By 1934, however, she had been forced to reassess. That August, officers of the Gestapo visited her apartment and ordered her to leave Germany. Her expulsion shocked the international community, and she hoped it would rally world opinion against Nazism. Hitler, she warned, "has gone to war already and the rest of the world does not believe it."[16]

Political scientist Robert Paxton has described fascism as less an ideology than a set of "mobilizing passions"; a hypermasculine attitude that elevates the group over the individual, stresses the need for political chieftains, rejects reason in exchange for urges and instincts, and regards the nation as the central actor in history.[17] Thompson had seen these forces taking over Germany, and upon her return to America, she began to notice them in her native country, as well. Thus, although she had begun as a supporter of the New Deal, she changed her mind when the *Saturday Evening Post* hired her to investigate the bureaucratic mess the Roosevelt administration had created. The experience made her, at least temporarily, into one of the president's most formidable critics.

In July 1935, four months before Lewis published *It Can't Happen Here*, Thompson reported that, however benevolent the New Dealers' motives might be, their programs were actually dividing Americans into two separate classes: one made up of wage earners and another made up of people whose lives were controlled by bureaucrats in nearly every detail. Recipients of federal aid were becoming a "ghostly commonwealth," she wrote, whose members "work, but most of them do not receive wages, but 'budgets,' and the amount which they earn is not decided according to their merits, but according to their minimum needs—as determined for them by careful investigation." Confined to a "curiously infantile world," their lives were entirely supervised by social workers who monitored their expenditures, debts, and even their eating habits. And because these people owed their livelihoods to the favor of government leaders and lived outside the boundaries of the ordinary economic system, they were ripe for exploitation by politicians and demagogues.

Thompson did not think this was a form of socialism, so much as "a new form of benevolent serfdom" that laid a dangerous foundation for fascism.[18] Alongside that was the fact that New Dealers were nurturing a contempt for the democratic process, as were their Republican opponents. She detected a "growing tendency toward personal leadership and personal government" among both parties, which disconcertingly resembled what she saw in Germany.[19] Roosevelt had "vastly . . . extend[ed], under personal leadership, the powers of the executive branch of the government and the function of government in the social and economic field," and had become "the leader and formulator of policy."[20] Voters, in turn, seemed to view themselves as having a direct, personal relationship with him, or envisioned him as a vindicator of their personal resentments. That sense of spiritual kinship was one of the definitive symptoms of fascism, and it was central to Roosevelt's leadership style. He seemed to think there was a "mystical compact . . . between him personally and the American people," Thompson wrote, and that the constitutional system of checks and balances should be "used or circumvented according to whether they work or not within the spirit of that compact."[21] Yet instead of challenging him on these points, rivals such as Charles Lindbergh, Gerald L. K. Smith, Gerald Burton Winrod, and William Dudley Pelley were imitating him. "If things move in the present tempo," Thompson told her husband, "I think we may easily have a Republican-fascist dictatorship by 1940."[22]

Louisiana's Huey Long was a bellwether. Although Thompson considered him a "clown"—an epithet Lewis was also fond of using—he was a prime example of the worrisome trends she detected, particularly the way he encouraged people to view politics as a matter of "getting things done" without democratic deliberation or respect for the rights of dissenters. Elected governor in 1928 and senator in 1932—a position from which he maintained his control over the state—Long had emerged as a formidable opponent of the New Deal, not because he opposed its collectivist aims but because he considered it too moderate. He had started as a Roosevelt supporter, but the NIRA codes persuaded him that the New Deal was a fraud, only benefiting big business and banks. Portraying himself as the champion of the common man, he oversaw a massive public works program during his governorship, which he used, along with other forms of direct payouts of taxpayer cash, to finance his reelection prospects. He directed public funds to the districts of legislators who supported him, imposed taxes directly without legislative oversight, controlled practically every civil service job in Louisiana, and used the police and National Guard as a miniature Gestapo, to terrorize political opponents.[23] Once in the Senate, he began what he called the "Share Our Wealth" campaign, which promised to confiscate all income above a certain amount and dole out the proceeds to everyone else. His spellbinding speeches and folksy demeanor developed such a fanatical following that historian Arthur Schlesinger Jr. labeled him "the messiah of the rednecks."[24]

Long laughed off the accusation that he was a potential dictator, and it is true that he had no sophisticated political theory. But his viewpoint on politics was rooted in what social scientists call the "clientele system," whereby leaders reward loyalty with special privileges and in which the rule of law or the sanctity of individual rights is subordinated to the leader's power. His anti-intellectualism, thuggishness, and portrayal of himself as the personal patron of the downtrodden made him eerily like the dictators of Europe. He was not alone in these tactics, however. Roosevelt, too, exploited federal funding and jobs programs to increase his authority, turned the FBI and the IRS against his political enemies (including Long), and was "intent," as Thompson wrote in July 1935, "on substituting himself and his own ideas, his own policies, and his own hunches, for the checked and balanced government of this country."[25]

Thus the character of "Buzz" Windrip in *It Can't Happen Here* is based not only on Long but also on Roosevelt. Windrip's platform, called "Fifteen Points of Victory for the Forgotten Men," combines Long's own manifesto (published in 1935 as *My First Days in the White House*) with Roosevelt's "forgotten man" slogan. It calls for government control over all finance, including presidential authority to issue unilateral decrees controlling banks—a power Roosevelt had actually exercised in 1933—along with a cap on personal income and confiscatory taxation. Yet it simultaneously pledges to "guarantee Private Initiative and the Right to Private Property for all time," thus echoing the oxymoronic promises of the New Deal.[26] It gives the president power to "institute and execute all necessary measures for the conduct of the government during this critical epoch"—the same power Roosevelt called for in his first inaugural address—as well as rendering Congress "advisory" and depriving the Supreme Court of authority to declare laws unconstitutional—again, powers the administration had, in all essentials, actually sought. As much as *It Can't Happen Here* aimed its blows at Long, attentive readers recognized it as a charge against the president as well.[27]

Perversely, communist writers applauded the book, seeing it only as an attack on fascism. As part of their Popular Front effort, they even convened a dinner party for Lewis and Thompson in New York that November, under the auspices of the League of American Writers. When the introductory speeches ended, an intoxicated Lewis took to the podium to denounce his audience. "I don't believe any of you have *read* the book," he told them. "If you had, you would have seen I was telling all of you to go to hell."[28] Then he tried to get the audience to stand up and sing a satirical hymn.

Paterson was delighted. "It is rumored that the Literary Left takes *It Can't Happen Here* as propaganda for their cause," she reported in "Turns," "and that Sinclair Lewis has informed them quietly that they are mistaken. His meaning was that they could all go and sit on a tack—Fascisti, Communists, or what have you." It was her "fervent hope" that the novel would "do some good among the Babbitts, who have been saying for ten years past that 'what we need is a dictator.'"[29] And the novel was a hit; Winston Churchill even praised it in *Collier's*.[30] Lewis prepared a screenplay, but Hollywood refused to film it, reportedly by order of the Hays Office—the censorship agency studios created in 1922 to appease federal demands for control over motion pictures—which

Louisiana governor Huey Long helped inspire the fascist dictator "Buzz" Windrip in Sinclair Lewis's novel *It Can't Happen Here*—although Windrip was also based in part on Franklin Roosevelt.

feared offending the German and Italian governments. "All of this seems to me a fantastic exhibition of folly and cowardice," Lewis complained.[31] Yet no evidence shows that Germany or Italy objected to the proposed film, and the truth was that the studios were more afraid of domestic backlash against Lewis's message.[32] The author therefore turned *It Can't Happen Here* into a play, which was produced by the Federal Theatre Project in locations across the country in 1936. It actually became the FTP's most successful production.

Welcome as that was, however, Paterson could not help but observe that the federal government's sponsorship of the play was "the most extraordinary irony of the contemporary scene." "The only way it *can* happen here," she wrote, "is by the extension of the operations of the state—as, for instance, by running theaters. It doesn't matter whether any one intends the final result or not; if you set up the state machinery to that extent, you have the makings of Fascism."[33] Whether the erratic Lewis recognized the irony of using the FTP to stage *It Can't Happen Here* is uncertain. One friend called him a political chameleon who "could be a liberal, a radical, and a reactionary on three consecutive days," and a later critic remarked that he "lacked a framework for belief," and that his "ideas on politics or economy were ill-defined."[34] But Paterson's warning that government-funded drama would eventually turn into government-censored drama seemed vindicated only months later, when federal officials ordered the closure of an FTP-sponsored musical called *The Cradle Will Rock*. That play—which depicted the workers of Steeltown abandoning the false consciousness of capitalism and rising up against the greedy mogul Mr. Mister—was such a clumsily extravagant piece of communist propaganda that even the Roosevelt administration was embarrassed by it.[35] Lane, who saw it with some friends during a trip to New York, walked out during the first act, calling it "a Red Revolution play" that "sneers at America, at liberty, at law."[36] In the end, the musical was not actually censored; its producers, Orson Welles and John Houseman, rented a theater and paid for the production themselves.[37]

Cradle was only the most famous of many FTP plays that consciously spouted Communist Party talking points; others included Clifford Odets's *Waiting for Lefty*, which glorified the party while depicting a taxi driver's strike, and the children's play *Revolt of the Beavers*, in which forest animals unite to overthrow capitalism.[38] Such leftist proselytizing offended congressional Republicans, who demanded to know why tax dollars were being spent on political plays. Southern Democrats, too, objected that FTP dramas often advocated racial integration, which they viewed as another part of the communist program. In 1939, after an extensive investigation into its political activities, Congress chose to defund the project.

Far away from the FTP and the FWP, however, a genuine American literary movement was emerging in the 1930s, one rooted not in collectivist creeds but in a commitment to the inherent value and potential of the individual. Literary scholars have never given this genre a name, in part because it intersects with many different recognized styles and schools and includes writers from diverse backgrounds.[39] But it would best be described as the "resilience novel" because, in contrast to the proletarian novel, its characteristic themes are personal moral strength and individual choices rather than the forces of history. Resilience novels focus on fortitude in the face of daunting odds, and the conquest of nature instead of the organization of a new economic order. This category includes historical romances such as Margaret Mitchell's *Gone with the Wind*, LeGrand Cannon's *Look to the Mountain*, and Ethel Hueston's *Star of the West*; family stories such as *Vein of Iron* by Ellen Glasgow and Zora Neale Hurston's *Seraph of the Suwanee*; and portraits of foreign lands such as Pearl Buck's *The Good Earth*. Its descendants include Jack Shaefer's *Shane*, Alan LeMay's *The Searchers*, and the novels of Elmer Kelton and Larry McMurtry, which use the frontier experience to dramatize the virtues of perseverance that are threatened by the modern age. But among the most important early resilience novels were the *Little House* books by Laura Ingalls Wilder and Rose Wilder Lane.

Little House on the Prairie appeared in September 1935. Whereas the first two books in the series, *Little House in the Big Woods* and *Farmer Boy*, had been intended as standalone volumes that aimed at a young audience and focused mainly on how pioneers went about surviving in the wilderness, the third book featured a more advanced plot and initiated a saga that followed the Ingalls family through Laura's childhood. It depicts the family's effort to establish a farm on a section of Osage tribal land after rumors circulate that the federal government is planning to remove the tribe and open the area for white settlement. After many hardships—including a terrifying prairie fire that races across the grass and nearly destroys their home—they learn that the rumor is not true. Instead, the government will be sending soldiers to force them off the tribe's property. The book ends with Pa packing up and departing to the East, disappointed but unbowed.

The actual incidents on which the novel was based happened when Wilder was too young to remember, so she and her daughter did their best to research real-life details to create an air of authenticity. The result shows how their partnership surpassed anything they wrote alone. Few of Lane's solo writings—and none of Wilder's—equaled the beauty and simplicity of the prose in these books, such as at the end of Chapter 5, when the Ingalls family reaches its destination and sits around the campfire on the empty grasslands, taking in the splendor of the American landscape: "Everything was silent, listening to the nightingale's song. The bird sang on and on. The cool wind moved over the prairie and the song was round and clear above the grasses' whispering. The sky was like a bowl of light overturned on the flat black land."[40]

Although a children's book, *Little House in the Big Woods* also appealed to parents who read aloud to them and enjoyed the lessons it taught. Along with its vivid imagery, it drew readers with its accuracy of detail and its depiction of the Ingalls family as resolute, cheerful, and loving. Older pioneer books had often portrayed the settler experience in dark tones—as, for example, in the works of Hamlin Garland, whose novels and memoirs of his own pioneer days were written in what he called a "mood of bitterness."[41] Lane and Wilder, by contrast, treated the prairie life as hard but rewarding, and showcased in particular the value of personal independence for which the Ingalls family, especially Pa, are willing to exchange many of the comforts of civilization.[42]

The resilience novel reversed the Revolt from the Village formula. Where *Main Street* had regarded the mediocrity of the small town with revulsion, and yearned for an impossible escape, resilience novels found in rural America a source of moral strength and self-reliance worth celebrating. Bess Streeter Aldrich, the Nebraska author whose *Spring Came on Forever* also appeared in 1935, put the point well. The prairie novelist "does not pretend that it is idyllic," she wrote, or portray it "as bleak and uninteresting. He does not assert that it has attained to great heights of culture and art . . . nor will he sell it for thirty pieces of silver. But in some way [he] catches in his writings the gleam of the soul of the wide prairie, dim and deep and mysterious."[43] *Little House on the Prairie* and its successors fit this description perfectly.

▰▲◤

Much of the effectiveness of the resilience novel came from its engagement with personal adversity. "Too much hardship will prevent a writer from developing," wrote Paterson in a "Turns" column on May 31, 1936, yet writers "must be apprenticed to [their] craft," and must "quarry the material out of experience, forge the tools to reduce it to form, and then make what [they] can of it." Laura Ingalls Wilder was testament to that. But Paterson had a different writer in mind when she wrote those words: a young Russian émigré she had just learned of, who had published her first novel that month after fleeing the Soviet Union "because she preferred the terrific hazards she has surmounted to the 'security' of a 'planned society.'"[44] After working as a waitress and in the wardrobe department at a Hollywood studio, the young writer had scored a respectable success with a stage play and now had published a semiautobiographical novel about life and love in communist Russia. It was called *We the Living*, and the author's name was Ayn Rand.[45]

Rand was born Alisa Rosenbaum in St. Petersburg on February 2, 1905. She was the oldest daughter of a pharmacist named Zinovy Rosenbaum and his wife, an aspiring intellectual named Anna. They were middle-class, business-owning Jews of the type routinely targeted by the czar's pogroms and, later, by Bolshevik purges. A bright child, Rand was drawn at an early age to philosophical questions, and she decided at 13 that she was an atheist. That was years after she had announced that she wanted to become a writer. She had fallen in love with the hero of a magazine story called "The Mysterious Valley"—a British military officer who is seized by the enemy, but bravely uses his wits to escape—and pledged herself to writing stories like that. The hero of the story was named Cyrus, and she would give the Russian feminine version of that name, Kira, to the heroine of *We the Living*.

As a schoolgirl, she devoured the novels of Victor Hugo and the poetry of Alexander Blok. She was drawn to their passionate intensity and their belief in the superlative importance of beauty, victory, and life, and of pursuing one's values with one's entire heart. This yearning for justice and joy was characteristic of the late 19th-century Romantics, but Rand would always think of it as the spirit of "youth"—a "conviction that *ideas matter* . . . that knowledge matters, that truth matters, that one's mind matters," and that suffering and pain are both intolerable and, in a profound sense, insignificant features of life.[46] The philosopher Friedrich Nietzsche, whom Rand first read in college in the 1920s, expressed this conviction in his classic *Thus Spoke Zarathustra*. In a chapter titled "On the Tree on the Mountainside," the prophet Zarathustra encounters a young man sitting beneath a tree, gazing into the distance with hesitant longing. "I aspire to the height," he says, and as a result, "nobody trusts me any more." Zarathustra reassures him that idealism is not misguided. "You still feel noble, and the others too feel your nobility, though they bear you a grudge," he says. "I beseech you: do not throw away the hero in your soul! Hold holy your highest hope!"[47] Decades later, Rand would put these words into the mouth of one of the heroes of her novel, *Atlas Shrugged*.[48]

The Bolsheviks seized power when she was 12. They soon expropriated her father's store and ordered the family to share their home with strangers. After months of living on Soviet rations, the Rosenbaums fled south to Crimea, in hopes of escaping communist rule. There they remained for three years. Rand and her two sisters enrolled in a private school as her father struggled to provide in the face of war and government confiscations. It was here in

1920 or 1921 that she first read Aristotle and was struck with fascination by the power of syllogistic logic—while at the same time reading the stories of O. Henry (recently translated into Russian) and Edmond Rostand's 1897 play *Cyrano de Bergerac*, one of the crowning achievements of French Romantic literature, which she would pronounce the greatest play ever written.[49] These two things—the encyclopedic curiosity and rationality of Aristotle, and the devotion to beauty and truth embodied by Rostand's hero—became the twin pillars of Rand's worldview. But in the summer of 1921, forced back to St. Petersburg by the Bolshevik conquest of Crimea, the family was subjected to the dismal regimentation of Lenin's government. Her father refused to work for the communists, and the Rosenbaums were left destitute in a city with no running water or electricity.[50] Rand and her mother earned what money they could by teaching Russian soldiers to write and translating foreign books and magazines that cleared Soviet censorship.

A central tenet of the new communist state was the abolition of private property, as a step toward the ultimate eradication of individualism. According to Marxist doctrine, ownership was a socially created concept that deprived laborers of the wealth they created and kept them subservient for the benefit of the privileged elite. This situation was supposedly untenable, because the forces of history dictated that the people would rise up against their masters and, in a two-stage process, obliterate private property and transform society into one that would satisfy the needs of all. In the first step, the workers would take over the means of production—factories, capital, and so forth—and in the second, they would transcend their selfishness and create resources that society would distribute to people in the manner that best served the whole.

Between these two stages stood the "dictatorship of the proletariat," a transitional phase during which the state would control all economic institutions and manage them in accordance with political calculations. This dictatorship, said Vladimir Lenin, would exercise "power that is limited by nothing, by no laws, that is restrained by absolutely no rules, that rests directly on coercion."[51] It would usher in a new dispensation that would resolve the problem of poverty by creating and allocating wealth "rationally," as opposed to the allegedly haphazard manner of capitalist nations governed by personal selfishness.

Accomplishing this change would depend on reconstructing human nature so that instead of pursuing their own self-interest, people would serve the interest of the whole. Communism would achieve this transformation by fashioning the "new Soviet man"—an unselfish being who would feel no need for privacy because he would belong entirely to the state and would work for the benefit of his comrades. "Only if the proletariat and the poor peasants display sufficient class-consciousness, devotion to principle, self-sacrifice and perseverance will the victory of the socialist revolution be assured," Lenin claimed.[52] According to his supporters, this was not oppression, because communism would create a new psychology, in which the individual's need for fulfillment would be replaced by commitment to the collective.

These arguments were nothing new. Plato had imagined that if people shared all property (as well as their spouses and children), they would be purged of selfishness and become a perfectly ordered community. Jean-Jacques Rousseau, too, argued that if people would surrender their self-concern and submit to the "general will" of the collective, private ownership and greed would wither away, and with them poverty and alienation. Efforts to create communist societies were undertaken repeatedly during the 19th century, including among many religious groups in the United States, which sought, in the words of one commune's leader, to "construct each in [its] own way, great compound hives for human beings."[53] These efforts to make humans more insect-like invariably failed, because, as Paterson put it in one column, "nothing is more salutary for theorists than contact with reality."[54] Yet the Soviet experiment would devote far more energy to making communism succeed than had ever been attempted before.

During the first stage of the Soviet Revolution, Lenin's government adopted a program later called "war communism," in which the government nationalized all major industries, prohibited private trade, and placed the economy under a government-controlled "plan" that substituted coerced labor for profit-driven enterprise. This move led to economic collapse and widespread food shortages.[55] Lenin's policies of confiscating grain harvests (some of which Lane had witnessed in Georgia) precipitated a famine that historian Richard Pipes called "the greatest human disaster in European history until then, other than those caused by war, since the Black Death."[56]

The severity of the crisis forced Soviet leaders into a slight retreat from their strict party line. Adopting what they called the New Economic Policy (NEP), they allowed some small businesses to operate, replaced grain seizures with a regular tax, and let peasants sell surplus crops on a tightly restricted market. This caused a modest thawing of the economy, including the reintroduction of money, which had been eliminated under war communism.[57] But the government treated those who tried to operate businesses under the NEP with suspicion and restricted their operations so severely that most closed up shop within a few years. They were subjected to official persecution afterward.[58] Meanwhile, the NEP also initiated a tightening of the Communist Party's ideological ranks through the first of what became the party's infamous "purges."[59]

It was in the midst of this that, in October 1921, Rand entered Petrograd State University, majoring in history, with a minor in philosophy. By this time, she had become fascinated by Nietzsche, whose electrifying literary style and bold individualism made a profound impression on her.[60] Although scholars have tended to focus on the influence on Rand of his notion of the *Übermensch*—the "overman" who would transcend the moral attitudes of contemporary society—equally important was his concept of ressentiment, the hostility toward success and achievement that leads weak people to despise, and seek revenge against, those who are strong and able. This, Rand thought, was what really motivated many communists, not any desire to improve the lives of the poor. In fact, she would write decades later that ressentiment—or as she termed it, "hatred of the good for being the good"—was the defining characteristic of the 20th century, the one common theme uniting communism, fascism, and other forms of collectivism.[61]

It was not just a matter of politics, however. Even in other areas of life, the people around her often seemed motivated by hostility toward anyone who was intelligent, successful, and enterprising, precisely on account of those virtues. That was one of the themes masterfully dramatized by Nietzsche's contemporary, the Norwegian playwright Henrik Ibsen, whose 1883 play *An Enemy of the People* explored the ways in which "the majority" often seek to destroy independent thinkers and strong individuals. "The majority is never right!" cries the play's title character. "All these majority-truths are like salt meat that's been kept too long. . . . The truths the masses recognize now are the truths that were established by the frontier guard in the days of our grandfathers."[62]

Rand's family seems to have revered Ibsen—her sister Nora was named for the heroine of his 1875 drama *A Doll's House*—and Rand found in him, as in Nietzsche, a devastating critique of traditional values, one that went beyond familiar concerns about majority tyranny and focused on the way conformity and dogmatism stifle superlative individuals. These dangerous tendencies, both writers thought, were built into the very fabric of modern society. That was a perspective as incompatible with social conservatism as it was with communism, and Rand must have thrilled at the climax of *A Doll's House*, in which Nora chooses to leave her unhappy marriage and pursue a life of independence, regardless of social consequences. When her husband Torvald insists that her foremost duty is to be a wife and mother, she answers no. "First and foremost, I'm a human being," she tells him. "I'm aware that most people agree with you, Torvald, and that your opinion is backed up by plenty of books. But I can't be satisfied any more with what most people say, or what's written in the books. Now I've got to think these things through myself."[63]

Standing at the opposite end of the spectrum from *A Doll's House* was Leo Tolstoy's *Anna Karenina*, which Rand also read around this time and which she later called "the most evil novel in world literature." Its theme was "that it is futile to look for happiness. . . . The author's message is as follows: 'Right or wrong, you have to obey the social standards of your surroundings, even if they are irrational—even if you are miserable. Accept, submit, and conform. If you attempt to rebel against social convention, you will be punished.'"[64] The book was not a protest against the stifling culture against which the title character rebels, but an indictment of her and of her lover Vronsky for the fact that they *do* rebel. Tolstoy's point seemed to be "that there is no such thing as a world of independent goals."[65] Little wonder that Tolstoy despised both Ibsen and Nietzsche.[66]

In her student years, Rand would come to see this dichotomy as manifesting a deeper crisis of individualism—one with its roots in moral philosophy. Communist politics was built on a morality of self-sacrifice, as Dorothy Thompson herself observed while visiting the Soviet Union in 1927. "What fundamentally distinguishes Russian education," Thompson wrote, "is that it is not interested in developing in children those qualities which make it possible for them to 'stand on their own two feet.' . . . It regards the 'collective' as something . . . which demands not the expression of the individual, but sacrifice of him; and it teaches the child to believe and more than that to *feel* that in yielding up his individuality, his person, his life and his will to the collective life and will, he merges himself in something so much grander and loftier than he can ever be. . . . The Collective in this atheistic state is God."[67] Rand saw this conception of self-sacrifice as rooted in the morality of altruism, which holds that the individual's moral worth is a function of his service to others. She rejected that view in favor of the moral tradition known as ethical egoism, which holds that the individual is responsible for himself—not the state, tribe, or class—and that his primary goal in life is his own flourishing, not the helping of others. In later years, Rand would be better known for her advocacy of ethical egoism than for any of her other philosophical views. But although it was a mainstay of ancient Greek philosophy, and was commonplace in the 18th-century Enlightenment, ethical egoism had come under fire during the 19th century, and had been largely rejected by leading philosophers and political thinkers, including in the United States by the 1930s. By the time of the New Deal, altruism was largely taken for granted.[68]

Along with the works of Ibsen and Nietzsche, Rand found spiritual solace in motion pictures. Going to the theater felt like having "a private avenue of seeing the world outside," and she saved her money for the chance to see any American film, hoping to glimpse the Manhattan skyline in the background.[69] Its tall buildings transfixed her, and skyscrapers would forever serve as a personal symbol of mankind's potential, if given the freedom to build. She was fascinated, too, by exotic movies about historical figures and faraway places. She began writing down brief ideas for stories to make into her own movies someday, featuring larger-than-life heroes modeled on 19th-century Romantic literature. Like Carol Kennicott in *Main Street*, she dreamed of a life of authenticity and meaning—only to find herself engulfed in a sea of ordinariness and uniformity. In *We the Living*, she would paint the suffocating atmosphere of Soviet communism in haunting detail, dramatizing the way it destroyed one's spiritual independence. Perhaps the novel's most nakedly candid moment is one in which the heroine Kira is forced to attend a communist political rally. She catches a glimpse of a foreign visitor reviewing the parade:

> She was tall, thin, not young, with the worried face of a school teacher. But she wore a tan sports coat and that coat yelled louder than the hurrahs of the crowd, louder than the "Internationale," that it was *foreign*. . . . And suddenly Kira wanted to scream and to hurl herself at the stand, and to grab these thin, glittering legs and hang on with her teeth as to an anchor, and be carried away with them into their world which was possible somewhere, which was now here, close, within hearing of a cry for help. But she only swayed a little and closed her eyes.[70]

Shortly before graduation, Rand was expelled from the university for being politically undesirable. She may have been too careless in her speech. "I knew enough, in my college days to know that it was useless to attempt political protests in Soviet Russia," she later wrote. "But that knowledge broke down, involuntarily, many times."[71] When a group of Western visitors objected to the purge, the university reversed its decision and allowed her to graduate, but her future in Russia was obviously bleak. Her movie ideas were already explicitly anti-communist, and the plan she concocted of trying to earn a living by writing subtly anti-Soviet screenplays was not realistic. After graduating, she enrolled in the official school for film production, while nursing a vague hope of escaping to the United States.

That hope became a reality in 1925, when her mother wrote to three cousins living in Chicago, to ask if they would sponsor her daughter for a six-month visit. They said yes, and Soviet officials—told she intended to study movie-making techniques that she could use in making propaganda films for the government—issued her a visa. The 21-year-old prepared for what her family knew would be a one-way trip. She later told Isabel Paterson that a young man approached her at a small gathering before her departure and "said to her quietly: 'When you get out, tell the rest of the world that we are dying here.'"[72] She intended to do just that.

Rand arrived in New York City in February 1926. "I'll never forget it," she said. "It seemed so incredibly cheerful and frivolous, so non-Soviet!"[73] Looking up at the 57-story Woolworth Building, then the tallest building in the world, she burst into tears at its beauty.[74] Adopting the name Ayn Rand—creating a new identity for herself in a way that countless other escapees from tyranny have done over the ages—she soon caught a train for Chicago, where she spent six months with relatives writing out ideas for screenplays and watching movies (138, in all) before setting out for Hollywood. One of her cousins arranged a letter of introduction to someone working for Cecil B. DeMille, in hopes that it might help her get a job. Amazingly, she managed to meet DeMille in person shortly after arriving in Hollywood. The director, who was then making his biblical epic *King of Kings*, was sitting in his car and noticed Rand staring at him, so he called out and asked who she was. When she stammered that she was looking for work in the movies, DeMille hired her as an extra.

During a break on the set one day, Rand met a handsome young actor named Frank O'Connor, and set about attracting his attention. She purposely tripped him as an excuse to apologize and start a conversation. A quiet and gentle man, he had small roles in such films as *Orphans of the Storm* (1922) and *Cimarron* (1931), and later in life displayed a gift for painting. By all accounts, Rand adored him, and they married in April 1929.

DeMille gave Rand an opportunity to pitch some of her story ideas to his staff. Although they were rejected for being too outlandish, she impressed him enough that he gave her a full-time job reviewing and summarizing potential film scripts. Already possessed of firm convictions about the kind of movies she wanted to see made, she focused on thrilling romantic stories with important themes. "Achievement is the aim of life," she wrote in her notes on one proposal— and then repeated it for emphasis: "Life is achievement."[75] But the studio bought none of her ideas, and shortly before the Depression struck, DeMille closed his studio to take a job at MGM. Rand found work as a waitress—although that did not last long, as she later told Paterson, because with her still-tentative English, she did not even know what a hamburger was.[76] After a few other short-lived jobs, Rand was hired by the costume department of RKO Studios, which enabled her to pay the bills and send money to her parents.

She had not abandoned her dream of becoming a writer, of course. On the contrary, to prepare herself, she devoured critically acclaimed American literature, especially Sinclair Lewis, who had just published his novel *Dodsworth* and who swiftly became her favorite American writer.[77] Aside from his masterful prose style and his pitch-perfect ear for the national idiom, Rand found in Lewis an echo of the yearning that she felt for a deeper significance in life. The theme of *Main Street*—which she later identified as "the struggle of a girl of more intellectual trends to bring culture to [her] town—her struggle with the materialistic small-town attitude of everybody around her"[78]—resonated with her, and she studied Lewis's style minutely.

Main Street likely brought to mind the contrast between *Anna Karenina* and *A Doll's House*. All three feature female main characters who yearn for a life premised on authentic values as opposed to social convention. Nora ends *A Doll's House* triumphantly, liberated to pursue happiness on her own terms, whereas in both *Main Street* and *Anna Karenina*, the characters end by committing a kind of suicide (in Anna's case, literal; in Carol's, spiritual). Yet where Ibsen sympathized with Nora's ambitions, Tolstoy viewed Anna's longing as reprehensible and presented her demise as the legitimate consequence of her rebelliousness.[79] His novel begins with the biblical epigraph "Vengeance is mine; I will repay," and it appeared to Rand that the vengeance in question was being wreaked by Tolstoy himself upon his own characters for having sought a new and better life. In *Main Street*, by contrast, Lewis portrays Carol Kennicott's desire to escape the "village virus" as worthy and valid, and her failure as an injustice and a horror. The life she dreams of is worthy of desiring—but is so often betrayed or sacrificed by people who lack the fortitude to pursue it that in Lewis's novels it appears inevitably and tragically beyond reach.

Equally important was Lewis's recognition of the relationship between the "village virus" and collectivism, especially fascism.[80] Although *Babbitt* had implied this relationship with its "Good Citizens' League," Lewis made the point explicit in *It Can't Happen Here*, which dramatized the easy transition from small-town parochialism into a nationwide movement climaxing in dictatorship. Rand revered the novel, calling it "the greatest book of the century" in a fan letter to Lewis that identified him as "the only *living* mind I've heard, the best god of the very religious atheist that I am, the best hero of an embittered and incurable hero worshipper who believes in nothing on earth except heroes."[81] She singled out as her favorite passage a tiny detail in Chapter 19, in which Doremus Jessup is hauled before a fascist judge named Effingham Swan—recently commissioned a commander in "Buzz" Windrip's militarized bureaucracy—who orders Jessup to identify people hostile to Windrip's administration. Speaking with affected informality, Swan insists on sitting at a table instead of on a judicial bench and calls Jessup by his first name because "then we shall feel all friendly and secure." But when Jessup later calls him "Swan," the judge corrects him. "*Commander*, my dear fellow—ridiculous matter of military discipline, y'know—*such* rot!"[82] The line, Rand said, made her feel like she was being slapped in the face. Lewis's subtlety in depicting the way modern tyranny disguises its essential violence beneath platitudes made his book "immortal."[83]

Lewis's impact on Rand has been insufficiently appreciated by scholars of her work, although it is evident in much of her writing, particularly in *The Fountainhead*. Yet she was his opposite in one important respect: Lewis viewed his characters' longing for a life of significance as doomed, and his novels typically end on a tone of resignation. Rand emphatically rejected this attitude. That became obvious in one of her earliest efforts at writing a novel: a story called *The Little Street*, which she began sketching out in 1928. The book, which she never completed, would have riffed on Lewis's contemptuous treatment of bourgeois Middle America in *Main Street*, but with a shot of romanticism that defied Lewis's resigned conclusion. Her plan involved combining Lewis-style observational caricature with a ripped-from-the-headlines murder story based on an actual crime in Los Angeles that year—in order, as she wrote in her journal, to "show that *humanity is petty*" and "that *the world is nothing but a little street*. That this little street is its king and master, its essence and spirit."[84]

Where Lewis found no cure for the "village virus," *The Little Street* would have, but would have pitched it in a tragic key, by featuring a defiant anti-hero: the accused murderer, Danny Renahan. A misunderstood visionary—brilliant, proud, and uncompromising, but lost and ignored in the pettiness of the world—Renahan would be portrayed murdering a popular clergyman who unjustly insults him. After a sensational trial, he would escape from jail, only to be lynched by a mob. "The only moment when Danny is afraid of death," according to her notes, would have come at the story's end, when he looks out of his jail cell window at the silhouette of a skyscraper against the night sky. The sight makes him feel "that he is in some other world, on another planet, where life is clear, pure and luminous like the sky he looks into. And he wants that life, he loves it with all the passion of his life-hungry soul."[85] Renahan, in short, is Lewis's Carol Kennicott transformed from a frustrated and resigned figure into a violent rebel who refuses to surrender his devotion to the good and beautiful. "The real, one and only horror," Rand wrote in her *Little Street* outline, was "*the horror of mediocrity.*"[86] Although she never went beyond these notes, she channeled the idea of a crime-and-trial story into several later works.

Rand finally made her first Hollywood sale in 1932, when Universal bought *Red Pawn*, a film idea set in Soviet Russia and heavily influenced by Victor Hugo. The movie was never made, but Rand gained important experience working with studios, which eventually led to her writing several successful scripts. She also tried expanding *Red Pawn* into a novel, in hopes of publication in the *Saturday Evening Post*, which she thought had a "decided anti-Soviet tone,"[87] but nothing came of that. In the meantime, however, she began working on a play—a courtroom drama ultimately called *Night of January 16th*—that became a breakthrough success.

The play was inspired in part by the financial scandal sparked by the multimillionaire Ivar Kreuger, known as the "Match King" for the enormous match company he owned. Aside from that business, he was also heavily invested in everything from banks to ball bearing manufacturers, and was believed to be worth hundreds of millions of dollars. But when he was found dead from suicide in his Paris apartment on March 12, 1932, the legend began to unravel. Accountants soon revealed that he was a cheat: the match company was insolvent, and Kreuger had forged important financial documents. Newspaper reports about Kreuger's schemes transfixed American readers and became one of the primary motivating factors for the adoption of federal securities laws by the Roosevelt administration a year later. But although Kreuger had committed fraud, he was also a business genius who fashioned many legitimate innovations that are commonplace in today's economy. Some people, particularly in his native Sweden, admired him as a self-made tycoon, and his most recent biographer concludes that he was "a builder, as well as a destroyer . . . a hero, as well as a villain."[88]

Tales of Kreuger's charisma and his ability to dominate other people proved fascinating reading. Isabel Paterson was especially astounded that so many important investors had never bothered to check on his creditworthiness, but were willing to trust Kreuger with enormous sums of their money. "Particularly curious is the episode of the big business man (American) who brought down Kreuger's house of cards by insisting upon an inspection of the books and assets," she wrote in "Turns." "He didn't insist until *after* he had handed Kreuger ten million dollars!"[89] Such financial irresponsibility seemed to her a sign of the times.

But it struck Rand that many reporters seemed less shocked by Kreuger's lying than by the fact that he had been wealthy to begin with. "It was not a crook that they were denouncing, but greatness as such," she thought.[90] In a book about the affair published months after Kreuger's death, author Trevor

Allen wrote damningly of the man's "all-conquering" ambition. "Not once in his life, so far as one can judge, was he satisfied with what he had," Allen sneered. "Mere greed of money can never wholly explain the all-conquering ambition of a man like Kreuger. . . . What gave zest to his labours was the lust of conquest, the sense of power."[91] Such language seemed to go beyond condemning dishonesty; it sounded to Rand like the grumblings of Main Streeters against someone with the temerity to rise above the average. Always on the lookout for unusual, philosophically trenchant plot ideas, Rand decided to use the story for a play—not about the millionaire crook himself, but about the effects that an ambitious personality has on other people.

The play she ended up writing, however, owed as much to Sinclair Lewis and Henrik Ibsen as it did to Ivar Kreuger. Ibsen's captivating philosophical dramas often focused on the relationships between men intensely devoted to their values—men of all-conquering ambition, in fact—and the women who long to share their visions. The title character of his 1865 play *Brand* is an ascetic, obsessive priest whose devotion to God's absolute truth is totally, even cruelly, uncompromising—and whose fiancée Agnes is wholly committed to supporting him in that pursuit. In *The Master Builder* (1892), an aging architect named Halvard Solness is inspired by a young devotee named Hilda to overcome his vertigo and climb to the top of the steeple of a church he is constructing. Solness falls to his death, but Hilda, obsessed with veneration, views his act as a moment of triumph. And *John Gabriel Borkman*, one of Ibsen's last plays, featured some particularly striking parallels with the real-life story of Kreuger; its title character is an industrialist released from a prison sentence for financial crimes. In the final scene, he tries to explain—to people incapable of understanding—that he envisions the coal from his mines giving life to the factories and ships of what he calls "my kingdom," and that, without his protection, lie "exposed to all the robbers and plunderers." As he dies, Borkman cries out to his kingdom and the "prisoned millions" whom his industrial genius will liberate: "I can see the veins of metal stretch out their winding, branching, luring arms to me. . . . I love you, unborn treasures, yearning for the light!"[92]

Rand seemed to find in Ibsen the utter devotion to integrity—the principle of reverence—that cured the "village virus." In *Main Street*, Carol Kennicott bemoaned the lack of anyone "big enough or pitiful enough to sacrifice for"[93]— a sentiment Ibsen's Agnes and Hilda would have understood. To Rand, too, it was not enough to rebel against the village; one also needed a bright star to steer by. "A man can't live just for things that do nothing to him—inside, I mean," said a character in *Ideal*, a manuscript she began writing around this time. "There should be something that he's afraid of—afraid and happy. . . . Something he can look up to."[94] And in *Night of January 16th*, she aimed to challenge the audience's own commitment to values. In fact, she employed a dramatic gimmick whereby audience members were recruited to serve as an on-stage jury to determine the guilt or innocence of the main character, Karen Andre, who is standing trial for the murder of her former boss, Bjorn Faulkner.

Prosecutors explain that police initially thought Faulkner had jumped to his death from a skyscraper after embezzling money from his business, but later discovered that the suicide note was a forgery. Now they've accused Andre, who had been engaged in an extramarital affair with Faulkner, of killing him. On the stand, she openly admits the affair; in fact, she explains that she worshipped Faulkner for his heroic personality. He seized life as though he wanted to cast a net over the whole world and claim it as his, and she could not help but devote herself to him. "Bjorn never thought of things as right or wrong," she testifies. "To him it was only: you can or you can't. He always could." Faulkner had been a stern, demanding presence—"a man born with life singing in his veins," who seemed to be "cracking a whip over an animal" whenever he looked at her.[95] She longed for the kind of world in which such giant spirits could thrive.

It is revealed over the course of the play that Faulkner's suicide was, indeed, faked—but not quite the way prosecutors thought. Instead, he and Andre had devised a plan to escape from a blackmail scheme that one of Faulkner's creditors was running. They intended to run away together with millions of dollars that, we learn, Faulkner did not actually steal. But the plan went awry, and now Faulkner really *is* dead. In despair, Andre confesses the entire story and pleads her cause as a woman who "felt a longing for greatness."[96]

Like Ibsen's Brand, Faulkner is idealized as a man unwilling to compromise by descending to ordinary things. And like Nietzsche's Zarathustra, he is a superlative aristocratic figure, with values beyond the mundane, to whom each individual responds in keeping with his or her own sense of greatness. But Rand's Faulkner is neither a criminal nor a Nietzschean superman—although some dialogue, such as Andre's reference to a "whip," certainly suggested otherwise. Meanwhile, Andre, like Carol from *Main Street* and Agnes from *Brand*, finds meaning in her admiration for, and partnership with, the superlative. Rand later called her philosophy "man worship," and that sense of devotion pervades the play.[97] It is a paean to what she called "an exalted view of self-esteem"—and the imperative to "live up to your highest vision of yourself no matter what the circumstances."[98]

This would prove to be a lifelong theme for Rand, whose novels are suffused with a sense of exaltation and awe, as contrasted with the trivial and dull. Reverence was always one of her principal values. The paradox of her life was that she was at once an atheist and deeply devout, and one of her primary literary goals was to reconcile her sense of sacredness with the secular, commercial values of modern capitalism. *Night of January 16th* represented an early attempt, in the character of Karen Andre (whose name means "man" and who feels she must "kneel" to the greatness in Bjorn Faulkner), to articulate that sense of worldly piety.

The play was successful enough, when staged in Hollywood in 1934, to be taken to New York City, where it opened on Broadway the following autumn after lengthy disputes with producers. In the interim, Rand turned her attention to completing her first novel, which she was calling *Airtight*. Loosely based on her own life, she hoped it would become "the *Uncle Tom's Cabin* of Soviet Russia."[99] It was, she told her agent, "the *first* story written by a Russian who knows the living conditions" of Stalin's empire; "the first one by a person who *knows* the facts and also *can tell* them."[100] But the novel was not meant as a mere documentary account. On the contrary, Rand opposed the literary method of naturalism, which prioritized a faithful depiction of real life, and instead embraced the romanticism of writers such as Hugo and Dostoyevsky, whose stories, although often inspired by real life, were concerned with highlighting moral principles rather than faithful depiction of facts. Indeed, for all her admiration of the arch-naturalist Sinclair Lewis, Rand's primary influence in this novel was Hugo, and it bears less resemblance to either *Main Street* or to Harriet Beecher Stowe's *Uncle Tom's Cabin* than to Hugo's *Les Misérables* or *Ninety-Three*.

Its plot concerns a teenager named Kira Arguanova, an engineering student in St. Petersburg (now renamed Petrograd). Driven solely by her dream of building skyscrapers and bridges, she feels alienated from her sister, who devotes herself to trivialities, and she despises the communists who demand that she serve the state. By chance, she meets an individualistic university student named Leo, who is persona non grata among the communists because of his father's counterrevolutionary activities. She falls in love with him and moves in with him when her family—scandalized that she sleeps with him before being married—throws her out. At the same time, she meets Andrei, leader of the student communists, whose political beliefs she despises, but whose personal integrity and commitment to principle she cannot help but admire. Andrei falls in love with her, and much of the novel's tension derives from the love triangle that ensues when Leo contracts tuberculosis and Kira begins an affair with Andrei in order to afford medical care to keep Leo alive.

She succeeds in concealing her relationship with Leo from Andrei, but when Leo is arrested for selling black-market merchandise, Andrei learns the truth. Soured on the corruption of Soviet bureaucrats, however, and discovering that Kira was right in her belief that some things in life are too personal and precious to surrender to the collective, Andrei arranges to have Leo released from prison and—in an echo of Javert's death in *Les Misérables*—commits suicide. Leo's liberation comes too late, though: stripped of any opportunity to provide for himself, he succumbs to despair, begins drinking, and runs away with another woman. Kira tries to escape alone across the border, but is killed by a patrolman who fails to even realize that he has shot her.

Although written in the shadow of the 19th-century Romantics, the novel is also modern in tone, with an eye on the concerns expressed by Sinclair Lewis. In fact, one of its chief themes is the way in which the Soviet state drowns its citizens in the dullness of the village, by penalizing spiritual independence, condemning personal ambition as anti-social, and wallowing in a sense of the lowest common denominator, enforced by unremitting officiousness. Rand—who thought "the hallmark of the twentieth century" was the way intellectual leaders used a "mawkish concern with and compassion for the feeble, the flawed, the suffering, [and] the guilty" to conceal a "hatred for the innocent, the strong, the able, the successful, the virtuous, the confident, [and] the happy"[101]—viewed communism as a hypertrophy of the mediocritism that Lewis so effectively satirized. Far from liberating people, it suffocated their uniqueness and obliterated their dreams.

This observation was not entirely new; Dorothy Thompson had seen during her visit that notwithstanding the "grandiose conception of the Soviet Republic," communism created an atmosphere of "airlessness." "Gaiety," she wrote, "is singularly lacking everywhere in Russia"—although, in a self-contradiction that was to become typical of her style, she concluded that "Russia . . . has that which Europe has lost. . . . Russia has hope."[102] Poet E. E. Cummings came closer to the truth in his own travelogue, when he declared the USSR a land of smothering smallness in which "the glorious future of mankind" consisted of "everyone ecstatically minding everyone else's business."[103]

But Rand wrote from firsthand experience, combined with a literary romanticism that made clear how the purported worker's paradise was actually a land of anonymity and despair. In one of *Airtight*'s most dramatic moments, a disillusioned sailor cries out that Westerners think the Soviet Union is "a huge beast," but they're wrong: "They don't know that it's made of cockroaches. Little, glossy, brown cockroaches packed tight, one on the other, into a huge wall."[104] In another passage, in which a Soviet clerk fills out Kira's application for a passport,[105] Rand elegantly expressed how communism swamps individual uniqueness in the dismal and ordinary. Although Kira's eyes are "the gray of storm clouds from behind which the sun can be expected at any moment," and reflect "a deep, confident calm that seemed to tell men her sight was too clear"—the clerk simply writes that they are "gray." Although Kira was born in a mansion where "a maid in black fastened the clasps of her [mother's] diamond necklaces," the clerk merely lists her birthplace as "Petrograd." Kira's body "was slender, too slender, and when she moved with a sharp, swift, geometrical precision, people were conscious of the movement alone," but in the space for "height" the clerk jots down only "medium."[106] Here and elsewhere, the novel dramatizes the extermination of uniqueness by a totalitarian doctrine that focuses on making everything the same. Alone in their apartment together, Kira and Leo insist on dressing up in their finest clothes, in an effort to create an above-average private little world. When they go to work in the morning, they must don drab and threadbare outfits—to "act like trash for the benefit of trash," as Leo puts it.[107]

In its own way, *Airtight* was a resilience novel. Kira's victory lies in her refusal to surrender her vision of a better life, and her insistence on living in a larger sense, even if it means her death—whereas Leo, like one of Sinclair Lewis's characters, ends up surrendering. Rand even takes time to satirize the proletarian novels of the age when she describes Leo's job translating Western books into Russian for the government printing house: "They were novels by foreign authors in which a poor, honest worker was always sent to jail for stealing a loaf of bread to feed the starving mother of his pretty, young wife who had been raped by a capitalist and committed suicide thereafter, for which the all-powerful capitalist fired her husband from the factory, so that their child had to beg on the streets and was run over by the capitalist's limousine with sparkling fenders and a chauffeur in uniform."[108] Such literature was detestable for the same reason that communism itself was: because it left no room for what Rand calls "the sublime in the human race."[109]

Airtight was distinctive in capturing the essential evil at the heart of Soviet oppression. In fact, Rand insisted it was "not merely an argument against Communism," but an attack on "all forms of collectivism, against any manner of sacrilege toward the Individual," because the definitive characteristic of such tyrannies was the principle that people must live for the sake of the group—the state, the race, the tribe—and that one's worth is determined by the degree to which one sacrifices for the needs of others.[110] "Don't you know," says Kira in an argument with Andrei, "that there are things, in the best of us, which no outside hand should dare to touch? Things sacred because, and only because, one can say: 'This is *mine*'?"[111] Rand's critique of the Soviet regime was not merely that it censored and robbed millions of people, but that it left them no room for *aspiration*—a word that suggestively shares the same root as the word for breathing. Rand's original title for the book derives from her view that collectivism deprived people of any opportunity to rise above the commonplace. "What do you think is alive in me?" Kira demands of Andrei. "Because I breathe and work and produce more food to digest? Or because I know what I want and that something which knows how to want—isn't that life itself? You came and forbade life to the living. You've driven us all into an iron cellar and you've closed all the doors and you've locked us airtight."[112]

Airtight was a promising debut for this future crusader for individualism, and a remarkable feat for a 31-year-old writer who had spoken English for little more than a decade. Yet it also reflected Rand's lingering interest in Nietzsche, whose views she later called a form of pseudo-individualism. In several passages, which she omitted from the second edition decades later, her characters spoke in the language of Nietzschean aristocrats, instead of classical liberals. In the most striking instance, Andrei tells Kira, "I know what you're going to say. You're going to say, as so many of our enemies do, that you admire our ideals, but loathe our methods." But Kira says no. "I loathe your ideas. I admire your methods. If one believes one's right, one shouldn't wait to convince millions of fools, one might just as well force them. Except that I don't know, however, whether I'd include blood in my methods." When the second edition appeared, Rand edited Kira's reply to say simply, "I loathe your ideals."[113]

Despite the novel's merits, Rand's agent found it hard to interest publishers until a screenwriter Rand met at Universal offered to send the manuscript to H. L. Mencken, then still working for the *American Mercury*, and still one of the nation's foremost critics. Mencken admired the book—and was unsurprised that publishers were rejecting it. Communism was so trendy in the literary world that dissenting voices had a hard time being heard, he grumbled. "Most of the American publishers who print Russian stuff lean toward the Trotskys."[114] Weeks later, Rand took the opportunity to write to Mencken directly. Admitting that she was starstruck addressing "the foremost champion of individualism in this country," and "the greatest representative of a philosophy to which I want to dedicate my whole life," she thanked him for his compliments on the novel and asked if he would consider sending it to Dutton, a publisher willing to print anti-communist books.[115] He did, but it came to nothing. Only after changing literary agents—hiring Ann Watkins, who also represented Sinclair Lewis—did Rand finally find a publisher. The book was released by Macmillan in April 1936 under its new title, *We the Living*.

Rand was prepared to get "plenty of hell from our good Red reviewers," and some were indeed hostile—the *New York Times* called it "slavishly warped to the dictates of [anti-Soviet] propaganda" and *The Nation* sneered at Rand's hostility toward the communist "experiment."[116] But most reviews were positive, and the book made decent sales. That it did not sell better was due partly to its tragic nature—one reviewer, while lauding it, called it "distinctly depressing" and full of "hopelessness and futility"—and partly to Macmillan's inadequate publicity campaign.[117] But the publisher did make sure to send its promotional material to the reliably anti-communist Isabel Paterson. She was impressed. Rand's flight to America, she wrote in "Turns," was proof that good writing cannot be produced in a "planned society." In fact, she noted, when Plato imagined his utopia in the *Republic*, he had stipulated that writers must be banished from it.[118] It was therefore especially ironic that so many contemporary American authors were now advocating communism—and that the one new author who had actually experienced it denounced it with such eloquence.

◢◣

Rand got a chance to meet Paterson at a cocktail party that year, but although the encounter meant much to Rand, Paterson later said she did not remember it.

Not for another four years would the young Russian become a friend and, to some degree, a protégée. Instead, Paterson had turned her attention to Rose Wilder Lane's latest book. Titled *Give Me Liberty*, it was Lane's first effort at a political statement, and it presented an impassioned protest against the New Deal. While reading it, Paterson found herself pausing to reflect with "wonder" that Americans "could have so far forgotten what they were about." In 1776, they had pledged themselves to the principles of individual freedom and personal responsibility. Now they were clamoring for handouts and government protection against the responsibilities of life.[119]

Lane had not started out to write *Give Me Liberty*. Her original plan had been to write a book about Missouri, inspired by her reading of Charles and Mary Beard's two-volume blockbuster *The Rise of American Civilization*, originally published in 1927. This was the same Charles Beard who scoffed at the "myth" of individualism, and *Rise*, with its irreverent tone and encyclopedic scope, was on its way becoming one of the most influential works ever published on American history.[120] Aiming to debunk what they saw as "schoolbook fictions," and treating long-cherished principles of American cultural identity as false idols, the Beards wrote history in terms of economic forces and class conflicts instead of ideas or the achievements of outstanding individuals.[121] They believed, as Charles and his colleagues in the American Historical Association put it in a 1934 report, that "the age of individualism and *laissez-faire* in economy and government is closing and a new age of collectivism is emerging."[122] Although pervasively anti-capitalist, *Rise* was rooted less in Marxist theory than in the Beards' aesthetic revulsion at the vulgarity of commercial enterprise.[123] Readers were left with the impression that American civilization was not a unique experiment in constitutional liberty, but a clash of mercenary interests masquerading behind dubious slogans.[124]

Still, its scholarly depth and insight, not to mention its comprehensive scope and elegant prose, made it more than a polemic. In fact, Lane found much to admire in it—particularly the Beards' view that American civilization was based on a conscious rejection of the feudalism that served as the foundation of European societies. What she thought they got wrong was their emphasis on democracy instead of individualism. They argued that the American Revolution had been motivated by a social trend of "leveling" that was irreconcilable with the hierarchical structure of European civilization.[125] What was significant about America, they claimed, was its "invulnerable faith in democracy, in the ability of the undistinguished masses, as contrasted with heroes and classes."[126] As for "frontier individualism," they considered it a mirage. Westerners may have rhapsodized about "the freedom of hardy men and women, taut of muscle and bronzed by sun and rain and wind, working with their hands," but the pioneers had been subsidized all along by the government.[127]

Lane agreed that the essential quality of American institutions was their contrast with European feudalism, but in her view, this was a consequence of the nation's fundamental commitment to the sanctity of the individual. That was as central to American society as the abolition of private property was to socialist nations. True, subsidies had existed in the past, but the Beards' own book showed how these often proved counterproductive. In any case, she thought their contemptuous treatment of individualism was merely an excuse for intellectuals who harbored what she called a "moral scorn of the American Constitution as a mere outworn trick of crooked exploiters."[128]

Thus when her agent obtained a commission to write a short guidebook for travelers about Missouri, Lane quickly became obsessed with the idea of turning the project into a rebuttal of the Beards' theories. Although publishers had asked for a simple overview of the Show Me State, she soon sketched a plan to write an in-depth analysis of the state's culture and history. In July 1935, she moved away from her parents' farm to the luxurious Tiger Hotel in Columbia, near the University of Missouri's research archives, and devoted months to the project. What she ended up writing was a novelistic history of the settlement of her home state, which she called *The Name Is Mizzoury.* Unsurprisingly, the publishers rejected it, but she would find the work useful when it came time to compose her novel *Free Land* and, later, her manifesto, *The Discovery of Freedom.* At the time, however, Lane tempered her disappointment at the book's rejection with gratitude that the project had "got me away from that damned farm."[129]

Evidently, her uneasy relationship with her mother had reached a crisis. Around this time, Wilder ordered Lane to return home and evict one of her friends, who had been living at the Mansfield farm for years, and with whom Wilder never got along. In fact, Wilder grew so angry that she ordered a hired man to kill Lane's dog. Recognizing that she could not bear to live with her parents any more, Lane stayed in Columbia for two years and eventually moved to Connecticut.

In the meantime, her spirits were lifted when Garet Garett, the reporter she had first met more than a decade before on the ship home from Europe, arrived in Columbia. Now regularly publishing articles about economics in the *Saturday Evening Post*, Garrett was 57 and an accomplished author—Isabel Paterson named his 1932 book *The Bubble that Broke the World* the best analysis of the causes of the Depression.[130] Now he was traveling through the Midwest to interview farmers for a *Post* article about the effects of a new federal program called the Resettlement Administration (RA), and he asked Lane to accompany him.

It was a natural request, given that Lane had published a similar article in the *Post* two years before, after interviewing wheat farmers who were reeling from the first waves of the Dust Bowl. That article had concerned the New Deal's muddled agricultural policies, which had been fashioned at a time when American farmers were enjoying crop surpluses, but which were thrown into disarray shortly afterward when drought and dust storms threatened to turn those surpluses into shortages. The Agricultural Adjustment Act had taxed farmers who grew "too much," in order to prevent prices from falling, but now those artificially high prices risked causing shortfalls. Lane had written in her diary in May 1933 that despite the fact that "violent weather everywhere" could wreck the harvest, federal officials were still holding conferences to encourage farmers to reduce production. "Our politicians seem never to have heard of weather."[131] A month after that, noting that "cities have suddenly become aware of a 'major agricultural catastrophe,'" she obtained the *Post*'s commission to travel through Oklahoma and Kansas, to report on the Dust Bowl's effects.[132] The result was a ghostwritten article bylined "A Wheat

Grower," in which she explained that heat and dust were "accomplishing an acreage reduction on a scale that made the Government's offer of a subsidy to farmers not to grow wheat seem needless."[133] If things did not change, she predicted, government planning would cause a food crisis.

But instead of reconsidering its scheme, the Roosevelt administration hatched a new one: it would move impoverished farmers off depleted farms and onto more productive land. Thus was born the RA, brainchild of social-ist Brain Truster Rexford Tugwell, who thought the principle of private farm ownership was obsolete and that agriculture should be managed by government bureaucracies. The RA was also inspired in part by Roosevelt's own senti-mental notion of reviving a yeoman farmer economy—a fashionable idea at the time.[134] In his inaugural address, he had spoken of the need to "provide a better use of the land for those best fitted for the land," and the RA accord-ingly aimed to establish new "subsistence homesteads" for farmers whom the government would transplant—coercively, if necessary. Thus notwithstanding its Jeffersonian rhetoric, the RA embodied, in historian Paul Conkin's words, a fundamentally "anti-individualistic, anti-Jefferson, collectivist approach" to agriculture.[135] It was this program that Garett was setting out to investigate in 1935, taking Lane with him on a two-week journey through the Midwest.

What they found reminded Lane of things she had witnessed in Soviet Georgia a decade before. The RA oversaw construction of new model communi-ties and induced farmers to move there—or forced them to—even though many could not afford to live in their newly designated homes.[136] The RA contradicted other New Deal programs that were trying to help farmers stay on their land instead of moving, or were encouraging them to plant less, whereas the RA sought to move them to where they could plant more. Moreover, the program was widely despised by the growers themselves, who had no desire to serve as a sociological experiment for bureaucrats who rejected the principle of private property. After two years of operation, the RA was struck down by a federal court that found its effort to condemn land for resettlement was "not justified by any reasonable construction of the Constitution."[137] In the meantime, many farmers refused to cooperate and gave a chilly reception to RA officials who tried to persuade them.

"In Kansas, I met a rabble-rousing New Dealer from Washington who took me to a farmer's meeting where he spoke with real conviction and eloquence," Lane recalled. "The audience listened absolutely noncommittal, until he worked up to an incandescent peroration: 'We went down there to Washington and got you all a Ford. Now we're going to get you a Cadillac!' The temperature suddenly fell below freezing. . . . That ended the speech; the whole audience rose and walked out. The orator later said to me, 'Those damned numbskulls! the only thing to use on them is a club.'"[138]

When farmers refused the government's offers of help, some officials did resort to compulsion. In southern Illinois, RA bureaucrats "took no nonsense," Lane told a friend. "They condemned the land—every farm; offered the owners $7 an acre, or nothing; this was a model project, tearing down houses, building new roads, surveying a Community Center all blueprinted." The government claimed its actions were necessary because the land suffered from so much erosion that it was unusable, but "when I asked to be shown the erosion, the answer was, it is sheet erosion. That is, the constant effect of rainfall on all Earth." In reality, the land was well maintained, and families had lived there for generations. "None of them wanted to be rehabilitated. None of them would speak to Garet or to me until we *proved* that we did not come from the Government."[139]

The articles Garrett published that autumn publicized the incoherence of both the AAA and the RA. "Never in modern times could the idea have occurred to industry, when it had to stop producing for want of demand, that the way out would be to produce still less and raise the price," he wrote. Yet that was exactly what Roosevelt was attempting—and the effort had one obvious flaw: if retail prices for crops rose, farmers would naturally produce more, which would drive down prices and undermine the AAA's efforts to keep prices up. "It is impossible really to control agricultural production unless you control also the surplus land and the conditions under which people may have access to it," Garrett explained. This was why the RA was trying to remove land from production by acquiring 10 million acres and transporting its residents elsewhere.

Naturally, if RA officials succeeded in transferring planters to better land, the farmers would inevitably produce more crops, which would "wreck the AAA program." The only way to make sense of the contradictions of New Deal agricultural planning, Garrett concluded, was to understand that its true purpose was not to help farmers, but to transform American society from one based on personal initiative and free choice into one planned and organized by an "all-seeing, all-powerful, all-wise" government. Bureaucrats would undertake "to administer the lives of [the] people, to mind them in their occupations, to arrange their incomes, to correct their past individualistic mistakes, to absorb their troubles, to regroup them to the land, to admit them conditionally to agriculture, to appoint what they may grow to eat and what they may grow to sell."[140]

Garrett described some of the farmers who did not want to participate. "In a lovely log cabin with a shaded porch, flowers and vines around it, is a woman who says no," he wrote. "She loves the log cabin. She likes to show it to you. Her man built it. She was born on this ground. It may not be much, only she is attached to it. Can the government take it from them, really? She asks you." Elsewhere, Garrett and Lane interviewed a 70-year-old woman and her husband on the porch of a home they had built together. She told them she could not grasp why the RA was trying to evict them. "Why does the Government want their land? It wants the land because it is no good . . . ! Why not? All these years they have lived on it. There is nothing the matter with it, only that it has been a little overcorned."

During their travels together, Garrett's feelings toward Lane seem to have briefly deepened. "Rose, dear," he wrote, "you shake me in the fixed principle of my life. . . . We two! We ought to be in a row boat somewhere in the middle of the Pacific or on a distant island. I want to see you and yet I dread it."[141] But there is no proof that his wistful comments came to anything. In fact, Lane was perplexed by Garrett, both because of his resolute pessimism and his odd, sometimes self-contradictory political beliefs. "I like[d] him very much, and admired him," she remarked 20 years later. "[But] we never agreed in principle. He said that I am a mystic ruined by materialism, and that he was a materialist ruined by mysticism. (I don't agree with that, either.)" She thought he "spoiled everything he wrote" with intense cynicism. "Hopelessness was his constant mood."[142] Yet she found their conversations stimulating, and he may have been partly responsible for what was to become Lane's most successful novel, *Free Land*.

▚

Since the New Deal's inception, its champions had maintained that the makeover of American society was necessitated by the closing of the western frontier. According to this theory, 19th-century westward expansion—subsidized by the federal government through measures such as the 1862 Homestead Act—had created prosperity by giving farmers "free land," which absorbed "excess" labor. This created a scarcity of workers that kept wages high—and high wages were the key to prosperity.

According to the celebrated historian Frederick Jackson Turner, whose 1893 essay "The Significance of the Frontier in American History" became one of the most influential scholarly papers ever published in America, the pioneer experience had also generated the "striking characteristics" of "the American intellect," including its "restless, nervous energy," its "buoyancy and exuberance," and its "dominant individualism." But the country had grown so rapidly, Turner thought, that by the 1890s, the frontier had vanished, "and with its going has closed the first period of American history."[143]

In the eyes of New Dealers, that meant there was no longer any outlet for "excess labor," which doomed American workers to poverty unless the next period of national history replaced capitalist individualism with a new, planned economy. "As long as we had free land," Roosevelt told a San Francisco audience in September 1932, only six months after Turner's death, "society chose to give the ambitious man free play." But now that "there is practically no more free land," the "freedom to farm has ceased," and society should focus "not [on] discovery, or exploitation of natural resources," but on "the sober, less dramatic business of administering resources and plants already in hand." Simply put, the day of individual enterprise was over, and "the day of enlightened administration has come."[144]

Roosevelt often repeated this point. Government policy, he declared in his book, *Looking Forward*, should "think less about the producer" and focus more on an "equitable distribution of the national income." Rather than encouraging the ambitions of people who sought "the prospect of being a millionaire," policymakers should aim "toward stability" and "greater security."[145] In a 1935 radio speech, he told listeners that "the American spirit of individualism" could no longer cope with the world's challenges, because "we can no longer escape into virgin territory."[146] NIRA enforcer Hugh Johnson agreed. "We must substitute for the old safety valve of free land and new horizons a new safety valve of economic readjustment," he declared. "The real trouble . . . was rugged individualism."[147]

Charles and Mary Beard went further. In *The Rise of American Civilization*, they argued that the Homestead Act had actually been fashioned with the intent of preventing socialist revolution. They claimed the act had originally been meant to distract workers who "in the normal course of affairs would have been devoted to building up trade unions" by giving land "to the hungry proletariat as a free gift, more significant than bread and circuses."[148] After the frontier closed and "the free land was gone," workers briefly found employment in mines and on railroads. But now a "point of saturation" was at hand, and the time had come for a salutary wave of collectivist regulation.[149] Even Garet Garrett seemed to share this opinion, although he viewed it as an unfortunate development. In his 1928 book *The American Omen*, he remarked that Europeans had long believed that American liberty could only exist as long as there was western land available for settlement—and he, too, wondered whether freedom would survive now that "the refuge of free virgin land is exhausted" and Americans had "begun to crowd up."[150]

Lane demurred. Decades later, she recalled how "professional thinkers" of the 1930s had fashioned the idea that

> these United States matured, abruptly, in 1933; therefore Wendell Phillips's remark, "The cardinal principle of our national life is that God gives every man the sense to manage his own affairs," is no

longer true. It was true before the American frontier disappeared, but now the American economy is mature. The adult economy removes from my skull the brain which God formerly placed there, and gives someone else the sense to manage my affairs. Why does an adult economy do this? Because it is so complex. All this seems quite clear to the Walter Lippmanns and Charles Beards, but it isn't to me.[151]

She was particularly offended by the phrase "free land."[152] There had never been any "free" land, and the government had not given away land for free in the 1860s. The Homestead Act required participants to make a down payment and then live on the land for five years and make improvements on it, where-upon they became eligible to pay a fee and register the land as their own. It was more of a dare than a subsidy: the government bet pioneers they could not survive on homesteaded farms, and if they managed to, the property was their reward. But living on and improving the western frontier was an arduous task, and most people, including Laura Ingalls Wilder's parents, had failed at it.

In their 1939 *Little House* novel, *By the Shores of Silver Lake*, Lane and Wilder would characterize the act as a wager: "Well, girls," Pa tells his wife and daughter, "I've bet Uncle Sam fourteen dollars against a hundred and sixty acres of land, that we can make out to live on the claim for five years. Going to help me win the bet?"[153] To win, Charles Ingalls and countless others like him were forced to draw on the virtues of thrift and patient toil. To characterize the Homestead Act as a form of government handout was therefore absurd, as was the suggestion that modern Americans lacked the gumption to with-stand the economic challenge of the Depression without the government's "enlightened administration." Lane had hoped to discuss this in *The Name Is Mizzoury*, but after it was rejected, she started contemplating a new novel that would refute the idea of "free land."

Before getting to work on that project, however, she wrote a long nonfic-tion article comparing what she had seen on her trip with Garrett with what she had witnessed in Europe in the 1920s. Part of it appeared in the *Saturday Evening Post* in March 1936—and *Reader's Digest* two months later—under the simple title "Credo." It recounted her own transformation from a self-proclaimed communist to a proponent of individualism. In the 1920s, she had thought that communism was "an extension of democracy" and even of the American dream, "a dream of a new world of freedom, justice, and equality." Socialists, she then believed, fought against an "economic tyranny" that resembled the political tyranny of the Old World. But now she recognized the "dominant fallacy" in such thinking: it assumed that bureaucrats would do a better job of managing society than individuals themselves could. In reality, there was no reason to think government officials would be exempt from the shortsightedness, corruption, or ignorance that plagued the decisions of private citizens. The flaw in all government planning, in fact, lay in the notion that the state is somehow immune from human weaknesses, whereas there is really no such thing as "the state." There are only human beings, and those in office are just as fallible as those they purport to govern. Putting official planners in charge cannot eliminate foolishness or corruption. It merely puts "economic power in the hands of rulers, so that the livelihood, the lives, of multitudes of men [are] once more at their rulers' disposal."

Just as a word like "state" could be misleading, so Lane thought the word "capitalism" could also be deceptive. Capitalism is not an entity or a plan. It is just a term for individuals making their own economic choices—coming together of their own free will to create businesses and compete against one another, knowing that success or failure "depends upon satisfying [consumers'] chaotic wants and pleasing unpredictable tastes." Unlike the permanent fortunes of Old World monarchs, wealth in America consists of "innumerable streams of power . . . flowing through the mechanisms that produce the vast quantities of goods consumed by the multitudes, and the men who are called the owners can hardly be said even to control the wealth that stands recorded as theirs."

Freedom is obviously no panacea; it imposes a harsh principle of self-discipline. Lane called it "a slavery in which one is one's own master bearing a double burden of toil and of responsibility." But allowing people to take their own risks had generated unimaginable wealth and progress—taking the world from the age of steam to the age of electricity. The "anarchy of individualism" also "distributed wealth to an unprecedented and elsewhere unparalleled degree," and did so "without plan or any such definite purpose." Obviously, far too many people were still in poverty, but that poverty was "not the chronic state of certain classes," as in other countries. It was usually temporary, and Americans had the freedom to escape it. Their economic liberty also generated a paradox: the world's most individualistic nation was also the world's most charitable. Americans more willingly helped the unfortunate than did the people of any other society—precisely because they were so free and so wealthy.

Now, however, this "anarchic individualism" was under fire from advocates of government planning who, notwithstanding their claim that they represented the wave of the future, were actually arguing for a retreat from modernity and a return to the antique political superstition that rulers are immune from the weaknesses and incentives of ordinary people. "There is nothing new in planned and controlled economy. Human beings have lived under various forms of it for 6000 years." Yet politicians such as Roosevelt, and intellectuals such as the Beards, were so infatuated with collectivism that Lane thought the only hope of rescue lay in resistance by ordinary people who were "still paying the price of individual liberty, which is individual responsibility and insecurity."[154]

A month after "Credo" appeared in the *Post*, an expanded version was published as a 62-page book titled *Give Me Liberty*. To her original article, Lane added an insightful critique of the logic of economic planning: to truly organize an economy, she argued, government bureaucrats would, in principle, need infinite knowledge. Lane used soap as an example: "The entire economic circulation-system of a modern country is affected by the number of its people who wash behind the ears. This somewhat private matter affects the import and production of vegetable oils; the use of fat from farm animals; the manufacture of chemicals, perfumes, colors," and so on.[155] Because the prices of soap's ingredients are connected to the prices and supplies of all other products, planners who sought to control the soap market would ultimately be forced to control all personal behavior. If they were to relax control over any aspect of production, the result would inevitably undo the government's plan.

In short, government regulation can never stop halfway, but must constantly expand, until the government controls even the tiniest details of personal life, regulating even "such questions as: how many yards of cloth shall be used in a woman's dress? Shall lipstick be permitted? Is there any economic value in chewing-gum?"[156]

Anticipating the arguments of economists such as Ludwig von Mises and F. A. Hayek, Lane contrasted the idea of government planning with the spontaneous order found in a free society. It was not true that government intervention is necessary to avoid chaos, she argued. On the contrary, there is a "certain instinct of orderliness and of self-preservation which enables multitudes of free human beings to get together"[157]—a mechanism of self-organization arising from individual decisionmaking.

Lane illustrated her point by comparing the way an audience leaves a theater with the way a teacher tries to maintain control of a classroom full of children. "No crowd leaves a theater with any efficiency," she wrote, "yet we usually reach the sidewalk without a fight." In a school, by contrast, "any teacher knows that order cannot be maintained without regulation, supervision, and discipline."[158] The difference lay in the fact that the theatergoers pursue their own purposes as responsible individuals, whereas schoolchildren are not mature adults trusted to make their own choices, and must therefore be constantly monitored and controlled. Likewise, in an economy, people left to their own devices will fashion solutions to problems through mutual bargaining. But taking away their freedom, as the regulatory state does, infantilizes them—treats them like schoolchildren, who must be bossed around. That might work in European societies that never developed an individualistic ethos, but Americans, "the most reckless and lawless of peoples," are unsuited to such a notion.[159] Their "principal desire" was "to do as they pleased," and they did not view themselves as children, or as servants of "community spirit," but as self-directed beings. "In America, a man works, but he is not Labor. . . . An American raises wheat, but he is not The Wheatgrower. . . . There is no *system* here."[160]

America's prosperity and its relative economic equality, Lane concluded, were the fruits of a culture that prioritized the individual, leaving people free to pursue their own aims, and to bear the costs and enjoy the rewards of their decisions. "Free land will not explain our wealth," she concluded (adding that "incidentally, it is an error to suppose that land in this country cost nothing").[161] Instead, the high standard of living in the United States was rooted in its culture of liberty. But that culture could only survive if people were willing to defend it. Lane would soon offer such a defense in her fiction.

At his inauguration in 1933, Franklin Roosevelt was hailed
by some intellectuals, who argued that the United States needed a dictator.
To many, the dozen years that followed seemed to approach dictatorship.

6

The Revolutionary

The 1936 presidential election was a spectacular victory for the Democratic Party. The Republicans had barely even tried to oppose Roosevelt. There had not seemed much point. After years of New Dealing, so many Americans owed their livelihoods to the bureaucratic welfare state he had constructed—and to his political and economic patronage—that Paterson called it "the first election in our history to be decided by votes paid for out of the public treasury."[1] But along with his spending, Roosevelt had also been more willing to employ the rhetoric of class conflict than he had been four years before. Eschewing the moderate tone he affected in 1932, he now told voters that "economic royalists" and the "forces of selfishness" were trying to undo the progress he had made, and that he "welcomed" the plutocrats' "hatred."[2]

To those who resisted the New Deal, such language looked like an attempt to distract Americans from the fact that government planning was not working. Federal spending had doubled, yet unemployment was still nearly 17 percent.[3] Gross national product remained below 1929 levels, and much of the apparent recovery consisted of government purchases rather than self-sustaining market improvements.[4] Despite these facts, opponents of the New Deal were almost comically ineffectual. The most well-known opposition group was the American Liberty League—an affiliation of business leaders whose vast wealth made them easy to caricature as heartless fatcats—which folded within two years.[5] Nor did the Republican Party offer a genuine alternative when the election came. Their nominee was Kansas governor Alf Landon, a Progressive and a pragmatist with no clear ideological convictions, who ran a campaign so slipshod that he made no speeches for two months after his nomination. Newspapers published satirical articles labeling him a "missing person." When he finally did appear, he underwhelmed. "The issues in this campaign," wrote Dorothy Thompson on election eve, "have been difficult to find."[6]

In fact, Landon offered voters only diluted versions of what Roosevelt already promised. He pledged to balance the federal budget, but added, "It is not going to be balanced by depriving our needy unemployed of the relief that is their right."[7] At times, he spoke forcefully against such measures as the NIRA and AAA, but in general he vowed to keep New Deal programs in place and run them more effectively. As his biographer put it, Landon "was unable to explain satisfactorily how he could lower trade barriers and yet afford additional tariff protection for farmers; how he could maintain and possibly expand existing services and yet balance the budget and perhaps reduce taxes; how he could effectively use state and local governments to conduct nationwide relief and social security programs."[8] H. L. Mencken was more direct. Landon "may be a convinced Jeffersonian," he wrote, "but as a practical matter, he is a Kansan." That meant he considered it "axiomatic" that "the Treasury was set up to pay the debts of clod-hoppers."[9] Added to these shortcomings was the ineptitude of Landon's managers. In hopes of making Roosevelt appear offensively elitist, they kept their candidate's image folksy and his speeches unintellectual. That backfired.[10]

Long before the election, it became clear that Landon's campaign was doomed. Roosevelt won all but two states, beating Landon even in his own home state. Democrats also gained 12 seats in the House and 5 in the Senate. Reading the news, Rose Wilder Lane wrote to a friend that she "cried in my embittered soul, O why didn't the Republicans nominate Mickey Mouse?"[11] The election was such a landslide that, according to historian Thomas Fleming, "Roosevelt began his second term as the most powerful political figure on the globe."[12] Even Stalin and Hitler faced significant opposition parties in their legislatures, but Roosevelt did not. "This is a personal victory, and an acknowledgment of personal leadership unique in our history," declared Dorothy Thompson. "It brings about an unhealthy state of affairs."[13]

Indeed, the danger she and other Roosevelt opponents most feared soon materialized, when the president announced plans to take control of the only federal institution he did not yet dominate: the Supreme Court. A showdown with the judiciary had been looming for some time, but the justices were slow to challenge the president directly. In fact, a year after Roosevelt's first inauguration, they issued decisions sweeping away long-standing legal doctrines that stood as obstacles to the New Deal.[14] Those cases involved state laws, not Roosevelt's federal programs, but they seemed favorable to the administration because they eliminated rules against price controls and the nullification of private contracts. Yet in the year that followed, the Court revealed that its willingness to indulge expansive *state* power would not necessarily extend to the *federal* government. A direct confrontation seemed unavoidable in January 1935, when the justices considered the constitutionality of Roosevelt's actions nullifying gold clauses in contracts.

Anticipating an adverse ruling, the president prepared a defiant message in which he planned to announce his determination to ignore the Court's decision and "take such steps as may be necessary, by proclamation" to implement his will regardless.[15] That message was never delivered, because the judges ended up ruling in his favor, but the peace was short-lived.[16] In May, the Court issued a group of decisions that invalidated important portions of the New Deal, most significantly the NIRA. Throwing out the government's prosecution of the Schechter family's poultry business, the justices ruled unanimously that the act exceeded Congress's powers.[17] Eight months later, they also declared the AAA invalid.[18]

Roosevelt had already considered "packing" the Court by replacing justices whose views he considered too constraining with others who would support his policies. Now two weeks after his second inauguration, he unveiled a bill that gave himself power to appoint a new justice for each one over the age of 70 who declined to retire. That bill would let him place a new majority of loyal judges on the nation's highest tribunal.

Caroline and Charles Ingalls, Laura Ingalls Wilder's parents,
appear as Ma and Pa in the *Little House* novels and as Caroline and Charles
in Lane's *Let the Hurricane Roar.*

The proposal proved extraordinarily unpopular, not just among Republicans but also among Democrats, who, among other things, feared that a new majority of liberal northern justices might limit or end racial segregation in the south.[19] Nor were Democrats united on the idea of undermining an institution widely viewed as the guardian of the nation's fundamental principles. Roosevelt's supporters tried to portray the court-packing plan as a matter of reining in "judicial activism" and vindicating democracy; conservative justices, they argued, were overriding the political will of the majority and dictating the nation's economic policy in the guise of legal interpretation. But this was disingenuous. The rulings against the administration contained no reference to economic or political considerations, and were based on long-standing legal precedents. The *Schechter Poultry* decision had even been joined by such Progressive justices as Louis Brandeis and Benjamin Cardozo, and it was relatively popular even among New Dealers, given that by that time the NIRA had become—in Roosevelt's own words—"a headache."[20]

Paterson wrote in "Turns" that the real question in the court-packing debate was "simply whether the powers of government shall be limited or unlimited." It was "nonsense" to characterize Roosevelt's scheme as reining in an out-of-control judiciary. The whole point of the Supreme Court was to operate as a brake on the "democratic" branches of government. The Constitution gave Congress "definitely limited" powers, and for those limitations to be effective there must be "some actual operative instrument which checks up legislative action against the granted power." The judicial branch was the "only possible instrument" for doing this.[21] To enable the president to control the Court would destroy any meaningful legal limits on the government.

The court-packing plan was so unpopular that it eventually fizzled out, but not before months of internal disputes created the first real cracks in the New Deal coalition. During that time, Republicans had the wisdom to remain mostly silent, recognizing that Democratic infighting was the best thing they could hope for. Roosevelt, however, never repented of the plan, and even devoted the next months to campaigning against fellow Democrats who had opposed it. In the end, he lost the battle but won the war. By the time court-packing failed in the summer of 1937, the retirement of one justice and a dramatic change of opinion by another ensured that the Court would never again demonstrate the same resistance to the administration's proposals that it had when it invalidated the NIRA and the AAA.

▰▲▰

Among the most important inroads of Roosevelt's Second New Deal was the Social Security Act of 1935. Touted by the administration as a retirement savings plan whereby workers would deposit a portion of their paychecks into accounts that would be refunded upon retirement, the program actually did no such thing. Instead, it imposed a tax on wages during employment, followed in old age by entitlement payments that swiftly exceeded whatever amount the worker had "paid in"—meaning that the system resembled the "Ponzi scheme" of financial fraud more than any genuine insurance system. It used a "peculiar method of 'investment' of the proceeds by spending the cash on something else and substituting I.O.U.s.," Paterson explained in "Turns," and unlike private debts, these IOUs were not backed by future productivity. Instead, government's credit "is sound as long as it can tax its victims some more."[22] There was no need for the federal government to operate a retirement system anyway; states already had old-age pension programs, and the private market had offered options for retirement insurance for decades, which paid better than Social Security. Privately run insurance companies, however, had to balance their books by operating in ways that provided more benefits than costs, whereas Social Security was funded by the government's power to tax, meaning that it had little incentive to remain solvent. Paterson also despised the phrase "Social Security," and insisted on the term "wage-tax" instead. For the rest of her life, she kept her Social Security card in an envelope marked "'Social Security' Swindle."[23] Upon retirement, she refused to accept payments.

Like the rest of the Second New Deal, Social Security signaled a drastic change in the relationship between Americans and their government. Intrusive and irrational as Hoover's policies may have been, they and many of the First

New Deal's measures had been viewed as temporary. But the Social Security Act, like other Second New Deal legislation, made no pretense at being short term. These laws erected permanent institutions designed to transform government from the servant of the American people into their caretaker and supervisor. This marked an apparently irreversible transition from a society based on individuals' right to lead their own lives toward a society in which they served the state as part of its effort to equalize outcomes.[24] In fact, Roosevelt told the audience at his second inauguration in January 1937 that government was no longer a system for preserving freedom; that was an "untruth" that had now been "unlearned," and replaced with the idea that government is "the instrument of our united purpose to solve for the individual the ever-rising problems of a complex civilization."

To Paterson and Lane, this seemed like the final triumph of *Main Street*-style dullness over the enterprising spirit of individualism. Americans who once rebelled against coddling were now prepared to meekly accept it. As historian C. Vann Woodward notes, the most striking phenomenon of the Depression era was the public's "prevailing submissiveness. . . . Much more common than rebellion among Americans of those years was a sense of shame and a loss of self-respect."[25] "If we had children," Paterson wrote in "Turns," "we'd be rather ashamed to look at them and reflect that we were born free, and had sold them down the river—and at that, for 'only a promise to pay. . . .' Will anyone now say that the sheeplike docility of the people actually worked for the general good?"[26] But the notion that self-reliance had been rendered obsolete in the modern age was now becoming almost a cliché, as New Dealers argued that it was time to abandon economic freedom and replace it with bureaucratic organization.[27] Like Charles Beard, who saw individualism as a relic of "days of primitive agriculture and industry,"[28] sociologist Robert MacIver argued that individualism, though "rooted in the mores of this country," had been superseded because "the frontier in American history has disappeared."[29] Roosevelt deputy Joseph P. Kennedy agreed. "An awakened people can no longer be deluded with talk of rugged individualism," he declared in his 1936 book, *I'm for Roosevelt*.[30] "The more complex the society the greater the demand for planning."[31]

Lane and her mother disagreed. However much circumstances might have changed, they saw no reason to think the lessons of the frontier needed to be "unlearned." On the contrary, as Lane argued in *Give Me Liberty*, the more complex a society became, the *less* likely it was that bureaucrats could organize it, or see to the needs of 128 million Americans. What was needed was not more government regimentation but more individual resolve, and novels such as *Little House on the Prairie*—published in September 1935—sought to reinvigorate the spirit of initiative that had seen Americans through previous economic downturns. Speaking to a woman's club months after that novel appeared, Laura Ingalls Wilder explained that the point of her books was to do precisely that. "In the depression following the Civil War my parents, as so many others, lost all their savings," she said.

> For two years in succession they lost their crops to the grasshoppers on the banks of Plum Creek. They suffered cold and heat, hard work and privation as did others of their time. When possible, they turned the bad into good. If not possible, they endured it. No other person, nor the government, owed them a living. They owed that to themselves and in some way they paid the debt. And they found their own way. Their old fashioned character values are worth as much today as they ever were to help us over the rough places. We need today courage, self-reliance and integrity. When we remember that our hardest times would have been easy times for our forefathers it should help us to be of good courage.[32]

The next *Little House* novel, *On the Banks of Plum Creek*, was published in October 1937. Among the most memorable and effective books in the series, it included Wilder's recollections of one of the worst natural disasters in American history: the grasshopper plagues of 1873–1877, when swarms of perhaps 3.5 trillion "Rocky Mountain locusts" devastated crops in Minnesota, Iowa, and the Dakota Territory.[33] After landing and eating their fill, the insects had laid eggs and started walking west, crawling over every surface that stood in their way, until there was not "any green thing in sight and the ground looked like a honeycomb it was so full of the little round holes where the grasshoppers had laid their eggs."[34] Laura's father Charles had tried in vain to save his wheat crop. He was finally forced to get work harvesting for eastern farms that had survived the attacks.

The infestations were still a living memory to many midwestern farmers—Roosevelt had even mentioned them in his first inaugural address—but to Lane and Wilder, there was a difference: 19th-century homesteaders had not expected the government to rescue them from such disasters. This was only partly true; the Minnesota legislature had, in fact, extended the deadline for tax payments and made a modest appropriation to help farmers buy seed for the year after the swarm. But that was all, and even then it had imposed stringent means testing.[35] Otherwise, state lawmakers had left responsibility for caring for the needy primarily to private charities and contributions from wealthy citizens, railroad companies, and fraternal organizations such as the Grange. At the time, many had characterized this response as a stingy lack of compassion, but the result was that government relief efforts minimized the moral hazard of deterring hard work and thrift, and left the state without more debt. Nor had lawmakers resorted to taxes that might deplete the private capital needed for future economic growth. Farmers like Charles Ingalls had taken jobs where there was a market demand, instead of continuing in profitless labor on the farm. "There were no jobs lying around to go begging while the government hired men as now," as Wilder put it.[36] In short, people had endured hard times and prevailed. There was no reason a similar approach could not succeed in 1937.

As with *Let the Hurricane Roar*, Lane decided to prepare a version of the *Plum Creek* story for adult readers also. But while she drew on her mother's *Pioneer Girl* material, the book she wrote next would tell the story of her father's life, while including the grasshopper attacks as well as the horrendous blizzards of 1880–1881. It would also draw on the research she had done while writing *The Name Is Mizzoury*. Her primary goal would be to emphasize that individualism was not a vestige of a bygone era; on the contrary, it was the principle that had allowed Americans to emerge from a simpler, more impoverished age and enjoy the astounding benefits of modern civilization. It would refute in fiction the intellectually lazy slogans about the disappearance of "free land."

Lane found it hard to get started on the project, given the immense personal stresses in her life at the time. She had decided not to return to her parents' farm after a bitter argument with her mother, and, as always, she was struggling with finances. She was still sending money to Rexh Meta in Albania—who had just written to say he was engaged—and she had taken in two new "adopted sons" whom she was sending to school as she had Meta. Roosevelt's reelection also brought on a bout of her recurrent depression. At such moments, it seemed that the America she cherished—proud, self-reliant, and unafraid—was gone forever. "One thing I hate about the New Deal," she told a friend in January 1937, "is that it is killing what, to me, is the American pioneering spirit." In Roosevelt's America, "all the old character-values seem simply insane from a practical point of view."[37] What point was there in working hard to earn a fortune, if it would only be confiscated through taxation and regulation?—and when foolhardiness, laziness, and dependency were subsidized instead? She struggled to remain optimistic, telling Garet Garrett that after "a hundred years, or five hundred," those values might "begin to stir again in history," but it was hard to keep up hope.[38] Garrett himself had little to offer. People were not interested in the economic common sense he had been publishing in the *Saturday Evening Post*, he told her. "They wanted manna and water out of the rock. I wanted people to stay hard and fit and self responsible."[39] Lane grew so despondent that she even fantasized about killing Roosevelt. By April, however, her feelings of despair had passed. She wrote in her diary that she was "feeling alive" once more, and producing about 1,000 words a day on the novel she was calling *Free Land*.[40]

▚

As the New Deal's fifth anniversary approached, Americans took stock of the expansion of government power and the immensity of the administration's spending. And although they still liked Roosevelt personally, their political support began to ebb. The court-packing fight left lasting ill will within the Democratic Party, and Republicans pointed out that productivity gains were unimpressive and unemployment still remained high; even if the millions now working for the government counted as "employed," the jobless rate remained at nearly 10 percent. Then in August 1937, the economy began to slump again. The stock market crashed, worse than in 1929, and manufacturing collapsed. Wages fell by more than 35 percent and 4 million workers lost their jobs.[41] New Dealers were shocked. "We are floundering," Democratic representative Maury Maverick told his House colleagues. "We have pulled all the rabbits out of the hat, and there are no more rabbits."[42]

Economists still debate the causes of this Depression within a Depression. Some attribute it to the Federal Reserve's efforts to reduce the money supply after a long period of dangerous expansion, which may have stalled the economy because so much of what seemed like growth in previous years had been built on inflationary federal spending instead of actual consumer demand. In fact, private investment in industry during this period was negative—meaning that businesses were funding production by depleting their capital base, the equivalent of a steamship captain burning the vessel itself to feed the boiler.[43]

But a larger factor was a drastic increase in the cost of labor, caused by the heavy taxes imposed on businesses, and the increased power of unions that resulted from the new National Labor Relations Act (NLRA). That act essentially forced businesses to acquiesce in union demands for higher wages and benefits, thus making it more expensive and complicated to employ people or start new businesses. It compelled employers to negotiate even with unions that lacked support from most workers—which meant a small percentage of employees could dictate the terms of employment for an entire company. In April 1937, the Supreme Court upheld the NLRA in a decision that, in principle, gave the federal government power to supervise the terms of every employment contract in the nation—a ruling that made clear that business owners could no longer hope for the Court to discipline the New Dealers.[44]

The NLRA sparked a wave of strikes, most famously against General Motors' facilities in Flint, Michigan, where for six weeks union members occupied buildings and shot at strikebreakers and police. When GM officials asked the government to evict the trespassers, both Roosevelt and Michigan governor Frank Murphy refused, which forced the company to capitulate.[45] Shortly afterward, when the Steel Workers Organizing Committee (SWOC)—a militant subsidiary of the newly formed Congress of Industrial Organizations (CIO)—threatened to copy that strike at foundries across the country, U.S. Steel's chairman caved without a struggle.[46]

Confrontations at smaller steel plants (known as "Little Steel") ended less peacefully. After Republic Steel's president Tom Girdler refused to sign an agreement with the CIO—his workers preferred their own union, instead—SWOC marched on Republic's facilities and on other Little Steel companies nationwide. At Republic's Chicago plant, SWOC protestors stormed the front gates armed with clubs, rocks, and slingshots. Police officers opened fire, killing 10 marchers in an incident that was captured by newsreel cameras and came to be known as the "Memorial Day Massacre." Many in the press unfairly blamed Girdler for the bloodshed, but after similar violent incidents occurred at foundries in Ohio, Michigan, and Indiana, public opinion went against SWOC. And when union leaders appealed to Roosevelt for help, the president, fearing political backlash, declined to intervene on either side.[47]

Union victories against GM and U.S. Steel resulted in few significant improvements for workers. But unions themselves gained by forcing managers to negotiate with them in exchange for labor. These negotiations were far from equal, since the NLRA enabled unions to trespass on business's land and to insist on "closed shops"—prohibiting employers from choosing to hire nonunion workers. The unions promptly pressed these advantages, forcing companies to increase wage rates by more than 10 percent. This hike in employment costs deterred investment and discouraged firms from hiring new workers.[48] Thus the administration's pro-union laws worsened unemployment by as much as six percentage points.[49]

None of this came as a shock to Paterson. She was not at all anti-union—she thought unions existed "by inalienable right"[50]—but laws such as the NLRA were bound to be counterproductive, because no law to settle labor disputes "can be effective while we have either personal liberty or private property." The reason was simple: in the event of a strike, such a law must either compel laborers to work or force management to meet strikers' demands. But forcing people to work "is slavery," she wrote. "No matter what new word may be found for it, that's the old word." And forcing management to concede "also requires force. The only conceivable means is confiscation of the property, in whole or in part, by fines or seizure, or perhaps closing the premises."[51] In fact, a few years later, when Montgomery Ward chairman Sewell Avery refused to comply with the Roosevelt administration's order that he accede to union demands, federal officials seized the company and soldiers carried Ward out of his office in his chair.[52]

Although the costs of higher wages might seem to fall on wealthy business owners, Paterson explained, they are ultimately borne by workers. "Who has actually gained by the [NLRA]?" she asked. "Not labor. It has lost an incalculable amount in employment." The real winner was government, which obtained power over both employers and job-seekers.[53] This was particularly true given that until 1947, it was legal for unions to donate money to political candidates, but not for corporations to do so. Thus politicians profited from union gains under the NLRA, which enabled them to receive subsidies taken directly out of workers' paychecks. Government also enriched itself from new taxes such as the Social Security "wage tax" and the "undistributed profits tax" that drained capital and thereby hindered the economy's ability to base recovery on anything other than government subsidies. Certain "high-minded persons" seemed to think that taxes or government borrowing could create money out of nowhere, or draw it from "outside the economy," but this was nonsense. "All such money has to come from production," so government spending inherently "represents a cut from all wages."[54] That was why every time political leaders claimed to be able to alleviate poverty, they nonetheless ended up "lifting pennies from the baby's bank."[55]

Just as the Social Security tax penalized employment, Roosevelt's 1936 undistributed profits tax punished businesses for reinvesting earnings toward further growth instead of paying dividends. It mandated that any business keeping one percent of net income to invest in expansion would lose ten percent of it in taxes. Because small businesses were less likely to qualify for loans, and were therefore especially reliant on reinvesting profits, the undistributed profits tax hurt them more than it hurt big businesses.[56] Both of these taxes were on top of a drastic series of other levies that more than doubled the income tax; eliminated exemptions; applied new taxes on liquor, gasoline, cars, gifts, and estates; and added a "wealth tax" of 75 percent on incomes above $1 million. In the end, the Roosevelt administration tripled taxes and imposed a 90 percent rate on the highest bracket.[57] States also nearly quadrupled their charges during this period. As one economist observed a decade later, these confiscatory rates "were high enough to paralyze initiative" by those most likely to invest in business expansion.[58]

The administration's ever-growing power over the economy not only signaled to owners and shareholders that they were vulnerable to new types of expropriation, but also made both producers and consumers fearful about where government might go next.[59] So much investment and productivity now depended on the will of political authorities that a single presidential speech or congressional vote could spell doom for major enterprises. Potential investors therefore chose to remain on the sidelines, and many businesses avoided new hires. Yet as the economy worsened—in what Roosevelt called a "recession," because he thought it sounded better than "depression"—the White House chose not to examine the disincentives it had created, but instead accused business owners of engaging in an intentional act of economic sabotage. The president called it the "capital strike."[60]

In October 1937, Roosevelt told Democratic Party chairman Jim Farley that the recession was "the result of a concentrated effort by big business and concentrated wealth to drive the market down just to create a situation unfavorable to me."[61] He was certain it was a conspiracy. "Business, particularly the banking industry, has ganged up on me," he told Farley again a few weeks later. "They are a pretty selfish lot."[62] Two months after that, Attorney General Robert Jackson, speaking before the American Political Science Association, said business owners were trying to "liquidate the New Deal" and establish "a new manifestation of 'aristocratic anarchy'" by refusing to invest or hire.[63] Four days later, Interior secretary Harold Ickes gave a radio address claiming that the nation's "sixty richest families" were engaged in a "general sit-down strike—not of labor . . . [but] of capital."[64] Roosevelt told voters shortly afterward that the recession was the fault of a "handful" of "bankers and industrialists" who were trying to "fight to the last ditch to retain such autocratic control over the industry and finances of the country as they now possess."[65] He demanded that the FBI begin investigating bankers and business leaders.[66]

In truth, there was no such conspiracy; business owners and investors were simply reacting to the economic incentives created by the administration, which punished economic growth and seized earnings.[67] Yet Roosevelt's scapegoating was all too familiar to students of political history. Leaders in Russia and Germany were simultaneously blaming their own economic setbacks on "saboteurs" and secretive "counter-revolutionary forces," and the conspiracy theory of a "capital strike" was, as one Roosevelt ally later admitted, a consequence of "the cross-pollination of one or another kind of self-styled Communists and New Dealers."[68] The administration's opponents began to fear that the "capital strike" might be used as an excuse for reviving something like the NIRA, with its economy-crushing "codes," or even an outright government takeover of capital.[69]

That was a chilling prospect. One of socialism's chief goals was to establish state control not only over factories but over the nation's investment apparatus, to enable bureaucrats, rather than private owners, to decide which industries would receive how much capital. If Roosevelt's advisers truly thought financiers and business owners were "striking" against the national interest, what was to stop them from crushing that strike by confiscating wealth and ordering investors to obey political commands? Prominent New Deal leaders such as Rexford Tugwell spoke openly of their belief that "the flow of new capital into different uses" should "be supervised" by the government, and in the years to come, several other nations would adopt measures to "conscript capital."[70] Even more moderate thinkers agreed. Only months after the "capital strike" slogan gained currency, economist Arthur Dahlberg published a book titled *When Capital Goes on Strike*, which recommended taxing people's savings accounts in order to instill a "fear of loss" in anyone who "hoarded" their savings.[71] Around the same time, federal officials chose a 12-foot limestone statue to grace the Federal Trade Commission's headquarters in Washington, DC. Executed in Socialist realist style, the sculpture depicted a muscle-bound worker brutally hauling backward on the bridle of a horse as it struggled for freedom. It was titled *Man Controlling Trade*.

Such things made Paterson "considerably worried about the possibility of Fascism."[72] There was no reason that conscription of capital would not also include conscription of *human* capital—that is, compulsory government service. In fact, given the administration's expansive public works projects, its effort to eliminate unemployment by swelling government job rolls, and its emphasis on the obligation of every citizen to serve others, that seemed the next logical step. Eleanor Roosevelt had long supported the idea of forcing American teenagers to "volunteer" for community service.[73] "I know people are afraid of making a thing like that compulsory because it seems like something the Fascist countries have done," she admitted. "But remember, everything we do must go through Congress."[74] That was little comfort in light of the fact that many states, mostly but not exclusively in the South, were already using vagrancy laws to "recruit" the unemployed for countless public projects.[75] In 1936, the Los Angeles Police Department announced a "bum blockade": any jobless person entering California would be returned home or sentenced to 80 days of hard labor.[76] And prominent voices were already calling for programs that would mimic the compulsory work camps already being established abroad—not only in Germany, Austria, and Italy, but even in Switzerland and Great Britain.[77] In Canada, Prime Minister R. B. Bennett—Paterson's former employer—oversaw the establishment of "voluntary" labor camps for the unemployed; any man out of work who refused to go would be arrested.[78] The U.S. Forest Service's John D. Guthrie, charged with overseeing the Civilian Conservation Corps (CCC) told an audience in Connecticut that he thought the Nazi labor camps being created in Austria were comparable to those the CCC was erecting in the Midwest.[79] Even Dorothy

Thompson, in one of her characteristically inconsistent moments, endorsed mandatory labor in a *Ladies' Home Journal* article in which she said that there was "nothing in the least undemocratic" about forcing young Americans into "work camps."[80] Horrified, Paterson declared in "Turns" that this was arguing "for slavery, pure and simple. . . . Compulsory labor is slavery. Miss Dorothy Thompson is in favor of it."[81]

The White House, however, responded to the alleged capital strike not with outright conscription or confiscation, but with the establishment in April 1938 of the Temporary National Economic Committee (TNEC), charged with investigating the nation's "concentration of wealth." When it wrapped up three years later, the TNEC issued a report blandly urging that "all organizations," including private businesses, be made "democratic," and recommending more vigorous enforcement of antitrust laws.[82] But by then, the TNEC had served its real purpose, which was to humiliate and frighten business leaders and to gain concessions of the sort the administration extracted from U.S. Steel president Edward Stettinius Jr. shortly before the 1938 elections.

Suffering drastic shortfalls due to the "recession," Stettinius's company decided to cut wages at its plants, but, afraid this would incur the wrath of federal regulators or the CIO, he traveled to Washington days after the TNEC was organized to meet privately with Attorney General Robert Jackson and other administration representatives. He asked them not to bring antitrust charges against his company, and Roosevelt's deputies, fearing the political consequences of a wage reduction, counteroffered: they would divert all of the government's steel orders to U.S. Steel if it promised to keep wages high. Stettinius's board of directors rejected that idea, fearing the backlash if such a secret deal became known. Then, in September, Stettinius met directly with Roosevelt, showed him the firm's confidential financial information, and again begged him to permit a wage reduction. Roosevelt once more refused, threatening to have U.S. Steel investigated by the TNEC, prosecuted by the antitrust lawyers, or even seized outright by the government if it tried to cut pay. Finally, they reached a compromise: the company could make cuts after the November elections. Not long afterward, the administration gave the CIO authority over some important machinists unions on the West Coast, in part to dissuade them from protesting the wage reductions at U.S. Steel.[83]

In the meantime, rumors of a secret arrangement with Roosevelt had leaked to the press, causing stock prices to go up and then back down. "It is not a very pretty thought that the market rose on rumors of a wage cut and was set back by the expectation of wage maintenance," wrote Paterson when the news broke. "But it is even more disquieting . . . that the market operations originated in Washington. There are far too many vague 'explanations' all around."[84] The incident seemed typical of the type of political wheeling and dealing that resulted from government entanglement in business.

In a May 1938 editorial, Paterson pointed out why the whole idea of a capital strike was fallacious. The "recession" was no conspiracy—it was caused by the fact that "any form of investment may be clubbed over the head by arbitrary rate fixing, or by property seizures, with violence, winked at in exchange for political contributions; or by punitive 'investigations' . . . or by taxes piled on taxes." Confiscatory government policies were the problem, not any intentional business boycott. "If there are sound opportunities which the banks pettishly refuse to take advantage of, will the 'capital strike' theorists name even one—some person or firm who has without reason been refused a loan, for proper and profitable use?"[85] Yet despite the lack of any such evidence, the administration maintained its "capital strike" rhetoric by implementing an aggressive new campaign of antitrust litigation.

In 1936, Congress had adopted the Robinson-Patman Act or the "anti–chain store" law, which was intended to protect small retailers against competition from grocery store chains such as A&P and Safeway. A relatively new idea at the time, chain stores used innovative business techniques to reduce prices, increase convenience, and expand purchasing options. But smaller businesses that could not compete economically viewed them as a threat not only to their own financial survival but to the stability and virtues of the American small town.[86] They celebrated the act's passage as a protection for their jobs—even though it increased the cost of food in the nation's worst economic crisis—and as a vindicator of traditional values.[87] "The Chain store is not owned by anyone in your town," proclaimed Indiana congressman Charles Halleck, who insisted that "if we ever get out of this depression," it would only be by eliminating the "absentee ownership" that "broaden[s] the gap between Main Street and Wall Street."[88] Dorothy Thompson pierced such rhetoric in her column. "The Robinson anti-chain store bill," she declared, "is an entirely reactionary measure" by people who, "for sentimental reasons" wanted to defend their "main street of shops . . . at the cost of all of us."[89]

Meanwhile, the administration entrusted antitrust prosecutions to a former law professor named Thurman Arnold, who, shortly before joining the Justice Department, published his anti-corporate views in a book titled *The Folklore of Capitalism*. In a pugnacious, sarcastic tone, Arnold heaped ridicule on the principle of economic freedom and characterized the American economy as a species of feudalism controlled by corporate overlords. Such notions as individual choice or personal autonomy, he claimed, were only empty dogmas fabricated by capitalist elites to keep citizens in subjection and scare voters away from government interventions that might help them.

Believing that "the best government is that which we find in an insane asylum"—because its "aim is to make the inmates of the asylum as comfortable as possible regardless of their respective moral deserts"—Arnold concluded that American "theories of government" were "the most unrealistic in the world."[90] To discuss ideas such as freedom or the proper role of government was pointless: "It doesn't get anywhere and it doesn't mean anything. . . . It is a form of prayer."[91] Indeed, he believed that "social creeds, law, economics, and so on" were all "mysticism" and had "*no meaning whatever* apart from the organization to which they are attached."[92] In the case of capitalism, that "organization" was masterminded by big business owners, who used such notions as individualism as tricks to maintain their power.[93] Indeed, they had fabricated the "illusion that we [are] living under a pioneer economy composed of self-sufficient men" in order to hinder the work of government experts who were trying to organize the economy.[94] Still, Arnold was confident that Americans would soon learn to accept the "new conception of the state," in which "government has a new role to play in providing for the security of individuals in their jobs and in the distribution of goods."[95] The "religion of individualism," he claimed, "has lost this potent magic."[96]

Commenting on the book in "Turns," Paterson expressed revulsion at Arnold's attempt to characterize moral debates over individual freedom as meaningless squabbles about mythologies. Arnold had "either read Machiavelli or else read someone who has read Machiavelli," she thought. His slick, often self-contradictory language and tone of worldly cynicism were carefully fashioned to obscure the real, crucial issues at stake. "His is the doctrine of expediency. Never mind high principles. . . . Moral catchwords may be useful to get people to do what you want them to do . . . but these slogans really mean nothing in regard to 'social institutions.'"[97] Paterson considered this species of argument both a devious tactic for manipulating readers and a naive way of deluding oneself. In truth, the moral consequences of government policies could not be avoided or dismissed as illusions, because the bills—ethical as well as financial—inevitably came due. Arnold might think himself one of those "modern thinkers" who "try to get rid of 'values'—in order to substitute 'workability,'" but this was foolhardy because "they have to make the attempt in words, and words are charged with values."[98]

Paterson argued that the administration's antitrust prosecutions were irrational, in part because the antitrust laws were so vaguely written that practically every economic behavior could be declared illegal, and in part because genuine monopolies can only exist by government intervention. It was not business owners who acted like feudal lords, but bureaucrats—including Arnold himself—who used the "mysticism" of antitrust law to act as kingmakers. For example—although Paterson did not know it—at the September 1938 meeting in which Edward Stettinius had pleaded for permission to cut wages, Arnold had asked the steel magnate if he would consider going into the aluminum business. When Stettinius asked why, Arnold explained that the Aluminum Company of America (ALCOA) was giving the administration trouble, and if U.S. Steel would consider entering the aluminum industry—which no other firm had tried to do, given ALCOA's overwhelming expertise—it would help the Justice Department bring antitrust charges against ALCOA. "Between you and myself, I don't know whether or not the [TNEC] boys are going to get to first base," Arnold told him. "I am much more interested in proper antitrust procedure than I am in any damn fool monopoly investigation. [But] I am going to put on a show regardless, and give the American public what they expect and demand."[99] Other administration officials approached steel magnate Henry Kaiser with the same request.[100] Both businessmen demurred, but their willingness to collaborate with the administration on other matters was eventually rewarded with official appointments and billions of dollars in government contracts and loans. Stettinius was made secretary of state, and Kaiser purchased ALCOA assets at bargain prices when the company was forced to divest.

Yet as Paterson observed, the same federal government that was pursuing ALCOA had already spent the better part of a decade creating monopolies throughout the industrial and agricultural sectors. "The government has restrained [trade], intentionally and forcibly," she wrote, by restricting competition, dictating the output of farms and factories, and setting prices for products and services. Arnold raised no objection to these programs, which proved he was not actually concerned with the consequences of monopolies.[101] Why was price fixing by private industry prosecuted as a crime, whereas price fixing by politicians praised as democratic? The consequences are the same; in fact, they are worse in the latter case, because although consumers are free to shop elsewhere, taxpayers are not. The only explanation for this paradox was that the New Dealers' true goal was not to protect people but to expand their own power.

Arnold's double-talk struck Paterson as a dangerous portent. Individualism was not a mere dogma or tradition, as Arnold suggested; it was part of the "logic of reality," as inescapable as the laws of electricity or mechanics.[102] Any politician who claimed individualism was obsolete was simply aiming to substitute government compulsion for freedom of choice. Arnold's antitrust lawsuits were a perfect example: he sued firms that succeeded through innovation and efficiency, while acting as a power broker for business leaders who made deals with the administration. Unless stopped, he and his colleagues would usher in an era of genuine monopolies—in which economic success was determined by political favoritism instead of hard work and skill. That was already how the Russian, German, and Italian economies operated, and they showed what the consequences were: "a breadline—economic serfdom, an autocratic, bureaucratic, supreme state."[103] There was immense danger, therefore, in America's shift away from individualism. "The moral outlook," Paterson thought, "is none too bright."[104]

Around this time, business and political leaders started warning that the final collapse of the free market might be imminent. "We are approaching a day when individual liberty will vanish," wrote Robert Lund, vice president of the Lambert Pharmaceutical Company, in a book called *Truth about the New Deal*.[105] Stewart Utley, general manager of the Detroit Steel Casting Company, agreed, declaring in *The American System: Shall We Destroy It?* that "the financial losses of the depression have been heavy, but they are insignificant as compared with the intellectual and moral degeneration which has swept over the American people." As a result of this degeneration, "those endowed with ambition, thrift, energy, and resourcefulness" were being "plundered in order that the loot may be given to those who do not possess [these qualities]."[106] But Lund and Utley were exceptions. Instead of defending themselves, it appeared to Paterson that most business owners were suffering from a failure of nerve. "The great loss is the habit of thinking for oneself and speaking one's mind," she wrote. "Timidity, plain cowardice, is the prevailing vice." This was true both of politicians, who were terrified of standing on principle and risking disapproval, and of ordinary citizens, who had come to view themselves not as responsible individuals but as victims of circumstance or servants of society. It seemed to Paterson that "when he gets stepped on," the modern business owner "apologizes for being in the way."[107]

The country appeared gripped by an obsession with conformity or an attitude of learned helplessness, and both "contain[ed] the germs of national death."[108] The administration's "capital strike" rhetoric only raised the stakes. In June 1938, Hugh Johnson—who had left the administration on bad terms and was now a Roosevelt critic—told a convention of steel industry executives that after the Supreme Court's decision in the *Schechter Poultry* case two years earlier, the president had said to him, "Business has bucked me, and when business wants to play with me again, it will be on its hands and knees."[109] Paterson was astounded that nobody seemed outraged by such "grave and repulsive" language. "'Industry on its hands and knees' is not a pretty idea," she wrote. "What can be the state of mind which could anticipate that condition as something to 'play with'?" But instead of speaking up in their own defense, "acquiescent" businesspeople chose to remain silent. "If they don't resent [such treatment]," she thought, "they may come near deserving it."[110]

▰▲◣

Paterson and Lane believed that the failure of businessmen to defend themselves indicated a worrisome erosion in national morale. This shift in mood was obvious to many others, too. Business journalist B. C. Forbes noted in May 1938 that industry leaders seemed "confused, bewildered, not to say disheartened," as a result of the "anti-business political agitation [and] anti-business legislation" coming from Washington.[111] A year later, Indiana businessman Wendell Willkie, who would soon run for president, remarked on the "spiritless" "atmosphere" of "melancholia" caused by "legislative policies that discourage the use of private capital for the development of industry."[112] Even Treasury Secretary Henry Morgenthau told reporters that he feared the "what's-the-use attitude" that was "holding back a number of business men from expanding their businesses and from taking normal risks."[113] Laborers also appeared to be succumbing to hopelessness. "People drive me wild," Laura Ingalls Wilder told Lane. "'What's the use' they ask, 'it won't do any good,' they say. . . . If we had such opportunities when we were young we would have been rich. . . . I can have no least sympathy for people who can do, and will only holler that there are no chances for them now."[114]

One disturbing portent of the national trend was the fate of William Randolph Hearst. A populist demagogue of fantastic wealth, the 74-year-old Hearst had spent decades alternately defying public opinion and craving its approval. In some ways, he was the last of the 19th-century tycoons, having revolutionized the newspaper industry and become one of the world's wealthiest men, thanks to a superb talent for appealing to the lowest common denominator. His newspapers combined prurience and prudishness, offering readers salacious photos of seminude dancers on some pages and moralizing investigations into the corruption of the wealthy on others. Lacking a coherent political philosophy, he articulated what he called "Americanism," which combined nativist and patriotic sloganeering with a boisterous endorsement of democracy, vaguely understood. As one contemporary put it, Hearst dedicated the enormous megaphone of his publishing empire "to ignorance and prejudice, hatred of the rich simply because they are rich . . . to socialism, discontent, envy, to the basest of human passions."[115] He paid Mussolini and Hitler to write for his papers because he endorsed their anti-Soviet policies and vaguely hoped he could persuade them to stop persecuting Jews.

In 1932, he helped engineer Franklin Roosevelt's nomination and showered him with flattery, but then came to loathe the NIRA, which he viewed as a threat to free enterprise and the First Amendment. For a while he remained frenemies with Roosevelt, alternately savaging the New Deal as "Nonsensical, Ridiculous, Asinine interference," and dining convivially at the White House.[116] Yet he grew persuaded that the administration was infested with communist schemers and posed an unprecedented threat to democracy, either in itself, or because its semisocialist policies would provoke a fascist reaction. When he decided the Communist Party was making drastic inroads in Hollywood, he called—without any apparent sense of irony—for the federal government to "take over the film companies . . . and see that they are conducted on a patriotic American basis."[117] He ordered his newspapers to begin investigating and exposing party activities—to which the communists responded by organizing strikes and boycotts of Hearst publications and newsreels. When, in January 1935, Roosevelt personally overturned a bureaucratic ruling in favor of a union at one of Hearst's papers—to repay the publisher for not endorsing Republicans in the previous fall's elections—communist leaders pointed to it as proof that Hearst and Roosevelt were really capitalists in cahoots.[118] But by then, the two had actually fallen out. Three months later, when Roosevelt told a Hearst deputy that it might be "necessary to throw the forty-six men who are reported to have incomes in excess of $1,000,000 to the wolves . . . in other words, to limit incomes through taxation," as well as to confiscate "vast estates," the publisher decided to support Alf Landon's campaign for president in 1936.[119] He threw himself into the work, which only triggered more boycotts by readers who had been raised on nearly a half-century of Hearst's crusades against wealthy capitalists. They cancelled subscriptions by the droves, attended anti-Hearst rallies—one organized by the Communist Party in Manhattan drew 15,000 people—and took to wearing buttons trumpeting "I don't read Hearst!"[120] Leading intellectuals hosted a convention in Atlantic City to condemn him, where the keynote speaker was Charles Beard. In his speech, Beard labeled Hearst an "enemy to everything that is noblest and best in our American tradition."[121]

Although initially defiant—"Landon will be overwhelmingly elected and I'll stake my reputation on it," he told reporters—the aging publisher's vitality waned after Landon's devastating loss. The boycotts had crippled his business, and when Roosevelt retaliated for his betrayal by ordering the IRS to investigate his taxes, things got worse.[122] Hearst's flagship paper, the *New York American*, was forced to merge with the *New York Evening Journal*, and by autumn 1938, it was apparent that his business empire was insolvent. It was placed in a trust, and Hearst was even forced to sell much of his world-famous art collection in a series of humiliating auctions.[123] His demoralization was evident in his newspapers, which lost their editorial edge. The giant of journalism retreated to writing weekly columns about his childhood memories and his favorite dogs. His fall from the status of industrial giant to that of an ostracized has-been would inspire some of the era's most successful artists: Aldous Huxley's 1939 novel *After Many a Summer*, Orson Welles's 1941 film *Citizen Kane*, and Ayn Rand's 1943 novel *The Fountainhead* all drew heavily on his biography.

Yet the nation's psychological shift seemed to run deeper than economics or politics, and Paterson thought it was especially noticeable in men. "There isn't a *man* left in the country," she groused. "They all want to be 'saved,' have their noses wiped for them by Mussolini, or Roosevelt, or somebody. . . . I will say flatly, that I think a man may still be a man even if he's panhandling in the street, asking for handouts at kitchen doors, but not if he's in a government 'camp.'"[124] Dorothy Thompson agreed. "This whole country is full of impotent men," she raged in her diary. "Hopeless as lovers, all scared of their wives, undeveloped, childish, arrested."[125] Not long afterward, sociologists Mirra Komarovsky and Winona Morgan would publish important studies documenting the disastrous effects of the Depression and joblessness on men's sense of themselves.[126] But Paterson and Lane would examine the relationship between work and masculinity on a deeper level in their fiction.

In March 1938, Lane's *Free Land* began appearing as a *Saturday Evening Post* serial. Released in hardback in May, it became her best-selling book and her most concentrated attempt yet to vindicate the individualist ideal in fiction. Yet while it contained occasional political statements, the novel was not propagandistic, and it made no effort to romanticize frontier life. It told the story of David Beaton, a young farmer who defies the skepticism of his father, James, by trying his hand at homesteading on the Dakota prairie in the 1880s. James disapproves of the Homestead Act because it looks to him like a government handout. "He did not believe in giving, or getting, something for nothing. He believed in every man's paying his own way. . . . 'Who supports the government?' he had asked. . . . 'We do, don't we? the people? Well, then don't it stand to reason the Government can't support the people?'"[127] But David overcomes his father's qualms. He builds a dugout and brings his wife, Mary, from New York to live with him on their claim.

Their trials are extreme and begin almost immediately. The couple are trapped in a blizzard on the way to the dugout and must huddle under their overturned sled to survive the storm. Later, the town is surrounded by Indians angry that another settler has stolen a mummy from a Native burial ground. David and his neighbors manage to stop the man and return the body before violence ensues. David is unable to earn enough in his first season and must take a job on the railroad—after which he tallies up his gains and losses, and finds he has earned very little. Still, he tells Mary, "We've lived, don't forget that."[128]

Mary becomes pregnant, and David sends her back East so she will not have to endure the winter on the plains, but he chooses not to accompany her, partly out of shame that he is still in debt.[129] When Mary returns with the new baby that spring, she learns that David cannot afford the farm equipment he needs and must trade his prized horses for oxen. It feels like a degrading concession to poverty. Time and again, Lane shows the family surviving on wits and hard work, their only recompense being their sense of pride in having lived on the awesome American frontier. "Bare endurance becomes a kind of progress," David tells himself, "when not giving up is the most that can be done."[130]

The ordeal is hardest on Mary. She despises the prairie, with its dust, debt, and dullness. "Weeping furiously in the shelter of her sunbonnet," she confesses, "I hate it, every bit of it. If it wasn't for David—but I hate it so, I can't hardly stand it!"[131] In her boredom and wretchedness, she and David begin to quarrel, and he briefly considers leaving her for another woman. Mary is so exhausted she hardly has strength to argue with him. When she becomes pregnant a second time, she hits rock bottom. "We're going to have another baby," she groans. "I wish I was dead."[132]

Yet in the spring, the family goes out for a picnic (they can only afford to make a few sandwiches out of cold beans and molasses) and they relish the beautiful scenery. "That was a perfect hour. No more troubles than shadows were under that blaze of sun. . . . The sun's heat quivered through muscles and bones, the whole earth was alive in heat, the grasses and the insects were in tune."[133] That is their only reward, and it is enough. Aware that many other families are worse off than they are, Mary admits that their deprivations are "storing up" for better days in the future.[134] The novel reaches its subtle climax when the time comes to decide whether to sign a new mortgage and stay on the land. Mary signs without hesitation, and David is surprised.

She put away the ink and pen and went on peeling potatoes while he blew on the writing to dry it. He said finally, "I appreciate you signing this."

She began scooping up the potatoes from the rinse water and dropping them into the kettle. "I don't know's I ever told you, David, I made up my mind the winter Davy was born, back east and you out here snowed in, that if I ever got back to you I was going to stay with you through thick and thin. No matter what happened."[135]

The novel ends with a visit from David's parents. Embarrassed at their destitution, David borrows more money to spruce up the homestead before they arrive, but James is not fooled. When David confesses that he is deep in debt, James decides to give him $2,000, enough to pay off everything. "Ever since you young ones was born to mother and me," James tells him, "I wanted you to have an easier time than we did."[136]

Heavily influenced by Lane's reading of *The Rise of American Civilization* and her own aborted *The Name Is Mizzoury*, *Free Land* was intended as a portrait of the frontier character. David is self-reliant and industrious, with a "pig-headed" stubbornness and hard-won common sense that focuses on making a living out of the earth.[137] That stubbornness—not financial success—is the novel's theme, for at the end, David has not actually prevailed; he remains almost as poor as he was to start with. His triumph lies not in profit, but in his deserved pride at having earned his bread by the sweat of his brow.

For this reason, *Free Land* is not only a resilience novel, like *Let the Hurricane Roar* and the *Little House* books, but also a reverse of the proletarian novels being published at the time. Where proletarian literature focused on the need for revolution to liberate the oppressed working class from capitalist domination, Lane's novel highlights the psychological values of self-reliance and perseverance in the American common man. David represents an entire society and culture, but his triumph is his own, and it consists of pursuing his own happiness through hard work and respect for his neighbors, not class solidarity or social consciousness. In fact, Lane's Beaton family is the exact opposite of the Joad family in John Steinbeck's proletarian novel *The Grapes of Wrath*, which appeared less than a year later. The Joads flee their farm, and in the process lose their most precious possession—their selves—at the hands of irresistible social and economic forces. They see their sole hope of salvation in mutual servitude, as symbolized by the famous climax in which the daughter, Rose, suckles a starving man with her breastmilk—almost literally submitting herself to be cannibalized. The Beatons, by contrast, stay on the land, and although, like the Joads, they remain poor at the end of their story, they feel a deserved sense of achievement at having survived the test. They are *un*-beaten.[138]

Thus *Free Land* makes a political statement—it replies to the Beards' version of history—but does so as part of its portrayal of the distinctively individualistic nature of what Lane called the ongoing American Revolution. The same year it was published, Lane authored a magazine article urging American mothers not to send their children to college because they would get "no experience in actual life" there, nor face any situation in which they "must depend upon [their] own efforts, where bare survival may exhaust [their] last ounce of determination and creative energy, where success demands fierce resolution, self-discipline, concentration, and where it is man's business to attack his environment and change it."[139] *Free Land* sought to fill that void. Thus its title had multiple meanings. It was not only an ironic answer to those who referred to the homesteaders as beneficiaries of handouts, but also a reference to the harsh process whereby the land actually *freed* the people.

This view was to prove a lasting source of controversy. Lane's detractors claimed—and still claim—that westward expansion was only made possible through government subsidies, and that farmers survived hard times by sacrificing their pretenses to individualism. This, it is asserted, disproves the novel's thesis. In 2017, literary scholar Caroline Fraser condemned *Free Land* for "glossing over individuals' responsibility for embarking on complex agricultural enterprises without the capital to pay for them,"[140] and argued that, contrary to Lane's rhetoric, settlers actually resorted to "socialism" to survive.[141] Yet the book was never intended as an economic defense of the Homestead Act. Indeed, some critics at the time saw it as a "harsh critique" of the act.[142] Instead, Lane meant *Free Land* as an account of the costs of such land, and a refutation of the claim that the frontier had created prosperity, as many New Deal economists claimed.[143]

As for frontier "socialism," Fraser's examples consist not of actual socialism—which means state ownership of the means of production—but of "cooperative ventures" such as "creameries, grain elevators, and warehouses."[144] Lane, however, never denied that western settlers found voluntary and cooperative means such as these to ease the risks of frontier living. On the contrary, she celebrated that fact as one of liberty's benefits. "America is producing an infinity of experiments," she wrote in the *Saturday Evening Post* months after *Free Land* appeared. "Everywhere, new social mechanisms created in this country meet the candid eye; mutual banking, insurance, countless methods of profit sharing and of ownership distribution, farmers' and consumers' cooperatives, innumerable forms of labor-management relationships, of community action, of free association for mutual aid."[145] She regarded these as blessings. What she opposed was the New Deal's effort to supplant such community-based, voluntary forms of assistance with a national, compulsory welfare state. She differentiated between what she called "neighborliness" or "cooperation"—which she considered essential frontier virtues—and "duty to others" or "community spirit," which she viewed as perverse and artificial New Deal substitutes.[146] Mutual assistance was compatible with freedom; a culture of dependence supported by government-mandated redistribution was not. In fact, Lane put so much emphasis on the virtue of aiding others in need that both Paterson and Rand would later distance themselves from her, fearing that her rhetoric sounded too much like collectivism.

Fraser also claims that Lane "never questioned the gullibility" of homesteaders who typically failed in their efforts.[147] But the opposite is true: Lane acknowledged in *Free Land* that the Homestead Act was a form of government aid and that most homesteaders failed.[148] Far from "glossing over" the question of responsibility, the entire point of the novel was to show where that responsibility properly fell—and to dramatize the virtues of those who accepted it rather than shirking it. That was why *Free Land* stressed the importance of family. David gives up his infatuation with another woman in light of his responsibility toward his wife and children. His father lends him money and pays his debts out of a sense of family commitment. As for his responsibility for embarking on a complex enterprise without capital, he and his extended family bear that responsibility themselves, rather than expecting others to shoulder it as a matter of duty.

In one telling passage early in the book, David muses about the experiences of his own ancestors and uses that thought to steady himself through a particularly rough time. "He reflected that this grass was nothing to the forest that his grandfather had cleared." He has a good plow and access to supplies via the railroad that his forebears never enjoyed. "It had taken his grandfather three years to put the plow to land which it would merely scratch because of the great roots."[149] David rallies his spirits with the thought of what his family survived. *Free Land* aimed to rally readers' spirits through a similar act of homage: celebrating character traits that saw previous generations through hard times, and that were under assault in 1930s from intellectuals who viewed individualism as obsolete and had little compunction about creating a mendicant class of Americans.

▰▰

Free Land became a best seller, and its success earned Lane enough money to buy a house in Danbury, Connecticut, only 20 miles from Isabel Paterson's home in Stamford. Soon they began exchanging visits, sometimes spending weekends together, listening to the radio, and discussing all manner of subjects—religious, political, historical, and literary. Lane admired Paterson almost without reservation, often transcribing their conversations in her diary as though they were too precious to let go. Paterson, in turn, enjoyed printing Lane's remarks in "Turns." She liked Lane's ironic sense of humor, although she was sometimes put off by Lane's habit of free-association talking—"she just wanders off in all directions," she once told Rand[150]—and was bothered by her tendency to say what sounded right, without thinking through the implications. She was also troubled by Lane's habit of exaggerating.[151] In *Never Ask the End*, in which Lane appears as the character Donna, Paterson described her as "rattling on," and "possess[ing] a constructive memory."[152] These things would eventually contribute to their falling out.

But Paterson could be grating, too. One day, she dropped by while Lane was still moving into her house and noticed some books lying unpacked in boxes. While she examined the titles, Lane explained that she had set that box aside because she intended to tell her contractor to paint the bookshelves a blue that matched the covers. Somehow, Paterson got the impression that Lane bought books based on the colors of their jackets, and teased her about it for years, much to Lane's annoyance.[153] It became the first example of what Lane called a habit in Paterson of stubbornly seizing on misimpressions and not letting them go even when corrected.

In May 1938, Paterson attended a party at Lane's house to celebrate *Free Land*'s release, along with their friends journalist Isaac Don Levine and his wife Ruth.[154] Newspapers from coast to coast were praising it as "gripping," "thrilling," and "stirring"; the *New York Times* even said it deserved a Pulitzer Prize.[155] Yet Paterson protested that many reviewers seemed to miss its central point, which was contained in Lane's ironic title. The novel, she explained, was aimed at demonstrating that "'free land' cost the settler as much as if he had paid for the same acreage in developed country." She hoped the book would "expose the falsity of the perennial statement of amateur economists that 'the frontier' and free land was formerly the remedy which pulled us out of depressions, and therefore, since that recourse no longer exists, we have to have a totalitarian state." Paterson knew firsthand that the frontier had not been a source of easy wealth but was "a long-term investment, if it *was* an investment." In fact, settling the West had usually drained capital rather than generating profit. During hard times, "people came back from the frontier instead of going there."[156]

"The lot of those pioneers in Dakota was preferable to the lot of any protected individual under any totalitarian state," Lane told a reporter that summer, but "it was not an easy lot. It meant fighting, standing the gaff on tough things. But in the end it meant roads, houses, electric refrigeration, automobiles." People were facing a similar struggle now. "You can see families moving on to new areas today, their goods in a wheelbarrow, their food nothing but carrots. They face loneliness, illness, taxes. They don't know what will come of it. Neither do we. . . . But we do know the American spirit is constant."[157] The novel resonated with readers because it was not a political tract, let alone a Pollyanna tale, but a resilience novel—a work of literature that celebrated the struggles and sympathized with the failures of an American family in the often-painful sweep of history. It was, Lane said, a "literary effort toward making the American spirit more self-conscious by explaining it to itself in rationally intelligible terms."[158]

▰▲▰

Paterson was taking her own look at the self-reliant character in the novel she was then writing, titled *If It Prove Fair Weather*. Intended as a love story—she even declared it, with some grandiosity, "the only love story ever written"[159]— the book also reflected Paterson's concerns about the change in the American psyche, particularly the male psyche, which she had observed over the previous decade. "Modern men," she wrote in "Turns," seemed to be displaying a quality of "uncertainty" that she had never seen before the Depression. "It isn't an 'economic' or political problem," she thought. "It is really personal and psychological." Men naturally sought a sense of challenge and of "mastery of the material world through intelligence." In ancient days, they had satisfied this need through military valor. That was no longer considered worthy in modern society, yet modernity offered men no real substitute. The only obvious one—entrepreneurialism—was scorned and treated as vulgar by cultural leaders. "Hence the most able and intelligent men are the least heard in our time, and the incompetent and unintelligent grab dictatorships and start drilling for war as a means of aggrandizing their egos."[160] The industrialists and explorers of the 19th century seemed to have disappeared, replaced by bureaucrats and seekers after privilege—as if all the nation's men had been "mysteriously turned into trolls overnight."[161]

She had touched on this matter briefly in *The Golden Vanity*—"There were far too many women in the world," reflects Charlotte Siddall toward the end of that book, "and no men at all"[162]—but where *The Golden Vanity* had viewed the change in male character through the eyes of its three female protagonists, *Fair Weather* is the story of one woman, Emmy Cruger (a transparent stand-in for Paterson herself). Emmy is having a tepid and uncertain love affair with a married man named James Wishart, who, although smitten with her, resists actually taking her to bed. He writes her letters that are carefully designed not to incriminate him in the event that they are discovered, and he avoids either making any serious commitment to her or breaking things off entirely. Emmy, too, cannot bring herself to end the relationship, because she loves him. Yet his dithering makes her feel slightly ashamed even of that.

Matters become more complicated when a new man, Jervis Huntley, enters the picture. He is assertive and laconic, where Wishart is noncommittal—their names suggest that where James merely wishes, Jervis pursues—and he and Emmy begin an affair of their own. But they do not love each other, and their relationship evaporates. Long afterward, Wishart reappears and invites Emmy to lunch. His wife, he explains, has been diagnosed with cancer, and he seeks to end the affair with Emmy that was never consummated to begin with. Repulsed by what she sees as Wishart's blend of self-righteousness and timidity, she refuses his farewell gift and sits bitterly through their final meal. She cannot actually despise him because her feelings were genuine, yet the entire experience leaves her feeling hollow.

Emptiness, in fact, pervades the novel. More even than *The Golden Vanity*, the book exudes an overwhelming sense of loss—not so much the loss of a world, but of manhood and conviction. Paterson's exasperation at a culture in which nobody seems to act on principle, even on a wrong principle, becomes clear in one passage in which Emmy fears she might "yield through lassitude" to Wishart's inept romantic signals.[163] That, she thinks, would be "to love without delight," and "nothing could be worse."[164] She longs for a world where people do what *matters* to them, rather than surrendering to what seems inevitable.

Paterson is at her best in creating a sense of place and interlacing her characters' inner thoughts with their spoken words. These and other effects skillfully draw the reader into Emmy's own mind. As with *The Golden Vanity*, *If It Prove Fair Weather* is shot through with melancholy and nostalgia, as when Emmy stares into her mirror and becomes "aware of its illusory, shadowy depths, as if it were a door into some timeless region, where, if they could pass through, there would be no limitations, nothing but themselves."[165] Yet the novel lacks a strong plot or admirable characters, and it fails in its ambition to depict the theme of love, given that none of the characters are shown to actually share any mutual values or enthusiasm, beyond a vaguely described sense of affection.

Critics were harsh. They saw little romance in the book and were puzzled by Wishart's indecisive pursuit of Emmy. Readers, one said, "will be more confused" than the characters themselves.[166] Another declared that "Miss Paterson, who reviews books herself and ought to know, calls this a love story. Doubtless she has her reasons. . . . This isn't a love story. . . . Merely following Miss Paterson's rambling and sidelong style is at times real work."[167] Another simply concluded that she was "not gifted as a novelist."[168]

Paterson defended her book in an essay in the *Saturday Review*, which urged readers to sympathize with her characters' dilemmas.[169] "Human beings are inevitably in an appalling predicament between their emotions and their obligations," she argued. "The two elements are not even conveniently distinct, but inextricably snarled in a cat's-cradle. And the more you try to untangle it, the worse it becomes." Wishart's uncertainty toward Emmy and his sense of his obligations as a husband were the consequences of a genuine ethical conundrum. If a man found himself in love with a woman not his wife, conventional morality told him that it was his "duty to repress and restrain such feelings," which "sounds very lofty" but was still unsatisfactory because it left the husband caring for his wife out of a sense of compulsion rather than genuine affection. "It is not so nice to be the recipient of duty." But the alternative—"to discard the inconvenient obligations and go ahead on the new path," which "twenty years ago" had been "thought to be a complete answer"—was no longer acceptable. Doing that only left behind "a trail of wreckage."[170] In fact, the entire idea of combining love with duty, or marrying someone "out of sheer altruism," was repulsive.

As for women, Paterson thought them largely responsible for the dilemma modern men faced. They claimed to admire the masculine senses of duty and honor, but in truth, they did not. "When a woman might have to think whether her husband must put his duty or herself first, she really believes he ought to do both, and could if he put his mind to it."[171] This and the cultural shift away from individualism—especially the scorn contemporary culture leveled against businessmen—were causing modern society to lose its sense of what masculinity meant. "Whatever a man's occupation," she wrote in *Fair Weather*, "his success derives from his virile quality, his faith in himself."[172] Yet in contemporary society, businessmen were typically treated as dullards, crooks, or Babbitts. Paterson thought this perverse. Business was "sheer imagination, the creative factor responsible for a world so complex, so fantastic, that it has us dazed. Nobody knows how it works. Even the men who do it don't know. And the ones who can't want to pull it down."[173]

Paterson often stressed this point. Quoting some lines by the Irish poet Padraic Colum ("An old man said, I saw / The chief of the things that are gone . . . / They passed, they that carried the swiftness, / And the pride of long ago") she lamented in "Turns" that "liberty, even the idea of freedom" seemed to be fading in America, replaced by an unmanly desire for "security."[174] Unless that changed, it would destroy the nation—which, after all, was only as strong as its cultural institutions. Foremost among these was individualism, which had to be fostered by a society that honored and rewarded its wealth creators.

In other words, Paterson was arguing for what economist Deirdre McCloskey later termed "bourgeois dignity"—meaning a culture that celebrates the willingness to innovate, invest, toil, earn, and take economic risks.[175] These virtues can only persist if society encourages them, and Paterson thought it was the obligation of intellectuals, perhaps especially of women, to preserve that culture as part of the national spirit. In "Turns," she recounted a conversation with Lane in which the two decided that "even if liberty is lost in this country—it may not be altogether lost, but suppose it is—the unique memory of a great free country will remain, the record in history, like the intellectual achievement of Greece in its Athenian age, a light for men to struggle toward once more."[176] At a time when the virtues of productivity and enterprise were under assault, the two writers hoped at least to preserve the moral foundations of freedom.

▰

The clouds of tyranny were indeed growing darker throughout the world. Mussolini's Italy had invaded Ethiopia. In the Soviet Union, Stalin was engaged in the Great Terror, which would result in the slaughter of perhaps 1.2 million people. Civil war was raging in Spain between fascist troops supported by the Nazi dictatorship and leftist forces subsidized by Stalin's Comintern. And in Germany, *Kristallnacht* marked another step in the worsening persecution of the Jews. Lane watched these developments with dread. "Russia and Germany," she thought, were "not civilized," but represented throwbacks to a barbarian stage of political development, revivals of prehistoric social systems in which government was based on mere physical force instead of the rational rule of law.[177] She hoped America would stay out of their quarrels, and in the coming months, her alarm at the prospect of another world war would lead to her first direct participation in a political campaign.

The conflict between fascists and communists struck Lane as a clash of two evils, and the idea of "fighting for Stalin against Hitler," as she told Dorothy Thompson, seemed just as "insane" as the notion of a "fight for Hitler against Stalin to save 'democracy' for the world."[178] Thus in September 1938, when British prime minister Neville Chamberlain announced that he had reached an accommodation with Germany, Lane regarded it as preferable to any likely alternatives. If Britain went to war, she thought, the United States would almost certainly become involved, and given the drastic shift away from individualism that Americans had already experienced under the New Deal, it seemed clear that "this country would instantly [become] a dictatorship" if that happened. She thought Chamberlain's peace had "given us this war-free space of time" in which to try to preserve American liberty before it was too late.[179]

Dorothy Thompson, wife to Sinclair Lewis and one of the most
important journalists of her day. Thompson and Lane were close friends,
and possibly lovers, in the 1920s. But they found themselves at odds
when Thompson—a fierce critic of Franklin Roosevelt in the 1930s—
reversed herself and endorsed Roosevelt in 1940.

Many Americans agreed.[180] "I would leave these two scoundrels Hitler and Stalin to fight it out," wrote the Progressive California senator Hiram Johnson to his son. Rep. Hamilton Fish agreed: an alliance with Stalin against Hitler, he thought, would mean sending American soldiers to their deaths "to make the world safe for Communism." Herbert Hoover told radio listeners that America should "stand aside in watchful waiting, armed to the teeth, while these men exhaust themselves."[181] Paterson, too, could not abide the notion of joining forces with Stalin. Not only would that inevitably get blood on American hands, but it was also unnecessary. Americans would defend themselves if the country were invaded, she thought, so there was no reason to jump into a European conflict. And if the United States did eventually have to fight Hitler, she could see no advantage in assisting the Soviet dictatorship, which could not even build cars without copying plans from American companies.[182]

Dorothy Thompson, however, disagreed. In 1936, she had started publishing her column "On the Record" in Paterson's own *Herald Tribune.* Syndicated to hundreds of other newspapers around the country, and stuffed with her own wide-ranging interests and interviews, it expanded Thompson's already significant star power and served as a platform for her to sound the alarm about Hitler. She thought Chamberlain was "a dupe and a tool," and he was not the only one. Fascists—who had a surprisingly large number of supporters in America—were getting away with brutality worldwide precisely because they scared good people into thinking that the only alternative was communism. Chamberlain's arrangement with Hitler was only "a hurriedly concocted armistice made in advance of a war to permit the occupation by German troops of a territory which by sheer threat and demonstration of force they have conquered by 'agreement.'"[183]

Her repeated warnings about the Nazis were often met with hate mail, either from racists who supported the German government, or anticommunists who accused her of downplaying the Soviet threat.[184] But Thompson was no defender of Stalin. She simply thought Hitler posed the more immediate danger, and this sometimes led her to minimize the dangers communism posed.

("Russia is a country of vast area, without territorial ambitions," she wrote in one especially fanciful moment, before accusing Nazi propagandists of "seek[ing] to represent Russia as a warlike power," when there was "no evidence to support this."[185]) Nevertheless, readers often called her a communist and a warmonger, and they sent her angry letters such as the one from a mother who expressed the wish that "the first bomb dropped on the U.S. will hit your son."[186]

Thompson shared many of Lane's and Paterson's objections to the New Deal. She often warned in "On the Record" that Roosevelt was laying the groundwork for dictatorship. On one occasion, she devoted her column to quotations from a book titled *Economic Foundations of Fascism* to show that it was identical to Roosevelt's schemes.[187] Yet her intellectual inconsistencies were often glaring, and she frequently expressed herself in mushy phrases, as when she faulted the Republican Party for having "failed to mobilize the vital spirit of evolution which is the breath of every living democracy," or argued that society should be viewed as "a collective, whose power and beauty depend upon manifold activities."[188] Billed as a "liberal conservative," her equivocations were a source of tooth-grinding annoyance to Isabel Paterson. "We seldom try to figure out what Dorothy Thompson means," she declared in "Turns," "because it would be a full-time job with incommensurate results."[189] Yet she sensed that Thompson was overreacting to the threat of European fascism by advocating domestic policies that were also unjust. When it was reported that Thompson had recommended canceling the 1940 presidential election, for instance, Paterson remarked that it was "most amazing" to "read diatribes against Nazism or Fascism by people who advocate the very measures which specifically *are* Nazism."[190] And when Thompson denounced opponents of Roosevelt's welfare state programs for engaging in "pure obstruction," and argued that Republicans were obligated to offer "constructive and precise counter-proposals," Paterson replied that this was like arguing that "if we catch somebody setting our house on fire, we mustn't say stop."[191] Republicans had no duty to offer their own versions of the welfare state.

But the approach of war, and Thompson's seeming willingness to discount the Soviet threat in her campaign against Hitler, would set the stage for her unhappy falling out with Lane in May 1939. The incident involved a speech Thompson gave to a group of journalists in which she referred to a recent series of *Saturday Evening Post* articles signed by a Soviet defector named Walter Krivitsky, but cowritten by Lane and Paterson's friend Isaac Don Levine. Part of Thompson's remarks focused on the need for journalists to maintain objectivity and strict accuracy in a partisan atmosphere, and to illustrate the point, she cited the Krivitsky articles in a way that seemed to cast doubt on his credibility, and, by extension, Levine's. That, at least, was the story Lane heard, and she challenged Thompson in an angry letter for calling Levine a liar. Thompson's efforts to explain came to nothing, and Lane called off the friendship.

It was an overreaction—Thompson had not actually attacked Krivitsky or Levine—but the real source of Lane's fury was the fact that her old friend seemed to welcome the coming war, and even appeared willing to overlook Stalin's evil in order to focus on Hitler. "I see rotten trick after rotten trick, half-truth and propaganda-slant in your [column]," Lane wrote. Thompson's comments on Krivitsky and Levine were just the latest example of giving aid and comfort to communist tyranny. "Once you were a fine person," Lane concluded. "Now you are coarse and stupid."[192]

By the time she wrote these angry words, Lane had thrown herself into an effort to prevent a second world war, by amending the Constitution to require that voters preapprove the nation's entry into any overseas conflict. This was the brainchild of Louis Ludlow, an Indiana congressman who had been a reporter during World War I, and who, like many Americans, thought the Wilson administration had sent American boys to European battlefields against the nation's will, partly to enrich munitions makers and international bankers. That idea seemed to have been vindicated by a 1935 Senate investigation that concluded that Wilson's deputies had made a secret agreement with Britain promising to back the British militarily if they went to war with Germany.[193] The revelation appeared to prove that even while Wilson had campaigned for reelection on the promise to keep America out of the war, he had been covertly arranging to join it. Such a thing, Ludlow argued, must never be allowed to happen again. He drafted a constitutional amendment providing that "except in the event of an invasion of the United States or its territorial possessions and attack upon its citizens residing therein, the authority of Congress to declare war shall not become effective until confirmed by a majority of all votes cast thereon in a national referendum."

Roosevelt opposed the amendment, arguing that it would hobble international diplomacy, because other nations would feel that the United States could not back up any threats of force. He tried at first to ignore the proposal, but interest in the amendment spiked in December 1937, when Japanese forces fighting against China attacked and sank an American warship, and voters began to fear that the administration might use the incident as grounds for joining the fight in Asia. When polls showed as many as three-quarters of Americans supporting the amendment, the White House began pushing harder against it, labeling it "rigid isolationism," which was not entirely fair, since the amendment would not have reduced the size of the military or limited international economic or political relations.[194] The amendment was narrowly defeated in an important procedural vote in Congress in January 1938, but Ludlow kept campaigning for it as the Sino-Japanese War intensified. Lane's mother grew interested in Ludlow's efforts and rallied her neighbors to write their representatives about the proposal.[195] She drafted a form letter addressed "To American Mothers," urging them to support it, which Ludlow's allies sent to voters nationwide.[196] Meanwhile, Lane advocated for the amendment in a series of articles for *Woman's Day*, *Liberty*, and *Good Housekeeping*.

Her *Liberty* article began by citing the senatorial investigation about Wilson. The consequences of World War I had been "a wasted generation," she wrote, "a crumbling of religion and morals; billions owed for unpaid debts; a collapse of overexpanded farming and industry; a first war depression (in 1924); an era of frenzied speculation; a price collapse, and the real war depression, not ended yet." There was no reason why the Roosevelt administration might not take the same deceitful path, with the same tragic consequences. And since the nation's leaders had proved themselves untrustworthy, the solution was to let the people decide. A referendum requirement involved no risk to national security, since it would not apply in case of invasion. As for the argument that it would handicap the nation's diplomatic efforts by making it harder to threaten other countries, Lane thought the reverse was true: "It might strengthen our diplomacy to let the world know that when or if we should fight, we will fight with united enthusiasm, not as a divided and conscripted people."[197]

The article drew a reply from Eleanor Roosevelt a week later. The idea that elected officials cannot be trusted "does not seem to me a very realistic viewpoint," she declared. If Americans do not trust politicians, "our remedy is to watch them more closely and keep them better informed as to our opinions." Besides, if war was so important that it required a national referendum, why not require the same for other, equally important matters, such as laws relating to health care, or even traffic laws? After all, more Americans die in car accidents than in war. More importantly, government officials are privy to secret information that ordinary citizens do not know, which meant a referendum might result in foolhardy choices by voters unaware of real threats. "No, Miss Lane," the first lady concluded. "I want no Ludlow Amendment and I want people to believe in their representative form of government. . . . If we cannot trust our representatives, then I think we cannot trust ourselves."[198]

Laura Ingalls Wilder was delighted by her daughter's article. It was "great, so plain and fair and true." Roosevelt's, by contrast, was an attempt "to scare people" by ignoring the fact that the amendment would not require a vote if the nation were attacked. "I simply gnashed my teeth when I read [it]," she told Lane. "My opinion is that Roosevelt has already made his secret agreement [with England] and Eleanor knows it. Your article touched them in a tender spot. . . . I am scared about what we are coming to."[199]

On May 10, 1939, Lane appeared before the U.S. Senate Judiciary Committee alongside American Civil Liberties Union attorney Morris Ernst to testify in favor of the amendment. "I am not a pacifist," she began. "I am a revolutionist, and I advocate this amendment as a measure which seems to me essential for the preservation of the principles of the American Revolution." The bedrock of that revolution was individual liberty, which could only be secured by a system of checks and balances. The Ludlow Amendment was simply "another check upon government, in line with the fundamental American method." In an argument she probably borrowed from Paterson, she pointed out that the Second Amendment, with its reference to a "well-regulated militia," showed that the Founding Fathers had expected "that the attitude of the American people toward a war would be voluntary."[200] The word "militia" referred to "a free corps of volunteer fighters," fighters who "refused to obey orders if [they] did not like them." But that safeguard against war making had been destroyed in the modern era, with its national conscript army—and that made it all the more necessary that the public enjoy some new "veto power" over any decision to fight. In theory, Congress's authority to declare war should have provided this protection, but the Senate's findings about the Wilson agreement showed why that was inadequate. At this point, New Mexico senator Carl Hatch interrupted. "Congress really reflects the attitude of the President: is that your feeling?"

"My feeling," Lane replied, "is that Congress—I do not know what happened. The American people did not know what happened. The power of the Executive grows to an extent that is alarming. . . . I cannot believe that Congress in 1917, without pressure and emotional pressure, perhaps—that in its sane mind Congress would have declared war in 1917. Look at the pressures—"

Now Idaho senator William Borah spoke up. "Are you sure the people will follow the President or follow Congress?"

"That is the question," she answered. "I do not know. . . . I do not want to leave to any body of men who are capable of evading the great responsibility of acting as protectors and defenders of the greatest freedom in earth—I do not want to leave to them the question involved in this matter."

Bothered by Lane's description of herself as a "revolutionist," which could be easily mischaracterized in the press, Borah tried to correct her. "Would it not have been better to call it 'Americanism'?" But Lane would not be deterred. "I prefer to call it a revolution, because it stands in opposition to everything else in the world; it is a new thing."

"In that respect it is Americanism," Borah maintained.

"In that respect it is Americanism, yes," Lane persisted. "But I think of it as a revolution; and it must stand, if not against the rest of the world, against the counter-revolution existing in this country."

Struggling to avoid handing rhetorical ammunition to the amendment's opponents, Borah tried again. "If we get Americanism, that is enough, is it not?"

"I think this amendment contributes to it, because I think it protects the liberty of the people," answered Lane, "and because a man cannot be put into his uniform against his will."

"We certainly have no business over there, so far as Americanism is concerned," Borah concluded, and the committee adjourned.[201]

Although Lane's insistence on calling herself a "revolutionist" discomfited the senators, she used that word deliberately because she was trying to speak in fundamental terms. She had explained what she meant in a January *Saturday Evening Post* article in which she argued that the term "liberal" was being abused by Roosevelt's supporters. True liberalism meant the defense of individual freedom, not support for government bureaucracy and compulsory regimentation. Freedom meant personal choice, the very opposite of the "disciplined and simple order" that New Deal planners were imposing. Their version of "order" was essentially reactionary, a throwback to an ancient, illiberal conception that viewed people as mere tools of society. That stood in contrast to the American system, which was based on the principle that people are self-directed beings, with a right to run their own lives. *This* was the truly "revolutionary" idea in the history of politics.[202]

But only four months after her trip to Washington, everything in the world changed. On September 1, 1939, Lane wrote in her diary, "Germany takes Poland. England will fight."[203] The war she and Paterson had expected for so long was about to begin.

Playwright Channing Pollock helped introduce Ayn Rand to
Isabel Paterson in 1940.

7

The Dark Horse

Two days after Germany invaded Poland, President Roosevelt told Americans that joining the war was the furthest thing from his mind. In a radio address two days after the attack, he insisted that the United States "will remain a neutral nation" and "no man or woman" should "thoughtlessly or falsely talk of America sending its armies to European fields."[1] But in truth, his administration was already finding ways to arm the forces fighting Germany, and Roosevelt—persuaded that Americans would soon have to enter the war themselves—decided to run for a third term so he would be in office when that happened. This, too, he kept secret.

One reason for his duplicity was that some Republicans thought they might have a chance at the White House in 1940, given that two full terms of New Dealing had still not cured the Depression. Even the president admitted that a third of the people remained "ill-housed, ill-clad, and ill-nourished."[2] But few Republicans could compete with Roosevelt on the campaign trail. He remained popular, thanks in part to his ebullient personality, in part to his careful image management, and in part to outright payments to political supporters. Although the Hatch Act of 1939 put some limits on the administration's use of federal funds for political purposes, it came only after half a dozen years of patronage and payoffs had entrenched the Democrats and cut deeply into Republican support. Nor would it become illegal until after his death for labor unions—among Roosevelt's most steadfast supporters—to donate directly to candidates' campaigns.

For opponents of the New Deal, the prospect of a third term seemed like another step toward dictatorship. The traditional two-term limit—not made part of the Constitution until 1951—had been challenged before, notably by the president's cousin Theodore, whose 1912 campaign had made a respectable showing. But with the New Deal having already obliterated so many cultural and legal precedents, some feared a third term would effectively end legal democracy.

Isabel Paterson was hardly surprised when Roosevelt announced in the summer of 1940 that he was prepared to run again. She had predicted it four years before, calling him the "permanent nominee" of the Democratic Party.[3] Now she forecast that he would play coy, "hesitat[ing] modestly" before arranging to "be 'drafted.'"[4] She was right: Roosevelt spent months refusing to confirm or deny his interest in a third term—thereby effectively preventing any other Democrat from mounting a campaign—and then saw to it that delegates at the party's July convention nominated him in his absence, thus creating the impression that breaking the two-term precedent was their idea, not his.[5]

That May, Lane and her friends Isaac Don Levine and Ruth Levine dropped by Paterson's house to admire her garden. Lane was on the edge of panic at the thought of war, writing in her diary that she was seriously considering suicide. She was convinced that if America joined the war, the nation would descend into dictatorship and perhaps armed revolution. Thus she was shocked to discover that the Levines seemed to want America to join the war. The Nazis had just attacked France, and that day she affronted the Levines by saying that she still thought it was not an American concern. "Don says, [the attack on France] means we go in," she recorded in her diary. "Japan will attack the Dutch East Indies. Hitler will seize Brazil. F.D.R. will *certainly* be reelected." The Levines welcomed that development, and when Lane resisted, "they both (Ruth and Don) turned against me three times." Ruth tried to explain that they felt so strongly because of their Jewish ancestry, but this made no sense to Lane. "Ruth, you are no more Jewish than I am English," she said. "We are *Americans*."[6]

Lane had not meant to sound callous or anti-Semitic—on the contrary, she considered anti-Semitism a "threat to the safety of every American" and "an attack on the foundations of this Republic."[7] But she thought of Americans as a distinct people regardless of their ancestry. For the Levines to distinguish themselves from her on the basis of their Jewish roots stung her as an assertion of "differentness, apartness."[8] Naturally, it was not so simple to the Levines. As the European war intensified, it became increasingly difficult to stake out a position against American involvement that was not at least insensitive to the plight of the Jews.

The confrontation with the Levines must have been especially painful, given that Lane had recently ended her relationship with Dorothy Thompson over what she thought was an affront to Don Levine's honor. In fact, both quarrels were largely consequences of her terror at the prospect of war. Lane's and Thompson's views had grown so different by that time that in October, Thompson abruptly endorsed Roosevelt's third-term bid, after having spent all summer supporting his opponent, Wendell Willkie. She had backed Willkie, where she could not support other Republicans, because he appeared to reject the GOP's anti-interventionist position, and his flip-flop on that issue late in the campaign instantly caused her to revoke her endorsement. In a column published days before the election, she called Roosevelt—whom she had recently characterized as a type of fascist—"a man of peace" who had proven himself "a great man in 1933." She singled out for particular praise his willingness to become "the first President in our whole history to dare call for conscription in the midst of an election campaign."[9]

Disgusted, Paterson wrote in "Turns" that Thompson's U-turn only proved the foolishness of joining any group solely on the grounds that it opposed Nazism. "On such premises, the joiner will soon find himself committed to 'leadership' demanding—we quote Miss Dorothy Thompson—'for President Roosevelt the power and authority completely to organize the economic and moral strength of this country' on 'a total war footing.' What more did Hitler ever ask? What more is there *to* ask?"[10] There was no point

Frank Lloyd Wright's career helped inspire *The Fountainhead*, although Rand later said his philosophical views were "almost the opposite" of her own.

in opposing dictatorship by imitating it, Paterson thought. Besides, American involvement in the war was impractical. "Japan will not attack our Navy," she told Lane one evening as they listened to the news together. And there was nothing the United States could realistically do about Germany. "If England and France lose, are Americans to declare a new war and reconquer all Europe?" Hitler had to know that destroying the capitalist nations would be "inherently suicidal," because the "essential base" of modern civilization "is liberty and private property." Even if Germany did manage to conquer the world, it "*can* not live."[11]

Yet over the following weeks, horror at the war news reduced Lane to transcribing into her diary the radio reports she heard about the retreat of the free nations. The rapidity with which semisocialist countries such as France and the Netherlands fell before the Nazi onslaught only seemed to confirm her and Paterson's views about the way bureaucratization rendered societies impotent. "The Allies have not fought," Paterson told her, because they were so "rotten with collectivism, [made] false by the Marxian lie."[12] It was "characteristic of these times," she thought, that "rulers are paper-minded men, with no experience of making things work."[13]

Despite everything, Roosevelt maintained throughout the election that a third term would not mean an American war. He claimed he had asked Congress for more military spending and a draft only to prepare defenses. Lane did not believe it, putting conspicuous quotation marks around the word "defenses" when noting this in her diary. When France collapsed in June, she recorded "panic in Washington" and talk of giving "Gestapo power to [the] FBI." "The whole world," she concluded, "is mad."[14]

Thus as she helplessly copied the horrifying news in her journals, Lane began to doubt the long-term viability of freedom herself. "I ask 'myself,' may it be possible that the whole effort of human freedom was a mistake? that the effort is too great for the results, which after all are too largely material?"[15] As autumn came, despair hung over her. She found it impossible to work and could not even write the review of Paterson's *If It Prove Fair Weather* that she had promised the *Herald Tribune*.[16] When Congress adopted a conscription bill that September—the first peacetime draft in American history—she wrote in her diary that "liberty is extinguished on the whole earth."[17]

▰

Yet although she seems never to have realized it, Lane was actually in the midst of producing her greatest literary achievement: her collaboration with her mother on the *Little House* series. The fourth volume, *On the Banks of Plum Creek*, had received a Newberry Honor in 1938, as had its successor, *By the Shores of Silver Lake*, in 1939. Then in June 1940, they published *The Long Winter*, which covered Laura Ingalls Wilder's experiences during the legendary blizzards of 1880–1881, when she was 14.

That winter was infamous for its massive snowstorms, which began in October and continued with only brief intermissions until April. Railroad companies, unable to clear their tracks, had suspended service for months, cutting off settlers' supplies and contact with the outside world. Crops were destroyed and thousands of cattle killed. Settlers were forced to survive on what supplies they had stored. As with the previous novels, *The Long Winter* detailed these events while incorporating principles of individual freedom and responsibility that Wilder and Lane thought were under attack in the New Deal era. The works were not didactic, but written in ways that dramatized these values in the lives of the Ingalls family as they labored to establish their farm.

The novel opens in the autumn of 1880, with the family living in a shanty on land that Charles Ingalls is claiming under the Homestead Act. To prove up their claim and gain title, the Ingallses must reside there for five years and improve it. Working in the fields one day, Pa finds a muskrat house. He shows it to Laura, pointing out that it resembles a human habitation—and that its thick walls indicate that the animal somehow senses an especially severe winter coming. "How can the muskrats know?" Laura asks, to which he replies that God tells them through their inborn instincts. Why then, Laura wonders, does God not tell human beings?

"Because," said Pa, "we're not animals. We're humans, and, like it says in the Declaration of Independence, God created us free. That means we got to take care of ourselves."

Laura said faintly, "I thought God takes care of us."

"He does," Pa said, "so far as we do what's right. And He gives us a conscience and brains to know what's right. But He leaves it to us to do as we please. That's the difference between us and everything else in creation."

"Can't muskrats do what they please?" Laura asked, amazed.

"No," said Pa. "I don't know why they can't but you can see they can't. Look at that muskrat house. Muskrats have to build that kind of house. They always have and they always will. It's plain they can't build any other kind. But folks build all kinds of houses. A man can build any kind of house he can think of. So if his house don't keep out the weather, that's *his* look-out; he's free and independent."[18]

This passage is a condensed version of an argument Lane would make for the rest of her life about the nature of individual liberty. Political freedom is not a function of mere cultural preference or tradition, but "a fact"—an inescapable quality of human nature.[19] Humanity's possession of rationality and free will, as opposed to the muskrat's instinct, means people can only survive by applying reason to the challenges of existence. That requires that they be free to think for themselves and enjoy the rewards of wise choices or bear the costs of unwise ones. Humans need freedom the same way muskrats need water and grass.

Alarmed by other signs that a bad winter is approaching, Pa decides to move the family into town, where they will be safer in the event of severe weather. In October, his forebodings prove justified when the storms hit. The Ingallses eventually use up their firewood and are forced to use hay instead— which requires them to keep constantly at work twisting it into thick braids that will burn slowly. The work is drudgery, and food supplies run so low that eventually they must grind what little wheat they have in a tabletop coffee mill to prepare bread. At last, the wheat, too, runs out.

Left with no alternative, Pa makes his way through the snowstorms to a store maintained by Royal and Almanzo Wilder, bachelor brothers who live across the road. He knows Almanzo (later to become Laura's husband) has hidden his "seed wheat" to preserve it for planting next season, and he is determined to buy some. Almanzo is equally determined not to sell and has concealed the wheat behind a false wall in the store. When Royal teases him about hiding it, Almanzo explains: "They'll bid up prices sky-high before a train gets through. I'll be out hauling hay or somewhere and you'll figure that I wouldn't refuse such a price, or you'll think you know better than I do what's for my best interests. . . . I'm nailing up my seed wheat so nobody'll see it and nobody'll bring up any question about it and it'll be right here when seedtime comes."[20]

Almanzo's stubborn refusal to use or sell his seed wheat echoes a common Depression-era metaphor about the dangers of foolhardy government spending. In explaining the difference between capital goods and consumption goods, economists of the period often used stock seed as an example: farmers keep it to plant the next year's crops, and eat or sell only the gains that exceed those savings. To consume one's stock seed would endanger the future of one's farm. Government spending is analogous to consuming the stock seed because it is financed by taxes (such as the "undistributed profits tax") extracted from wealth creators, or by borrowing (which turns into inflation and deprives existing dollars of their value), and is therefore a means of confiscating savings that are needed for investment. That endangers all future prosperity.[21]

In *The Long Winter*, Almanzo prudently refuses to touch his seed wheat even when the town's food supplies dwindle. But when Charles Ingalls appears at his store with an empty pail, having run out of every scrap of food, he relents and lets Ingalls have some. Such charity is not sustainable, however—Almanzo cannot afford to feed the whole town—so he decides to walk to a farm a few miles south that is rumored to have more grain in storage, and buy some to supply the villagers. Royal urges him not to, because the storms are too fierce. But Almanzo insists. "I'm free and independent," he tells his brother. "I do as I please."[22] Royal decides to go along. After a treacherous journey, they arrive at the farm, only to find the owner is equally reluctant to let go of his wheat. Eventually, he agrees to sell at an exorbitant price—he'll plant oats next year, instead—and Almanzo returns home a hero. Like "Country Jake" in *Old Home Town*, he has demonstrated the kind of entrepreneurial risk taking that enables people to survive crises and even to prosper.

But when another storekeeper in town tries to sell the wheat at an even higher price, the townspeople lose their temper. They burst into the store in a fury, intending to take it. Charles Ingalls calms the crowd, but tells the manager that while they won't seize it by force, they will remember his stinginess and boycott his business when spring comes. At that threat, the storekeeper backs down and sells the wheat to the people at cost. The lesson is clear: self-reliance and mutual aid reinforce each other.

One of the finest of the resilience novel genre, *The Long Winter* is at once thrilling in its details and elegant in its language and pacing. Its characters are both realistic and stylized in ways that articulate values—values that Wilder scholar John Miller identifies as "hard work, deferred gratification, self-control, community, respect for the authority of teachers and parents, deference to the wisdom of elders, and the blessings of harmonious, cooperative families." And it is all done in a way that is engaging and memorable for both adults and children. It is bizarre, continues Miller, that Lane's detractors have come to label these values "conservative," which if anything is "shortchanging [to] liberals."[23] Lane and Wilder considered them fundamentally *American* virtues—elements of a culture of self-reliance that they believed was under assault.

◢▲◣

Although Alf Landon had never stood much chance against Roosevelt in 1936, some hoped Republicans could rally four years later. Yet the party's leadership was still notably lacking. The two most likely candidates for the party's nomination in 1940 were Ohio senator Robert Taft, the GOP's elder statesman, and the respected Michigan senator Arthur Vandenburg, an eloquent New Deal opponent whom Sinclair Lewis had used as a model for one of his anti-fascist heroes in *It Can't Happen Here*.[24] Both, however, were well-known for their insistence that the United States should take no part in the European war, a position that looked increasingly untenable in light of growing fascist belligerence. France fell to the Nazis only days before the Republican convention, and party insiders decided that nominating an anti-war nominee would be political suicide.

Instead, they turned to Wendell Willkie, a businessman with virtually no political experience, who only two years before had been a registered Democrat. Young and enthusiastic, Willkie enjoyed intellectual conversation, but had little aptitude for political theory, and was at most only a tepid opponent of the New Deal. He also had a tendency toward amateurish rhetoric and gaffes. When Roosevelt transferred some American warships to British control without legal authority, Willkie called it "the most arbitrary and dictatorial action ever taken by any President in the history of the United States," an exaggeration that hurt his credibility.[25] On another occasion he claimed that Roosevelt had secretly negotiated to turn over Czechoslovakia to Hitler.[26] Many found his boyish nature charming, but that counted little against an experienced campaigner like Roosevelt.

Paterson knew Willkie. In fact, he was carrying on an affair with her boss, Irita Van Doren, and he attended at least one of Paterson's weekly salons at the *Herald Tribune* offices. She apparently saw him often, and he even published some reviews in the paper's book section.[27] His relationship with Van Doren was politically advantageous because she was close to the *Trib's* publishers, Ogden and Helen Reid, who were influential in the Republican Party and who, along with other prominent Republican media figures, were looking to back a candidate who rejected the party's noninterventionist position on the war. Willkie also impressed magazine publishers Russell Davenport and Henry Luce when he engaged in an on-air debate with Attorney General Robert Jackson and law professor Felix Frankfurter about the administration's regulatory policies.[28] Other Republicans might have done the same, but unlike them, Willkie also advocated helping the British "in every way we can, short of declaring war." When Taft suggested that it made no difference who won the war in Europe, Willkie called him "blind, foolish, and silly."[29]

Such comments made Willkie seem, in the summer of 1940, a viable candidate for those who opposed the administration domestically but were willing to fight the Nazis.

Willkie opened his campaign with a solid statement about domestic policy—defending the "desirability" of private profit and pointing out that "a planned economy calls for rigid control of prices and production; and this control in turn leads to the suppression of civil freedom." In a series of articles in the *Atlantic Monthly*, the *Saturday Evening Post*, and the *Trib*, he argued that New Dealers had put the nation's economy in a "straightjacket," which might be enough to "keep a man out of trouble," but was "not a suitable garment in which to work." After years of "strict regulation and taxation of industry," he noted, the administration still had "as many people unemployed as at the beginning of the period." What was needed was a reduction in government meddling and more freedom for businesses to expand.[30]

Lane had reservations about Willkie, but she had a hard time articulating why. When she heard his first campaign speech, she was disappointed and confided to Paterson that she had a gut instinct he could never beat Roosevelt. Why? Paterson demanded—but Lane could not explain. It was just a feeling, she said, and given that most voters based their choices on feelings, and she was a typical Middle American, her inarticulable hunch was a dangerous portent.[31] Paterson thought the comment bizarre; years later, she would cite it as proof that Lane acted on emotions instead of logic. It would prove to be one of the first cracks in their friendship.

◣▲◥

One of those who volunteered to work on Willkie's presidential campaign was Ayn Rand, now living in New York and taking a break from the novel she had begun writing four years before.

After the success of *Night of January 16th*, she had hoped a stage version of *We the Living* might attract audiences. But when it appeared on Broadway under the title *The Unconquered*, it flopped. She remained interested in writing drama, however, and still hoped to find a literary outlet for the theme of idealism versus mediocrity. In 1934, she tried with a short novel called *Ideal*, which she later turned into a play. Again reflecting the influences of Henrik Ibsen and Sinclair Lewis, *Ideal* centers on a beautiful and reclusive movie star named Kay Gonda, who vanishes after apparently murdering a famous millionaire. She seeks refuge by visiting fans who have sent her admiring letters, in hopes that one will help her hide from the police. Each, however, betrays her in ways that reveal that they are not genuine idealists after all—either because they admire her for the wrong reasons, or because they value money or fame more than principle. Reduced almost to nihilism by this apparently universal lack of integrity, Gonda finally meets a fan named Johnnie who really does share her own aspiration for a life of beauty and significance—as well as her disappointment at the way others betray such yearnings. "Have you ever been in a temple and seen men kneeling silently, reverently, their souls raised to the greatest height they can reach?" he asks. "Then have you wondered why that has to exist only in a temple? Why men can't carry it also into their lives?"[32] The problem is not that people cannot dream—but that they *only* dream. Like Gonda, Johnnie wants to see that vision made real. His idealism rescues her from despair, and the story reaches its climax when Johnnie heroically saves her by framing himself for the millionaire's murder and then committing suicide.

Rand was dissatisfied with the novel, and theaters were not interested in the play, so she tried writing another script, called *Think Twice*—a murder mystery with a philosophical edge, in which an alleged humanitarian turns out to be a killer. It, too, failed to sell. She had better success with *Anthem*, a dystopian science fiction novella about a future in which every shred of individualism has been erased and people refer to themselves as "we" instead of "I." In the story's climax, the hero rediscovers the principle of independent thinking, along with the electric light, symbolizing the connection between individualism and technological progress. But American publishers rejected it, and although it appeared in Britain in 1938, it failed to reach American audiences.

Still seeking to express the theme of longing for value in a world of mediocrity, Rand began in 1935 to plan a new novel she called *Second-Hand Lives*. The idea originated in a conversation with a colleague at the RKO wardrobe office, where she had been working since 1929. When Rand asked the woman what her life's dream was, her reply was that she wanted more than her neighbors had; if her neighbor had a car, she would want two cars. Rand was appalled by the fact that the woman measured her life entirely by comparison to other people, instead of by her own achievements in the real world. Such a person seemed to approach life "second-hand," as Rand wrote in her journal, because she "place[d] [her] basic reality in other people's eyes."[33] This was literal *self*lessness. Lacking principles of their own, such people tended to settle for mediocrity, to shrink away from pursuing their dreams, and to embrace ill-conceived dogmas handed to them by others, instead of acting on their own judgment.

Rand thought this phenomenon explained why many idealistic people were drawn to communism. She reflected in her journal that people repulsed by ordinariness and smallness—who fled the "village virus," in other words—were often attracted to Marxist rhetoric because it "at least, offers a definite goal, inspiration and an *ideal, a positive faith*."[34] Yet it was a false ideal, for it actually represented the ultimate triumph of mediocrity: the subordination of the self to the lowest common denominator of society. The true solution, she believed, was the principle of individual creativity: the spiritual and intellectual spark that enables people to build and thrive. The Revolt from the Village represented a worthy desire for something more real than the drabness of materialistic, bourgeois, bureaucratized society—and the world did need "a new set of values" to "combat this modern dreariness." But instead of collectivism, the "new faith" that was called for was "*Individualism* . . . a revival (or perhaps the first birth) of the word 'I' as the holiest of holies."[35] The escape from mediocrity must begin with the individual who measures himself not by comparison with others, but in terms of real achievement. Rand wanted to celebrate that individualism with the romantic and revolutionary tone she found in such works as *Brand* and *Les Misérables*.

She decided to attempt this with a novel about an architect—the ultimate firsthand life, since architects can only build on the basis of objective facts, not the opinions of others. Her hero would challenge society's stale platitudes in the name of his own creativity. A decade earlier, Paterson had written that one reason a true individualist literature had not emerged was because it was hard to dramatize the process of "drawing the plan of a skyscraper," but Rand now set out to do just that.[36] She began reading books about architecture and the lives of builders, especially the iconoclastic Frank Lloyd Wright.

In one sense, Wright was an odd choice, because he professed to hate cities and skyscrapers. Born in rural Wisconsin in 1867, he was primarily known as a homebuilder in the Midwest. Not until 1951 would he erect his one and only office tower—not in Manhattan, but in small-town Oklahoma. In 1926, when Rand arrived in the United States, Wright's career was in a slump, and although he was much in the headlines that year, it was on account of his scandalous lifestyle, not his buildings. Two decades earlier, he had abandoned his wife and six children to run away with a client's wife, who was afterward horrifically murdered by an ax-wielding madman who burned Wright's home, Taliesin, to the ground. Wright had rapidly remarried, to a mentally unstable woman whose violent outbursts frequently made the newspapers, and in 1926, she had him arrested on morals charges when he brought his soon-to-be third wife, Olgivanna, to live with him at the rebuilt Taliesin. Photos of Wright in jail made the front pages, and he and Olgivanna were shortly thereafter evicted from Taliesin because of his inability to pay his debts. When the Depression hit, Wright's commissions largely vanished.

A revolution was then underway in architecture—a period historians call the Second Skyscraper Era—and Art Deco towers such as the Chrysler Building, the Empire State Building, the Waldorf Astoria, and Rockefeller Center were beginning to soar over New York's horizon. With their clean, straight lines and elegant, streamlined curves, these immense buildings captured the imagination, as art critic Robert Hughes observed, because they "replayed the myth of frontier expansion."[37] Conquering a vertical wilderness instead of a Western one, their builders—from Raymond Hood to William

Lamb, to William Van Alen—were staking out the sky with unprecedented audacity, just as the pioneers had civilized the land. But these developments left Wright behind. By the early 1930s, designers were embracing the cubical, minimalistic "International" school of architecture instead of Wright's distinctive "Organic" style. Devoid of ornament and studiously anonymous, the International Style was effectively the opposite of the romantic, individualistic aesthetic Wright championed, and its practitioners began sneering at the 70-year-old Wright as "an aging individualist" and "the greatest architect of the nineteenth century."[38]

That all changed in 1936, when he began simultaneous construction of two of his finest masterpieces: a headquarters building for the Johnson Wax Company in Wisconsin and the house called Fallingwater in Pennsylvania. Together, they vindicated his reputation as America's greatest architect. When local bureaucrats blocked completion of the Johnson Wax Building because they thought the lily pad–shaped columns holding up the ceiling were too slender to bear the weight, Wright—who never held an architect's license, refused to join the American Institute of Architects, and sometimes built without the required permits—insisted on a public demonstration. His assistants piled six times the expected load on a test column before it collapsed. Anyone looking for a model of defiant genius needed to look no further. In January 1938, that building and the breathtaking Fallingwater were featured in a special issue of *Architectural Forum* and on the cover of *Time*. That same month, Manhattan's Museum of Modern Art (MOMA)—which was occupying temporary quarters at the newly finished One Rockefeller Plaza—staged a small show of photographs of Fallingwater, then nearing completion.[39] In February 1939, MOMA mounted another, larger exhibit that again gave Wright a prominent place. Offering his distinctively American twist on the International Style, Fallingwater was, as one scholar puts it, "an unsurpassed example of art improving nature, of man making the world a better place."[40] It rapidly became a cultural icon. Rand loved it so much that she eventually used it as the basis for three different houses that her novel's hero Howard Roark builds.[41]

In addition to studying Wright's work and his *Autobiography*,[42] Rand took a job in 1937 in the office of Manhattan architect Ely Jacques Kahn, writing lengthy notes in her journals about Kahn, Wright, and others. She had admired American skyscrapers since first seeing them in films while in Russia, and had arrived in America in the middle of the Second Skyscraper Era. The Great Depression had ended the construction boom of the twenties, but one massive undertaking went on, and it was then the main topic of conversation in any New York architect's office: Rockefeller Center, the largest development project ever attempted by private capital. Overseen by John David Rockefeller, Jr., the wealthiest man in America, it sparked artistic as well as economic controversies. When a model of the Center was unveiled in 1931, *New Yorker* architecture critic Lewis Mumford loathed everything about it. He made it the target of weekly columns of unhinged vitriol. "If Radio City is the best our architects can do with freedom," he thundered, "they deserve to remain in chains."[43] (Mumford would inspire the villain Ellsworth Toohey in Rand's novel.) Two years later, the artistic world was scandalized when the Rockefeller family ordered the destruction of a fresco painted in the lobby of the complex's central building by the communist artist Diego Rivera. Commissioned by John's son Nelson—who, like Rockefeller's wife, Abby, was an enthusiast for Rivera's work—it was titled *Man at the Crossroads*, and it heralded the coming socialist revolution with images of greedy capitalists spreading venereal diseases and causing war on one side, and heroic portraits of Karl Marx and Vladimir Lenin bringing peace to the proletariat on the other. When Nelson saw the completed work, shortly before it was to be unveiled, he had the entire thing jackhammered out of the wall.[44]

Rand made slow but steady progress on her novel, but she periodically set it aside to work on other projects such as *Anthem*. Then in 1940, she took an even longer break to join the Wendell Willkie campaign as an unpaid volunteer. She helped by preparing campaign literature and speaking to audiences who viewed pro-Willkie films at a movie theater the campaign rented in Manhattan. She had approached the campaign convinced that Roosevelt's push for a third term meant it was "now or never as far as capitalism is concerned."[45] The New Deal appeared to her as little more than a variation on the collectivist politics of the Russia she had fled. The president's rhetoric of focusing not on the creation of wealth, but on the distribution of wealth already created, sounded like the "dullness made God" dramatized in *Main Street*. The efforts to cartelize major industries as with the National Industrial Recovery Act, and to prosecute successful businesses for "monopolistic" behavior, seemed to manifest the ressentiment that Nietzsche and Mencken had railed against. And the possibility that Roosevelt might now remain in office for life seemed to foreshadow the destruction of American freedom.

As a volunteer for Willkie, she often found herself speaking to would-be voters directly, on stages and street corners, about the evils of statism and the need for economic liberty. She was a compelling speaker, but she was soon disappointed by her own candidate. Aside from the now-legendary amateurishness of Willkie's campaign, the man was simply not a principled defender of individualism or free markets. In fact, he was not philosophically opposed to the New Deal at all, and on the campaign trail, he promised to retain every aspect of Roosevelt's program, from crop insurance to the National Labor Relations Act, and to expand Social Security.[46] When other Republicans urged him to attack the administration directly, he refused, preferring vague slogans about the need for vigorous leadership. "This is a campaign of revitalization, which looks forward rather than back, [and] which is not political in its nature," he wrote in an *Atlantic Monthly* article that concluded that Americans "do not need" to "reject the principle of federal supervision over industrial activities."[47] When he did criticize Roosevelt, he couched it in vague and even alarming phrases, such as when he told an audience: "The time has come when the government must cease giving to the people. The time has come for the people to give to the government."[48] Such tactics turned off many Republicans without attracting any Democratic votes. William Randolph Hearst, who had endorsed Willkie early on, remarked in September that "every time Mr. Willkie speaks he says something—but it is generally something Mr. Roosevelt has said before and said better."[49]

Worse was to come. The main reason Willkie had been nominated was that his opposition to isolationism made him attractive to voters disaffected with the Republican's anti-interventionist foreign policy. Yet as polls shifted—first showing him tantalizingly close and then losing ground—Willkie in desperation began to express anti-interventionist views himself, thus alienating influential figures such as Dorothy Thompson. Then, as Election Day approached, Roosevelt decided to pull out all the stops. He told a Boston campaign rally seven days before the polls opened, "Your boys are not going to be sent into any foreign wars."[50] It was a promise he had no intention of keeping, but it helped him beat Willkie by a convincing 54 to 45 percent.

Paterson was disheartened by Willkie's limp defense of economic freedom and suspicious of his last-minute opposition to Roosevelt's foreign policy. Likely because her boss was Willkie's mistress and ghostwriter, she made virtually no mention of him in print—referring to him only once in "Turns," when she declared, with barely concealed derision, that she would vote for him "no matter what."[51] She thought the main lesson of his campaign was that anything short of a vigorous and principled attack on the New Deal was a pointless exercise. Many others agreed. H. L. Mencken wrote in his diary that it was absurd for Republicans to offer voters only "mild New Dealers—in other words, inferior Roosevelts."[52] There was no way to "beat a demagogue by swallowing four fifths of his buncombe and then trying to alarm the boobs over the little that is left."[53]

That was a view Rand shared. She had found the experience of working on the campaign exasperating. One of her jobs had been to distribute literature making the case for free markets against Roosevelt's government planning. Yet it had proved almost impossible to *find* any published material that made a strong, intellectual case for free markets. "We received letters by the thousands, begging us for information," she told a friend. "They begged us for answers."[54] But the campaign offered none. She and other volunteers signed up "for one purpose only—to work for a cause they believed [in]," only to watch their own candidate sabotage that effort.[55] Running a principled and consistent campaign might have failed, she concluded, but a campaign whose theme was "me too" could never deserve to succeed.

On election night, Paterson and Lane followed the returns on the radio at Lane's house. Roosevelt's reelection, they agreed, was a doleful sign for the nation. "It's the crowd, the mass," Lane said. Voters had absorbed collectivism so deeply that they could no longer think for themselves. With Europe overtaken by one variety of socialism or another, America had been individualism's final stronghold. Now a third Roosevelt term would be interpreted as an endorsement of the government-controlled economy in the United States—and it almost guaranteed a second world war. That seemed to spell the end of the Industrial Revolution, which meant the end of human progress and perhaps an eventual collapse into universal slavery.[56]

Paterson agreed. "The power will explode," she told Lane. Conscription, confiscation, censorship, and the extinguishment of individualism in America would combine with a potentially endless series of wars between European tyrannies that would destroy industry and agriculture, leading to mass starvation. That would only increase the power of dictators, because "where government is the source of food, the hungry go to it," even if that means enslavement. The result would be an unending cycle that would erase a century of human progress.

The source of that disaster was not primarily economic, however. It was moral. Americans had been misled by irrational ethical arguments to support the New Deal. Consciously evil people, whether criminals or political leaders, have little power to destroy the world, Paterson told Lane; instead, it was "the large number of the well-meaning" people who—ignorant of what morality truly required—were seduced into supporting collectivism by the rhetoric of concern for the underprivileged, and ended up giving authoritarian government power over their lives. "All the harm is done by 'good' people," she concluded. Recording the conversation in her diary, Lane agreed: deceived by false, anti-individualistic morality, Americans had finally "lost respect for human rights."[57]

Ayn Rand, too, thought the lack of resistance to Roosevelt had moral, rather than economic, roots. What was needed was a philosophical campaign to make the case for individualism and build a foundation for long-term success. The American Liberty League, having amounted to nothing, dissolved in September 1940, leaving the National Association of Manufacturers as the only significant organization opposing the New Deal. But its efforts were tentative, nonideological, and fruitless. Other allies had fallen by the wayside. Sen. William Borah, a leading New Deal critic, died that January—the same month that Sen. Arthur Vandenberg, who had led the Republicans in opposing Roosevelt's Second New Deal—announced that as a "realist" he now thought it "cannot and should not be reversed."[58] Dorothy Thompson had joined Roosevelt's party. William Randolph Hearst was regarded as a bankrupt relic, notably mocked in the newly released *Citizen Kane*. Mencken, having retired from the *American Mercury*, found his philippics against the New Deal so unpopular that he ended his newspaper column and started writing his memoirs instead.

Rand thought it was time to rally the remaining forces of individualism—not by lobbying the government or running political campaigns, but by formulating and advocating better ideas.[59] In 1937, she had written to the editor of the *Herald Tribune* urging the formation of "a committee, an organization, or headquarters" to "lead and centralize the activity of all those who are eager to join their efforts in protest. . . . 'It can't happen here,' you think? Well, it's happened already!"[60] Now, in late 1940, she prepared a manifesto addressed to business owners whom she called "innocent fifth columnists" because, by compromising or remaining silent in the face of the government's ever-growing control over society, they bore the most blame for threatening the future of freedom. "Don't say smugly that 'it can't happen here,'" she warned. "One idea—and one only" brought about totalitarian dictatorship in Russia, Germany, or anywhere else, and that was the idea *"that the State is superior to the individual."* There was no reason this idea could not gain traction in the United States; in fact, it already had, even among alleged defenders of freedom. "They 'oppose' Totalitarianism and they 'defend' Democracy—by preaching their own version of Totalitarianism, some form of 'collective good,' 'collective rights,' 'collective will,' etc."[61]

The reason groups like the American Liberty League failed, she thought, was that they offered no intelligent alternative to the New Dealers' *moral* arguments.[62] Roosevelt and his supporters took idealistic positions that appealed to ethical principles—helping others, serving the nation, ending poverty—but conservatives merely complained about the details of the administration's plans and spoke blandly of a return to traditions that many considered outdated—or worse, of "democracy," defined as mere majoritarianism instead of a constitutional system centered on protecting individual rights. What the country needed was an intellectual movement for individualism that would focus on fundamentals. "Let us offer the world *our* philosophy of life," she wrote. "Let us drop all compromise, all cooperation or collaboration with those preaching any brand of Totalitarianism in letter or in spirit. . . . Of every law and of every conception we shall demand the maximum freedom for the individual and the minimum power for the government necessary to achieve any given social objective."[63]

In the spring of 1941, she sent a copy of her essay to playwright Channing Pollock. A self-made man who thought plays should "urge the enteral verities,"[64] the deeply conservative Pollock shared with Rand an admiration for drama with strong moral themes, and he loathed what he called the "theater habitués and sons of habitués" who preferred literary "realism."[65] By 1940, these views had essentially forced him out of the theater, and he had taken up politics instead. He feared that "if the government fulfills its promise to protect us from the consequences of our own failings and follies," Americans would "find [themselves] existing only for the State, instead [of] . . . the old State that existed only for its citizens," and he wrote extensively against the New Deal, while crossing the country on a lecture tour.[66] He liked Rand's idea of a new organization and encouraged her to expand on her draft. She began preparing a more thorough work, called "The Individualist Manifesto," and in the months that followed, she, Pollock, and others tried to get the organization going. One person they tried to recruit was Isabel Paterson.

Paterson did not like joining groups—she had just lectured Dorothy Thompson in print that May that doing so risked compromising one's principles[67]—and she and Lane sometimes joked about founding a "Society for Non-Communication."[68] "If you wish to join it," Paterson explained in "Turns," "you simply do not let [Lane] know, do not write her, do not call, go into silence." (Paterson added that she herself "[could not] become a full member of the society" for "obvious reasons.") Thus, when Rand received no answer to her invitation and called to follow up, Paterson suggested that she visit her at the *Trib's* headquarters instead. At that meeting, the 35-year-old Russian must have impressed the 54-year-old Canadian, because Rand was soon a frequent participant in Paterson's weekly salons, held on Monday evenings as she and her friends finalized that week's "books" page and the "Turns with a Bookworm" column.

The two women hit it off right away. Earnestly intellectual and intensely curious about Paterson's historical and literary knowledge, Rand was fascinated by the older woman, and Paterson was charmed in return. Rand was "elegant," she reported in "Turns," with "smooth black hair, round eyes that look black and aren't, neat figure and just that turn of the head and direct gaze and natural simplicity of manner."[69] And Paterson's weekly gatherings seem to have been great fun at times. "When Pat is in a good mood, she is like quicksand," Rand told a friend, "completely irresistible."[70] Paterson's best friend, the humorist Will Cuppy, was a frequent guest at these get-togethers. On one occasion, he teased Rand about the common literary cliché whereby novels about Russia always seemed to include a passage in which a sled is pursued by a pack of wolves.[71] Why didn't people take extra passengers with them on sleds, he joked, in order to toss them to the wolves and escape? Rand replied that she had never known any actual Russian sled to be pursued by wolves. "All she knew of that subject she had learned in Hollywood." "We could only marvel at her comparative illiteracy," Paterson continued. "Every American child knew that story in our younger years." But Rand replied that as a child in Russia, she had naturally been taught all about "American Indians toma-hawking settlers," to which Paterson—who had grown up near Indian country herself—answered by "explain[ing] kindly that that seldom occurred within our memory, or not to any of our acquaintance."[72] Paterson also delighted in Rand's occasional stumbles over American idioms. She laughed, for instance, when Rand suggested that Paterson write her autobiography because "I can't do myself justice."[73]

Rand had progressed enough on *Second-Hand Lives*—which, just before publication, she retitled *The Fountainhead*—that she knew much of its plot would center on a newspaper. Paterson arranged to show her the printing presses, to gather realistic detail. She eventually invited Rand to visit her Connecticut home, and soon the young writer was a regular guest, joining Paterson for weekends during which they stayed up late discussing literature, history, and philosophy. At other times, Paterson spent evenings at Rand's Manhattan apartment, talking until sunrise about profound ideas, or joking about books and politics. Rand loved the experience. She particularly trea-sured the memory of one late-night conversation about consciousness, during which the pair tried to figure out what goes on inside the mind of a beaver.[74] (They evidently decided that beavers do not regard themselves as consciously able to act.[75]) Rand even worked a subtle reference to this exchange into a passage of her novel in which newspaper magnate Gail Wynand recalls how, when he was young and poor, he would sometimes escape his unhappy sur-roundings by thinking about his pet kitten, who "was clean—clean in the absolute sense, because it had no capacity to conceive of the world's ugliness. I can't tell you what relief there was in trying to imagine the state of conscious-ness inside that little brain, trying to share it, a living consciousness, but clean and free."[76]

In fact, the friendship between Wynand and *The Fountainhead*'s hero, Howard Roark, appears to owe much to the feelings that developed between Paterson and herself. Around this time, Paterson inscribed a copy of *If It Prove Fair Weather* to Rand, with a touching quotation from the 16th-century French essayist Michel de Montaigne: "Because he was himself; because I was myself." It was a line Montaigne used to describe his relationship with Étienne de La Boétie, which Montaigne had offered as the ideal companionship—one in which "souls are mingled and confounded in so universal a blending that they efface the seam which joins them together."[77] Rand later reciprocated with a copy of *The Fountainhead* in which she wrote, "You have been the one encounter in my life that can never be repeated"—a line that in the novel is spoken by Wynand to Roark as an expression of the deepest possible rapport.[78]

Yet as much as she enjoyed her time with Paterson, Rand may have also felt intimidated by the older woman's brilliant mind and abrasive personality. Only a few years later, she told a friend that she had "never approved of Pat's incredibly offensive manner toward people," but could not figure out how to react when she witnessed it, because she had so much admiration for Paterson's "fierce intellectual honesty [and] her strict devotion to ideas."[79]

Although the exact content of the pair's midnight discussions cannot be reconstructed today, they must have included the philosophical ideas that Rand was putting together into the system she later called Objectivism. In its mature form, Objectivism seemed to combine the scientific rationality and virtue-oriented ethics of Aristotle with the romantic individualism of Friedrich Nietzsche—although Paterson insisted in a letter to Rand: "Your idea is *new*. It is not Nietzsche."[80] When asked years later to describe her philosophy as briefly as possible, Rand replied, "Metaphysics: Objective Reality, Epistemology: Reason, Ethics: Self-interest, Politics: Capitalism."[81] This meant that she rejected any appeal to supernaturalism and believed the world exists independently of human consciousness; believed that comprehension is exclusively a matter of reason and logic, rather than faith or intuition; and, in morality, held that people should pursue their own interests, rather than serving the needs of others. Consequently, she believed in undiluted laissez faire capitalism, with government limited exclusively to defending individual rights.

Of all the elements of her philosophy, the one that would draw the most criticism in the years to follow was her rejection of the principle of self-sacrifice, and her belief that selfishness—by which she meant rational self-interest—is a virtue. This theory of ethical egoism had been shared by Aristotle, Epicurus, and other Greek and Roman philosophers, as well as many Enlightenment-era thinkers.[82] But by the 1940s, much of that legacy had been supplanted by altruism, which saw morality as consisting essentially of obligations toward other people or society in general. Rand viewed herself as "challenging the cultural tradition of two and a half thousand years," but Paterson shared Rand's ethical philosophy.[83] A morality of rational self-interest, she thought, was proper for human beings, who are inherently individual beings responsible for their own lives. It was also the only sound basis for political freedom. "'Sacrifice' and 'unselfishness' seem to be the motives causing wholesale destruction, devoted to death," she wrote in "Turns." "When men relapse into 'selfish' and unsacrificial motives they create a living human world—grow food, build houses, invent and construct and produce, strictly 'for themselves.'" Freedom must mean the freedom of each person to pursue his own life for its own sake—an inherently self-interested proposition. "After all, wasn't it selfish of the slaves to want to be free? Why weren't they satisfied to live for their masters and die for them too . . . [?] The masters said it was for the good of society that they kept slaves, and their argument was quite as sound as any other argument for the good of society."[84] Modern intellectuals who invoked service to others as a virtue were perverting the very vocabulary of ethics to make it seem as if freedom was oppression and vice versa. In fact, preaching self-sacrifice was worse than outright slavery, since slaves are innocent victims of violence, whereas altruism tries to fool people into enslaving themselves.

Because altruism regards human beings as fundamentally needy, Paterson continued, people who actually try to live on the basis of that morality "can't have any relationship at all with persons retaining a shred of independent capacity or self-respect."[85] Modern intellectuals were drawn to this moral view precisely because it "call[s] for the antecedent need or misery of its objects," and therefore gives them grounds to demand power over others and "make themselves important."[86] Thus in *The God of the Machine*, Paterson would condemn what she called the "purest altruism" of "the communal cult,"[87] because it stood opposed to the principle that "every person is born with a right to a life of his own."[88]

Whether these ideas were owing to Rand's influence or whether Paterson reached them on her own cannot be teased out now; neither can the extent of Paterson's influence on Rand. Although one observer said that during their late-night conversations, Rand sat at Paterson's feet while Paterson served as "guru and teacher," Rand had actually finished most of the plan for *The Fountainhead* before the two met and had already thought through much of the groundwork for Objectivism.[89] Years later, Rand told Paterson that she distinctly remembered talking her out of a belief in altruism. "Positively not," Paterson replied. What Rand had done was to explain how "the theory and historic fact of 'enlightened *self*-interest' which to me seemed right, rational, fundamentally true" could apply to the complicated question of the duties between parents and children. "I could see that even in such a relationship, it isn't really 'altruistic,' as the parent has incurred the obligation to begin with, and is morally bound by his or her own previous voluntary and initiatory action," she told Rand. "But I had failed to see the plain fact that you brought out, that the well-being, the very survival, of the child is still dependent on the parent acting for *himself*, on his *own* interest."[90] In short, Paterson recalled Rand having helped her understand one specific example, not persuading her to reject altruism generally.[91]

The difficulty of deciphering precisely who generated which ideas in Paterson and Rand's relationship—a matter on which the two later quarreled—is illustrated by a letter Paterson sent Rand after *The Fountainhead* was published, which urged on her friend the idea that "*there is no such thing as the collective.*" Some things, she explained, take on new properties when combined with others of that same kind; concrete, for example. But the same is not true of human beings. They always remain essentially and unalterably individual. No matter how they are combined, or in what numbers, each person always acts on his or her own judgment (or lack thereof), which means there is no sense in speaking of "the collective" or "the race" or "the proletariat" behaving in a particular way.[92] It was a persuasive point, and one Rand often made in later writings. Yet by the time Paterson wrote this, Rand had already said the same thing in *The Fountainhead* itself, as when Howard Roark says, "There is no such thing as a collective brain."[93] It seems unlikely that Paterson taught this idea to Rand or vice versa. Both being devoted individualists, it probably struck them simultaneously.

Rand's notebooks give intriguing hints of their other conversations. In one note from 1943, after *The Fountainhead* was published, Rand mused on the distinction between different "style[s] of soul[s]"—that is, the discrepancy between people whose mental image of humanity is heroic and those whose image of humanity is one of desperation, poverty, and loss. She cited as an example of the latter "the worm who wrote to Pat about the Wright brothers—the deliberate belittling of greatness."[94] This was a reference to a series of "Turns" columns Paterson had published commenting on a new biography of the airplane's inventors. Writing as a member of the Airplane Generation, Paterson had remarked that the Wright brothers were fortunate to have done their work before the New Deal; had they been working in the 1940s, the government would have forced them to fill out reams of paperwork, obtain permits from multiple bureaucracies, and join "a co-operative social group to study leadership" before letting them fly.[95] In short, the Wrights had been creators—self-starters—not joiners who spent their time focusing on relationships. She returned to the point in several later columns, observing that "the airplane was invented in the United States precisely because this was the only country on earth, the only country that ever existed in which people had a right to be let alone and to mind their own business."[96] New Dealers should ask themselves, she said, what would happen if innovators and inventors—whom Paterson called the "Intelligence Section" of society—were "put out of action by a system of 'economic controls,' rationing, political restriction, and a devouring plague of bureaucrats throughout the world."[97]

Her comments provoked a letter from a reader who insisted that it was "unfair" to describe the Wrights as having "needed nothing whatever except their own earnings," because it was well known that the Wrights' sister Katherine helped subsidize their experiments with her income. Paterson replied that although this was a popular legend, it was not true; Katherine Wright herself had denied it.[98] "She knew where recognition was due, and gave it—to her brothers, the men who invented the airplane, by their own intelligence and their own means." But, Paterson added, it was also instructive to ask why "such sentimental fables" persisted. She thought it was because some people wanted "to detract from the just credit due to originality and independence."[99] This exchange over the Wright brothers, Paterson concluded, proved that Rand was right to say that contemporary culture was hostile toward the intellectual independence of inventors and entrepreneurs—and that this hostility was rooted in envy.

Rand and Paterson did not agree on everything, however. They especially differed in their literary views. An adherent to the tradition of 19th-century Romanticism, Rand could not admire the plotlessness of *The Golden Vanity* or the stream-of-consciousness quality of *Never Ask the End*. She valued Romanticism because it sought to dramatize abstract ideas, rather than to present the world "as it is," which was the goal of naturalism. Paterson, by contrast, respected the Romantic approach but was committed to naturalism in her own novels.[100] Nor did they admire the same writers; Paterson disliked Hugo, Dostoyevsky, and the mystery stories Rand enjoyed, and Rand took no interest in works such as *The Tale of Genji*, which was Paterson's favorite. Paterson told Rand outright that she did not care for *Anthem*, and she harbored private doubts about Rand's later work. In fact, with only three exceptions, Rand's published fiction shows little indication of any debt to Paterson.

In 1958, Rand told a group of students that she had originally intended for Howard Roark to mention Hitler and Stalin in the climactic courtroom speech of *The Fountainhead*, but that when Paterson saw the outline, she urged Rand to remove those references. Incorporating such specific examples would date the novel, Paterson thought, and reduce its impact in years to come. That was good advice, and Rand followed it, helping give her book a sense of timeless relevance. The second of Paterson's influences can be found in a letter that postdates *The Fountainhead*, which reflects her recommendation that Rand omit unnecessary descriptive passages. "I have been engaged in a wild orgy of weeding," Rand wrote back, "not of devil's grass, but of adjectives."[101] It is unlikely that Rand was unfamiliar with this age-old rule of good writing before encountering Paterson, but the critic's recommendation was probably a helpful reminder.

The third element in Rand's fiction traceable to Paterson's influence is more significant. Paterson was fond of invoking the myth of Atlantis as a metaphor for the way the frontier ethos of the America she had known in her youth seemed to have vanished. In *Never Ask the End*, Marta—who represents Paterson herself—recalls a trip she took across the western prairie years earlier: "This is a wild land," she had thought at the time. "It has never been plowed or fenced." Now, grown older, she thinks the people of her generation "belong to a sunken continent; lost Atlantis, submerged under the westward tide of the peoples of the world. Our little towns are drowned, too. One used to come to the end of a board sidewalk and step off upon virgin sod. . . . After us, nobody will know what it was like."[102] In Paterson's mind, Atlantis symbolized the America that the Airplane Generation had known—a pre-war, pre-Depression, pre–New Deal country full of boundless possibilities and brilliant innovators. Now that all seemed lost, replaced with a national gloom in which economists deprecated entrepreneurialism, historians deemed individualism a myth, and politicians proclaimed a future of collectivism, conformity, and conscription.

Twenty years later, Rand would incorporate the image of Atlantis into the book Paterson helped inspire, *Atlas Shrugged*. There, the name refers to the secret valley where the world's great geniuses hide after going on strike. Rumors of this refuge's existence circulate early in the novel, and Atlantis is first mentioned at a cocktail party—not unlike one of Paterson's literary teas. An unnamed woman approaches the heroine, Dagny Taggart and, in a "soft, mysterious tone," tells her that "an old friend of a great-aunt of mine" once actually saw Atlantis. "The Isles of the Blessed. That is what the Greeks called it, thousands of years ago. They said Atlantis was a place where hero-spirits lived. . . . Perhaps what they were thinking of was America." When Dagny seems doubtful, the woman becomes "belligerent" and "brusque," and insists, "My friend saw it with his own eyes"—precisely the kind of stubborn response characteristic of Paterson. Rand—who also included herself in a cameo in another passage of the book—had given her mentor a walk-on part in the novel.[103]

But the connection ran even deeper. For Paterson, Atlantis symbolized that element of human nature that remained unsurveyed and unlimited; the terrain of the psyche America had left each person free to discover. In short, it stood for the openness and opportunity of the frontier. In Rand's novel, it stands as a metaphor for youth: the "sensation of independence from the starting years of your childhood."[104] It may seem strange that Rand, who always saw Manhattan as her spiritual home, would employ the West as her symbol of liberty, but it was so, and thanks largely to Paterson.[105]

During their evenings together, Paterson helped teach Rand about American history and politics, especially constitutional government, and recounted details and gossip about left-wing intellectuals and avant-garde writers. Rand may also have picked up a certain wry sense of humor from Paterson, who was firmly convinced that a novel "has to include the element of comedy, or we can't enter into it."[106] Little of Rand's work before her meeting with Paterson contains any element of humor, but most of the writing she produced afterward incorporates a degree of observational comedy that often parallels Paterson's own. For example, just as the columnist often ridiculed Gertrude Stein, whom she considered a phony, so Rand added a delightful caricature of Stein to *The Fountainhead*: a writer named Lois Cook, whose writing consists of such lines as "toothbrush in the jaw toothbrush brush brush tooth jaw foam dome in the foam Roman dome."[107] And in a note to herself while developing the character of the villainous Ellsworth Toohey, Rand remarked: "It would be Toohey who'd find philosophical significance in Donald Duck. . . . It's not Donald Duck that he's boosting. It's philosophy that he's destroying."[108] This mirrors a passage in Paterson's *Golden Vanity*, in which the communist writers on the Siddall family's payroll "discovered a profound philosophy in [the comic strip] Krazy Kat."[109] Rand's observational humor owes much to the satire of Sinclair Lewis, of course, whom she had admired long before meeting Paterson, and whose influence can also be detected in such works as *The Little Street* and *Ideal*. But there, Rand had treated mediocrity with a tone of bitter indignation noticeably different from the ironic touch of her later works. Although it is impossible to prove, Paterson may have helped Rand move from the darkness of her earlier writing toward the comparatively brighter tenor of *The Fountainhead*.

Another common thread in Rand's and Paterson's work concerned the naive, or conniving, willingness of businessmen to collaborate in their own destruction. In *The Golden Vanity*, the Siddalls willingly subsidize publication of a communist magazine, just as steel tycoon Hank Rearden in *Atlas Shrugged* writes checks to his brother-in-law's anti-capitalist charity. "Isabel was particularly scornful of the 'deckle-edged speeches' of the businessmen of the mid-'40s who had cravenly accepted the inevitability of a mixed, or Fabian, economy that kept edging toward socialism," wrote Paterson's friend, John Chamberlain. "Isabel was the first to talk about the need of business to support its own press, its own electronic media, its own schools and universities."[110] Rand, too, spent the last four decades of her life urging business owners to defend themselves—to support a "civil liberties union for businessmen" or, at a minimum, to withhold support from institutions that were expressly hostile to free enterprise.[111] In her final public appearance in 1982, she reiterated this point. "Some of the worst anti-business, anti-capitalism propaganda has been financed by businessmen," she warned. "It is a moral crime to give money to support your own destroyers. Yet that is what businessmen are doing with such reckless irresponsibility."[112]

Together, Paterson and Rand helped each other develop a theory of the psychological connection between the creative personality and political freedom—and, by contrast, between the people who impugn innovation— who seek to constrain, control, or belittle it—and political demands for greater government control over individual choices. Paterson would write in *The God of the Machine* that "the philanthropist, the politician, and the pimp are inevitably found in alliance because they have the same motives, they seek the same ends, to exist for, through, and by others,"[113] whereas "the productive man . . . does not like to live at the expense of others."[114] These and other passages echo the primary theme of *The Fountainhead*, which, in Rand's words, addressed the difference between collectivism and individualism, not in politics, but in the souls of particular people.

At a time when leading intellectuals and politicians spoke openly of the eclipse of individualism and highlighted not inventors, scholars, and creators, but classes, masses, races, and social engineering by the state—and in which totalitarian governments were murdering millions in Europe and Asia for the express purpose of creating utopias—Paterson, Lane, and Rand found inspiration and intellectual support in each other's company. They would devote themselves in the coming years to championing the cause of freedom both in intellectual argument and in literature.

Part Three

A New Birth of Freedom

Newspaperman William Randolph Hearst started out as a Roosevelt supporter, only to turn against Roosevelt in 1936. He inspired the character of Gail Wynand in Rand's *The Fountainhead*.

8

The Self-Starter

Paterson, Lane, and Rand had expected the New Deal to eventually end in war one way or another, because war is inherent in the logic of collectivist societies. A government focused on redistributing wealth rather than protecting the rights of individuals to enjoy the fruits of their labors will eventually run out of wealth to redistribute, whereupon it must seize it from unpopular domestic minorities—by conscripting capital—or go to war to take it from despised foreigners.[1] As Paterson put it in *The God of the Machine*, "the slave economies of Soviet Russia and Germany" could not even "maintain their mechanical equipment without continual replacements from free nations," and if the free, productive countries refused to hand over their treasures voluntarily, communist and fascist rulers would try to grab it by force.[2] "The mob is the most perfect example of 'collectivism,'" she declared, "and its most distinctive activity is the lynching party."[3]

Moreover, collectivized economies are built essentially on the model of wartime conditions; they treat workers as national resources, commanded by officials to serve a single purpose, as opposed to a free, civilian society in which people pursue their own happiness as they choose.[4] In their rhetoric and imagery, New Dealers fetishized war—starting with Roosevelt's first inaugural address, in which he invoked the war analogy as the basis of his entire agenda.[5] New Deal programs then began imposing a bureaucratic discipline on the nation not far removed from actual wartime conditions. Thus as America came increasingly to resemble the command-and-control economies of Europe, it became more likely that the administration would take the nation to war for one reason or another.

Paterson, Lane, and Rand were not alone in this worry. In early 1941, communist folk singer Pete Seeger would write the song "Plow Under," likening the world war to the New Deal's economic policies:

> Remember when the AAA,
> Killed a million hogs a day?
> Instead of hogs, it's men today. . . .
> The price of cotton wouldn't rise;
> They said, we've got to fertilize. . . .
> They said our system wouldn't work
> Until we killed the surplus off. . . .
> Plow under, plow under,
> Plow under every fourth American boy.[6]

Paterson feared that if a second world war came, it could very well destroy civilization, not only because of the drastic improvements in weapons since the first war, but because with much of mankind already enslaved to communist or fascist regimes, America appeared to be the only refuge left for human creativity. Yet the New Deal imposed increasingly stringent limits on that freedom, and the arrival of war might easily erase what elements of it remained, whether through conscription of manpower and wealth, or censorship of news, debate, and entertainment, or punishment for so-called subversives, or the establishment of internment camps—all of which would permanently damage the constitutional order. Added to this was the fact that some New Dealers openly advocated replacing modern industrial society with subsistence agriculture overseen by the state. As Wolfgang Schivelbusch puts it, the Industrial Revolution was "a relatively recent historical event, [in the 1930s] only two generations in the past. Given its relative youth, industrialization had no claim to irreversibility."[7] Paterson, Lane, and Rand had good reason to fear that a second world war could inaugurate a new Dark Ages.[8]

Thus when the war came in December 1941, Paterson lamented but was unsurprised. The Axis powers were certainly monstrous and deserved to be defeated, and although she had no fear that the Allies might lose, she did worry about the harm the United States might inflict on itself in the interim. From ancient Greece to revolutionary France, history had plenty of examples of nations going to war, only to lose their freedom on the way to victory. Indeed, America's very industrial strength might set the nation up for an especially awful reckoning. "A regime of popularity is effective for starting a war," she noted, and if that nation is productive and vigorous enough, then "the regime is likely to begin with an appearance of enormous success in aggression," only to "end by disintegrating in civil war and possibly subjection to a foreign power."[9]

The White House began shifting the New Deal onto a wartime footing by establishing new agencies, including the War Production Board, with jurisdiction over manufacturing and supply, and the National War Labor Board, with authority over manpower, as well as the Office of Censorship, with authority over all communications going in or out of the country. It revitalized the Office of Price Administration (OPA), which had actually been created before the war, to control the prices of such goods as tires, nylon, and meat. It also doubled income taxes and reduced the personal exemptions threshold so drastically that 13 million new taxpayers were liable. This transformed what had been a tax on the top 5 percent of income earners into a form of mass expropriation and an annual ritual of obligatory service. "The government is so hard up," Paterson told her readers, "that if you only make $16 a week it needs your help."[10] The government also implemented the withholding system, which made income taxes essentially invisible to many workers, and started a national propaganda campaign to persuade Americans to accept the new taxes.[11]

Paterson thought such economic restrictions were counterproductive. Less government control would better ensure the productivity necessary to supply the nation's military and civilian needs. Expanding government power over industry would likely cause shortages and would mean that goods and services were doled out by favoritism—by "pull"—instead of being allocated on the basis of individuals' actual needs. Whenever government is given

Rockefeller Center, the largest development project ever undertaken by
private capital, transformed Manhattan and helped inspire *The Fountainhead*.

authority to decide how resources are used, she warned, the result is to transfer decisionmaking from individuals to bureaucrats, who become a cadre of economic kingmakers. Riding on the bus one day, Paterson overheard the driver ask a passenger what was in the package he was carrying. "Meat," the man answered. "I'm going home and get my dinner." In reply, the bus driver snorted, "Aristocrat!" It was, Paterson wrote, "a spontaneous recognition of the fact that the political power of rationing institutes a class society; whatever you get, it is by favor, permission or privilege."[12]

Paterson's warning was prescient. The administration's wartime planning consisted largely of putting the country's biggest corporations in charge of military production. Government contracting was dominated by the most powerful companies, with General Motors alone gaining 10 percent of the business.[13] Meanwhile, control over the civilian economy soon extended to nearly every decision citizens could make. When the OPA's price restrictions caused shortages, the government implemented rationing—and federal bureaucracies began dictating everything from how much gasoline people could use each week to the kinds of fabrics they could use for making clothes. When Lane was told she could not buy some slacks because they included too much wool, she grumbled to Paterson, "The OPA has little to do meddling with my pants[!]"[14]

▰▰

But if freedom was going to be so drastically sacrificed, what were Americans being asked to die for? On January 6, 1941, 11 months before war was declared, Roosevelt delivered a State of the Union address in which he identified the "four essential freedoms" at stake in the European conflict: freedom of speech, freedom of religion, freedom from fear, and freedom from want. Notably absent was the right to private property or the liberty to make one's own economic choices. And although freedoms of speech and religion were, of course, long-cherished elements of the classical liberalism to which Paterson, Lane, and Rand subscribed, the freedoms from want or fear were incompatible with any previous conception of liberty. Want, Paterson observed, can only be cured by forcing some people to produce goods and services for others. And the eradication of fear can only be realized by an omniscient, omnipotent, omnibenevolent state.[15] In truth, even that would not succeed, since as a practical matter a totalitarian government can never create sufficient productivity or safety. Phrases like "freedom from want" are "are nonsense," she concluded. "Freedom is just freedom from restraint. And what Communism, government control, brings about is freedom from soap, freedom from shoes, freedom from food."[16] Lane agreed: freedom could refer only to a person's "own control of his living self"—not to access to wealth others create.[17]

Roosevelt's speech seemed to both women just another attempt to twist language to bewilder the populace and obfuscate the principles at issue. Not only was it impossible for the state to eliminate want, but the attempt to do so was a perversion of the word "freedom" because it rested on the assumption that freedom consists of specific permissions given out by the ruler. That was what Paterson called "the European idea of 'liberties' instead of the American liberty."[18] In fact, she hated to see that word used in the plural. *Liberty* was what people had a natural right to as freeborn individuals; *liberties* were permissions given to people by all-powerful kings.

Then in August 1941, Roosevelt updated his "four freedoms" with the Atlantic Charter, which announced that the British and their American supporters were fighting for "a better future" defined by "improved labor standards, economic advancement and social security," "the right of all peoples to choose the form of government under which they will live," and two of the "four freedoms"—"freedom from fear and want"—somewhat ominously omitting freedoms of speech and religion.

Language like this seemed designed to serve what Paterson, Lane, and Rand saw as a worrisome trend of elevating democracy over liberty as a central constitutional value. For nearly a decade, New Dealers had made a virtual fetish of the word "democracy"—whether expressly in terms of political control, or more abstractly in terms of the national spirit—perpetuating the notion that majority rule is more important than, or is even the basic source of, individual freedom.

To Paterson, this represented a dangerous reversal of priorities. "Liberty is the last word you'll find in contemporary books or speeches," she observed in "Turns" in early 1940. "When it is mentioned at all, it is only in order to explain that by liberty the speaker doesn't really mean liberty, so don't worry; he means some form of coercion."[19] Throughout that year, she returned to the point time and again. The American political system, she argued, was not based on democracy—which "contains no other principle than majority rule," and is therefore "fatal to liberty"—but on "the inalienable right of the individual."[20]

When celebrated historian Henry Steele Commager wrote to ask Paterson facetiously what form of government she preferred, if she was so opposed to democracy, her answer was simple: "a republic." The American Founders had chosen a republican system, with a constitutionally limited form of democracy, to create "safeguards for individual liberty against any majority." They did so knowing that the "specific meaning" of the word "democracy" was the unlimited power of the majority, which inevitably meant the eradication of freedom. Commager was only pretending to be ignorant of this, she continued—in reality he was intentionally trying to twist the language to prioritize political control over the individual rights that give government its legitimacy in the first place.[21] (Unpersuaded, Commager would take time in a series of 1943 lectures on democracy to list the "shrill" Paterson alongside the pro-slavery intellectuals of the 19th century as exemplars of "the anti-majority theory" of the Constitution.[22])

A similar perversion of language was noticeable in the transformation of the word "liberal" from a term that referred to supporters of political and economic freedom into a label for advocates of the regulatory welfare state. Walter Lippmann and Dorothy Thompson, among others, were calling themselves "liberals" even while advocating expansive state control. This was what Paterson called "the 'redefinition' process," whereby "a facile liar is 'defined' as a man of 'integrity' and 'democracy' signifies abracadabra."[23] When Thompson wrote in her 1942 book *Listen, Hans* that "people want a freedom in which their work, the creative expression of their lives, is not regarded as a commodity to be bought and sold like so much soap," Paterson objected to the implication that paid labor is undignified. "We like soap," she declared in "Turns," and "we don't at all mind our 'work' being bought and sold like soap—meaning for money."[24] People must earn a living, and to do so they must be free to sell their labor as they choose.

Paterson had been similarly underwhelmed by Thompson's 1938 book, *Dorothy Thompson's Political Guide*, in which the columnist defined liberalism not as a coherent philosophy of individual freedom, but as a "kind of spirit" that holds "that there is good in every nature," and that "a good society is one in which that goodness can be given the greatest possibility to expand and develop."[25] Thompson's version of liberalism aimed at the "development and perfection" of the human soul, by freeing people from poverty "in order that they might enjoy independence, and therefore have courage and character."[26] Paterson thought such "lofty flights of oratory" were nonsense.[27] To view freedom not as an end in itself but as a means to accomplish some larger object meant that "some one—and who else but the speaker?—is to define that 'object,' is to judge whether or not other people are using their freedom in the manner prescribed, and may revoke it if they do not do as they are told."

Thompson's vague, even backward definition of liberalism "contains a tacit assumption that men are born under orders to fill our passport applications for living, declaring some purpose or object which is subject to approval or refusal beforehand."[28] For the same reason, Paterson dismissed Thompson's argument that after the war, nations should foster "tolerance." "'Tolerance' cannot be 'created,'" she declared. Rather, the goal should be "to abolish the political power which alone [makes] slavery possible. . . . The proper alternative to making a man a slave, if you do not wish to associate with him on any other terms, is to let him alone. . . . You have a right to be let alone, or to leave anyone else alone, and so has he. And that is all there is to it, now and forever."[29]

▰▲◣

War, Paterson thought, risked destroying precisely the freedom it was supposed to protect, especially if the government adopted conscription. Although the draft had been eliminated at the end of World War I, talk of compulsory government service became increasingly common in the late 1930s, both among those who, like Eleanor Roosevelt, argued that America's youth should be forced into civilian community service, and those such as the American Legion, which called for mandatory military service in preparation for war. At last, on September 16, 1940, Roosevelt signed the nation's first peacetime conscription law.

Paterson was horrified. It represented an abandonment of American principles and the adoption of a basic element of totalitarianism.[30] "If men cherish their liberty," she wrote, "conscription is the perfect expression of what they must fight against."[31] She thought there was no real need for such a measure; Americans had always been willing to fight for their own freedom when attacked. But to implement a draft in a time of peace was likely to give politicians an incentive to seek war, since hostilities would result in more money and power for them to control. Worse, it was morally irrational for Americans to embrace the tactics of their fascist enemies by forcing people into service against their will in the name of protecting freedom.

It took courage for Paterson to voice these objections openly. By this time, leading politicians in both parties were openly advocating censorship and even the prosecution of anyone engaged in "anti-democratic propaganda," and she could easily remember that similar arguments during World War I had led to widespread punishment of dissenters.[32] Twenty years after that war, both the Sedition Act of 1917 and the Supreme Court's decisions upholding it remained on the books (as they still do), and as a new war loomed, there was a genuine possibility that such terror could return. In the Senate, Hugo Black's Lobby Investigation Committee was already engaged in highly publicized inquisitions into the administration's opponents, and in the House, the Special Committee on Un-American Activities—already almost a decade old—was taken over by Texas representative Martin Dies, who began using his position to investigate fascist and communist infiltration in the United States. The committee's inquiries cast a shadow over all dissenting voices, particularly those who might be accused of undermining morale in a national emergency. Meanwhile, the FBI began collecting information on "subversive activities," including "the distribution of literature . . . opposed to the American way of life."[33] Among others, it monitored Sinclair Lewis, whom it suspected of being a communist; H. L. Mencken, whom it labeled a Hitler sympathizer; Frank Lloyd Wright, who had discouraged his apprentices from joining the military; and novelist Pearl S. Buck, a friend of both Paterson and Lane, who spoke against the draft.[34] Lane herself would soon be targeted.

The Alien Registration Act, adopted in June 1940, and better known as the Smith Act, made it a crime to "influence the loyalty, morale, or discipline of the military or naval forces," and federal officials enforced it against opponents of conscription. In March 1941, the War Department sent a letter to Professor Edward Harwood, founder of an anti–New Deal think tank called the American Institute for Economic Research, ordering him to cease allowing "matter critical of the President of the United States" to appear in the institute's newsletter.[35] The administration used the Smith Act to charge scores of dissenters with sedition in the years that followed, especially for opposing the draft; one 1944 trial against 30 defendants was the largest sedition trial in American history. Among those charged was George Viereck, whose son Peter was a correspondent of Paterson's.[36] Roosevelt himself took a hand in curtailing some of the journalists who criticized him. After the *Yale Review* published an article by John T. Flynn, one of the nation's leading anti–New Deal writers, the president wrote to the editor to complain. "Flynn should be barred hereafter from the columns of any presentable daily paper, monthly magazine or national quarterly, such as the *Yale Review*," he insisted. The editor obeyed.[37]

State leaders also openly abused their powers. Only days after Paterson published a column attacking conscription, Jersey City's mayor Frank Hague called for the establishment of concentration camps for union leaders and other subversives. The previous November, he had delivered his infamous pronouncement, "I am the law!"—which Sinclair Lewis used in his ongoing national lecture tour as proof that fascism was, in fact, happening in America.[38] When a reporter asked Hague, "You don't believe in civil rights?" the mayor replied, "Whenever you hear that sort of cry about civil rights, you find the man saying it has a Russian flag under his coat."[39] Staunchly anti-communist as she was, Paterson reviled any form of censorship, because, as she observed in her next column, arguments for jailing subversives today would be exploited by tomorrow's politicians. Hague might invoke the "Russian flag" as a cliché to override freedom of expression, but next time around, some other cliché would serve as an excuse. "The *Russian flag* is pretty good," she wrote, "but not as novel and arresting as a *horse-and-buggy* or an *economic royalist*. . . . He might have justified suppression of speech 'against the government' the next day, with comparative safety."[40] And Hague did, in fact, broaden his calls for censorship, even banning Dorothy Thompson from giving a speech in Jersey City a few months later.[41]

Paterson was therefore well aware of the risks of dissent. To openly oppose the draft, she wrote in "Turns" in November 1939, "would get us nowhere at present, unless into the hoosegow, especially in what are called 'liberal' circles. So we'll say nothing of the sort."[42] But in fact she denounced the draft in a series of articles leading up to the war, and opposed the Dies Committee's investigations, as well. They would "accomplish nothing," she thought, and were likely to prove counterproductive. For one thing, fascism and communism were "merely different labels for collectivism, and government ownership and control, and the extinction of individual rights, including private property." If Congress wanted to root out that ideology, it would have to start by cleaning its own house, since these were the principles animating the previous decade of American politics. "Will Chairman Dies turn his attention to his legislative colleagues, and check up how far they have advanced the common purpose of Communism and Fascism—which is government ownership and control—by their own measures?" If the answer was no, then the hearings would likely only become "a smoke screen in partisan maneuvers to achieve what it professes to denounce."[43] As for the Smith Act, she wrote, it was "unconstitutional and subverts the first principles of the American political structure."[44]

Once the war began, however, it became clear that Americans could expect even stricter limits on their freedom. Roosevelt had issued a proclamation in September 1939 declaring a "limited national emergency" to "preserve neutrality"—a set of oxymorons that essentially amounted to an unofficial declaration of war—and in May 1941, he announced a new, "unlimited" national emergency that expanded his powers even further. When hostilities officially began that December, his authority became virtually limitless. A federal Office of Censorship was established, alongside several propaganda agencies, and although the government initiated relatively few sedition prosecutions, this was due more to Attorney General Francis Biddle's refusal to obey the president's orders than to any White House commitment to free speech.[45] Most often, Roosevelt's critics censored themselves, out of fear of reprisals or ostracism. Publishers told conservative writer Zora Neale Hurston to delete passages from her 1942 memoir *Dust Tracks on a Road* because they criticized him for supporting European colonial rule in Asia and refusing to condemn segregation at home.[46] Garet Garrett, who had written vigorously against American entry into the war, was fired from the *Saturday Evening Post*, as were other writers who had opposed military involvement. "You can't say what you think now and it is wartime," Paterson told Rand. "God damn them all to hell is what I say."[47]

In the years that followed, the government drafted some 10 million men into the military, confined 120,000 Japanese Americans (and many Italian and German Americans) in internment camps, confiscated $5 billion in "alien"-owned property, censored newspapers and mail, wiretapped countless Americans—including even Eleanor Roosevelt—and ordered the execution of suspected German saboteurs without trial.[48]

Nevertheless, the hope remained that Allied victory might not only vanquish tyranny abroad, but also reignite a love of liberty at home. Thus it was in the midst of the war that Paterson, Lane, and Rand would produce their lasting testaments to the principles they cherished. In 1943, after years of patient labor, the three "furies" published the books that together articulated a vision of individual freedom that had been under assault for more than a decade.

▰▰

Friends and readers had been urging Paterson to write a book about politics for years, or to change "Turns with a Bookworm" into a column focusing on politics. She tried the latter in 1938 when she began writing a column called "I Sometimes Think" for the *Herald Tribune*. It was circulated widely when Dorothy Thompson went on an extended vacation and newspapers around the country substituted Paterson's column for Thompson's. But "I Sometimes Think" never took off, and it was soon canceled.[49] Instead, Paterson turned her attention to writing a book, and by November 1941—after working many late nights and weekends—she had finished the outline for *The God of the Machine*.

Her plan was to discuss economics and politics in engineering terms—to develop her idea that a free economy represented what she called the "long circuit of energy in production"—which she insisted was "not a figure of speech or analogy, but a specific physical description" of the economic process.[50] She was not referring simply to the chemical or electrical energy involved in manufacture or trade, but to the way political relationships, moral beliefs, and economic institutions generate and transmit the human energy of individual creativity.

The book's 23 chapters address everything from education policy and the meaning of money to significant provisions of the U.S. Constitution. Its general thesis is that economic exchange is a kind of "circuit" whereby individuals, acting on their own local knowledge and circumstances, can cooperate to create and distribute wealth throughout society, while respecting each person's freedom to run his or her own life. This distinguishes it from centralized, command-and-control economies in which people are compelled to pursue a single, unified goal, and where they occupy social positions determined by the authorities.

Because a free society lets people make choices based on their own circumstances, capitalism empowers them to gather resources or to disburse them in ways that serve their own needs. Dictatorships or bureaucracies, by contrast, make people subservient to others, bar them from using the knowledge available to them, or divert their resources to serve the rulers' purposes rather than their own. Anticipating the economic theory of "spontaneous order," Paterson concludes that free markets are "fully able to carry out by voluntary association vast and complex operations of which collectivism is utterly incapable."[51] Because "throughout the longest series of exchanges, every person has a direct interest in getting the goods through, or producing them," the "general sequence creates the long circuit of energy, by an unbroken transmission."[52] By contrast, "no collectivist society can even permit co-operation; it relies upon compulsion; hence it remains static."[53]

In a passage that strikingly echoes the theme of Rand's *Fountainhead*, Paterson distinguished between two different conceptions of "power": power directed toward "the mastery of nature" and "power over other men." The latter is the essential characteristic of collectivism and "is most easily disguised under humanitarian or philanthropic motives."[54] Such a focus on power over people leads to a society that is frozen and changeless, as opposed to the fluid, ever-evolving society of freedom created by a culture that concerns itself with mastering nature. Making an argument Karl Popper would advance two years later in *The Open Society and Its Enemies*, Paterson wrote that what utopias such as those of Plato or Marx have in common "is that all of them are final; they are arrangements in which human beings fit as specialized parts of a pattern. . . . They are static societies."[55] Static societies cannot invent or innovate, because "creative processes do not function to order."[56] To live, people must think, and to think, they must be free. This explains why collectivist countries such as the Soviet Union stagnate, or are forced to borrow or steal technology from freer societies.

In fact, the idea of controlling humanity's creative energies was socialism's central fallacy, a fallacy Paterson likened to the crackpot theories behind perpetual motion machines. "The perpetual motion crank," she wrote, "admits that he has to get his engine *started* by a normal introduction of energy from an external source. After that, he says, it will keep on running on its own indefinitely. . . . The theory of Marxist Communism is precisely that of the Perpetual Motion Machine, point by point, for it stipulates that the productive system created by free enterprise is a pre-requisite, to be taken over by the Communist machine." The laws of thermodynamics dictate that all machinery will run down and will need replenishment from outside sources. Likewise, an economy must be kept going by an influx of individual creativity and thought. Yet collectivist thinkers ignored this need, simply assuming that productivity would continue in the absence of the profit motive.[57]

The book's most celebrated chapter is "The Humanitarian with the Guillotine," which makes the case that the mass-scale horrors of totalitarianism are the inevitable consequences of one central idea: that the *primary* justification of existence" is "to do good to others." Concentration camps and mass murder do not come about merely from the idiosyncrasies of corrupt dictators, Paterson argues; on the contrary, their "root" is "ethical, philosophical, and religious" doctrines that preach the subservience of the individual.[58] These doctrines are often portrayed as the essence of compassion: to serve other people is made to sound like charity. But that is a pretense. Anyone genuinely concerned with helping others would favor economic liberty, since it is essential for creating the alms to be distributed to the needy. Yet collectivists do not take this route, because their true goal is not to aid the unfortunate but to expand their own power and feel good about themselves. Given that "humanitarian" redistribution can only continue as long as there are needy people, modern "humanitarians" seek not to cure poverty but to make it sustainable and permanent. And for the same reason, modern collectivists have replaced the idea of charity as a religious principle—which Paterson thought incompatible with the idea of compulsion—with "humanitarian or philanthropic" notions that justify state-enforced redistribution. That explained why they view economic producers as existing "only for the sake of the non-producer, the well for the sake of the ill, the competent for the sake of the incompetent."[59]

Worse, government charity infantilizes its beneficiaries, treating them as incapable of running their own lives. "What the humanitarian actually proposes is that *he* shall do what he thinks is good for everybody," and this inevitably leads to tyranny, because the only way the "humanitarian" can retain authority is to control the lives of both the recipients of charity and the producers whose work funds it.[60] That was what distinguished the New Deal welfare state from the private forms of aid that existed in the frontier society of Paterson's youth. New Dealers typically argued that the private charities of that era had not been well enough funded to eliminate poverty—but the same was true of the new government assistance programs. The real difference was that private charity did not seek to "perpetuate the dependence of its beneficiaries." In fact, before the New Deal, the general atmosphere even in hard times had always been one of hope: "in the most distressful periods, there was no real famine, no black despair, but a queer kind of angry, active optimism and an unfaltering belief in better times ahead." By contrast, the compulsory relief of the Roosevelt age was demoralizing. It prolonged dependence and imposed countless meddlesome restrictions on the lives of the needy—rules that dehumanized them and made them into statistics. This occurs because the social worker is "taught that it is right to 'live for others,'" and "as long as he can believe he is doing that, he will not ask himself what he is necessarily doing *to* others, nor where the means must come from to support him."[61]

These passages reflected Paterson's belief in ethical egoism. Yet she failed to advance an explicit argument for this principle, a point on which Rand would later criticize her. When *The God of the Machine* was published, Rand called it "the greatest book written in the last three hundred years," but upon rereading it in the 1960s, she decided that "The Humanitarian with a Guillotine" was not as good as she had remembered, because Paterson never expressly argued that the individual has a right to exist for his own sake.[62] Nevertheless, other passages did make clear that Paterson believed this: for example, in a chapter likening the political institutions of the Japanese Empire to the cultural trends in America, she wrote that the "social ideal" of the society against which the United States was then at war could be found in "the purest altruism, in the communal cult," which admitted "no possibility of personal initiative or choice," and no notion of "the right to do as one pleases."[63]

Paterson's reference to Japanese society reflected a lifelong fascination with that country. Relying on the work of sociologist Lafcadio Hearn, she characterized Japan as a place where every instinct toward individualism was rigorously stamped out by cultural and educational institutions. In a chapter titled "Our Japanized Educational System," she condemned Progressive education reforms in the United States that seemed to aim at the same goal. Modern schools, she argued, were "the complete model of the totalitarian state," because they sought not to teach children the skills of independent living, but to extinguish critical thinking and individualism.[64] This extended even to pedagogic methods that emphasized memorization—such as "pictographic reading," later known as the "look-say" method—over critical thinking and obedience instead of creativity. A quarter century later, Rand would develop this point in a long essay of which she was especially proud.[65]

Another passage of *The God of the Machine*, however, was to generate lasting conflict between the two women. Although the book employs the language of mechanical and electrical engineering, Paterson also insisted that the case for individual liberty necessarily depends on the existence of God. The reason people have a right to freedom, she argued, is because they have free will—the proper role of government being to protect their right to make decisions, safe from robbers and thieves. Thus political freedom is, in Paterson's words, "essentially a secular application of the Christian doctrine of the individual soul." And because free will can only be explained by "a divine source," an atheistic philosophy "can admit no rights whatsoever."[66]

Rand apparently objected to this section when she read Paterson's manuscript before publication.[67] She thought the case for individualism did not logically depend on the existence *or* nonexistence of God, because divine creation could at best provide a historical account of humanity, whereas the claim that humans have rights depends not on the history of human nature, but on its qualities. As she put it in a 1963 essay, "The issue of man's origin does not alter the fact that he is an entity of a specific kind . . . and that rights are a necessary condition of his particular mode of survival."[68] Rand's attitude toward God's existence was therefore akin to that of the mathematician Pierre-Simon Laplace, who is reported to have answered, when asked why he left God out of his mathematical calculations, that he "had no need for that hypothesis."[69] Rand thought Paterson agreed with that position, but within a few years, it would become a source of contention, as Paterson came to believe that Rand's atheism undermined her case for individualism.[70]

▰▲◣

Paterson's description of economics in mechanical or electronic terms is provocative, intriguing, and sometimes puzzling. One reviewer said she "rides her analogy to death," and another that her "almost obscure" sentences were "by no means easy reading."[71] But there was merit in her insistence that she was not using an analogy or a metaphor, but speaking literally. Economic activity does indeed involve the transformation and movement of different kinds of energy: a farmer who uses a harvester is changing the fuel that runs the machine into a different kind of energy, in the form of the grain he harvests; when that grain is consumed, energy is again transformed into the movement of a living person's body. When that person engages in work, he or she once more changes that energy into action—and those actions can store up or release other types of energy, as where the person devises an equation that helps release the previously untapped energies of the atom. Viewed in this way, the investment of capital can be viewed as the movement, storage, or release of different energies.

Still, Paterson's mechanical terminology is less accurate than if she had used the language of biology or information theory, as a later generation of economists did. Economic exchange is more analogous to an organic, complex adaptive process such as evolution than to a mechanical or electronic device. Machines are made, whereas biological processes—and free markets—are grown.[72] And whereas "energy" refers to that property that must be applied to an object to perform work on it, "information" refers to a *qualitative* property— specifically, the resolution of uncertainty, or the arrangement of things into useful forms. Paterson was writing years before information theory became well known, but her contention that economic markets should be viewed as a means of transforming and transferring resources through intricately complex networks has since been vindicated by the "information economics" pioneered by George Stigler, Kenneth Arrow, and others.

In fact, the most striking aspect of Paterson's "machine" theory is the degree to which it parallels the "Austrian school" of economists, despite the fact that she was not deeply familiar with their work.[73] At the time Paterson was writing, these economists—Carl Menger, Eugen von Böhm-Bawerk, Ludwig von Mises, and F. A. Hayek—were developing the theory that prices, far from representing any kind of inherent worth, are actually signals about comparative demands for resources. In what economic historians later called the "marginal revolution," these thinkers refuted Karl Marx's "labor theory of value" and showed that socialism is unworkable because if the state owns everything, it becomes impossible to calculate relative costs and benefits.[74] Paterson was not aware of their writing, much of which was published in scholarly journals and in German. A year after *The God of the Machine* appeared, Hayek would begin publicizing their insights and developing a broader argument that, left to their own devices, people will generate new social and cultural institutions without necessarily intending to do so—thus eliminating any need for government planning. That theory would win him the Nobel Prize in 1974. Paterson's argument that the economy is just an enormously complex system for transmitting productive energies—and that any attempt to control that system through force is "bound to result in explosion"—represented a prescient insight into the same phenomenon.[75] Yet she appears never to have read Hayek's work.

When *The God of the Machine* was published, the cantankerous Paterson refused to send copies to reviewers at the *New York Post*, the *Saturday Review*, the *Chicago Sun*, *The Nation*, or the *New Republic*, who she assumed would pan it.[76] But it received favorable notices in the *L.A. Times*, the *New York Times*, and elsewhere.[77] Two years after its publication, Lane reviewed it in the *National Economic Council Review of Books*, a newsletter she began editing in August 1945.[78] It "smashes to bits the whole basis of nearly all previous work in political economy," she declared. It was "the first approach ever made to a scientific study of the relations between production (the operation of human energy in converting the materials of this earth into forms of wealth and distributing them) and the structure of the political mechanism, the State, in which this energy so operates." Lane thought the most valuable aspect of Paterson's analysis was its intense "realism"—its refusal to ignore the fact that all production and exchange must take place within natural laws that cannot be remade by "the will of the people or an Act of Congress." Rand, too, enthused about the book in letters to publishers, business executives, and fans. It was "the greatest defense of capitalism I have ever read," she told one. "It does for capitalism what *Das Kapital* did for the Reds."[79] It "could literally save the world," she told another, "if enough people knew of it and read it."[80]

But Paterson was surprised to learn the identity of another admirer: former president Herbert Hoover, who likely read the book on Lane's recommendation. Paterson reacted with puzzled amusement when he wrote her a complimentary letter about the book, given that she had long considered him a dangerous fool. But knowing he might be able to help publicize her work, she agreed when Lane arranged for her to have lunch with him at the Waldorf Astoria in New York.

It was a waste of time. Writing to Rand afterward, Paterson reported that Hoover proved to be every bit as dull as she had expected. Self-obsessed, fond of meaningless phrases and clichés, he annoyed Paterson by referring to her book's mechanistic and electrical terms as mere metaphors. "I said they weren't metaphors but engineering descriptions. He said very well, but I insisted that was an important distinction"—whereupon Hoover changed the subject. He had bad table manners, too, and insisted on keeping the door open throughout the meeting "so the two girl secretaries could doubtless preserve his virtue if it came to the worst."[81] But he irritated Paterson even more when, in response to her complaint that business leaders refused to stand up for themselves, he observed that this was understandable, given that executives were so busy working. "Whereas you and I," Paterson growled, "with the extraordinary advantages we have possessed—being women, with a living to earn as best we can, and no backing, and the dishes to wash, and no firsthand experience in the engineering and industrial field, and with the aforesaid prominent men cutting our throats by endowing every triple-asterisk Pink in the country and supporting the same on all the periodicals—it is obvious that we can very well do the thinking, is it not?" She was pleased that Hoover seemed to understand a few of her arguments, but came away from the meeting repulsed at the idea "that I am asked to accept such a man as an intellectual equal."[82] There was no chance the Great Engineer would help promote her book.

◢◣

Where *The God of the Machine* focused on the mechanics of political and economic liberty, Lane's *The Discovery of Freedom* focused on its history.

Like Paterson's book, it began with the concept of "energy," but Lane meant something subtly different by the term. For Paterson, the energy with which the economy deals is the mechanism by which economic productivity generates value in the world. But for Lane, human energy means the self-directed capacity of living things to create meaning in a universe of inanimate matter. The locus of this energy is the individual, which Lane highlights as the crucial fact of her argument.[83] The fact that this creative capacity belongs inherently and inescapably to individual humans, not to groups, is why collectivism can never succeed. Political authorities may punish, enslave, and kill people—but they can never actually penetrate a person's self, to compel that person to feel, think, or believe. Lane's energy metaphor is therefore an effort to articulate what America's Founding Fathers meant when they spoke in the Declaration of Independence of the "inalienability" of individual rights. "The nature of human energy," she wrote, is that "each person is self-controlling, and therefore . . . every human being, by his nature, is free."[84] This meant individual liberty was not just a cultural preference, but a fact about human beings—just as the shelter-building instinct is a fact about muskrats. This showed, too, that man's need for freedom could not be superseded by changes in social or economic circumstances. Thus although Lane's focus was on history, her argument was not essentially historical. She viewed liberty not as tradition created over time, but as a law of nature, like those of biology or medicine. Liberty is literally *discovered*, not constructed.

In Lane's telling, the "first attempt" to realize the principle of inherent individual freedom came with the monotheism of the biblical Abraham, who took the first step toward the concept of the rule of law. Drawing on the book of Samuel, Lane relates how the Israelites feared freedom and clamored for a ruler, because they shared what she calls the "pagan" notion that human beings must be commanded by an authority figure in order to live their lives. The Israelites had wanted "to be 'like all the other nations.' But to be like any other people, they must forget that men are free."[85] And as the prophets warned, the consequence of that shortsightedness had, indeed, been tyranny. The Samuel story taught what Lane considered Judaism's most important principle: that people must necessarily govern themselves by rules, rather than subordinating themselves to worldly dictators. In fact, Lane thought the centrality of this idea in Judaism explained why tyrannical governments throughout history have so often been anti-Semitic. "Wherever tyranny is strongest—in 15th-century Spain, in Czarist Russia, in Nazi Germany—attacks upon the Jew are most mercilessly atrocious" precisely because "four thousand years ago, a Jew said that men are free."[86] Jesus's mission, too, was based on this central truth. "He spoke of the God of Abraham, the God that is Rightness, and does not control any man but judges every man's acts."[87]

According to Lane, the "second attempt" to vindicate individual liberty in world history came with the advent of Islam. Drawing on what were by then two decades of interest in Muslim history, she argued that Mohammed's message was one of freedom and equality. The Prophet taught that "there is no superior *kind* of man; men are humanly equal," and therefore "there should be no priests. Each individual must recognize his direct relation to God, his self-controlling, personal responsibility."[88] That insight gave birth to "the first scientific civilization"[89]—the Islamic Golden Age—during the same period in which the Christian West was mired in medieval dogma and oppression. Alas, after generations of peace and progress, the Muslim world abandoned the principle of human freedom and lapsed again into the "pagan" principle of rule by Authority. That had happened because after the Crusades, Muslims ceased to think of Allah as a rational principle of lawfulness and came to think of Him instead as an incomprehensible mystery Who rules the universe by decree. Piety, they decided, consists of "submission to the Unknowable" in a "static, changeless universe" governed by "the controlling Authority."[90] That idea rendered the Islamic world "stagnant for six centuries." Lane believed a similar trend could be observed in the contemporary world, "as communists and fascists and Nazis submit to The Party, and as some Americans believe that individuals should and must submit to an enforced Social Good, to the Will of the Majority, to a Planned Economy, to many other pagan gods that do not exist."[91]

Humanity's "third attempt" to realize the principles of freedom began with the American Revolution, which liberated people from the control of the state.

It was a leaderless revolution; a social movement in which people living on the frontier abandoned feudalism and saw themselves not as servants of the crown, but as individuals worthy of the liberty to create lives for themselves through economic productivity and exchange. The revolutionaries did not fight for "democracy." Instead, they "stood against both monarchy and democracy, because they knew that when men set up an imaginary Authority armed with force, they destroy all opportunity to exercise their natural freedom."[92]

Illustrated with dozens of examples, some entertaining and unusual, drawn from Lane's autodidactic reading in history and philosophy and citing everything from the works of Thomas Paine to the Quran, *The Discovery of Freedom* is, in the words of historian Brian Doherty, "an eccentric and spirited statement of a certain strain of the modern libertarian character: historically visionary, rooted in American experience yet foreseeing the whole world transformed by a political/ideological spirit that could and should be universal."[93] The book makes little pretense to scholarly precision, but aims instead to offer a personal view, one that emphasizes liberty as a motive force in society's evolution, in the same way that Charles Beard and others had emphasized the role of class conflicts and the power of economic elites.

Discovery contains some clumsy passages, such as the paragraph that asserts "because no man can control another . . . a great many—one by one—must stop believing in pagan gods, and know the real nature of human life-energy, before that energy can operate effectively to make a world fit for human beings to live in"—which comes off sounding like a commercial for a New Age medicine.[94] Some of Lane's efforts at philosophy are also dubious, such as her statement that "consciousness itself is an act of faith. No one can prove that he exists. No evidence of the senses, and no effort of logic, can demonstrate the existence of the element that everyone means when he says 'I.'"[95] But the book hardly deserved the ridicule it received at the hands of some reviewers, such as the *Baltimore Sun* writer who called it "inaccurate," "nervous," and "pungent."[96] Others lauded it, however, most notably newspaper publisher R. C. Hoiles, who repeatedly praised it alongside *The God of the Machine* in his syndicated column, and J. A. Rogers, editor of the *Pittsburgh Courier*, the nation's leading black newspaper, to which Lane had begun contributing regular columns in October 1942.[97]

Two ideas in *Discovery* would, however, cause conflict with Paterson and Rand. First, in her discussion of property rights, which she considered essential to individual freedom, Lane nevertheless used equivocal language that must have alarmed her colleagues. "The right to own property is not an inalienable natural right, as life and liberty are," she declared, but "a legal right, absolutely essential to an individual's exercise of his natural rights." Nobody owned property in primitive societies, she claimed, or under feudalism. It was America's Founding Fathers who had invented this brand-new principle.[98]

As a historical assertion, this was false—many societies antedating the American Revolution had recognized property rights—but more distressing to Paterson and Rand was the implication that private property was merely a social construct, which suggested a dangerous moral relativism. Although Lane obviously considered property crucial, calling it a function of positive law rather than a natural right implied that it was merely a privilege given to people by the state, and that the government could legitimately replace it with some other principle if necessary. Lane herself would later repudiate her wording when R. C. Hoiles wrote to complain.[99] It was an "appalling error," she admitted.[100] "I was contradicting myself. . . . The theory that ownership of property is not a 'natural right' but a 'civil' right, *granted* to a person or persons by the Whole (the King, Legislature, State, Society, or Community) rests on [a] collectivist fallacy."[101]

A more lasting problem originated in a phrase Lane had long ago become attached to, and which she employed repeatedly in *Discovery*: "All men are brothers." What precisely she meant by this is unclear. She seems to have been seeking to combine the long-standing principle that "all men are created equal"—meaning that human beings have the same rights regardless of race or sex—with the deeper cultural traditions and social mores that cause people to respect their neighbors' rights and assist others in need, an idea she vaguely associated with the "invisible hand" phenomenon identified by Adam Smith. In Lane's view, social habits play a greater role in securing individual liberty than do laws or constitutions, and she wrote in *Discovery* that "the real protection of life and property, always and everywhere, is the general recognition of the brotherhood of man," not the laws enforced by the state.[102] "How much of the time is any American within sight of a policeman? Our lives and property are protected by the way nearly everyone feels about another person's life and property."[103] As those habits and conventions of mutual respect expand to encompass a whole nation or even the whole world, the result is to lift the standard of living for all—not just in a material sense, but also in a spiritual sense.

Lane had groped toward this idea a dozen years earlier in a letter to Dorothy Thompson in which she laid out her thoughts about the destruction of bourgeois ethics in the previous decade. "What [people] need is an object, an aim, which will compel us to accomplish a purpose by indirection," she wrote. "The greatest good to the greatest number will obviously be reached when each individual of the greatest number is doing the greatest good to himself. That is why the Brotherhood of Man is all right, if and when each man is primarily concerned with his own relationship to God. And the hell of it is, we have no God. He's gone completely. We absolutely must make a new one."[104] Now, she had come to view this sense of fraternity—which she insisted was "not a pretty phrase nor a beautiful ideal," but "one of the brutal realities of human life on this inhuman planet"[105]—as an idea that could indirectly accomplish that purpose: connecting personal morality with political liberty and economic prosperity.

But Paterson objected to the vagueness of Lane's brotherhood concept. Did Lane mean to imply that every person owes a moral duty to serve other people's interests? If so, what room remained for insisting on one's right to private property in the face of those who sought to confiscate it to provide for the "needy"? Lane seemed to be embracing an idea of subservience that undermined the cause of freedom. Or did she mean to imply a sort of relativism whereby people were obliged to ignore significant moral distinctions? "Stalin is no brother of *mine*," Paterson insisted whenever Lane recited her brotherhood principle. "After a year of hearing that," Lane later told a friend, "one day I said to her 'Nobody agrees with you more heartily than Stalin.'"[106] Their long-simmering disputes seem to have exploded at that point. Lane later told Rand that in the argument that ensued, Paterson, in a rage, called her a "liar" and a "communist."[107]

In fact, Paterson did not like Lane's book. She mentioned it only twice in "Turns," and then only briefly.[108] Lane was later to complain that her failure to publicize it destroyed sales. Paterson told Rand that fall that Lane had even sent her an indignant letter accusing her of *"acting with* the Pinks" by "suppressing" *Discovery*.[109] Paterson made a crushing reply: nobody, she told Lane, had the right to use such language with her, certainly not a former communist.[110] Two years later, Lane confronted her about it again. This time, Paterson responded with a withering offer to tell Lane just *exactly* what she thought of the book. Embarrassed, Lane declined, and dropped the subject. In the end, *The Discovery of Freedom* sold fewer than 1,000 copies, and a crestfallen Lane felt obliged to return the publisher's advance.[111] It can have come as little comfort that Laura Ingalls Wilder considered it her daughter's best work.[112]

▰▲◣

Critics may have been puzzled by *The God of the Machine* and put off by *The Discovery of Freedom*, but they were shocked by *The Fountainhead*. It was an audacious novel, incisively modern but defiantly romantic, which combined the observational satire of Sinclair Lewis with the passionate idealism of Victor Hugo. It represented the culmination of Rand's efforts since *The Little Street* and *Ideal* to address the Revolt from the Village without surrendering to the cynicism and despair that dogged Lewis's own work. Indeed, Rand saw the rebellion against mediocrity as representing what Hugo called mankind's "celestial quality"[113]—the craving in every human soul for truth and beauty— and she sought to celebrate that drive in her novel, by contrasting the creative "self-starting" personality with the conformist mindset of those who live by and through the opinions of others.

The action revolves around brilliant young architect Howard Roark, who is expelled from architecture school because he is too gifted and the school's dean fears his radical genius. Deprived of a degree, he becomes an apprentice to an inspired builder named Henry Cameron, whose work has fallen out of fashion. Roark's reputation gradually grows, but his defiant refusal to compromise the integrity of his designs causes repeated conflicts with corporate boards and civic groups who fear to be associated with his unorthodox designs. Unable to find clients on his own terms, Roark is reduced to earning a living as a manual laborer in a granite quarry.

While there, he begins an affair with Dominique Francon, daughter of a prominent architect whose employees include Peter Keating, one of Roark's classmates from the architecture school. Keating is a hack who squanders his talents by focusing on social climbing instead. He knows all the right people—he eventually even marries Dominique—and rises in his profession through social connections instead of ingenuity. He becomes a protégé of a prominent art critic named Ellsworth Toohey, who writes a column for the *New York Banner*. Vaguely resembling Julius from Paterson's *The Golden Vanity*, Toohey is a sly and cynical manipulator whose perverse collectivist philosophy is consciously committed to the destruction of greatness and the elevation of mediocrity.

When businessman Hopton Stoddard decides to fund construction of a nondenominational temple, he asks Toohey to recommend an architect, and Toohey suggests Roark. It's a trap: Toohey knows Roark's design will be so radical that it will spark a controversy he can exploit for the purpose of destroying Roark's career. It works: the church scandalizes the artistic community and Toohey persuades Stoddard to sue Roark for breach of contract. Dominique, meanwhile, is so certain that greatness is impossible in a world that rewards banal conformity that she testifies against Roark at the trial, despite the fact that she loves him and had even posed for the statue that forms the temple's centerpiece. The court rules against Roark, and the temple is destroyed. Yet the publicity surrounding the trial benefits Roark in the long run, because people who read about his work in the newspapers come to admire it and seek him out for commissions.

In the interim, Dominique—in a masochistic effort to destroy her own idealism—divorces Keating and marries Gail Wynand, a newspaper tycoon modeled after William Randolph Hearst. Wynand is a self-made million-aire with strongly individualistic personal values, and he genuinely loves Dominique. Yet he shares with her a contempt for the ordinariness of the world, and his newspaper reflects it. For years he has pandered to readers, becoming rich by cynically aiming at the lowest common denominator and sacrificing his own integrity because he considers it valueless in a world that does not care about principles. When he hires Roark to build a house for him-self and Dominique, however, the two men become friends, and the friendship gradually reignites the idealism of Wynand's youth. He finds himself vaguely ashamed of having built his wealth on mere popularity, without achieving something of lasting value. Their comradery also tortures Dominique, who loves Roark despite herself. He is everything she had once dreamed of seeing in the world and had long ago abandoned.

That reawakening of Wynand's integrity becomes central to the final quarter of the novel. Keating persuades Roark to help him design an ingenious new government housing project called Courtland Homes. The task is too complicated for Keating's meager skills, whereas Roark—who can do it—is too controversial to be considered by the managing committee. Thus they make a *Cyrano de Bergerac*–style arrangement: Roark will secretly design the project merely for the sake of the challenge, while Keating takes the money and credit. Roark's one demand is that Keating not allow the plans to be altered. It is a promise Keating cannot keep, and Courtland Homes is hid-eously compromised with redesigns by dozens of second-rate architects. Roark decides to vindicate his rights to his own creation. With Dominique's help, he dynamites the project (without harming anyone) and surrenders himself to authorities for trial.

Wynand, his idealism fully rekindled, tries to defend Roark in the *Banner*. "We have never made an effort to understand what is greatness in man and how to recognize it," he writes.

> We have come to hold, in a kind of mawkish stupor, that greatness is to be gauged by self-sacrifice. . . . Is sacrifice a virtue? Can a man

sacrifice his integrity? His honor? His freedom? His ideal . . . ? But these are a man's supreme possessions. Anything he gives up for them is not a sacrifice but an easy bargain. They, however, are above sacrificing to any cause or consideration. . . . It is precisely the self that cannot and must not be sacrificed.[114]

But public outrage over the trial becomes so intense that *Banner* readers begin canceling subscriptions, boycotting his papers, and picketing his offices with signs that proclaim "We don't read Wynand!"[115] Soon the paper faces bankruptcy. Wynand discovers that he has neglected the realm of ideas for too long. Like Hearst publishing Mussolini's and Hitler's columns in his real-life newspapers, he has allowed Toohey to propagandize against individualism until it has become too late to reverse course. When he fires Toohey, the staff goes on strike and eventually Wynand is compelled to surrender. He reverses the paper's editorial position, calls for Roark's conviction, and retreats into despair.

At his trial, Roark gives a dramatic speech, explaining that the case boils down to a clash between two visions of life: that of the creator, whose focus is on conquering nature, and who has the right to decide the terms on which he will create—and that of the second-hander, who exists only through his relationships to other people, and whose motive is to gain power over them. Second-handers "feel they have a right to anyone's property, spiritual or material," and by propagandizing for self-sacrifice, they often persuade creators to submit, and to produce for the benefit of others rather than for themselves.[116] But that is a shameful self-betrayal, for every person has the right to exist for his own sake. "I did not receive the payment I asked," Roark tells the jury. "They took the benefit of my work and made me contribute it as a gift. But I am not an altruist. . . . I do not recognize anyone's right to one minute of my life. Nor to any part of my energy."[117] Roark asks for no favors—only the freedom to apply his mind to the problems of building and creating—and he has a right to insist that everyone else respect his freedom and honor their obligations to him.

The jury vindicates Roark, but Wynand has destroyed his business and himself: he closes the *Banner* and divorces Dominique, who marries Roark. But as a farewell gesture, Wynand hires Roark to build a project he had long dreamed of: New York's greatest skyscraper, to be called the Wynand Building. "Build it," he tells Roark, "as a monument to that spirit which is yours . . . and could have been mine."[118]

The Fountainhead is not an essentially political novel. Virtually none of its characters are government officials, and its conflict focuses not on the role of the state, but on Roark's clashes with social convention—with squeamish businessmen and materialistic mediocrities such as Keating, who abandon their artistic values in hopes of commercial popularity. In short, the novel is a hymn to individualism, and at its core is the moral principle that every person has the right to pursue his or her own happiness. Although this idea that self-sacrifice is evil would come to be most closely associated with Rand, thanks to such writings as her 1964 book *The Virtue of Selfishness*, it was a view Paterson and Lane shared. None of them were *hedonists*, in the sense of pursuing pleasure for its own sake, but all three believed people can and should aim their actions toward their own well-being, and that it is positively immoral to subordinate one's own rational interests to those of others (or to sacrifice others for oneself). In their eyes, the argument for self-sacrifice was typically used as a way to trick people into subordinating themselves to the state. "If the primary objective of the philanthropist, his justification for living, is to help others," Paterson wrote, "his ultimate good requires that others shall be in want. His happiness is the obverse of their misery."[119]

Lane, too, considered altruism immoral. In 1948, she recounted a conversation with an English friend who told her that although he agreed with everything Lane said about freedom, still, he thought it was the responsibility of the upper classes to "look out for the lower classes. . . . And really, how can we without pushing them around a bit?"

The only answer [Lane continued] is, "You can't." As Isabel Paterson said, "The power to do things for you is the power to do things to you." But the idea of simply letting every person, even an "underprivi-leged" person, live his own life because God endows him with self-control and responsibility which no one can alienate from him—this idea flatly denies the concept of Christian altruism which churches have inculcated for two thousand years: the belief that goodness con-sists in living for others, which can't be done without pushing them around.[120]

The hero of Rand's novel makes his position unmistakable. "I am a man who does not exist for others," Roark says at his trial.[121] The political implica-tions are clear, but Rand's focus is on her character's spiritual independence and artistic integrity, not his political views. Rand biographer Anne Heller calls Roark "as American as Huckleberry Finn or Holden Caulfield," but he is better seen as Rand's answer to the questions J. D. Salinger's *Catcher in the Rye* would pose in 1945 about authenticity in a world of phoniness—and that Sinclair Lewis had raised in *Main Street* about greatness in a society that cel-ebrates the insipid and ordinary.[122]

Some critics have noted Roark's resemblance to Nietzsche's fictional prophet Zarathustra, especially in the passage that opens the novel's fourth section, which bears a notable resemblance to the chapter in Nietzsche's book titled "On the Tree on the Mountainside." Yet by this point in her life, Rand had come to distance herself from the German philosopher. For instance, she abandoned a plan to include quotations from Nietzsche's books—as well as the Bible—in the novel, and if Roark resembles Nietzsche's vision of the "well turned-out person," who "has reverence for himself," he is actually closer in spirit to the "great-souled man" described by Aristotle, who is "of few deeds, but of great and notable ones," and is "unable to make his life revolve round another, unless it be a friend; for this is slavish."[123] As for Roark's likeness to Huckleberry Finn, Paterson, too, noticed the resemblance. Roark, she told Rand, "is what an American boy wants to be. . . . A sort of composite Revolu-tionary soldier who knew what he was fighting for, and like Leatherstocking whose rule of conduct was to act 'according to his nature,' and Kit Carson and Daniel Boone and Jim Bridger on their simple level—now what is the common denominator? I would say that it is the fact that they had their own business to be concerned with. I believe there is a vague feeling that the type had to do with 'the frontier.'"[124]

Perhaps ironically, one person Roark bears little resemblance to is the real-life architect Frank Lloyd Wright. An occasionally careless designer and an often unscrupulous businessman, the real Wright designed buildings that are gorgeous, ingenious, and awe-inspiring, but his grasp of individualism, while sincere, was eccentric; he called Soviet communism "a heroic endeavor," for example, while simultaneously holding that "there is probably no great society where individual possession is not something to be respected and encouraged."[125] Rand had studied his autobiography in preparation for the novel and based some of its plot on his actual career—the Stoddard Temple owes much to Wright's 1908 Unity Temple and 1913 Midway Gardens—and she admired his defiant romanticism as well as many of his public statements (such as "individuality realized is the supreme attainment of the human soul"[126]). But she could not understand how he reconciled that with his praise of the Soviet Union. "This is sheer drivel," she wrote in her journal, after reading one of Wright's statements.[127]

Paterson thought it was asking too much to expect Wright to be a philosophical sage. "The man has a streak of talent and a yard-wide phony streak," she told Rand. "I avoid such people because one never can tell which streak one will encounter, or when. . . . Plenty of men of ability have been half nuts also. That's a fact of record."[128] Rand never ceased to celebrate Wright's architecture—she even asked him to design a house for her in 1946—but she found good reason to clarify years later that "as a person—as a character—Roark's philosophy is almost the opposite of Wright's."[129]

A stronger influence on *The Fountainhead* was Sinclair Lewis.[130] Roark's relationship to his mentor, the elderly Henry Cameron, parallels not only Wright's relationship with his own teacher, Louis Sullivan—at least, as Wright characterized it in his memoir—but also the bond between the title character of Lewis's *Arrowsmith* and his professor, Max Gottlieb. And Rand's satirical portraits of modern intellectuals are cut with the same precision as Lewis's caricatures in *Babbitt* and *It Can't Happen Here*. Lewis's influence also helps explain the otherwise puzzling character of Dominique—whom Rand once called "quite stupid" if taken literally. Dominique is an intensely exaggerated version of *Main Street*'s Carol Kennicott—"an idealist paralyzed by disgust," as Rand explained.[131] Where Lewis's character ends up abandoning her dream of a meaningful life, Dominique tries to obliterate her ability to desire anything. Freedom, she thinks, means "to ask nothing. To expect nothing. To depend on nothing."[132] Yet in *We the Living*, Rand had argued that *wanting* is the essence of life. Dominique—in a desperate attempt to avoid being suffocated by the "village virus"—decides to sabotage her capacity to want in the first place.

As Lewis had done in *It Can't Happen Here*, Rand draws on several other real-life figures as bases for her characters. They include not only Wright as an inspiration for Roark, but also Lewis Mumford, Harold Laski, and Benito Mussolini as models for Ellsworth Toohey; H. L. Mencken as the basis for the character of journalist Austin Heller; and William Randolph Hearst as the model for Gail Wynand.

Rand had intended from the moment she began planning the novel to model a character on Hearst, one of the few remaining business leaders who resembled the industrial giants of the previous century. He fascinated Rand in part because he seemed to combine an extraordinary egotism with an absolute contempt for the power of ideas. He had "great influence," she wrote in a 1935 journal entry, "because he always sits on the fence and says only that which is 'box-office.'" He thought that made him independent, but it actually made him "the greatest of slaves," because it meant he based his very identity on other people's opinions.[133] His politics were notoriously inconsistent—championing Roosevelt in 1933, only to become Roosevelt's enemy two years later—with the result that by the time he tried to take a principled stand for freedom in opposing the New Deal, his credibility had been wasted. Rand would use his life to dramatize the betrayal of individualism committed by those who foolishly think that success means ruling other people. Just as Hearst had supported figures such as Mussolini, Wynand's cynical attempt to manipulate the public creates his own nemesis: Toohey, whom he thinks he controls but who actually controls him. *The Fountainhead*'s climax depicts Wynand deject-edly walking the streets of New York, discovering that he is not the master of popular taste, as he imagined, but its plaything. By sacrificing principles, he has come to exemplify the *Main Street*–style dullness he despised.

Neither Wynand nor any of Rand's other characters are journalistic cop-ies of their real-life models. Austin Heller, for example, shares Mencken's iconoclastic individualism—he is "devoted to the destruction of all forms of compulsion, private or public, in heaven or on earth," and has an encyclopedic knowledge of literature and music, as did the actual writer—but he is trans-formed in the novel into an Oxford-educated aristocrat with an English accent and a fondness for modern architecture (which the real Mencken disliked).[134] Even Sinclair Lewis may have helped inspire a character: Steven Mallory, the sculptor Roark hires to create the statute of Dominique at the center of the Stoddard Temple.

When the reader is introduced to Mallory, he is 24, embittered by rejec-tion from art critics who view his daring and exultant style as obsolete and insignificant. Although once intensely idealistic, he has been devoured by cynicism, so that his "eyes were like black holes left after a fire not quite put out."[135] Haunted by nightmares in which he is attacked by a faceless mon-ster that represents the "village virus," Mallory has been driven to alcoholism, and has so thoroughly abandoned any belief in the possibility of a world that prizes greatness that he pushes Roark away when the architect comes to hire him. Lewis, too, was hideously addicted to drink, a fact well known to gos-sip columnists at the time. As early as December 1931, Paterson told a friend that Lewis was "burnt-out" by alcohol. "Never saw such a pathetic wreck," she said, after seeing him at a party. "[He] looked like a goner."[136] A decade later, after grueling fights and tearful pledges of reform, he and Dorothy Thompson divorced. He had always dreamed of completing a great, idealistic novel, and conducted exhaustive research for it, but gave it up. After *It Can't Happen Here*, his career began to deteriorate. His later books received dismal reviews in prominent journals, and by the time he died in 1951, he had become a relic.[137] Rand understood that shattered idealism could lead to self-destructive behavior. In *We the Living*, Leo is driven to alcoholism out of rage at a society that denies him any opportunity to lead his own life. That character was likely based on real people Rand had known who became addicted after their dreams were destroyed by communist rule. Passages of *The Fountainhead* in which Mallory describes his recurring nightmare of being pursued by the beast of mediocrity suggest that Rand incorporated the source of Lewis's own tragedy into the book.

But unlike Lewis—a naturalist writer, focused on faithfully representing the actual world—Rand was a romanticist, who aimed at dramatizing abstract principles.[138] And where Lewis's novels tend to conclude either that idealists must resign themselves to the "village virus" or flee the village entirely, Rand's viewpoint is not nearly so anti-social. On the contrary, *The Fountainhead* is both idealistic and optimistic; cynicism, it says, is just another form of surrender. When Wynand, who sacrifices his profoundest values at the novel's climax, tells Roark that he expects the Wynand Building will be "the last achievement of man on earth before mankind destroys itself," Roark replies, "Mankind will never destroy itself."[139]

What's more, just as *Main Street* expressed a quiet sympathy for Carol Kennicott even while satirizing her pettiness, Rand's novel shows a surprising tenderness toward "second-handers." Peter Keating is treated less as a villain than as a case of self-sabotage—a man who wrecks his own potential, more by sins of omission than by overt wrongs.[140] Driven by a demanding and manipulative mother whom he lacks the fortitude to resist, he turns down the opportunity to study architecture at a great school and lets himself be bullied into an unhappy marriage and a job he does not particularly want. After years of squandering his talent, he comes to his senses and makes a last, feeble effort at psychological independence. Leaving a meeting with Roark, he pauses and pulls out some sketches of a building he drew in private. "I haven't shown it to anyone," he says. "Not to mother or Ellsworth Toohey. . . . I just want you to tell me if there's any. . . ." But the designs are no good, and Roark tells him so.

As he walks away, Roark feels a wave of pity for "a man without worth or hope."[141] Keating is no scoundrel, but the victim of a slow spiritual suicide, who—like Wynand—has thrown away his gifts piecemeal. The protagonists of Sinclair Lewis's novels, John Updike once said, typically end up "in a kind of hopeless surrender to the values satirized."[142] Similarly, Keating discovers only too late that he has condemned himself.

For all its Lewis-inflected satire, *The Fountainhead* is an overwhelmingly serious novel, concerned with the veneration of human potential. In *We the Living*, Rand had written that "the highest thing in man is not his god" but "that in him which knows the reverence due a god," and reverence served as one of *The Fountainhead*'s most significant themes.[143] "[The] feeling I want for Roark," Rand told herself in her preparatory notes, was "the difference between . . . art as a business and art as a religion . . . the burning reverence as against the 'meal-ticket' architecture."[144] In a passage she cut from the manuscript, Roark's girlfriend complains that she never feels relaxed in his presence. "It's like . . . like as if you had no weekdays at all in your life," she tells him, "nothing but Sundays."[145] Rand strove not only to depict who creators are and why they create, but also the sense of devotion toward human greatness that she saw as the only genuine rebellion against the village. "You're a profoundly religious man, Mr. Roark—in your own way," says a character in the finished book. In a solemn whisper, Roark replies, "That's true."[146]

▰▲◤

During *The Fountainhead*'s completion, Rand had joked with Paterson that she expected critics to label Howard Roark "ruthless." When Paterson asked why, she replied: "You'll see. He will be called worse than that, just because he doesn't want power over any one . . . because he asks nothing but individual freedom and independence. . . . You say that, and your hearers will be shocked; they'll exclaim: How cruel!" When the novel was published, Paterson wrote in "Turns" that Rand was right. "She knew the formula of the sentimentalists. And that's the thesis of her novel; it is explicitly against altruism, as the curse of the modern world. But apparently, it was such a jolt, the reviewers couldn't even bring themselves to state it."[147]

It was true that reviewers typically failed to discuss the book's philosophic elements, but most reviews were complimentary.[148] The *New York Times'* Lorine Pruette—a longtime friend of Paterson's—called it "the only novel of ideas by an American woman that I can recall."[149] Frank Lloyd Wright raved that he read "every word," and that Rand's "thesis is *the* great one."[150] One of the few hostile notices appeared in Paterson's own *Herald Tribune*. Written by left-wing Harvard professor Albert Guerard—who expressed his "fascinated eagerness" about the novel's "frankly intellectual" style and "exciting events and colorful characters"—it expressed discomfort with the way the book "haughtily denounces the herd."[151] Guerard thought Rand failed to recognize that even geniuses like Roark need supporters and helpers, who may be less talented but are still worthy of respect. This, like Guerard's claim that the book "scorns the Profit Motive," was oddly off-key, given that the novel features a cast of supporting characters who, although not geniuses, befriend and help Roark and are treated positively.[152] Of all the reviews she received, Rand singled out Guerard's as the one that bothered her most. For such a review to appear in the nation's leading Republican newspaper was distressing.

Paterson and Lane also harbored some private objections to the book, especially toward the scene in which Roark rapes Dominique—an incident that would become one of the novel's most polarizing elements, notwithstanding Rand's explanation that Dominique welcomes Roark's act and that the book could not be fairly interpreted as advocating sexual assault.[153] "I do not like it," Lane remarked when she read it. "Call me a prude."[154] Paterson's qualms were more abstract. Ambivalent about romanticism generally, she was concerned about the novel's uncompromising intensity. The romantic temperament, she explained, seeks excellence instead of mere sufficiency—it insists on the "difference between living and merely existing." But although that attitude is essential to the accomplishment of greatness, "the romantic illusion" can also generate "enormous crimes when it is linked to a petty ego and fourth-rate intelligence. That is the romanticism of all the conquerors and dictators."[155] Romanticists sometimes blurred the distinction between the "village virus" and the harmless joys of small-town life. In other words, their scorn for "bourgeois values" sometimes drew them toward self-destructive or violent gestures—or to utopian totalitarian movements—unless it was balanced by respect for the peaceful pursuit of happiness. As later events were to show, Paterson feared that the passionate intensity of Rand's literature was not sufficiently grounded in reason to avoid making the same mistake.

9

The Subversive

The nation's entry into World War II had caused many Americans to reexamine the attitudes they had adopted in the previous two decades—about patriotism, nationality, freedom, and the future. They began to more sharply define themselves in contrast to the authoritarian fascist states the country was fighting. Intellectuals such as Gunnar Myrdal, Carl Becker, and Max Lerner began writing with a new respect for American political and social values—values that clashed with the authoritarian politics of the New Deal era.[1]

Voters, too, were growing restive about the Roosevelt administration's "experiments" with the economy. Republican gains in the 1942 midterm elections revealed that they still liked the president, but were getting tired of New Deal schemes. It was "a bad November for extremists and prophets," wrote former Roosevelt aide Raymond Moley. "The American people have reminded the 'morale builders' in Washington that they don't want to be told what to think or how to feel."[2] Once the new Congress convened, it promptly abolished or scaled back the National Youth Administration, the National Resources Planning Board, the Farm Security Administration, and other bureaucracies. Meanwhile, the Supreme Court began showing a greater willingness to defend individual rights against schemes of social engineering. In 1943, it took the unusual step of overruling a decision from only three years before, in which it had allowed state schools to force children to pledge allegiance to the flag. Reversing themselves, the justices declared that "compelling the flag salute and pledge transcends constitutional limitations on their power

Tom Girdler, president of Republic Steel, served as a model for the character Hank Rearden in Ayn Rand's 1957 novel, *Atlas Shrugged*.

and invades the sphere of intellect and spirit which it is the purpose of the First Amendment to our Constitution to reserve from all official control."[3] By 1944, when Roosevelt sought a fourth term, he would find it necessary to abandon his ultra–New Dealer vice president, Henry Wallace, and pick as his running mate the less ideological Harry Truman.

The reevaluation of American society was not limited to politics, but encompassed the entire culture, which began to experience a reversal of the Revolt from the Village. Journalist Alistair Cooke told his British readers on the eve of Independence Day in 1943 that Americans were fighting not just for democracy but for "the right to live in their own house and bring their children up as they please, and go fishing on Sunday, and pitch horseshoes, and say what's on their mind whether Washington agrees or not."[4] A year later, the Pulitzer Prize for Fiction went to *A Bell for Adano*, John Hersey's comic novel about the American occupation of Sicily, in which the hero—an army officer charged with administering a small Italian village—tries to replace an antique church bell that was destroyed in the fighting. Steeped in a vision of America as a liberator and defender of pastoral small-town life, the book ends with the image of the Liberty Bell proclaiming freedom through all the land. In 1945, novelist Susan Glaspell, who started her career as an especially vocal Village Rebel, came full circle in her novel *Judd Rankin's Daughter*, which celebrated the small town she had once despised.[5] Filmmaker Frank Capra recapped the entire Revolt from the Village in miniature in *It's a Wonderful Life* in 1946. Jimmy Stewart starts out desperate to leave his provincial hometown, only to be forced to stay—and to decide that his ordinary but virtuous life is good enough.

Some critics began denouncing the entire Revolt from the Village movement in retrospect as a dangerously immature phase in American letters. As early as 1936, critic Gilbert Seldes had written in *Mainland*—a book Lane and Paterson loved—that "the dominant tone in American literature" before the Depression, especially the works of Sinclair Lewis and Sherwood Anderson, had been "a long sustained attack on the outcome of a century and a half of American life."[6] Now that Americans had been "compelled" to "cultivate [their] own garden," they had "begun to discover how fertile [their] garden may be."[7] Four years later, poet Archibald MacLeish, now serving as Librarian of Congress, published a controversial essay called "The Irresponsibles," which attacked the novelists and poets of the 1920s for shirking their "responsibility for the common culture," and thereby aiding in "the destruction of the whole system of ideas, the whole respect for the truth, the whole authority of excellence which places law above force, beauty above cruelty, singleness above numbers."[8] But in 1943, historian Bernard DeVoto went further, and unleashed a blistering criticism of the Village Rebels—particularly Lewis— for having "turned their backs on America."

In a series of lectures at Indiana University, DeVoto accused Lewis, Anderson, and other novelists of having completely "misrepresented their culture."[9] Ordinary Americans of the twenties, he argued, had been confident in the virtue and strength of their society—a society in which people enjoyed unprecedented economic opportunity and the freedom to live comfortable lives in peace. Yet the literary intellectuals of that decade, led chiefly by Lewis, had abruptly decided "that the promise of American life had ended," and began portraying American small-town life as "tawdry, venal, and corrupt, its culture barren, its life contemptible."[10] DeVoto admitted that Lewis was "the best novelist" of the era, but condemned him for persuading Americans that bourgeois life was "trivial, shallow, and mediocre," a position that was false to the facts and a form of treason toward the beauty of small-town life.[11]

Lewis had considered DeVoto a friend, and was so shocked when a portion of the lecture appeared in the *Saturday Review* in April 1944 that he replied with an essay of almost hysterical abuse in which he called DeVoto dishonest, stupid, and ugly, and ridiculed DeVoto's own novels.[12] He finished by insisting that the reason he had criticized America so harshly in *Main Street* and other books was because he loved his country and its potential. But although that was probably true, it was too facile an answer, and Isabel Paterson's explanation was more insightful. The reason writers of the twenties had viewed America with contempt, she explained in "Turns," was because they embraced "the doctrine of statism."[13] Bourgeois life in the pre–New Deal era had struck litterateurs as vulgar precisely because it was the culture of an unplanned society of free people, pursuing their own happiness instead of some romanticized vision of social greatness. Lewis himself may not have had a political agenda, but the contempt for American life that pervaded his novels resonated with those who scorned the commercial republic and reviled the "forgotten man who gets the necessary work of the world done."[14] What was needed now was a cultural and intellectual revival of individualism—a literary movement that would repair the damage the Village Rebels had inflicted.

That would not be accomplished, she continued, through bland sentimentalism about small-town folk. Indeed, she despised Hersey's *A Bell for Adano* for just this reason: its protagonist was a "little bureaucrat" who "bustle[d] around among the ruins shedding sweetness and light" and "made it impossible for people to lead any kind of life." She thought writers needed to *delve*, to understand the nature of modern heroism in a capitalist society—and portray the creative qualities that made for strong and healthy societies.

> We do live in a world which is the creation of the Mind. When we turn a switch, step into a train or motor car, use the telephone, take a bath, we aren't just using trivial gadgets, irrelevant to culture, intellect, or morals; all of those things are visible products and instruments of a high moral order. . . . Isn't there something wrong with literature when it can not or does not admit in its subject matter any human being who really belongs to that high level and is capable of creating, contributing to, or maintaining it? Literature rightly takes all humanity as its province; certainly not even the primitive savage is excluded; but is it not strange and ominous if only the civilized man is excluded?[15]

Creative entrepreneurs were seldom seen in contemporary novels, and virtually never in those the critics celebrated. In fact, Paterson wrote, "the only strictly American hero appeared mostly in popular fiction of the last fifty or sixty years." The technologist or the entrepreneur "marked a genuine change in human history: he was the man who built, made, invented, produced.

The French philosopher Étienne Gilson was one of Isabel Paterson's favorite writers. She encouraged Rand to read his books—but Rand found them unpersuasive.

He did something instead of striking an attitude. He is presented (on the grand scale) in only one recent novel, *The Fountainhead*."[16] Paterson, Lane, and Rand hoped to reignite individualism—not by appealing to "community spirit" or the "100 percent Americanism" that Village Rebels had satirized—but by awakening a sincere appreciation for the creative personality.

◢▲◣

In the midst of his fight with Lewis, Bernard DeVoto paused to review Lane's *Discovery of Freedom*. It was "exhilaratingly versatile," he declared, and although he objected to some of her historical claims ("one is forever saying *yes but*") and disagreed with her defense of capitalism, he thought the book was "on the side of the angels."[17] By the time that review was published, however, Lane had gone into full revolt against the state.

Refusing to participate in Social Security, Lane made every effort to keep her income below the income tax threshold, and when wartime price controls caused shortages and the government resorted to rationing, she decided to go "off the grid." She expanded her garden so she could grow food for herself and traded canned goods to neighbors for help on her farm. Then in April 1943, an incident occurred that was to become a small legend in the history of libertarianism.

Listening to a radio broadcast about Social Security—which she accurately saw as a mimic of German social welfare programs—Lane grew furious and mailed a postcard to the broadcaster on which she asked why the nation was bothering to fight Germany if it was simultaneously adopting that country's policies. "All these 'social security' laws are German," she wrote, "instituted by Bismarck and expanded by Hitler. Americans believe in freedom, not in being taxed for our own good and bossed by bureaucrats."[18] When the local postmaster saw Lane's postcard, he contacted the FBI. It dispatched a pair of state police officers to her home to interview her. Indignant, Lane demanded to know what right they had to investigate her political opinions. One officer replied that he did not like her attitude.

"*You* do not like *my* attitude!" Lane shouted back. "I am an American citizen. I hire you, I pay you. And you have the insolence to question *my* attitude? The point is that *I* don't like *your* attitude. What is this—the Gestapo?" The police officer tried to calm her, but Lane was having none of it. Was writing the postcard a "subversive activity?" she asked. The cop muttered yes, to which Lane replied, "Then I'm subversive as hell!" According to some versions of the story, she ended the confrontation by inviting the officers in for freshly baked cookies (a rumor she later denied).[19]

Lane wrote up the story in a pamphlet titled *What Is This—the Gestapo?* that was published by a conservative political organization called the National Economic Council. The story soon began appearing in newspapers. As with many of Lane's stories, it probably became embellished in the retelling, but when journalists asked the FBI, it admitted that the incident happened.[20] In fact, Lane's complaint became a personal embarrassment to FBI director J. Edgar Hoover when the American Civil Liberties Union's executive director Roger Baldwin, an acquaintance of Lane, wrote him directly to ask about it. Hoover replied that the whole thing had been blown out of proportion, and blamed the local cops. When Baldwin showed Lane Hoover's letter, she felt moved to write the director herself. "A secret police," she complained, "always holds a potential danger to individual freedom and human rights." She added ingratiatingly that she thought Hoover had no intention of making the FBI "an instrument of intimidation," but added that his "effort to keep the FBI strictly within the limitations of American principles" could succeed only if ordinary Americans "raise a loud yell" whenever any agent "puts so much as a toe of his boot across the line protecting any American right to free thought and speech."[21]

Lane had by this time reconciled with Dorothy Thompson, and she wrote to her younger friend about the confrontation, proud of the way she had stood up for herself. "It's really too bad that only the dandelions heard me."[22] What Thompson thought about it she did not say. She remained too far on the left politically for Lane's tastes, anyway. Lane thought she had a "basically European" attitude toward politics—meaning that she was convinced

America was composed of social classes, and believed the only relevant political question was whether the lower classes should rule or whether politics should be overseen by the wealthy and powerful. Lane, by contrast, thought America was not a class society. It was a free nation in which even those born poor had the liberty to work their way up to wealth. "When a state of affairs exists, in which a $40-a-month mechanic can become Henry Ford— or Lockheed—how can you say that 'unless they take direct action with guns, the people cannot redistribute ownership'?" Lane demanded of her friend. It was true that the wealthy tried to use government power for their own ends, but the solution to that problem was to restrict the bureaucrats' power, not to expand it further by letting government dictate all economic behavior in the name of the "people." In fact, the New Deal, as well as communist and fascist governments abroad, proved that government bureaucracies only expand the power of elites at the expense of the common man. "I do wish you would read my new book," she added. "If you would read that, and then read Isabel Paterson's (I think badly titled) *The God of the Machine*, perhaps you and I would have a few words that we could speak to each other. . . . I wish you were here now; I have just taken from the oven two beautiful rhubarb-cream pies topped with perfect meringue, if I do say so."[23] But to this, too, Thompson made no answer.

By this time, Lane was writing a regular column, called "Rose Lane Says," for the *Pittsburgh Courier*, and in 1945 she took over editorship of the monthly *National Economic Council Review of Books* (*NECRB*), previously edited by longtime free-market stalwart Albert Jay Nock. This work only brought in a little pocket money, but it gave her a forum to express her opinions on current affairs and intellectual trends. In her first month as editor, she lauded a new translation of works by the 19th-century French economist Frédéric Bastiat, a book by Fundamentalist preacher Carl McIntire, and *The Fountainhead*, which, in an extremely rare move, was climbing the bestseller lists two years after publication. The novel, Lane wrote, had become a "phenomenon."

The Fountainhead's unusual word-of-mouth success attracted Hollywood's attention, as did the influence of actress Barbara Stanwyck, who adored the novel and demanded that Warner Brothers buy the film rights.[24] Born into a poor family and orphaned at the age of four, Stanwyck had worked her way from office clerk to the peak of Hollywood stardom, and had just received an Oscar nomination for *Ball of Fire*. Warner listened. It offered Rand $50,000 to write the script—the same amount Margaret Mitchell had received for *Gone with the Wind*[25]—and to celebrate, Rand, at Paterson's urging, bought herself a mink coat. Rand and her husband soon packed up and moved to Los Angeles, settling in a sleek modern house. Soon afterward, Paterson sent her a congratulatory letter. She had never doubted Rand would triumph, she said, yet she was "always just as surprised as anybody else when something turns out right."[26] Lane, too, was delighted. "[Lane] said, out of her own head," Paterson reported, "that it is marvellous [*sic*] and heartening to think what you have done, against the maximum odds—coming from that hell-hole, she said, made it more significant, really a sign."[27]

Paterson was delighted by Rand's success. "You *are* the Wonder Girl," she told the woman she was calling "sister."[28] And Rand was exhilarated by Paterson's chatty, intelligent letters. "All my life, reading the published correspondence of famous people, I envied them because they received personal letters on important and abstract subjects," Rand told her. "And now I have one of those letters myself."[29] Over the next months, Paterson wrote long missives, quoting from poets and medieval philosophers, gossiping about journalists, critics, and Wendell Willkie, and advising Rand on business relations with her publisher, which was failing to meet certain parts of *The Fountainhead* contract. Yet Paterson's letters also reflected her growing exasperation with Lane. Their tension had boiled over at last during yet another conversation about Lane's "brotherhood" idea. "I asked Rose, what meaning did she attach to her repeated quotation, 'All men are brothers'? Biologically we all belong to the same species, by definition—but I said, if I am to be told that certain persons are my 'brothers,' what of it?" Lane had been "evidently puzzled" by the question, but Paterson insisted that "I am not in any such relationship with any of the parasite busybodies who are running around trying to get me killed."[30] The friendship was clearly fraying.

"What should one do with people like Rose?" Paterson asked Rand. She relayed her version of the conversation three years earlier, in which Lane had said she disliked Wendell Willkie but could not explain why. It was wrong to act on hunches, Paterson thought, and especially immoral to vote that way, since doing so had consequences for other people. When Lane insisted that it was possible to act morally based only on intuition, Paterson—who was fond of quoting John Erskine's famous statement that people have a "moral obligation to be intelligent"—had cried that this was "frightful rubbish." If people went about acting on their instincts, that was their own concern, she growled, but there "could be no warrant for you doing anything on a 'hunch' which must concern me." Morality obliged each person to consult reason, not emotion; to cast a vote based on feelings instead of careful attention to the facts was unethical. "I guess that old idiot annoyed me today unduly," Paterson concluded.[31]

Meanwhile, Rand raced to complete the screenplay for the film version of *The Fountainhead*. She finished it by the end of 1944. Then delays ensued, reportedly due to the federal War Production Board's objections that constructing the movie sets would exceed rationing limits.[32] As they waited, producer Hal Wallis, who had recently opened his own studio, offered Rand a job working on other films. She spent the next two years helping revise existing scripts and write new ones. She suggested that Wallis adapt Paterson's 1924 novel *The Singing Season*—a historical romance set in medieval Spain—but he showed no interest. Lane also asked Paterson to pass along the suggestion that *Free Land* would make a good movie, although there is no evidence Rand made that attempt. Rand did, however, manage to insert a subtle salute to Paterson into another script she wrote. *Love Letters*, released in 1945, stars Jennifer Jones and Joseph Cotten as a couple separated by a murder mystery with a values-oriented twist, in unmistakably Ayn Rand style. In one scene, a character holds up a toy boat he played with as a child. Its name, he says, is *The Golden Vanity*.

Rand found writing for Hollywood frustrating, even painful, especially when confronted by studio censors. "I don't like the fact that what actually reaches the screen is just a distorted mess of what I had intended," she told Paterson.[33] Needing energy to work long hours, she began taking Benzedrine, and when Paterson found out, she responded with motherly scolding that it was bad for her protégée's health.

Paterson whipped off stream-of-consciousness notes at a rapid pace, some a single page long, others five or even ten pages, all covered in a riot of typographical errors and strikeouts. Rand, by contrast, wrote slowly and precisely, and had her letters typed by a secretary. She would often spend an entire day composing a letter to Paterson. "There were many pages," her secretary recalled, "and she would want me to read it back, and then she would change it while I was reading it."[34] Rand relished the intellectual exchange, but it consumed time she should have been spending on scripts and books. As a result, her letters were infrequent, which brought a rebuke from Paterson, who wondered why she could not simply jot down a few lines now and then. "The first letters I ever wrote regularly were to my family in Russia, when I came here," Rand explained. "I had to be extremely careful of what I said. . . . I have not been able to write any kind of letter spontaneously ever since."[35]

And she was very busy. In addition to her movie work, she had also agreed to prepare a nonfiction follow-up to *The Fountainhead*, called *The Moral Basis of Individualism*. She struggled with the project throughout 1945, writing and reading about the history of philosophy. Some of the ideas of history's great thinkers made her "hair stand on end," she told Paterson. "But I must do it. . . . When I'm in New York I would like to talk to you about philosophers and help you to curse them."[36] That book, however, never progressed much beyond notes and rough outlines. In January 1944, *Reader's Digest* printed a portion of what she had written, titled "The Only Path to Tomorrow," which underscored the need for a principled defense of liberty against the ever-growing state. "No tyrant has ever lasted long by force of arms alone," she declared. "Men have been enslaved primarily by spiritual weapons. And the greatest of these is the collectivist doctrine that the supremacy of the state over the individual constitutes the common good. No dictator could rise if men held as a sacred faith the conviction that they have inalienable rights of which they cannot be deprived for any cause whatsoever, by any man whatsoever, neither by evildoer *nor supposed benefactor.*"[37]

Expanding on the theme of her novel, she contrasted two types of individual characters: the Active Man—who produces and creates, and whose "basic need is independence"—and the Passive Man—who "expects to be taken care of by others, who wishes to be given directives, to obey, to submit, to be regulated, to be told," or who desires to dominate, which is essentially the same thing. Although "some humanitarians demand a collective state because of their pity for the incompetent or Passive Man," their effort to "harness" the Active Man in order to compel him to produce for redistribution was both futile and wrong. "The Active Man cannot function in harness. And once he is destroyed, the destruction of the Passive Man follows automatically."[38]

Paterson applauded the article, although she couldn't resist teasing her friend that *Reader's Digest* printed it alongside a piece by Rand's nemesis, Wendell Willkie. She was pleased to hear that Rand was reading philosophy, and agreed that many ancient philosophers were "a bit weird." Paterson especially disliked Plato, whom she considered the godfather of central planners and communists, but she added that it was only to be expected that such pioneering thinkers would make errors along the way.[39]

Then she unleashed a startling criticism of Rand's own beliefs. Rand had detected "a frightening kind of rationality" in the mistakes of ancient philosophers—meaning that they seemed to commit the same kinds of fallacies, with the same types of real-life consequences.[40] Now Paterson accused her of sharing the same "frightening" characteristic. "You talk a lot of 'reason,' but frequently don't use it, because you make assumptions that are not valid," she claimed. Her specific example was that in an earlier conversation, Rand had accused her of being prejudiced against modern civilization—referring to an exchange in which Rand claimed that Paterson viewed innovations such as radios and airplanes as insignificant. But, Paterson insisted, that was not what she had actually said. She had only said that such inventions were not necessarily improvements over previous discoveries. It was Rand, she claimed, who had fallaciously argued that more recent inventions are necessarily of greater value.

Paterson went further. Reviving a dispute about religion that dated from their conversations over the manuscript of *The God of the Machine*, she accused Rand of irrationality: "You assume that 'if God exists, man is a slave.'. . . I believe your specific argument is that if God exists, He can arbitrarily interfere with what you are doing." But, Paterson said, that was false; God could be both perfect and benign, and His existence would not necessarily detract from man's distinct value.[41] On the contrary, she thought Rand's atheism had that consequence. Rand was advancing the same "'humanistic,' 'scientific,' theanthropic philosophy" that led inevitably to totalitarianism. Logic and reason alone could not give a complete account of humanity; that required something more—something supernatural. But then, after having defended the dignity of mankind, Paterson abruptly concluded by saying that "perhaps the human race had better destroy itself, judging by its present performance. I can't say I care any more."[42]

The letter shocked Rand. She had never claimed that new things were necessarily good, or old things bad, she replied. On the contrary, she sometimes considered herself a "reactionary" by the standards of the day, since she "want[ed] to go back to what we had before" the New Deal.[43] As for her "theanthropic" philosophy, if Paterson had specific arguments to offer, she would be happy to discuss them, but she could not respond to mere name-calling. She thought it bizarre that Paterson "found it necessary to take up with me the subject of God, at this time, by letter—when it is probably the most difficult subject of all," but she was prepared to defend her beliefs regarding God's existence, as long as the conversation only involved arguments based on reason; she would not debate the subject with anyone who appealed to "the fiat of revelation."[44] Since revelation is by definition beyond logical argument, she considered it pointless to assert it in any debate.

Rand denied the existence of God for several reasons. First, assuming He existed, His nature would necessarily be so far beyond human comprehension that it was irrational even to try to grasp His limits or characteristics. Second, the very concept of God seemed self-contradictory. He was typically assumed to be limitless and infinite, but that violated the law of noncontradiction, because "an entity is that which other entities are not"—and an infinite being would not be constrained by that limitation. That meant He would necessarily have to *be* everything. Such a pantheistic view of God-as-everything either resulted in triviality (by redefining God to a synonym for reality itself) or led to the conclusion that God is an irrational entity that cannot be understood "in human terms."

In any event, Rand denied that religion was necessary to a belief in individualism, and was content to leave it at that. In fact, she worried that an appeal to faith would undermine individualism, since faith-based arguments involve a type of "fiat"—an unprovable and arbitrary "because I say so"—that was not evidence, but just an unprovable assertion. That meant no theory premised on faith could persuade anybody who denied the validity of that religious assumption. Therefore, to contend that one could believe in individual rights only by first assuming the truth of a religious creed was to cripple one's argument at the outset.

Paterson replied by urging her friend to read the work of Catholic theologian Étienne Gilson.[45] Rand did so, but found his arguments unpersuasive. There could be no compromise between reason and revelation, she scribbled in the margins of his book *The Unity of Philosophical Experience.* "Once you have accepted the possibility of a compromise between two diametrically opposed, mutually-destructive conceptions—such as Reason and Faith—you have destroyed the validity of all clear, positive, absolute concepts. . . . And the destruction will show up, sooner or later, to destroy you."[46] The same inconsistency undermined the work of even the greatest philosophers, she told Paterson—for instance, Thomas Aquinas, the religious thinker Rand most respected, had endorsed the idea that the government should punish heresy.[47] Aquinas's errors, Rand believed, proved just how dangerous it was to try to argue for individualism on a religious basis.

Paterson responded by reiterating her position that it was impossible to make a reason-based argument for individualism *at all.*[48] The argument for individual rights is "self-evident," she thought, "and that which is self-evident is not a matter of proof. You see it or you don't. Some don't. I dunno what you can do about it."[49] As for Aquinas's support for religious persecution, that had not been based on his religious beliefs, but on the secular proposition that government should protect society from the influence of bad ideas. Wrong though that notion might be, it was not qualitatively religious. Yet Paterson left unaddressed Rand's deeper claim that arguments based on faith could not persuade, and therefore undermined, instead of strengthened, the case for individualism. Instead, she simply reasserted her position. "If you do start with a statement of atheism," she thought, "you won't have any basis for human rights."[50] That was that.

The exchange set a pattern that recurred for the rest of their relationship, and indeed throughout Rand's career. Although a confirmed atheist, she was less interested in the question of God's existence than in the conflict between reason and faith. What was needed in the world, she thought, was a vindication of individual rights in exclusively rational terms. To frame an argument for individual rights in terms that appealed to revelation rendered individualism vulnerable to those who argued that it was only an obsolete superstition. But Paterson thought materialism could provide no foundation for a belief in human uniqueness—no reason to think the human mind is qualitatively different from inert matter—and therefore no basis for concluding that a person's freedom to make his own choices is entitled to moral weight.

Strangely, Paterson appeared to reverse course only weeks later, in a letter that agreed with Rand that the case for individualism "would not need to be specifically either 'atheistic' or theological," and that it was "sheer absurdity" to base an argument for individual rights on "any other terms than those of our natural powers." She still thought something about the human capacity for free will "cannot and does not occur in wholly inanimate sequences," and therefore could not be explained in materialistic terms. Yet at the same time, she acknowledged that it was illogical to think "we could not be 'free' if we can't work magic."[51]

It was a weighty subject, and one Rand was uncomfortable discussing by letter. She was planning to visit New York in September 1945 and told her friend that they could finish that conversation in person. Intelligent and eloquent as she was, Paterson was never a systematic thinker, and her tendency to write in an epigrammatic, assertive style often made it hard to follow her reasoning from premises to conclusion. Rand hoped a face-to-face discussion might help resolve matters.

▰

There was another reason for Rand's trip East. Paterson wanted to introduce her to Jasper Crane, an executive with DuPont, who had written admiringly about *The God of the Machine* and seemed sincerely interested in helping promote the cause of individualism. The 64-year-old Crane had worked for DuPont for three decades, rising to the position of vice president by the time the Depression struck. He had consistently opposed the Roosevelt administration's schemes, and now he was preparing to spend retirement supporting broader efforts to teach Americans about economics and the principles of the Constitution. He had recently befriended Leonard Read, head of the Los Angeles branch of the U.S. Chamber of Commerce, who had an idea for how to do that.

Born in Michigan in 1898, Read had served in the Army Signal Corps in World War I, barely surviving when his troop transport was sunk by a German U-boat. After the war, he ran a small grocery business, then moved to California to go into real estate. He had initially supported the New Deal, only to be talked out of it by businessman William Mullendore, a former assistant to Herbert Hoover who in 1945 would become president of Southern California Edison. After his conversion to free-market economics, Read had published a book attacking the New Deal, and now he was looking to start an organization to promote a theoretical case for economic and political freedom—efforts that in 1946 culminated in the establishment of the Foundation for Economic Education, the nation's first libertarian think tank.[52] Crane and Mullendore would serve on its board.

Read had impressed Paterson and Lane at a lunch meeting where he and Crane explained their plan. A man of "unusual natural intelligence," as Paterson called him, Read was not a philosopher, but he understood the importance of explaining economics and politics to the lay person.[53] To that end, he had already launched his own publishing house, called Pamphleteers Inc., and soon began asking Lane for help with his efforts to produce a booklet of quotations about freedom from great thinkers in world history. After assembling a long and eclectic collection, he also wrote Rand to ask for her thoughts.

Rand strongly disapproved. Along with some powerful insights, the manuscript also included many meaningless slogans and quotations from figures such as Leon Trotsky—not exactly an ideal spokesman for liberty. Putting them together in this way was likely to be counterproductive, she told Read, because people would think "if this is the best that can be said for freedom and individualism, it ain't much!"[54] She urged him to delete the irrelevant or sentimental quotations and to add some material from Paterson. In fact, she felt "a little indignant" that he had included only two minor passages from *The God of the Machine*.[55] Read passed Rand's letter along to Lane, who immediately wrote Rand to express her agreement. The draft was a "botch," she said, and she welcomed Rand's suggestions.[56] Although Paterson had often mentioned Lane in her own letters to Rand, this marked the first time the two women had corresponded.

Through their connections with Leonard Read, Paterson, Lane, and Rand began to serve as intellectual gatekeepers for a small movement of free-market thinkers. It was a role they considered important but often found vexing, given how many professed advocates of liberty appeared to sabotage their own cause by contradicting themselves or wavering on fundamental issues. Indeed, contrary to the claims of some recent historians that the post–New Deal interest in free enterprise was brought about by a campaign of "businessmen" who "worked for more than forty years to undo the system of labor unions, federal social welfare programs, and government regulation of the economy" that Franklin Roosevelt established, the three "furies" usually found the opposite to be true: businessmen were typically hesitant to speak out against government control, and performed poorly when they tried.[57] "All our God-damn business men," Paterson told Rand, "are so 'busy,' they cannot spare any attention or time to think."[58] Considering themselves "practical" and "pragmatic," they typically preferred to keep their heads down than to openly oppose the confiscations of their earnings or the arbitrary burdens of government regulation. "Have you heard one objection from the [National

Association of Manufacturers], the United States Chamber of Commerce, the Old Guard Republicans, or any other group of capitalists, to any socialistic measure here, from the 'protective' tariff to the Wagner Act or the Smith Connally bill?" asked Lane in one of her newspaper columns. "If you ever do, let me know: send me a clipping. That will be *news*."[59]

Even when they made the attempt, business owners seemed incapable of making a principled case against government interference. In 1943, Paterson sent Rand an advance copy of *Boot Straps*, a memoir by Republic Steel president Tom Girdler, scheduled for publication that fall.[60] It had been Girdler's refusal to negotiate with the Steel Workers Organizing Committee that had precipitated violent demonstrations at Republic's plants and the "Memorial Day Massacre" in Chicago in 1937. Rand admired Girdler for his refusal to cave in to SWOC's demands, and his vivid description of the strikes would help give life to passages in *Atlas Shrugged* years later.[61] She would even base the character of steel magnate Hank Rearden in part on Girdler. But she found his memoir disappointing, as did Paterson, because he failed to grasp that the reason he was demonized in the press was not economic, but moral. In fact, Paterson thought the book's most remarkable feature was the contrast between Girdler's "enormous practical ability" and his "utter absence of general ideas."[62] He expressed bewilderment that while everyone agreed that workers had a right to strike, nobody spoke up for "the much more venerable and important right to work."[63] And he complained that "the rotten core in all of the New Deal thinking" was the presumption "that a man with payroll responsibilities is necessarily less of a humanitarian than people of prominence without such responsibility."[64]

"That is not true," admonished Rand in a long and patient letter she sent Girdler in July 1943. The real reason socialism was growing in popularity was "because we accepted altruism as an ideal." That allowed self-professed humanitarians to claim a moral high ground they did not deserve. "In principle and in fact," socialists were "parasites," because "they are primarily concerned with distribution, not with production, that is, with distributing what they have not produced. Parasites are neither honorable nor kindly. So it shocked me to read you, a great industrialist, saying in self-justification that you are just as good as a social worker. You are not. You are much better." She closed by urging him to read *The God of the Machine* and *The Fountainhead*.[65]

It wasn't just businessmen. Professors, politicians, and philosophers seemed equally inept at making the case for freedom, frequently offering weak or unprincipled arguments that ended up harming their own cause. One striking example was F. A. Hayek's 1944 book *The Road to Serfdom*, which argued in accessible, layman's terms that government planning, even if limited to just one area of the economy, must inevitably expand into political control over the whole society. The book became a bestseller, and helped usher in a free-market movement among economists. Yet while many of his arguments paralleled those that Rand, Lane, and Paterson, made in their books, Hayek was not a defender of laissez faire. His book did not even contain the word "rights," and it defined individualism as "recognition" of the individual's "views and tastes as supreme in his own sphere, *however narrowly that may be circumscribed*," which seemed to legitimize government efforts to circumscribe it narrowly.[66]

Hayek declared that "in the hands of private individuals, what is called economic power can be an instrument of coercion."[67] But Lane, Paterson, and Rand insisted that the word "coercion" must be reserved for physical force alone. Using it to refer to mere economic wealth, absent actual compulsion, played into the hands of those who argued that antitrust laws, price controls, and other restrictions on industry were needed to protect people from the economic "coercion" of high prices or property rights. Worst of all, Hayek thought the political philosophy of freedom was so flexible that there were "no hard-and-fast rules," and that liberty was compatible with government planning if it "deliberately creat[es] a system within which competition will work as beneficially as possible."[68] In the margin of her copy, Rand wrote: "*Here* is the whole case given away for good. If principles aren't 'hard and fast'—what is? What do we go by? Who decides what is 'beneficial' and what is 'possible'?"[69] It was almost inevitable that Hayek would conclude his argument by defending government wealth redistribution. There was "no reason," he declared, why bureaucrats could not guarantee "some minimum of food, shelter and clothing" as well as "a comprehensive system of social insurance" through a welfare state.[70]

Rand concluded that Hayek was a "compromiser" who would "do more good to the communist cause than to ours" by surrendering the case for liberty.[71] Lane agreed. Now editing the *NECRB*, she condemned him repeatedly for "cancel[ing] out his own argument" by "denying his own premise," and "betray[ing] the cause that he defends."[72] To support a moderate redistributive state, she thought, was like a doctor "advocat[ing] no more than a 5% injection of syphilis."[73] In the end, Hayek contributed important insights regarding political and economic liberty, but Rand and Lane thought his inconsistencies ruined his argument for freedom.

Other New Deal opponents struck the "furies" as so naive that they failed to anticipate how their arguments might be misrepresented. They were bothered, for example, when conservative journalist George Peck published a column about the testimony of Hitler's deputy Albert Speer at the war crimes trials then underway in Nuremberg.[74] Speer told the judges that Hitler once expressed frustration that Soviet factories outperformed those of the Nazis— a point Peck used to argue that the Germans were thwarted by their own commitment to government control over industry. But this argument did not work, Rand wrote Peck, because it "implied that Russia was free of such controls." He should have emphasized that the Soviet Union was no less tyrannical, and certainly no more productive, than Nazi Germany.[75] That was a significant concern at a time when American liberals were exaggerating Soviet economic productivity and downplaying its atrocities. Rand forwarded her complaints to Lane, who echoed her concern. "The question," she told Rand, "is what to *do* about the George Pecks."[76]

Most of all, Paterson, Lane, and Rand were troubled by economists who seemed unable or unwilling to offer a *moral* case for liberty. Whatever their disagreements, all three shared a belief that freedom could not be defended on exclusively economic grounds. Instead, the case must be made for the individual's right to his own life. Thus they were shocked when in 1946 Leonard

Read published *Roofs or Ceilings?: The Current Housing Problem*, a pamphlet by prominent economists Milton Friedman and George Stigler that criticized rent control. The two scholars used the word "rationing" to describe how housing stock is allocated in a free market, using it in its technical economic sense, as referring to any mechanism by which goods or services are distributed. But to the "furies," the word implied government coercion. Goods in a free market are not *rationed*, they thought, but bought and sold. Using such a label for the free choices of buyers and sellers was a dangerous equivocation. "The sense in which it has always been used," Rand told William Mullendore, was to refer to "the decision of an absolute authority, with the recipients having no choice." Employing the same word for both voluntary and involuntary practices obscured the quintessential *ethical* distinction, which was the presence or absence of government compulsion. Indeed, Friedman and Stigler's pamphlet entirely ignored the *immorality* of government rationing, focusing exclusively on the argument that it was unfeasible. "They say 'rationing by a public agency is unlikely to be accepted,'" Rand wrote. "Do they say that it *should not* be accepted? Why, no. . . . The public gets the impression that the proposal is desirable, in fact noble and idealistic, but people are too stupid or backward or selfish to accept it."[77]

Lane was outraged, too. "I saw that damnable *Roofs or Ceilings* in manuscript," she told Rand, "and I raised hell about its implications and its 'rationing' trickiness." She complained to one of Read's colleagues, who—without Friedman's or Stigler's approval—added a footnote to the article slightly modifying its language. Enraged, Friedman refused to have anything to do with Read for years.[78] Rand and Lane also held Read at arm's length after that incident. "He is thoroughly honest, not a compromiser, not a coward," Lane told Rand. But "he simply does not possess a mind that *grasps* abstract principles."[79]

Lane and Rand had similarly mixed feelings about Henry Hazlitt's 1946 book *Economics in One Lesson*, published the same year and destined to become a classic of free-market thinking. A skilled writer who had taken over editorship of the *American Mercury* after H. L. Mencken's retirement, Hazlitt made an eloquent and persuasive case for free markets based on the work of economist

Frédéric Bastiat, who had observed that although government policies often appear beneficial, that is typically an illusion caused by the fact that their true costs—which consist of the things people might otherwise have done with their wealth, had government not taken it—are often invisible. When government taxes a business's capital to fund construction of a bridge, that can look like a gain because people see the bridge—but they never see the factory the business would have built or the products it would have invented if it had been allowed to keep its money. The factory or the goods are the true cost of the government's policy. But because they are never created, that cost remains unseen, with the result that wasteful government policies seem constructive even while they worsen the economy. "The art of economics," Hazlitt argued, "consists in looking not merely at the immediate but at the longer effects of any act or policy."[80]

Elegant and convincing as Hazlitt's book was, Lane had concerns. In fact, she thought it was "basically all wrong," because it seemed to ground the argument for economic freedom in the idea that liberty is good for *society*, whereas capitalism's true justification is that it protects the right of *individuals* to run their own lives.[81] In the *NECRB*, she called the book "a major achievement," but expressed anxiety over its implicit assumption "that persons should consider and act for the general welfare." In reality, "there is no common good, no general welfare; the only human welfare is the welfare of individual persons." Everyone has an obligation "to promote his own good, care for his own welfare, pursue his [own] happiness," and not "intrude his attention upon other persons' affairs and act for their welfare, nor to sacrifice himself for it." By equivocating on this point, Hazlitt's book undermined the case for freedom.

Yet at the same time, Lane could not resist reviving her "brotherhood" theory. "'Love thy neighbor *as thyself*' is sound practical expediency," she wrote in her review, but she thought that phrase's deeper meaning was that every person has an obligation to be *self*-reliant. "Human beings survive (and possibly prosper) on this planet only by working together." But that cooperation consists in "production and in free exchange of goods," not the demeaning and dangerous practice of taking away people's freedom in the name of compassion. Voluntary transactions were, in Lane's view, an expression of mutual respect that reconciled the actions of responsible individuals with the general welfare, without the need for any kind of sacrifice. Hazlitt, however, seemed to be quietly endorsing the false idea that pursuing one's own welfare is inherently contrary to the general good—which implied that government must curtail people's freedom. "We must not be extremists, says Mr. Hazlitt; we must admit that groups must sometimes be sacrificed for the good of all." To this, Lane could not agree.[82]

Lane sent Rand a draft of her review in a letter that sought the younger woman's opinion. She wasn't asking "for such an effort as writing a considered judgment of the thing," she said; she would be "grateful for just an epithet." "I could depend on Isabel for it," she added wistfully, "but she doesn't telephone me any more."[83]

Rand liked Lane's review. She agreed that the book was unusually good, but that its effort "to divorce economics from ethics" was foolish and dangerous. Economics necessarily deals with values, and therefore cannot avoid the question of which values people pursue and why. One passage in particular bothered Rand; in it, Hazlitt argued that "the more [capital] that is diverted to producing frivolities and luxuries, the less there is left for producing the essentials of life for those who are in need of them."[84] This concept is economically fallacious because no intrinsic distinction exists between luxuries and necessities. On the contrary, free-market exchange is precisely the mechanism by which people figure out what they need and what they can do without.[85] Yet Rand's deeper objection was ethical: nobody has any moral obligation to refrain from spending on "frivolities," and to suggest otherwise implies that government may justly force people to forgo what bureaucrats consider luxuries in order to purchase "the essentials of life" for others. She thought Hazlitt's argument was "not true as economics" and "wrong as morality."[86]

Although the "furies" often expressed irritation at the failure of economists or journalists to articulate a consistent, principled case for freedom, Lane tended to be more patient, and she cautioned Rand not to write off those whose arguments seemed muddled—something she had often seen Paterson do. "It really is an error to hold (as Isabel so passionately does) that minds never need to learn to think, can't be helped to do it," she told Rand, after learning that Paterson had written a ferociously rude letter to a businessman who said he found *The God of the Machine* too hard to read. "Human beings learn to think as they learn to speak and talk," Lane thought. "If they hear nothing but French, they'll speak French and if they hear nothing but social-ism, they will think socialism until something shows them that socialism isn't the *only* way to think. . . . I think it is as absurd to demand that everyone who can read English understand *The God of the Machine* as it is to expect every child who can read a primer to understand *The Fountainhead.* There was a time when Isabel and you couldn't have understood either of them, and minds do not grow up at the same rate."[87] But although Rand agreed with that, she was to find herself confounded over the years by countless intellectuals whose failure to articulate the case for individualism seemed motivated by something other than mere misunderstanding.

◤▲◥

World War II proved to be the greatest disaster in history, and Paterson— now approaching 60—was disgusted by the daily spectacle of death. The war was "being conducted with abominable incompetence," she told Rand, "by hyenas who will use the torture and death of American soldiers to adver-tise themselves."[88] She was equally repulsed by the atomic obliteration of Hiroshima and Nagasaki that brought an end to the fighting. The atom bomb, she told Rand, seemed to herald a new age—one that "means 'be individualists or die,' and no compromise."[89] A few months later, Rand had an opportunity to put that observation into practice, when Hal Wallis, her boss at the movie studio, asked her to prepare a script for a movie about the Manhattan Project.

She took the assignment with a special seriousness. "The motion picture is a most powerful medium of influencing men's thinking," she wrote in a memo to Wallis, and "whether [the bomb is] used, and how it's used will depend on the *thinking* of men."[90] A film of this sort might therefore turn out to be even more important than the existence of the bomb itself. She proposed to tell the story in a way that would articulate the theme that *"statism leads men to war"*[91]—and making such a movie would require that "when we say 'men must be free or perish,' let us be specific and honest about what 'free' means. It means free from compulsion; it means free from rule by force; it means free from government control of enterprise."[92] She would dramatize this by showing that the Manhattan Project itself had succeeded by giving its scientific geniuses the utmost freedom of thought—whereas the totalitarian regimes of Germany and Italy had deprived their greatest minds of freedom, prompting scientists such as Albert Einstein, Enrico Fermi, and Leo Szilard to flee to the United States, where they contributed their insights toward the project's success. Tentatively titled *Top Secret*, the movie would use the Allied victory to show that liberty is superior to dictatorship, both in moral principle and practical results. "We must not start the picture with the final stage, something like Roosevelt calling the scientists together and saying: 'Boys, make me an atomic bomb,'" Rand wrote in her memo. "That's not the way it was done. If that were the way, Hitler would have done it." Simply put, the bomb "was *not* a creation of government—but of *the free cooperation of men*."[93]

Rand was inspired in part by the work of an English biologist named John Randal Baker, whose 1945 book *Science and the Planned State* argued that totalitarian countries might claim to be more efficient and progressive than capitalist countries, but in reality, central planning "gravely damage[s] science."[94] It did so not just because censorship and shortages handicap scientists' research, but also because the spirit of scientific inquiry is inherently anti-authoritarian. "The scientist takes nothing as true on anyone's authority."[95] Yet centrally planned societies are by definition based on loyalty and obedience—the very opposite of the questioning, even rebellious mindset that makes for good scientists. The consequences of statism could be seen at that moment in the Soviet Union, where authorities put the charlatan Trofim Lysenko in charge of biological research, banned criticisms of his pseudoscientific theories as "bourgeois," and dismissed or imprisoned scientists who refused to comply.[96] Anticipating arguments later advanced by Karl Popper, Jacob Bronowski, and others, Baker concluded that "freedom of association, freedom of inquiry, and freedom of speech and publication" are indispensable for technological advancement.[97] Paterson called Baker's book "fascinating" in "Turns," and Lane lauded it in the *NECRB* for "prov[ing] incontrovertibly that without individual freedom of thought, of speech, and of action there could be no scientific progress."[98] Rand agreed, writing in her journal that it showed that "invention, discovery, science and progress are possible *only* under a system of free enterprise."[99]

Along with Baker's book and other research, Rand also interviewed several members of the Manhattan Project, including its chief scientist, J. Robert Oppenheimer. He and the other physicists she spoke to stressed the informality and lack of hierarchy among the Project's participants. Scientists were "given [a] choice of problems" to solve, Oppenheimer told her. "No one ever gave an order at Los Alamos."[100] She thought that was a "magnificent" line and insisted that it be used in the picture.[101] The film, she hoped, would be "an epic of the American spirit," not in a "phony flag-waving way," but by "dramatiz[ing] that which is the essence of America": the freedom to think out one's own solutions to problems.[102] The atomic bomb project would be shown as a microcosm of a free society—one in which people worked freely to build, and overcame challenges by using reason, rather than focusing on social relationships or trying to please the group.

▰▰

Top Secret was never made, but Rand used the material she gathered from her meeting with Oppenheimer to develop the character of Robert Stadler, the brilliant but naive scientist in her 1957 novel *Atlas Shrugged*, who is manipulated by an increasingly dictatorial American government into designing a terrible new weapon. In fact, Rand was already working on that novel, having started it almost immediately after completing *The Fountainhead*.

The initial inspiration probably came almost a decade earlier, when the Roosevelt administration blamed the "recession" of 1937 on a "strike of capital." Although no such conspiracy had existed, the White House had furiously denounced industry leaders and engaged in a vigorous program of antitrust litigation. Attorney General Robert Jackson, who thought Roosevelt "was not given to thought in economic terms," believed the president saw antitrust law as a means of "punishing" his enemies. A cabal of rich industrialists seeking to wreck the economy by failing to perform made the perfect target.[103] Roosevelt's vendetta was especially aided by the fact that antitrust laws were written in extraordinarily vague terms, giving courts maximum flexibility to decide, ex post facto, which business practices were or were not legal. The 1890 Sherman Act, for instance, prohibited any "contract, combination in the form of trust or otherwise, or conspiracy, in restraint of trade," without explaining what qualified as a "restraint," and the Robinson-Patman Act of 1936 banned "discrimination" in prices if it "substantially lessened competition"—terms that were also left undefined. Little wonder that Paterson called antitrust laws "freak legislation." They were a revival of the idea of "status law," she argued, meaning laws that did not aim at specific wrongdoing by individuals, but sought to freeze the economy into permanent stasis by punishing businesses that deviated from what rulers considered the norm. "Nobody knows what it is [the antitrust laws] forbid," she concluded.[104] Businesses that charged too much could be accused of reaping monopoly profits; those that charged too little could be prosecuted for underselling competitors; those that charged the same as other firms were liable for price fixing.

This ambiguity was worsened by nonstop changes in the Roosevelt administration's own policies—all of which retained a single feature despite their many inconsistencies: they all increased bureaucratic power. Likening government to a sneaky child who finds excuses for getting into the cupboard where the cookies are kept, Paterson had observed in June 1938 that the Hoover and Roosevelt administrations had first blamed the Depression on excess production, and, later, on production shortfalls. "In short, no matter what was wrong, the remedy was the same—hand over the key to the pantry."[105] The same month, Justice Department antitrust chief Thurman Arnold—whose book *The Folklore of Capitalism* she had attacked in "Turns"—declared that "if an industry has gone so far on the path of monopoly control that competition can never be restored, Government regulation is necessary."[106] Yet, Paterson argued, no business can maintain monopoly control without using government power to prohibit competition against itself. Absent government's assistance, the threat of new competition always serves to discipline businesses.[107] The companies Arnold and his allies called monopolies were typically just successful because they satisfied customers—something that should be rewarded, not punished. *Actual* monopolies were created by government favoritism—the only means by which firms can outlaw competition—yet the administration made no attempt to end its economic interference. On the contrary, it created legal cartels, imposed regulations too costly for new businesses to satisfy, and limited government contracts to a few politically influential companies.[108] Arnold was not really interested in a competitive economy, Paterson concluded, but in a system of government controls over industry, which he absurdly called a "remedy" for the country's economic woes. "Europe," she concluded, "is [already] in convulsions from precisely that remedy."[109]

Two years later, after what was then the longest trial in American history, a federal court rejected Arnold's antitrust case against ALCOA, in a 200-page opinion that found "no warrant in fact or law" for Arnold's claims.[110] Yet the company's victory was short-lived. In 1945, an appeals court reversed the decision and ruled that ALCOA had violated the Sherman Act by "embracing each new opportunity as it opened" and "facing every [potential competitor] with new capacity already geared into a great organization, having the advantage of experience, trade connections, and the elite of personnel." In other words, ALCOA was being punished for doing its job well.

According to the appellate court, the antitrust laws prohibited not only dishonest activities, but any business practices "actuated" by a "desire to prevent competition."[111] Yet as the Shechter brothers had pointed out in their own trial a decade earlier, the nature of economic competition is to try to outperform other firms, and one business's professional excellence and skill necessarily mean it will be better able to satisfy customers than others. It was precisely that skill that attracted buyers to ALCOA. The Roosevelt administration was declaring ALCOA "anti-competitive" due solely to its competence, even while it was mandating price controls and imposing productivity quotas on businesses. As Rand would later summarize, this legal theory meant companies were liable to punishment for their virtues, while others were rewarded for their vices.[112] In the end, the principal beneficiaries of the ALCOA prosecution were not consumers, but political leaders—and the business owners who curried favor with them, such as Henry Kaiser, whose steel company acquired many of ALCOA's assets after it was forced to divest.[113]

Only three months before the ruling against ALCOA was announced, Rand had started outlining what would become her 1,000-page opus, *Atlas Shrugged*—then called *The Strike*. She and Paterson had often discussed what would happen if government bureaucracy and taxation forced the country's leading thinkers and innovators to give up. The result, they thought, would be social collapse. Ancient civilizations, after all, had vanished when creative thinkers chose to retire rather than participate in economic exchange. Could the same thing happen in America?

Paterson, who in 1930 had published a novel about barbarian tribes in Roman days, was likely familiar with Edward Gibbon's theory that the decline of Rome resulted in part from the early Christian Church's "condemnation of the wisest and most virtuous of the Pagans," which led talented individuals to retreat into monasteries where they were "contented with the silent, sedentary occupation of making wooden sandals, or of twisting the leaves of the palm-tree into mats and baskets" instead of maintaining the empire.[114] The Dark Ages that followed, Paterson thought, were "in the nature of a prolonged business depression."[115] A similar phenomenon had occurred in the Islamic world, which, as Lane noted in *Discovery of Freedom*, had once been a bastion of science and philosophy, but had retreated into dogma and stagnation in the years after the Crusades. In 1931, Paterson had written in "Turns" that "civilizations fall" because "citizens just walk off and leave things flat. . . . It would come to one noble Roman first—there'd have to be a first one. He would ask himself in a dazed moment, why am I standing here . . . ? And he never came back."[116] Thus when she and Rand discussed Roosevelt's purported "strike of capital," the answer seemed plain: civilizations could be destroyed by statism, which stifled or ruined the people of ability on whom progress and productivity depend. That, they thought, would make a fine theme for a novel.

In October 1943, Paterson sent Rand a quotation she had encountered in one of Étienne Gilson's books on philosophy. Discussing the conflict between Islamic philosophers and theologians in the Middle Ages, Gilson summarized the views of the Muslim thinker Averroës, who had recommended that his fellow philosophers stop trying to debate the mystics who claimed that truth was directly revealed to them by Allah. "The happy few whom God has endowed with a philosophical mind," Averroës wrote, should instead "content themselves with a solitary possession of rational truth."[117] Didn't that attitude of intellectual retreat, Paterson asked, explain how the Muslim world had lost its position as the world's intellectual leader? Indeed, it appeared to be just one example of a pattern that had ruined many civilizations. Whether it be the fall of Rome, the end of the Islamic Golden Age, or the self-destruction now underway in Germany—which before the 20th century had been labeled "the land of poets and philosophers"—any society would collapse if it persecuted self-starters so much that they decided to follow Averroës's advice to withdraw instead of learning and teaching.

Rand enjoyed the quotation. "I know that I will now have to write *The Strike*," she wrote back. "You'll push me into it."[118] She had already sketched out a rough plot in her notes. In a sense, it would be the reverse of *Top Secret*; where that movie would have shown that free societies outperform tyrannies by allowing thinkers the liberty to invent, *The Strike* would dramatize the collapse that ensues when society tries to persecute them.[119] In long, introspective journal entries, Rand puzzled out the process whereby nations lose their freedom. "Since the majority of people are second-handers by nature, will they necessarily and always destroy a free system[?]" she wondered. "Is every civilization only to have a very brief period (such as Greece's 150 years and America's 150 years) before the second-handers unavoidably destroy it . . . ? *Or are the second-handers in the majority?* That, perhaps, is the heart of the question. Maybe not. Maybe Pat is right—the fault is in men's thinking, not in man's nature."[120]

Rand began designing an epic novel about how collectivist ideas kill productive societies. Second-handers use humanitarian slogans to expand their power over the self-starters whose creativity is crucial to cultural growth, until at last the achievers refuse to cooperate. They withdraw from the world, and civilization crumbles. Paterson thought it was a powerful premise—indeed, she told Rand the book would be "an historic event," so "incalculably important" that "I do not now know of one single other person whose individual continued existence would matter in the same way as yours."[121] In August 1946, she told "Turns" readers that Rand was working on a novel that would "provoke a lot of controversy" when it appeared. But she warned them to be patient, because the book "won't be ready for a year or so yet."[122] In actuality, it would take more than a decade.

▼ 10 ◤

The Witness

Rand was intensely busy, after all. While working on *The Strike* and *Top Secret*, she was also writing a series of articles for *The Vigil*, a newsletter published by the Motion Picture Alliance for the Preservation of American Ideals—an anticommunist group that included such luminaries as Walt Disney and Ronald Reagan. Titled "A Textbook of Americanism," the articles were intended to help producers articulate individualist values in their films while avoiding clichés that served the interests of communist propaganda. The "Textbook" was designed in a question-and-answer format and covered such topics as "What is the basic principle of America?" and "What are rights?" To the latter, Rand answered "A right is the sanction of independent action. A right is that which can be exercised without anyone's permission. If you exist only because society permits you to exist—you have no right to your own life. A permission can be revoked at any time."[1]

She sent a copy to Lane, who lauded it in the *NECRB* as "incomparably the best writing obtainable on human rights," and asked Rand for extra copies to give to friends.[2] But she also challenged some of Rand's language.[3] Was it accurate to say that a right "can be" exercised without permission? Or was a right something even more essential than that? What exactly *is* the nature of rights? In what was probably a long letter, now lost, Lane appears to have elaborated on her own theory that rights are not just abstract moral principles, but more like a process—akin to Adam Smith's "invisible hand"—by which each person's self-interest is coordinated for the benefit of society.[4]

Rand began her answer by agreeing that she should have written that a right *is* exercised without permission, not only that it *can* be; whether or not others approve is simply not a factor in the question of individual rights. But as for what rights are, they are principles—they form a moral space around the individual where coercion is prohibited. This space was a necessity of human survival, since people must use reason to survive, and reason is a function of individual thought, which cannot operate under compulsion. Thus "if we accept as an axiom that man's survival is desirable, we have to recognize man's rights."[5]

Lane remained puzzled, however, by what philosophers call the "ontological status" of rights—that is, the manner in which they can be said to exist—and she pressed Rand in her next letter. "Is a 'right' a thing, a fact, existing unalterably in the essential nature of the four-dimensional world? in the same sense that, say, electrons *are*[?]" It seemed to her that the main difficulty in grasping the idea of rights was that they seemed like pure abstractions that belonged to some hypothetical other dimension, instead of actual things existing in the physical world. That was problematic because people tended to think of morality as an unattainable ideal, somehow at odds with the demands of real-world survival. People seemed to believe "that morality is a fine thing rewarded in Heaven (if you believe in Heaven) but suicidal as a 'practical' policy here and now, of course," and that was why it seemed whenever one asserted the idea of *rights* in a political argument, people always came back with "I agree with you in theory but we've got to be practical."

This dichotomy between justice and practicality, of ideal and real, was baseless, Lane continued. The "self-controlling" quality of human beings—that is, their autonomy—is a real thing, inherent in their nature, meaning that freedom is not just an abstract hope or a desirable tradition, but a life-or-death matter of fact, just like the need for food or the human capacity for language. "If life, liberty, ownership are natural functions of human beings, regarded as generators and controllers of a form of energy (human energy)," then "no human action *can* suppress or extinguish these human functions in this world. The attempt to do this is an attempt to do the *impossible*."

This conundrum dogged political philosophers throughout the rest of the century. Were rights merely social constructs, like rules of fashion or etiquette? If so, on what basis could one condemn crimes against humanity in other cultures, such as the Holocaust? In contrast, if rights are immutable, like the laws of biology or chemistry, how could so many societies fail to recognize them? The law of gravity cannot be violated, but laws against murder or theft can. That suggested there was something different about the two types of "law." In which category did moral law belong? Or as Lane put it in her letter, "Precisely what *is* my 'right' to live?" If it was a "spiritual, moral sanction," as Rand described it, then it seemed to be of little practical use in protecting one's life, since it could not actually stop a murderer from killing. Perhaps, then, the right to live is a quality of "life itself." But then why should one prioritize one's own life over the life of another person?

After several paragraphs of such philosophical brainstorming, studded with references to history and theology, Lane concluded, "You must recognize (and do, by now) that I'm only a fumbler, *trying* to think."[6] And Lane's questions did strike Rand as poorly formed. It was enough, Rand thought, to say rights are principles of human survival. They exist in the same manner that scientific propositions exist.[7] But she denied that they are categorical imperatives. Rights are conditional propositions, of the form "if you want to survive, then you must do X." Any deeper account of their metaphysical nature was unnecessary.[8] Like medical or dietary prescriptions, or rules of morality, the principles of individual rights could be disregarded, but doing so led unavoidably to deleterious consequences. As for valuing one's own life over others, Rand was firm: every person has a moral obligation to his own self, precisely because it is his own.

For that reason, Rand objected to Lane's assertion in her review of *Economics in One Lesson* that "'Love thy neighbor *as thyself*' is sound practical expediency."[9] She had "never agreed with that slogan," she told Lane. It was "impossible and improper." It was impossible because it is not literally feasible to accord the same concern to others' welfare as to oneself, if for no other reason than that one cannot know another's priorities. And it was improper because

Pierre Lecomte du Noüy's book *Human Destiny* sought to reconcile science and religion—which played an important role in ending the friendship between Ayn Rand, Isabel Paterson, and Rose Wilder Lane.

love can only be meaningful if it is an expression of one's *own* profoundest values. Any "love" motivated by duty—worse, duty toward people whose values one does not actually share—would be a form of masochism, even self-destruction. "What we owe our neighbors is respect," Rand thought, "*not* love."[10]

Lane replied in a long, scattershot letter that explored the love-thy-neighbor principle as she understood it. "The discordance about love thy neighbor as thyself probably is in the definition of 'love,'" she thought. "I don't exactly *love* myself; I preserve myself . . . and my interests require that I not jeopardize (and that if and when necessary, I protect) my neighbor's." Mutual assistance in a time of emergency—such as rushing to help one's neighbor put out a fire threatening his house—is a "*natural* human action, done with little or no reflection" because people view an emergency threatening other people as a personal concern, also. This might be rationally justified after the fact—perhaps the fire threatens the whole town unless it is extinguished—but people do not make such calculations in the moment; they simply act. And if that emotional impulse to aid others is so deeply embedded in the psyche, did that not suggest that there was a natural law leading humans to aid each other? This, Lane added in parentheses, was "[t]he point at which Isabel goes into a fury and calls me, violently, a communist."

Yet she thought Paterson was wrong to view this argument about an innate drive to help others as inconsistent with individualism. After all, was there not "a vital distinction between co-operation and collectivism?" Lane thought the impulse to help must relate to the principle of individual rights on some deep level. Perhaps rights were a mechanism by which each individual's free choices tended to help other people—the same way that Adam Smith had argued that each businessman's pursuit of personal profit tended, as if organized by an invisible hand, to raise everybody's standard of living. In fact, "it seems to me that the essential basis of co-operation is individualism." And if there were a natural law whereby the pursuit of self-interest also benefitted others, perhaps "love thy neighbor" was simply shorthand for that law. People tended to think this impulse to help others equated to self-sacrifice, but that was wrong because human flourishing depends on voluntary cooperation and exchange.

Thus we love our neighbors, in a sense, by respecting their property rights, or buying and selling things. "I think the collectivist view that individualism is 'atomizing' is totally false," she concluded. "It's collectivism that disintegrates natural human co-operation and comes to 'dog eat dog.'"[11] Whereas liberty seemed to manifest a kind of love toward one's neighbors.

Rand replied months later, in a long philosophical letter that explained her view of "loving one's neighbor." First, she argued, the injunction is literally impossible, because each person is inescapably in charge of his own destiny. But more importantly, it was not a worthy goal, even under Lane's idiosyncratic definition of "love." Assuming the slogan merely meant that one should *protect* others as much as oneself, rather than actually love or serve them, it still imposed a positive obligation on people against their will. "It's that element of *owing*, of moral duty, which is crucial," Rand thought. "If you *owe* your protection to your neighbor—then it is a claim which he can and must present against you, should you fail in your duty. And who would define the debt and the failure? You or he?" It was precisely this alleged duty to aid one's neighbors in emergencies that had led New Dealers to declare "one emergency after another. If you *must* help your neighbor in an emergency, then a man who is starving by reason of his own errors, shiftlessness or laziness is certainly in a state of emergency, he *needs* your help, so he would be justified in demanding it." Rand thought one might choose to help a neighbor in distress, but there could be no moral *obligation* to do so. That would conflict with a person's responsibility for his own life. In many circumstances, it would be rational to help a neighbor extinguish a house fire, but there were also cases in which it would not be—for example, if one's own home were already burning. In that situation, "whose house would you and *should* you save first? Of course, your own, and properly so. Therefore, you cannot 'love him as yourself.'"

Another problem with the "love thy neighbor" mandate was that it ignored relevant differences between people. Love, or any other feeling, could only be based on an appraisal of someone's specific behavior. "A blanket command to love is collectivism." Nor did Rand think that humans have any truly instinctual drive to aid one another. People, unlike beavers or muskrats, act based on reasons. That did not mean there was never good reason to feel benevolence toward others—in fact, feeling that way "is *natural* in the sense that there are good rational grounds for it"—but it was not a universal human sentiment, nor was it invariably a good thing.

Rand agreed with Lane's distinction between cooperation and collectivism, and her observation that the only real "dog eat dog" societies were the totalitarian ones. But that only proved that mutual aid could not be the *fundamental* principle of human relationships. "Only free, independent men can cooperate and feel benevolence toward one another" because "they know that cooperation will involve no pain or injury to them—that is, no demand for self-sacrifice."[12] Individual autonomy must come first, and cooperation second. "Men *are* brothers," Rand had written in *The Fountainhead*, "except in boards, unions, corporations, and other chain gangs."[13] Authentic brotherhood can only proceed on a basis of mutual independence. "Of course, Individualism doesn't mean isolation, aloofness, or escaping to a desert island," but it did mean respecting the *essential* independence of each person—their right and responsibility to direct their own lives.[14] It also meant the freedom to *decline* to cooperate with others.

Lane could not quite grasp this idea. "You have perhaps shown me that I am a collectivist," she replied. "Maybe the American frontier mores wasn't [*sic*] as individualistic as everyone, on the frontier, believed it was." She recalled how, during her childhood, people helped neighbors through hard times without thinking about consequences. "There was a typhoid epidemic in town when I was 13 or 14," she told Rand. "It never occurred to me to ask *why* I worked all day and sat up all night with one or other of the girls of my age who had typhoid; it was just what people did, of course. . . . The time my mother went back to Dakota because her father was sick, when I was 11, of course I did all the housework and cooking, laundry, etc., for my father; but when all the cherries were ripe on washday I went up the street to Betty's house and told her I couldn't handle it all, so of course she came and picked the cherries while I did the washing." Helping others had been more like an instinct than a rational calculation of costs and benefits. "I didn't feel grateful and she didn't expect me to." Lane concluded with a postscript: "Have you ever read my mother's books?"[15]

Before Rand could answer, Lane sent her another letter of six densely packed pages. "I do not know what a moral duty is," she began. Morality seemed to her something akin to physical laws—woven into the fabric of the universe—that can be discovered after the fact and explained by reason, but that are felt immediately as gut instincts. Principles of ethics are like a mother's warning to her child not to walk too close to a cliff. Such a warning can be accounted for by reason—to prevent the child from falling—but it is experienced as an instantaneous emotional impulse. Moral rules, too, are less like duties than like intuitions embodying the hard-earned wisdom of previous generations: they are "not a question of 'owing' or of 'moral duty,'" but more like evolved responses to the dangers of the world. Generosity, for example, is rationally defensible because it serves human welfare, but is subjectively felt as an intuition.

Lane thought generosity was consistent with self-interest—and she did not limit this generosity to her actual neighbors. Indeed, her idea that helping others benefits oneself was extremely broad. Even if her worst enemy's home were burning down, she would put out the fire, she told Rand—not to help him specifically, but because the destruction of any house is "a waste of human energy," and therefore a loss to all humanity. "Property per se is valuable *to me*, whether or not it is *my* property." By the same reasoning, it is in the best interests of ordinary people to defend the rights of great geniuses, and of great geniuses to assist those less gifted, because "either the genius or the 'lesser man' is totally ineffective without the other." In short, individualism "always, inevitably" results in a "co-operative economy," and in the modern era, it had created a "world-wide *co-operative* economy, which obviously is directly dependent for its existence upon individualism." The vast number of human interactions made possible by economic exchange were actually manifestations of the "principle of human co-operation" that "is implied by" the principle of loving one's neighbor.[16]

Lane thought this argument resolved what many of classical liberalism's opponents considered a vulnerable spot in the philosophy: why bother defending the freedom of one's fellow citizens? If individuals have no duties to others, why would they protect their neighbors from attacks by enemies or a tyrannical ruler? Lane's answer was that she felt an almost irresistible impulse to do so: when faced with a proposal to deprive people of freedom, she could not stop herself from speaking out. She did not calculate the risk to her own rights first. For example, although Social Security was bound for financial collapse, it was unlikely to fail within her own lifetime. Nevertheless, she felt bound to protest against it on behalf of future generations. To Rand, the love of freedom and a rational sense of benevolence toward others were sufficient reasons to oppose such measures, but Lane thought these alone could not explain her drive to defend her fellow citizens.[17]

Borrowing from radio preacher Carl McIntire—whose books tried to fuse libertarian politics with traditional Christian ethics—Lane argued that biblical principles revealed themselves in the world no less than scientific laws do.[18] ("I firmly believe that someday there will be a science of morality," she told Jasper Crane years later. "I think the First Principle of scientific morality is the American Declaration. . . . Atoms are endowed by the Creator with electrons, protons, ions, etc. We are endowed by our Creator with *our* functions and powers."[19]) And if the command to love one's neighbor was analogous to the principles of physics, then the fact that helping others ultimately redounds to one's own benefit was analogous to the observable phenomena by which scientists prove the laws of motion. The fact that economic liberty leads to greater prosperity proved that the universe's Creator designed people for freedom, not collectivism. Lane did not think moral behavior must be motivated by religious belief—on the contrary, because "moral principles exist in the nature of things," a person could be moral without realizing it, in the same way that he would obey the laws of physics without knowing their ultimate source.[20] Yet she did believe that all knowledge depends inherently on faith. The very existence of the material world, she told Rand, was only a "basic assumption" that cannot be proved.

Thus our knowledge of anything necessarily includes a leap of faith, as does our understanding of morality.

Rand began drafting a response, which ran to 22 pages of handwritten script, but she appears never to have completed it. Acknowledging that "a person's pursuit of his own personal advantage often does benefit other men," she argued that this was "only a secondary consequence," and not always or necessarily true. For example, an artist might work for years without being appreciated or recognized, but rather than giving up and finding some job that serves others, she thought it would be right for him to continue pursuing his artistic vision. And although some emergencies might demand extreme actions to save lives or property, "man's actual existence is on earth, not on a bare raft, and he must produce his own wealth, not wait for a voluntary handout (sharing) from another man, nor attempt to loot that other man's property."[21] There is obviously nothing wrong with helping other people if one has good reason to value them, but that was a fundamentally different question than whether one is morally bound to serve the interests of others across the board. Rand thought it was equally "vicious" for people to be "sacrificed by other men, through brute force (as in any concentration camp or political slaughter)" or to "sacrific[e] themselves, of their own volition, because they think it is proper to do so."

As for Lane's references to God, Rand considered that a topic for another day. "I do not know (nor care too greatly) whether man's consciousness is a special spiritual element," she wrote. "I am concerned only with how this consciousness works, here, on earth, what it can do, what it should do."[22] Although she did not agree with Lane that the world's existence can be explained only by a divine Creator, she objected more strongly to the assertion that reality cannot be proved to exist. On the contrary, she wrote, the world's existence is self-evident; any attempt to prove its existence would be otiose. As with all axioms, to deny the world's existence involved a self-contradiction. And the idea that one could only take the existence of reality on faith was dangerous because it lent a specious credibility to faith. "'An act of faith' is belief without evidence," she explained, and that "is the most vicious action of which men are capable; it is the root of all their sins, crime and misery." To accept faith as a legitimate method of understanding was to surrender the game, because "if any 'act of faith' is proper—then all acts of faith are proper."[23]

◤▲◥

Rand never sent this reply, nor did she ask about Lane's repeated allusions to her fight with Paterson. But Lane's hints suggested that the two had ceased speaking. The details are unclear because the letters Lane and Paterson exchanged were either lost or destroyed, but the immediate cause of the rupture was apparently the same argument Lane was now offering Rand about humanity's instinctual need to assist others. Paterson had complained before about the vagueness of Lane's "brotherhood" principle, and it appears that in late 1945 or early 1946, the two quarreled about it again, and that Paterson in a fit of anger called her a communist.[24] Such an accusation might seem bizarre, but Lane had in fact *been* a communist, or a communist sympathizer, 20 years earlier, and Paterson appears always to have viewed this as a sign of weak character.[25] Her discomfort was probably exacerbated by Lane's statements in *Discovery of Freedom* that "honest communists" based their beliefs on "the fact of human brotherhood," and that communism "recognizes the equality and the brotherhood of man."[26] Such wording must have made Paterson squint at Lane's repeated invocation of that word.

Lane thought she was drawing an important distinction between what she considered the kernels of truth in communism—its rejection of artificial social hierarchies such as race or sex and its rhetoric of aiding the poor—and the "fallacy" communists committed by assuming that equality requires subordination to the state or the destruction of individualism. She characterized this distinction as the difference between collectivism and cooperation, or between neighborliness and "community spirit." But Paterson thought her terminology was not only confusing, but inaccurate: communist "brotherhood" was a sham. Stalin showed no fraternal feeling toward the Ukrainians he starved, the Poles he massacred, or the Russians he enslaved.

The word "equality" in the context of communist thinking could only refer to the equality between fellow prisoners. *Genuine* fraternity is valid because it is chosen by free individuals—not emotionally, but for rational reasons. Lane's equivocation seemed to Paterson like one of the halfway defenses of freedom that she considered worse than outright opposition.

Another element in their conflict was Lane's habit of exaggeration. Lane later said that during the course of their argument Paterson called her a "liar," and Lane did indeed have a habit of bending the truth. Friends rolled their eyes, for example, at her claim that King Zog of Albania had once proposed to her.[27] Some of her stories were probably innocent errors—as, for example, her claim to have interviewed Joseph Stalin and met communist organizer Jack Reed in person—but in other cases, her embellishments were more self-serving.[28] Paterson seems to have finally grown tired of indulging her friend's tall tales.

On the other hand, Paterson was growing increasingly short-tempered with everybody. When Jasper Crane wrote her an admiring letter about *The God of the Machine*, he made the mistake of mentioning that he had asked some friends for their opinions about publicizing the book and they answered that it was too advanced for average readers. Paterson exploded in a letter that called Crane's friends stupid and cowardly, and likened herself to Newton and Euclid. She proudly forwarded a copy of the letter to Rand, who was shaken by its ferocity.[29] On another occasion, she chewed out a businessman so savagely for failing to support free-market ideas that he replied that he now understood how the Germans must have felt after being firebombed. "That is nothing," Paterson told Rand when relating the story. "I'll give him Hiroshima yet." If anyone were to "heedlessly inquire" whether lambasting people in this way was helpful, her answer was: "When I hit anyone with an axe it is not my intention to do them good; I am no philanthropist."[30]

Months later, Paterson apparently "screamed" at Leonard Read, then in the process of starting the Foundation for Economic Education, during a discussion about his plan to republish Rand's novel *Anthem*. Paterson had read *Anthem* years before and had told Rand at the time that she did not like it.

But her language with Read was apparently more explicit, and Read later told Rand that she had yelled at him for not reading *The God of the Machine* carefully enough to realize that Rand's ideas were borrowed from her own. When Read showed Rand an abusive letter Paterson had sent him, Rand replied that it "was a bad shock."[31] She knew her friend was temperamental and sometimes nasty, but things seemed to be getting worse.

In fact, Rand had been trying to comprehend her friend's behavior for a long time. She even wrote to Lane to ask if she had noticed Paterson's growing rage. A fragment of Lane's reply survives among Rand's papers. Yes, Lane said, relating the incident with the rosebush and other examples of Paterson's obstinacy. "An idea once in her head cannot be dislodged."[32]

Paterson's rage was increasingly forcing friends to avoid her—which only worsened her feelings of isolation and bitterness. And she was well aware of how off-putting she could be. "Slowly but surely I am fixing it so that I won't speak to anyone but you," she had told Rand three years earlier, "and if you then won't speak to me I'll be all set for peace and quiet, won't I just?"[33] A year later, her outlook had not changed. "Am I in a bad temper[?]—you bet, all the time. And what I think about the human race you can guess. Maybe the one thing it *is* right about is its evident determination to exterminate itself."[34] Around the same time, she quarreled about something with her closest friend, humorist Will Cuppy, and apparently never spoke to him again before his 1949 suicide.[35]

Rand mused in her journal about Paterson's abrasiveness, wondering what the older woman sought in their friendship and why she alternated between bitterness and a clingy need for attention. It seemed as though Paterson found in her some solace from the "spiritual emptiness, hopelessness, confusion, dullness, grayness, [and] fear" of the contemporary world.[36] She seemed to have been "wrecked by a fierce sense of injustice"—an indignation toward cruelty and irrationality, which erupted at times into "violent" misanthropy, "exaggerated pride," and "insane arbitrariness"—a tendency to assert "I am right because I'm right." Paterson had "given up" trying to persuade people, she thought, a habit that had grown so extreme that it "turned to hurting those whom she likes." This reaction was obviously self-defeating, because such a "Byronic" pose only ended up leaving her more lonesome, and her arguments more unheard. Rand decided that her mentor was a tragic case, someone who might have become "a great rational thinker," but was instead slowly withdrawing from the world.[37]

Rand composed these notes in preparation for *The Strike*, as she thought about whether to model a character on Paterson. She had started devoting more time to that novel after *Top Secret* was canceled. And in February 1948, she traveled to New York and Chicago to research railroads and steel mills—destined to be centerpieces of the book. Afterward she wrote Paterson a long, enthusiastic letter describing the trip. She had been treated to a behind-the-scenes look at the workings of modern trains, and the engineers even let her operate the engine itself. "Believe it or not," she beamed, "I have now driven the Twentieth Century Limited." There was "nothing as glamorous as a brilliant achievement of the human mind and a diesel engine is certainly that."[38]

In Chicago, she toured a Kaiser steel mill and was hosted at a special lunch by the company's executives—"not the financiers or the directors, but the real working executives of the mills." She found them "wearily resigned to getting nothing but smears from writers," and astonished that she wanted "to glorify them in a book." They shared with Rand "simply hair-raising" details of the government regulations hindering their business. "Here is a sample: The [Interstate Commerce Commission] now controls the distribution of freight cars. They have threatened an embargo on freight cars for deliveries to steel plants, which, if put into effect, would stop the entire steel production of the country."[39]

Paterson was delighted by Rand's letter, but chided her for being distracted. "I do not think you ought to be writing letters to any extent now, or certainly not in any time when you should be writing."[40] Rand was by then well into the work; far enough along that she showed part of the manuscript to Paterson, who offered some suggestions on what was to become Chapter 8. In this part of the story, the character Dagny Taggart, vice president of the Taggart Transcontinental railroad, accompanies steel magnate Hank Rearden on a train ride over an ingenious new bridge built out of Rearden's new invention: a lightweight, superstrong alloy called Rearden Metal. Reading Rand's description of the characters' sensations on the train sparked Paterson's joyful memories of watching and riding railroads on the prairie in her youth.

"A train streaming across the landscape," she told Rand, was "not quite like any other visual impression of things in motion." It was "not exactly a feeling of speed in the obvious way, as with a bird flying or a stone thrown or a creature running—not exactly that it is going 'fast,' but that it cuts space, it gets there so positively that the relative quality of 'speed' becomes unnoticeable; it's on another scale. Almost an effect of planetary motion." She urged Rand to keep her descriptive sentences streamlined, to convey that feeling of swiftness, and to eliminate adjectives that would weigh down the prose like "a donkey engine [hitched] on behind."[41]

Rand wrote back to say that she was, indeed, "weeding" adjectives, and the final version of this passage captured some of what Paterson was trying to describe: "[Dagny] felt no wheels under the floor. The motion was a smooth flight on a sustained impulse, as if the engine hung above the rails, riding a current. She felt no speed. . . . She had barely grasped the sparkle of a lake ahead—and in the next instant she was beside it, then past. It was a strange foreshortening between sight and touch, she thought, between wish and fulfillment."[42]

Rand had selected railroads as a primary setting of *The Strike* for just the reasons Paterson cited: they symbolized humanity's conquest of nature and the potential of free individuals to prevail over the forces arrayed against them. Paterson and Lane could easily remember the revolution railroads had brought about in American life. Lane had described them in *Free Land* as miracles of delight, and she and her mother had devoted a chapter to the subject in their 1939 *Little House* book, *By the Shores of Silver Lake*, in which 12-year-old Laura begs Pa to take her to see the railroad being built. Father and daughter marvel at the sight of construction crews preparing the ground for rails. Looking out at the immense grassland, Laura thinks that "someday the long steel tracks would lie level on the fills and through the cuts, and trains would come roaring, steaming with speed."[43] The railroad represents everything civilized: safety, abundance, and the creative mind at work. When horrendous blizzards cover the tracks in *Free Land* and *The Long Winter*, thriving villages are reduced to lonesome wastelands haunted by the prospect of famine.

The source of all the benefits manifested in the railroad is, of course, the human mind. "Are there railroads because people think of them first when they aren't there?" Laura asks Pa. "Yes," he replies. "That's what makes things happen, people think of them first. If enough people think of a thing and work hard enough at it, I guess it's pretty nearly bound to happen, wind and weather permitting."[44] Just as freedom was essential for the scientific discoveries that enabled Manhattan Project scientists to help win the war, so freedom to think and innovate was crucial to the development of the railroad and all the blessings it brought. Rand incorporated the same sense of bold innovation into *The Strike* in the character of Nathaniel Taggart, Dagny's 19th-century ancestor, who founded the railroad and whom Dagny reveres. In one passage, she looks at a rail map dating from his era, and at "the red arteries winding across a yellowed continent. There had been a time when the railroad was called the blood system of the nation, and the stream of trains had been like a living circuit of blood, bringing growth and wealth to every patch of wilderness it touched."[45]

Paterson, too, celebrated her memories of the railways in her novels. In *Never Ask the End*, Marta recalls the thrill of crossing the Rocky Mountains behind a powerful locomotive: "They put on four and sometimes six Mogul locomotives for the big transcontinental passenger trains," she says. "At night, hitting that three percent grade, two engines in front and two behind, pouring out streams of smoke and fire, it was like going to hell on a first-class ticket. Perched up in a sort of crow's nest in the observation car. There was a man from Pittsburgh asked me to elope with him. Made you feel like that."[46] Rand emphasized this theme in her manuscript. Halfway through the first part of the novel, Dagny walks the dark streets of New York in growing fear after several of the nation's leading industrialists have mysteriously vanished, and she thinks to herself of the way that "men on a dark prairie liked to see the lighted windows of a train going past," because it "gave them reassurance in the midst of empty miles and night" just to think that someone was going somewhere.[47]

More than any other creation—perhaps more than the airplane—the railroad represented to Paterson, Lane, and Rand, the future that industrial innovation had brought about in the 20th century—and that was now threatened by the political and cultural onslaught of collectivism.

◤▲◥

"People nowadays think that the universe *is* malevolent, that reality is evil, that by the essential nature of the world, man is doomed to suffering and frustration," Rand told Paterson in March 1948. "I am not certain, as I was before, that we will see an intellectual renaissance on a large scale in our lifetime."[48] The horrors of the war, the expansion of communism in Europe, and the beginning of an atomic arms race were especially gloomy portents. Paterson sensed it, too. She thought people were "afraid to look at the reality of anything, having got themselves into this monstrous mess." Yet strangely enough, she had begun feeling more hopeful. "I think there is a large chance of a turn in my own lifetime, though I hardly thought so a few years ago, and it does *look* worse now."[49] The problem was not that collectivist ideas were becoming more popular—on the contrary, Rand and Paterson both noticed a significant shift in public opinion since the war's end. The problem was that people "still talk about 'the middle of the road'" instead of taking a firm stand for liberty.[50]

A persistent obstacle was the morality of self-sacrifice, which taught people not to stand up for themselves but to surrender their freedom to the assertions of government leaders. It was a point on which Paterson and Rand agreed, despite their religious differences. As an atheist, Rand saw no foundation for the principle of self-sacrifice to begin with. And although Paterson did believe in some kind of God, she thought the Christian doctrine of self-sacrifice contained "inherent contradiction[s]"—particularly that, on the one hand, "it is a man's whole business to *save his own soul* . . . [that] he is him*self* and his real and sole concern," whereas on the other hand "*sacrifice* is the *means of salvation*," which would mean "he must also sacrifice himself to enter into that plan." Still, she gave Christianity credit for originating individualism, with its idea "that human beings are immortal and completely separate and full entities, persons." This "was the *new* idea in Christianity" when it was introduced in Roman times, and it "was bound to develop free 'capitalism' in its secular expression." Unfortunately, when that religion became the official faith of the Roman Empire and merged with imperial political institutions, its original individualism was lost and the idea of self-sacrifice was incorporated into Christian culture instead. Thus, Paterson concluded, the Catholic Church had been "*organized* on the idea of sacrifice," and naturally "could not be expected to countenance free capitalism" in the modern age.[51]

Paterson did not consider herself a Christian, but she was fascinated by religion, and throughout 1948, she enjoyed explaining the history of Christianity to Rand, occasionally teasing her protégée about having not read the Bible herself.[52] Paterson agreed with Rand that "received Catholic political philosophy" was "silly as well as deadly" because the principle of sacrifice led able and intelligent people to abandon their freedom and subordinate themselves to the service of others. But she did not believe Church leaders had purposely adopted what they knew to be false moral doctrines. "I don't think the human race has *consciously* 'penalized virtue for being virtue.'"[53] Rand replied that it was pointless to argue over their motives. "If the Catholic political philosophy contains all the elements which add up to opposing Capitalism because it makes man happy, but they have not consciously admitted to themselves that that is what it adds up to—it doesn't make them any the less guilty."[54] It was at least clear that the Church endorsed "a form of Statism run by the Church—which simply means that it hopes for a return of the days of the Inquisition."[55] Paterson agreed that the papacy's overt goal was "re-establishing the union of Church and State wherever possible," but she thought it "more plausible" that its embrace of the morality of sacrifice was "sheer earnest error, the mistaking of wrong for right."[56]

By this time, Rand also had finally met Lane in person for the first time—and found their religious differences insurmountable. Their brief exchange of letters about loving one's neighbor had been interrupted by work—Lane's on the *NECRB* and Rand's on the film version of *The Fountainhead*, which at last seemed to be getting underway—but in the autumn of 1947, Rand traveled to the East Coast to testify before the House Un-American Activities Committee about pro-Soviet propaganda in movies. She planned to combine that trip with some research for *The Strike*, and to visit Lane at her Connecticut home.

Rand's congressional testimony was part of the committee's examination of the degree to which Communist Party functionaries had influenced popular culture through movies. As a Russian refugee who had published a novel about life in the Soviet Union and was now working in Hollywood studios, Rand was an ideal witness. Happy to testify, she prepared a detailed presentation about several films, but never delivered it because the committee changed its plans at the last minute and asked her to rebut studio executive Louis B. Mayer, instead. Mayer had told the committee that the 1944 film *Song of Russia*—which egregiously whitewashed Stalin's brutal regime—was "little more than a pleasant musical romance."[57] Rand firmly disagreed. It portrayed Russians as content, even boldly idealistic, and explicitly likened the Soviet Revolution to the American Revolution. That was repulsive enough, but Rand thought the larger problem was Hollywood's "carelessness with ideas"—its willingness to disregard the inescapable clash between individualism and collectivism, which could only redound to the benefit of tyrants.[58] Defenders of movies like *Song of Russia* excused them on the grounds that they had been made during the war, in an attempt to strengthen the Soviet-American alliance. But Rand considered it immoral and unnecessary to "deceive the American people" about the nature of Stalin's tyranny.[59] Temporarily joining forces against a common enemy was one thing; persuading Americans that the USSR was a free and happy society was another.

Rand tried to contrast the American culture of optimism and self-confidence with the pervasive atmosphere of despair and privation she had known in Russia. The idea of a "pleasant musical romance" set in Stalin's dictatorship was a travesty. "In my time we were a bunch of ragged, starved, dirty, miserable people who had only two thoughts in our mind[s]," she told the committee. "That was our complete terror—afraid to look at one another, afraid to say anything for fear of who is listening and would report us—and where to get the next meal. You have no idea what it means to live in a country where nobody has any concern except food. . . . They have no idea of any pleasant romances or love—nothing but food and fear."[60]

"You paint a very dismal picture," said Pennsylvania congressman John McDowell when Rand finished. "Doesn't anybody smile in Russia anymore?"

"Well, if you ask me literally, pretty much no," Rand replied.

"They don't smile?" asked McDowell skeptically.

"If they do, it is privately and accidentally. Certainly, it is not social. They don't smile in approval of their system."

McDowell pressed. "That is a great change from the Russians I have always known. . . . Don't they do things at all like Americans? Don't they walk across town to visit their mother-in-law or somebody?"

"Look," Rand answered. "It is very hard to explain. It is almost impossible to convey to a free people what it is like to live in a totalitarian dictatorship. I can tell you a lot of details. I can never completely convince you, because you are free. It is in a way good that you can't even conceive of what it is like. Certainly they have friends and mothers-in-law. They try to live a human life, but you understand it is totally inhuman. Try to imagine what it is like if you are in constant terror from morning till night and at night you are waiting for the doorbell to ring, where you are afraid of anything and everybody, living in a country where human life is nothing."[61] It was an effective statement, but the committee did not ask to hear the rest of her presentation.

From Washington, Rand traveled to New York doing research for *The Strike*, and stopped en route at Lane's home. They likely discussed Lane's own travels in the Soviet Union a quarter century earlier, and Lane's falling out with Paterson a year before. But at some point, the conversation turned to religion. Rand left no record of the meeting, but 16 years later, Lane told Jasper Crane that the younger woman's atheism had given her "a terrific shock."[62] To her argument that the universe must have had a creator in order to exist, Rand replied by asking, "who created God?"—a question Lane considered "puerile" and "silly-childish," although she left no hint as to how she answered. "Any further discussion was certainly futile," she said, "so there wasn't any more and I haven't seen her since."

It does not appear, however, that Rand and Lane's meeting was actually as heated as this letter suggests. On the contrary, a day after Rand's visit, Lane sent her a long follow-up letter that firmly but pleasantly pressed her arguments. Echoing the writing of French biophysicist Pierre Lecomte du Noüy—whose 1947 book *Human Destiny* she had praised in the *NECRB* that April—Lane argued that the universe contains a natural principle (she called it "creativeness per se") that keeps the universe coherent, as opposed to it flying apart into randomness.[63] Given the fact that things tend toward disorder—the law of entropy—the only thing that could explain the persistence of material reality would be some kind of godhead (although Lane denied that this was "supernatural, spiritual, [or] superhuman" or a "'Supreme Intelligence' that rules the universe," an idea that she said "makes no sense to me"). Not only does this creativeness per se principle hold reality together, it also gives a direction to biological evolution. Indeed, its primary expression, du Noüy wrote, is in man's own ability to create.

Du Noüy's argument appeared to reconcile science and religion, and *Human Destiny* became fashionable in conservative circles as a result. Its central thesis was that "the harmonious majesty of the great laws" governing physics and biology reveals an overarching plan by which evolution is organized—a plan that guides both the development of lower life forms and the purpose of human consciousness.[64] According to du Noüy, the universe must be governed either by randomness—in which case the existence of animal life or of the human mind would be wildly improbable, and material existence would fall apart—or by some force that organizes matter into meaningful forms. Since only consciousness can do this, the universe must be permeated by a mind that gives it order and purpose, through a process of gradual evolutionary development.

"Orthogenetic" notions of this sort have been proposed for centuries— Julian Huxley and Pierre Teilhard de Chardin were advancing their own versions at the time—but unlike these others, du Noüy held that one of the principles implied by this organizing principle is the need for freedom.[65] "Natural evolution," he wrote, "has striven to evade the statistical hold which dominates the inorganic universe and has prepared the way for the advent of human liberty."[66] Single-celled creatures, by evolving into multicellular and then animal forms, expand their freedom to act, which du Noüy took as proof of a universal tendency toward greater freedom over time—a tendency that also governs the development of every individual.[67] To support this argument, he cited that "very remarkable and amazingly intelligent book, *The God of the Machine*."[68]

Paterson had in fact corresponded with du Noüy for years, and in 1956, she would publish a long feature about him in *National Review*, lauding his theories as an alternative to Darwinian evolution.[69] "The argument [of Darwin's *On the Origin of Species*] is that in the organic order, species originate from elementary types by variations (the variations are not accounted for, but are at least conceivable), and then by the survival of the variations best adapted to the environment," she wrote. "But in fact, the human species *does not* do anything of the kind; it survives by adapting the environment."[70] Humanity's unique capacity for invention or discovery could only be explained by something outside nature itself: a Creator responsible for making reality the way it is.

Lane, who probably read the book at Paterson's suggestion, thought it supported not only her view that "a materialist or determinist philosophy has deadly consequences in human affairs," but also her incipient "brotherhood" theory.[71] "I believe that existence is *created* and created for a *purpose*," she told a friend, and "that the Purpose is served by the created beings (any and each of them, including us) living according to the *nature* with which they are endowed by the Creator."[72] She did not think God was a person, however, or that He governed the lives of individuals or answered prayers. Instead, she seemed to believe in something like Aristotle's notion of a "prime mover"—an entity not motivated by will, choice, or desire, but more like an inerrant and constant force in the physical world, aware solely of itself.[73]

That theory, however, seemed to view God as a mere synonym for reality. To conceive of God as having no personality—as an invariant part of the universe, indifferent to human affairs—relegated Him to the role of a natural phenomenon akin to gravity or the Higgs field (created by the so-called God particle) that today's physicists believe is the source of matter's physicality. To the extent that this was an argument for God's existence, it was a God stripped of any of the characteristics traditionally ascribed to Him.[74] It seemed like the kind of God even an atheist could believe in.

Although Rand never addressed this matter in print, an intriguing note in the margin of her copy of Étienne Gilson's *The Unity of Philosophical Experience* suggests how she might have replied. Gilson—the theologian Paterson had urged Rand to read—described the belief of certain Muslim theologians that Allah continually creates all the atoms that make up matter, and that this accounts for their reality and coherence. This belief seemed silly to Rand, who wrote that such philosophers were "invent[ing] demons instead of accepting facts."[75] If God creates every particle anew every instant, and each instant can be infinitely subdivided into smaller instants, then God's creation must be a continuous process, one that goes on without a break through every fraction of every second, in keeping with invariant, coherent, rationally predictable laws. To call this "God" instead of "reality" seemed like a semantic trick.[76] What's more, this argument seemed to commit the same fallacy as the economic arguments that imagined government could spend money "outside the economy"—it was dualist thinking that assumed there could be something real outside of reality. Paterson herself had likened that to the goofy physics of the "perpetual motion machine."

Lane clearly relished sharing these ideas with Rand during their meeting. She concluded her follow-up letter by saying that it had been "grand seeing you," and "I do hope you come back."[77] But although Rand sketched out notes for a reply, she apparently never wrote one, and although they exchanged brief notes for some years to come, they never met again. Their correspondence petered out. Lane could not reconcile herself to Rand's atheism for the same reason that Paterson could not: both believed a purely mechanical universe had no room for free will or for the value of individual personality.[78]

What Lane and Paterson never grasped was that although Rand was an atheist, she was not a crusader on the subject, of the Richard Dawkins or Christopher Hitchens variety.[79] The metaphysical question of God's existence was less important to her than the epistemological question of whether a person based his beliefs on reasoned argument or an appeal to faith. Only the former, she thought, could provide a legitimate foundation for individualism—or any other idea—whereas the latter's inherent arbitrariness undermined any argument that employed it. If a case for individualism incorporated any proposition based on the "fiat of revelation," it was ultimately embracing a premise that left it vulnerable to challenge by those who appealed to a different revelation or who disputed the validity of revelations at all.

Questions like these would grow increasingly important at the end of the 1940s, a period that witnessed a surge in religious affiliation in the United States. Although religion had always been commonplace in American life, the Revolt from the Village had coincided with a secularizing trend that lasted from the 1920s through the war. When peace came, however, church membership grew so markedly that the media began to speak of a new "great awakening."[80] In part, this arose from the desire of homecoming veterans to return to a life of normal domesticity, but it was also an artifact of the Cold War, when religion became a proxy for the difference between communism and freedom. Carl McIntire's books *The Rise of the Tyrant* (1945) and *Author of Liberty* (1946) made Bible-based arguments against collectivism and reached a wide audience. In 1947, Billy Graham began his ministry, inaugurating a decades-long combination of Christianity and political activism. And a year later, Bishop Fulton J. Sheen published *Communism and the Conscience of the West*, which sharply criticized Soviet tyranny.[81] The trend continued such that by 1955, when the flagship conservative journal *National Review* was founded, religious and political lines were deeply drawn in a way that left Rand, as an atheist defender of capitalism, largely isolated.

Meanwhile, Lane gravitated toward the religious right. She never fully embraced Fundamentalism—indeed, she did not regard herself as a Christian— and she rejected the traditionalism of prominent religious conservatives such as

Russell Kirk, whom she called "true reactionaries" aiming to "take us all back to medievalism."[82] Yet she came to believe that "the connection between freedom and Christianity," with its doctrines of "persuasion, sacrifice and love," was "demonstrated" by "actual history."[83] By the 1950s, she had decided that Rand, with her "arrogant atheism" and "contempt of [ordinary] human beings," had it all wrong. In fact, Rand had "no understanding at all of individualist principles."[84]

11

The New Intellectual

Franklin Roosevelt's death in April 1945 marked the end of an epoch, but the change was not immediately obvious because of the smooth way in which the new president, Harry Truman, distanced himself from some of his predecessor's policies. A year earlier, Democrats had nominated him for vice president, instead of the incumbent Henry Wallace, because the latter was seen as a holdover from the radical New Deal liberalism of the 1930s, a position that had become unacceptable to voters. Wallace's guileless admiration for the USSR was also an embarrassment to the Roosevelt administration, and when, in early 1945, he was effectively demoted to secretary of commerce, Congress only confirmed him after a long debate that revealed just how much the New Deal's popularity had waned.[1] Roosevelt was unenthusiastic about making Truman his running mate, but his own failing health, and a national trend toward conservatism that would climax in Republicans taking Congress in 1946, forced him to moderate his tone.

In fact, the president barely knew Truman, who was far less deferential to the Soviets in foreign policy than his predecessor. Where Roosevelt and Wallace had persistently ignored communist atrocities, Truman began edging away from Stalin as soon as the war ended. On March 6, 1946, Winston Churchill told students at a Missouri college, with the new president in attendance, that the Soviets had wrung down an "iron curtain" across Europe. By then, the USSR was already at work on an atomic bomb, the first of which it tested on August 29, 1949, only two months before China also officially fell to communist rule. Despite the Allied victory over the fascists, freedom seemed to be in retreat worldwide. Half of Germany and all of Poland, the Baltic States, and Lane's beloved Balkans, would remain under communist domination for another 40 years. Communists also had considerable influence in Italy, waged a civil war in Greece, and were a major force in France. A socialist government even ruled in London. Throughout the Cold War, collectivism only seemed to expand. By the late 1970s, most of the world would be governed by one variety or other of collectivism.[2]

In the United States, however, peace brought a relaxing of government controls over enterprise, and a potent economic boom.[3] Republicans campaigned under the slogan "Have You Had Enough of the Alphabet?"—in reference to the New Deal's "alphabet soup" agencies—which was shortened to "Had Enough?" Voters answered yes. Once in control of Congress, Republicans trimmed federal spending, eliminated rationing and price controls, and cut taxes both directly and indirectly by adopting a system of joint returns for married couples, which for many families amounted to a 50 percent reduction.[4] The Administrative Procedures Act of 1946 brought a degree of discipline to the nation's regulatory agencies. A year later, the Taft-Hartley Act leveled the playing field between labor unions and management, and the General Agreement on Tariffs and Trade reduced international trade restrictions. The War Production Board, the War Labor Board, and the Office of Price Administration were dismantled, soldiers returned to the workforce, and factories the government had commandeered to build tanks and jeeps were sold back to private investors or allowed once again to produce for the private market. This reversal resulted in more choices for the public and encouraged private investment in place of government spending. At last America began to emerge from the Great Depression.

Much of this activity happened in spite of the new administration. Truman—whose resemblance to George F. Babbitt in Sinclair Lewis's novel was a frequent subject of comment—was persuaded, as many Democrats were, that the war's end would bring about an economic decline.[5] He called voters' desire to free the market "insane in [its] selfishness."[6] But the Republican Congress rejected his efforts to retain price controls, nationalize health care, mandate universal military training, and increase spending on public works and subsidies.[7] And although a brief and serious recession occurred in 1946, this policy of letting industry grow and giving employees, buyers, CEOs, and investors freedom to make their own economic decisions ensured a swift transition from war to a peacetime economy, and laid the foundation for a wave of prosperity in the 1950s.[8]

It would take longer to recoup many of the other losses of the New Deal era. Confiscatory tax rates remained on the books—incomes above $200,000 were taxed at 91 percent—as did arbitrary antitrust laws that penalized businesses for reducing prices and providing good service to customers. Surveillance of private citizens grew, the ownership of gold was still illegal, and the military draft remained in place. The Truman administration even threatened to use conscription to shut down a strike of railroad workers. Most of the bureaucracies and entitlement programs begun in the 1930s were never eliminated, and the entanglement of government and private industry that marked Roosevelt's approach to the economic crisis persisted—laying the groundwork for what President Dwight Eisenhower later called the "military-industrial complex."[9] As a result, the idea of a government-managed economy would strike the next generation as almost axiomatic.

▰▲◣

From her post as editor of the *NECRB*, Rose Wilder Lane was trying to rally scholars and writers to oppose collectivism, and particularly what she saw as the insidious and growing popularity of the ideas of economist John Maynard Keynes in the college classrooms of Truman's America.

Since 1936, Keynes's *General Theory of Employment, Interest, and Money* had served as a theoretical bible for New Dealers. Brushing aside the classical approach of thinkers such as Adam Smith—who underscored the role of individual choice in economics and viewed markets as self-correcting mechanisms of mutual exchange—Keynes argued that government could control the economy on a broad scale by borrowing and spending, and that economists who focused on production as the engine of growth were fundamentally misguided. He believed the focus should be on consumption, instead, which government should actively encourage by taxing the "hoarded" savings of private citizens and spending those dollars to "stimulate" economic activity.

In essence, Keynesian theory was a sort of "cargo cult" economics, which sought to replicate the surface appearance of a thriving market without addressing the legal and economic institutions that make for actual flourishing.[10] Spurring demand by penalizing thrift might result in visible phenomena such as manufacturing, or the construction of dams and bridges. But that production does not represent an economically legitimate form of prosperity because it is not generated by the actual demand of consumers. Such policies therefore made no more sense than if the government were to bulldoze people's homes and pay the dehoused residents to rebuild them.[11]

Moreover, as economists Peter Boettke and Patrick Newman note, one of the "unfortunate casualties" of Keynesian theory "was the prior belief that falling prices were good and a healthy growing economy would experience mild deflation from increases in productivity which did not need hands-on managing." Under Keynes's tutelage, economists instead came to view low prices as bad and encouraged government to prevent them by manipulating interest rates and the money supply. In reality, Boettke and Newman note, such efforts "would not successfully steer [the economy] but instead crash land it right into the rocky shore."[12] Since government spending to "stimulate" the economy is necessarily drawn from taxes imposed on the same private sector that is being stimulated, Keynesian theory was the economic equivalent of scooping water from one end of a swimming pool and pouring it back in the other end. Worse, when government funds programs with borrowing instead of taxes, it risks inflation, piles debt on future generations, and endangers the savings of every person in the country. As Paterson commented in "Turns" in 1941: "Some while ago, Mr. Keynes wrote . . . the following words 'Lenin is said to have declared that the best way to destroy the capitalist system was to debauch the currency. By a continuing inflation, governments can confiscate secretly and unobserved an important part of the wealth of their citizens. . . .' After making that statement, which history verifies, Mr. Keynes later advocated 'deficit spending.' Did he think Lenin was certainly right in working to overturn the existing basis of society? If not, why does he advocate measures of that nature?"[13]

For her part, Lane objected that Keynes confused activity with prosperity. "Keynesian economists," she wrote, "say in effect: 'Spending makes wealth,'" which was economically nonsensical and morally unsound. "Thriftlessness means irresponsibility, disregard for one's obligation to others, and indifference to the rights of others. That way lies trouble." Keynes merely offered another rationalization for government control over the economy. "If you know Marxian dogma, you can see numerous similarities between it and Keynesian doctrines," she told *NECRB* readers. It was "collectivistic and mechanistic. It deals with people in classes and masses, in averages and aggregates. It proposes to relieve the individual of responsibility in a variety of ways. It represents property rights as mere privileges from the state to be given or taken away according to the will of the ruler." Yet because Keynesians masqueraded as defenders of free enterprise, "they get a hearing in places which would be closed to a professed socialist."[14]

Among economists, the leading opponents of Keynes's theory were members of the Austrian school, led by Ludwig von Mises. Born in what is now Lviv, Ukraine, in 1881, Mises was originally trained as a lawyer but became a prominent economist for the government of the Austro-Hungarian Empire. When the Nazis came to power, he and his wife fled to the United States, and Mises began teaching at New York University. He published penetrating analyses of socialism, including *Omnipotent Government* in 1944—a book Paterson, Lane, and Rand admired—and five years later, released his masterwork, *Human Action*. Labeling Keynesian theory a "Santa Claus fable," he argued that it was merely another variation on the pro-inflationary policies common throughout history, all of which committed the same essential fallacy: regarding government as outside the economic realm, with the ability to fine-tune the processes of production and exchange, when in reality it "can spend or invest only what it takes away from its citizens." Government spending necessarily "curtails the citizens' spending and investment to the full extent of its quantity."[15]

Paterson appears never to have read *Human Action*, but Lane hailed it in the *NECRB* as "unquestionably the most powerful product of the human mind in our time," and Rand frequently recommended it as—in the words of one of her students—a book "of the first rank of importance."[16] They especially admired Mises's rigorous adherence to methodological individualism—his insistence that all economic phenomena must be evaluated in light of their consequences for specific people, not in terms of aggregates and abstract forces. But although this was congenial to their own ethical individualism, Mises himself actually rejected Lane's and Rand's moral views. He denied that ethics could have any objective validity because assertions about right and wrong cannot be experimentally proved. They are therefore "beyond any rational examination."[17] Morality was only a matter of personal preference, and, in a democratic society, the arbitrary value preferences endorsed by the majority simply *are* justice.

This ultrademocratic view led Mises to make such startling pronouncements as: "Everything that serves to preserve the social order is moral; everything that is detrimental to it is immoral. Accordingly, when we reach the conclusion that an institution is beneficial to society, one can no longer object that it is immoral."[18] Rand and Lane were distressed by such language; whatever their differences, they thought morality was objective—a set of prescriptions for human flourishing—and that the truth of ethical principles can be rationally demonstrated. In their view, any economic theory divorced from a conception of the human good was as senseless as an attempt to practice medicine while denying there is any such thing as health. Mises's subjectivism seemed to threaten the intellectual rigor of the case for liberty by suggesting that the value of freedom is merely a matter of personal taste, rather than a mandate of human nature.

Lane therefore declared in the *NECRB* that Mises was "absolutely sound" in economics, but "in politics he is bewildered."[19] Thoughtless political statements "sprinkle the pages" of his books, she complained, including his assertion that any political system could be made to function if only "the rulers are equal to their task."[20] This was "stuff and nonsense!" akin to saying that an automobile engine could work without pistons if the driver tried hard enough.[21] Rand seconded Lane's objections. She told Lane in 1946 that she thought Mises was the best contemporary economist, but his attempt "to divorce economics from morality" was "impossible," given that economics was inherently concerned with people pursuing values in order to survive and flourish.[22]

A year later, Lane challenged Mises directly in a letter. "You sincerely believe that you are opposed to socialism," she wrote, but he actually was not. The notion that justice is whatever the majority says was "in theory and in practice" the very "basis of socialism." Mises's reply made clear that he had no interest in discussing the subject. "I do not care whether or not you consider me sincere," he wrote. "It is my principle never to address any reviewer who calls my writing 'stuff and nonsense.'" Besides, "I know that all communists and ex-communists are fundamentally opposed to my theories."[23]

Lane's own showdown with Keynesian theory came only a month after this dispiriting exchange, in her review of a college textbook called *The Elements of Economics* by Stanford University professor Lorie Tarshis. It was the first American college textbook written from a Keynesian perspective, and Lane was startled by its "many lies of omission and distortion," such as Tarshis's claim that no economic depressions occurred before the mid-19th century.[24] Equally troubling were the "innumerable repetitions" and "implications" that gave the book an undeniable "slant" against free markets. Tarshis repeatedly emphasized the profits of businesses while omitting mention of their losses or the risks they faced, giving readers the impression that businesses were nefarious and greedy. He claimed free markets cause inequalities of wealth, when in fact they do not.[25] He described advertising as a form of economic waste, when it actually plays a valuable role in the marketplace.[26] He made no comment on the poverty and stagnation of the Soviet economy, and while characterizing 19th-century American individualism as ruthless, made no mention of the extraordinary improvement in living standards it created, including for the poor. He claimed that government should ensure that "the division of [wealth] among members of the society" is "compatible with the society's standards of justice"—which would necessitate a police state.[27] And faithful to Keynes's theories, he argued that the cause of unemployment and other ills was insufficient spending—"low consumption," he called it.[28] Government, he concluded, should take "active steps" to "raise the propensity to consume."[29] In practice this meant finding ways to confiscate savings.

Tarshis also ignored critiques of Keynesian theories. As William F. Buckley later noted, novice readers could finish his book and never learn "that some reputable economists have read Keynes *and disagreed with him!*"[30] Rather than discuss classical economic doctrines, Tarshis simply asserted that "the nature of our economy has changed."[31] And although he insisted that he was not defending centralized economic planning, he concluded the book by arguing that "considered, and concerted, action" by the government was the only way to achieve lasting prosperity.[32] All of this led even one sympathetic reviewer to conclude that his book would "need considerable revision before it will satisfy the needs for a text in introductory economics."[33]

Lane devoted the August 1947 *NECRB* to a thorough trouncing of the book, highlighting its support for command-and-control economics. "A little arithmetic would show Professor Tarshis that the Central Planning Board which he urges so plausibly upon trusting ignorance cannot possibly exist," she declared. Mustering arguments that Paterson, Hayek, and others had formulated in preceding years, she pointed out that it would be impossible for any bureaucracy to "determine equitable price-wage relationships" for the 50 million workers in America, and the billions or trillions of goods and services they produce—for even a single hour, let alone a year or decade. "Only a Gestapo could try to enforce 1937 wages and prices in 1945." By contrast, the decentralized decisionmaking process of free markets—individuals choosing for themselves without government oversight—managed to solve the complex coordination problem of determining how much goods and services should cost. "Every customer in every shop does a share of the job [of economic coordination], and for free," she observed. "Capitalism has created an economy so productive and so complex that it can't work on any basis but individual decisions, and can't exist where individuals are not permitted to make the decisions."

Worried that Tarshis's book would work as a form of propaganda just when the nation was poised to liberate the economy and create a postwar boom, Lane urged "every American" to "act to stop the teaching of these fallacies and lies in the schools and universities he supports." Subscribers soon responded. Merwin Hart, Lane's employer at the National Economic Council, organized a letter-writing campaign to university officials across the country, providing copies of Lane's review and asking them not to use the book in classes. Throughout the autumn, Lane continued to urge *NECRB* readers to write university administrators to protest against the book before it "convince[d] another generation of college students that nothing but unlimited Federal spending can preserve their country."[34] The campaign was successful, and the text was largely abandoned. A new one by Paul Samuelson became the standard in colleges, instead. To Lane, this was not much improvement, since Samuelson was no more a principled defender of free markets than Tarshis, but Samuelson's book at least offered students a glimpse at anti-Keynesian arguments. It was a small victory, but one she could be proud of.

▰▲▰

By the end of 1947, Isabel Paterson was looking for a way out of the *Herald Tribune*. The newspaper's leadership was drifting to the left, and at the age of 62, she wanted more time to write at length on subjects that interested her. She had long dreamed of establishing a new magazine devoted to individualist thought, but she insisted that it must generate income instead of being run at a loss, as so many magazines were. It was hard to raise capital, however. "I know such a magazine could be made to pay," she told Rand. But "when I think how dumb the 'practical men' are, not to see that such a magazine would go, I seethe with fury."[35] She, Lane, and Rand had now spent years in meetings with potential backers, and the prospect of a new magazine still seemed out of reach.

One obstacle was Paterson's abrasive personality. She told Rand that at one lunch meeting, she directly confronted the wife of the publisher of the *New York*

Daily News, demanding to know "what the hell is the matter with the rich people in this country? Why is there no periodical in this country for *ideas*— no publication in which anything rational can get printed?" Wealthy business owners "sit on their tails and whine, after subsidizing Communists to do them in."[36] The victim of this particular outburst took it in stride, but no startup capital was forthcoming, and other potential financiers were not so patient.

Another Paterson protégé, John Chamberlain, came close to arranging funds to start an independent magazine, but those plans fell through at the last minute. Instead, he began writing for an anti-communist journal called *Plain Talk*, which was founded in 1946 and was edited by Lane's friend Isaac Don Levine. Rand contributed an article a year later again urging Hollywood to stop naively producing anti-individualist films. ("Don't attack individual rights, individual freedom, private action, private initiative, and private property," she advised. "It is the proper wish of every decent American to stand on his own feet, earn his own living, and be as good at it as he can—that is, get as rich as he can by honest exchange."[37]) But Paterson refused to write for *Plain Talk*, because Levine supported the military draft. That by itself might not have been an insurmountable obstacle, but he shocked Paterson when he answered one of her arguments against conscription by saying he was "afraid of people with principles," specifically referring to Paterson and Rand. It was impractical, Levine thought, to expect the United States to defend itself with a volunteer army. When Paterson answered that it was self-defeating to force people to serve the state in the name of freedom, he demurred. "He will say 'Now come down to earth, etc.,'" she told Rand when relating the story. "I never did understand people who could talk as if one could be 'practical' without principles."[38] Four years later, when *Plain Talk* ceased publication and was succeeded by *The Freeman*, Chamberlain became its editor and invited Paterson to write for it. Again she refused, this time because Chamberlain did not pay enough.

In May 1948, she flew cross-country to visit Rand in Los Angeles, in hopes of interesting California investors in the magazine idea. The younger writer was "too excited to think straight" at the prospect of her friend's visit, and was particularly eager to show her around the studios where *The Fountainhead* was being filmed.[39] But the visit proved a disaster. Only Rand's version of the story survives, but it is plain that Paterson's bitter and confrontational behavior caused a permanent rift in their friendship. When Rand took her to a meeting of the Motion Picture Alliance for the Preservation of American Ideals, attended by prominent actors and Warner Brothers executives who were then working on *The Fountainhead*, Paterson spoke so rudely to one of Rand's coworkers that the man walked out. Then after a dinner with screenwriter Morrie Ryskind—a former socialist who had testified before the House Un-American Activities Committee and never worked in Hollywood again—Paterson made a clumsy joke about not liking "Jewish intellectuals."[40] Rand did not find it funny. "Then why do you like me?" she demanded.[41]

Paterson was again uncouth when Rand took her to a meeting that included William Mullendore, movie star Janet Gaynor, and Gaynor's husband, costume designer Adrian. During the conversation, Adrian suggested printing a sample issue of the proposed magazine so readers could see what it would look like. Paterson became enraged at the idea of doing such a thing for free. She turned to Mullendore—whose friendship with Rand had grown so close that she was showing him passages of her manuscript for *The Strike*—and demanded to know why industrialists refused to put their money where their mouths were. "None of the businessmen do anything! *None* of them!" Offended, Mullendore stormed out of the meeting. "That woman ought to be kept out of sight," Gaynor told Rand as she left.[42]

Finally, toward the end of her visit, Paterson mentioned to Rand that she had been offered the opportunity to review *The Fountainhead* five years earlier and had declined. This shocked Rand, who had been particularly bothered by the "horrible" review the *Herald Tribune* had published—and which would never have appeared if Paterson had been willing to review it herself.[43] Paterson may have considered it inappropriate at the time to review a novel by a close friend. But whatever her reasons, Rand felt betrayed. She told Paterson that she could never forgive the slight.

For years, Rand had struggled to understand her friend's temper and her habit of hurting those she was close to, but now she had had enough. She was 45, an accomplished writer with a bestseller, a major film, and a growing circle of friends and admirers. She felt no further obligation to make allowances for Paterson's behavior, and her former mentor's refusal to review the novel—even after having called Rand "a portent, a sign in the heavens," and the kind of "historic event" that "does not happen once in a hundred years, perhaps not one in a thousand"—must have cut deeply.[44] The two sank into bitterness, and Paterson decided to return to New York early. After a silent ride to the airport, Rand bid her goodbye at the gate. "I hope you'll be happier than you are," Rand told her.[45] They remained cordial in the coming years and corresponded about the possibility of a new magazine, but their friendship had essentially ended.

The film version of *The Fountainhead* was released a year later. It starred Gary Cooper as Howard Roark and Patricia Neal, instead of Barbara Stanwyck, as Dominique Francon. (Stanwyck, who had wanted the role so badly that she had insisted Warner Brothers buy the film rights, had been shouldered aside so rudely that she quit the studio.[46]) The film suffered from several weaknesses, including a mediocre score and poorly designed buildings that failed to substantiate Roark as an architectural genius. Cooper himself thought his performance stiff and unpersuasive. Yet Rand's screenplay skillfully reduced her nearly 800-page novel to under two hours by folding Roark's backstory into the first thirty minutes and entirely eliminating the Stoddard Temple subplot. Reducing Roark's climactic courtroom speech to five and a half minutes was a particular ordeal for Rand, especially given the studio's squeamishness about her ideas, and when the film appeared, reviewers snickered at its unusual length. "Cooper's wordy outburst," one columnist called it.[47] The movie was only moderately successful, but it considerably boosted the book's sales.

Paterson's fortunes were not as bright. Only months after *The Fountainhead* premiered, *Herald Tribune* editors canceled "Turns with a Bookworm." There were likely many reasons for that decision, but the primary one was the paper's leftward lean after publisher Ogden Reid died in 1947. The most striking evidence of this trend was the paper's reliance on Joseph Barnes, a communist sympathizer—and probably a party member—as leader of its foreign department. Some staff members even organized a Communist Club.[48] When efforts were made to unionize the newspaper's employees, Paterson openly opposed them, insisting she had the right to decide for herself whether to let a union represent her—a position that made her even more of an outcast than she already was. When economic circumstances led to layoffs, her ideological opponents in management saw an opportunity to eliminate her. Her last column appeared on January 30, 1949. It contained no reference to the fact that after 25 years and over 1,000 entries, "Turns" was coming to an end. Upsetting as it was, Paterson knew she had had a good run. "If I had got on any other paper," she wrote in a private note, "I would have been fired years before."[49]

She started writing a new novel, called *Joyous Gard*, which she tinkered with for almost a decade. In 1959, she contacted Ayn Rand to ask her opinion of the manuscript. Her visit was the first time in years that they had met in person. But Paterson now found it "impossible" to communicate with her old friend. The 54-year-old Rand had just published *The Strike*, retitled *Atlas Shrugged*, and although loathed by critics, it was selling well. Her confidence was growing just as Paterson's fortunes were diminishing, and the student had gained an emotional as well as intellectual distance from her former teacher. Unsurprisingly, Rand disapproved of *Joyous Gard*; they had never agreed on literary questions. Rand prized larger-than-life characters and highly dramatic stories, whereas Paterson wrote discursive, meandering tales heavy with introspection. "She really seemed to imply that I *could* write novels like hers if I tried," Paterson told a friend after their conversation. "It isn't talent, but Reason that does it, you see." But what Rand thought reason demanded differed from what Paterson believed.

Paterson apparently tried to steer their discussion toward religion, reiterating her belief that human energy is qualitatively special and cannot be accounted for in materialistic terms. Rand still disagreed. There was only one kind of reality, she thought—the natural, physical world—and the idea of a God Who stands outside that reality violated this basic principle, which she often summarized by the phrase "A is A." To Paterson, that slogan seemed like a meaningless mantra.[50] She did not back down in the conversation with Rand, but she lacked the energy to pursue the argument. "All the fire had burnt out," said Rand's associate Nathaniel Branden, who was present at the meeting. "Even the bitterness" seemed "perfunctory."[51] Paterson later said that Rand's atheism made her "bigoted," and grumbled that Rand had "decided, or is on the verge of coming to the conclusion, that I am not rational."[52] The two never met again.

Paterson was nevertheless excited about *Atlas Shrugged*, which fulfilled her prediction, more than a decade before, that Rand's follow-up to *The Fountainhead* would "provoke a cyclone of controversy."[53] The book is an intellectually ambitious epic in which the world's great thinkers and innovators— scientists, investors, philosophers, artists, even judges—join a philosophically astute engineer named John Galt in withdrawing from a world that increasingly demands that they sacrifice themselves. Paterson had long insisted that collectivism's war against the individual only succeeded because foolish or cowardly business leaders went along with it. *Atlas Shrugged* dramatizes this thesis in the form of a mystery novel that involves vivid, even cinematic incidents such as oil fires, train crashes, and prison escapes.

Where *The Fountainhead* was inspired in part by the novels of Sinclair Lewis, *Atlas Shrugged*'s foremost literary progenitor was Rand's idol, Victor Hugo. This approach is plain not only in its cast of heroes and its intricately designed plot, but also in the lengthy speeches given to characters throughout the book. Where Hugo habitually put his commentary into the words of his third-person narration and included long digressions in *Les Misérables* and *Notre-Dame de Paris* on such things as church architecture or the sewers of Paris, Rand placed her thoughts into dialogues and monologues. One reason many critics objected to her novel was that she wrote in the mode of 19th-century Romanticism at a time when that style was considered outmoded and even vaguely suspect. But the book is simultaneously modern in its focus and sensibility, and it reveals Lewis's influence, especially *It Can't Happen Here*, with its depiction of America's slide into despotism as a consequence of a cultural infatuation with mediocrity and egalitarianism.

Whatever her reservations about Romantic literature, Paterson was awed by Rand's carefully organized plot. It was "far more complex than *War and Peace*," she told a friend, and "cram-jammed with 'story,' with action." She disliked Galt's lengthy speech at the novel's climax—a 60-page manifesto Rand spent two years writing, which Paterson thought most readers would skip—and she thought Rand erred by having the novel's hero appear only toward the end. Yet his absence helped serve the novel's mystery element, and readers found that the plot's momentum kept their attention. The book was an immediate bestseller.

"The great fraternity of eggheads and deadheads, 'Liberals' and Commies and bureaucrats, are carrying on a deliberate campaign to kill the book, if they can," Paterson noted. "They are ganged up in close ranks."[54] Indeed, reviewers were almost uniformly hostile, denouncing its unwavering individualism and intense ideological content. One of the few positive reviews came from Paterson's acolyte, John Chamberlain, who wrote in the *Herald Tribune* that "a thorough comprehension of its massive reaches would be roughly equivalent to mastering a Ph.D.'s knowledge in the separate fields of ethics, economics, political science, physics, and psychology."[55] But left-wing critics detested it, calling it strident and cruel, and conservatives were no less outraged.[56] *National Review* was especially harsh. It published a review by Whittaker Chambers, a former communist who had converted to Christianity, who accused Rand of wanting to murder her ideological opponents. Paterson, who had written several articles for *National Review*, was incensed. She complained to editor William F. Buckley, calling the review libelous—a significant assertion by a woman with so much experience reviewing books—but Buckley dismissed her complaints and defended Chambers. Indeed, he denounced Rand for the rest of his life, commissioning a feature for his magazine a decade later that was aimed at destroying her reputation for good and publishing another attack upon her death in 1982.[57] He was disgusted by Rand's atheism, just as Rand could not accept his efforts to reconcile capitalism with religion or the ethics of self-sacrifice.[58]

Paterson was outraged not only by Buckley's treatment of Rand, but also by his refusal to publish an article of her own shortly after the *Atlas Shrugged* review appeared. Ostensibly an assessment of a book on business management by the president of the DuPont Corporation, the article was actually a disjointed tirade against business executives who failed to defend free enterprise—and it called out retired DuPont vice president Jasper Crane by name. Buckley insisted that Crane's name be removed from the piece, and when Paterson refused, her relationship with the magazine ended. She spent the rest of her life living on a modest pension and seeking a publisher for *Joyous Gard*. She died in January 1961, at the age of 75, and was buried in an unmarked grave at a church in Burlington, New Jersey. A short, unsigned obituary in the *Herald Tribune* noted that she had been "an open-minded liberal in her discussions of literary works," but "so extremely conservative" in her politics "that she was once called a philosophical anarchist."[59]

By then, Rand had gained a large following of her own. A year after Paterson's death, she began publishing the *Objectivist Newsletter*, which featured commentaries on current events and essays by a growing number of philosophical apprentices. In 1964, she printed her own review of *The God of the Machine*, which she labeled "a brilliant and extraordinary book" sparkling with "little gems of polemical fire" that ranged "from bright wit to the hard glitter of logic to the quiet radiance of a profound understanding." She thought its greatest strength lay in its recognition of the qualitative difference between government action and private action—that the essence of the former is physical force, whereas the latter is fundamentally voluntary. That seemingly simple distinction was often obscured in political debates, leading to such self-contradictory notions as the idea that a business was a monopoly merely because it was successful, or that poverty represented a form of oppression. By emphasizing the principled distinction between state and private action, Rand thought, Paterson's book avoided the pitfalls other writers fell into—ones that led them to argue oxymoronically that vindicating freedom requires government coercion.

Rand also praised Paterson's recognition that an economy is an energy-transmission device whereby the factors of production are efficiently allocated through the voluntary exchange of values. But she criticized the book's engineering terminology for being too "sketchy" and "fragmented."

Paterson's language tended to strike readers as "merely metaphorical," when it was clear that she was not speaking in metaphor. Rand also criticized the "occasional statements" in the book "attempting to connect freedom with religion," but thought these were so obviously "irrelevant and arbitrary" that they could be easily ignored without affecting the readers' comprehension.[60]

Paterson would have been appalled at the idea that her references to God were irrelevant.[61] In fact, in a chapter called "The Virgin and the Dynamo"—a phrase borrowed from Henry Adams—she had argued that the source of the human energies transmitted by the economy must be something outside the material universe. The "God" of the "machine" in her title was the quality of free will—which is "the genesis" of the "dynamo" of production—and which Paterson thought could not be accounted for by anything other than a supernatural cause. Like Paterson, Adams had been a student of medieval Christianity, and in his memoir he explained how he came to view the Virgin Mary as a symbol of the ineffable "power" of human creativity—a power that was more than merely mechanical. "All the steam in the world could not, like the Virgin, build Chartres," Adams wrote.[62] The "virgin," Paterson continued, represented "an unconstrained element, grace or mercy, which implies free will in man, being available to continual choice."[63] That spark of creativity was somehow exempt from the entropic forces that wear down all the material elements of the universe. Only death—or foolhardy political and economic policies such as slavery or collectivism—could extinguish it: "Being constructed according to the laws of mechanics, the dynamo itself is deterministic; that is to say, left to itself, it will stop," declared Paterson. "Then if it is to run, it must be by the will and intelligence of man."[64]

▰

Throughout the 1930s and 1940s, many of those who dissented from the New Deal had hoped a novel would appear that would articulate what they stood for: individualism, entrepreneurialism, and freedom from meddling bureaucracy. In 1945, H. L. Mencken urged the aging Sinclair Lewis to try.

"The country swarms with subjects" for novels of "the Roosevelt and post-Roosevelt eras," he told his friend. "The rich radical, the bogus expert, the numbskull newspaper proprietor (or editor), the career job-holder, the lady publicist, the crooked (or, more usually, idiotic) labor leader, the press-agent and so on."[65] But although Lewis still had important things to say—especially in *Kingsblood Royal*, his 1947 novel attacking racial segregation—the task was beyond his powers.[66] Increasingly embittered, he died of alcoholism in January 1951. Mencken himself suffered a stroke in 1948 that left him unable to write, and he died in 1956, a year before Laura Ingalls Wilder died at her Missouri home at the age of 90.

Paterson, Lane, and Rand all wrote novels of the Great Depression—novels aimed at addressing the moral, psychological, and political crises America had undergone in the "Roosevelt era." For Lane, it was *Free Land*, which sought to rally the self-reliant spirit of the American frontier. For Paterson, it was *The Golden Vanity*, which dramatized the mental and moral forces whittling away at the culture of prosperity and hope. And for Rand, it was *Atlas Shrugged*, which imagines a second Great Depression in an alternate future in which the war against individualism she witnessed in the 1930s reaches its climax and plunges the nation into economic and social catastrophe.

Although often called "prophetic," *Atlas Shrugged* looks backward as much as forward, and although not *about* the Depression, it echoes the New Deal experience throughout. Rand caricatures Brain Trust bureaucrats and their intellectual hangers-on with a Lewis-like precision that extends even to their names (Orren Boyle, Balph Eubank, Eugene Lawson), which are eerily similar to the unusual names of Roosevelt's real-life advisers (Ogden Mills, Rexford Tugwell, Raymond Moley). Many of the novel's characters are drawn from New Deal–era figures. Hank Rearden—the steel tycoon "torn by the naiveté of his own generosity"—is modeled in part on Republic Steel chairman Tom Girdler; writer Balph Eubank is loosely based on James M. Cain and other novelists of the period; railroad president James Taggart resembles Henry Kaiser and other businessmen who benefited from political favoritism; Emma Chalmers, the mother of a collectivist politician who rises to prominence through her family connections and champions boneheaded agricultural experiments, is drawn from Eleanor Roosevelt.[67]

Several of the novel's events are also inspired by actual incidents, such as when James Taggart squelches a small competitor under a government decree that restricts competition in the manner of the National Industrial Recovery Act. The government imposes a "Fair Share Law" that—like the mandates of federal antitrust law—forces businesses to sell products to all buyers rather than to those willing to pay more. As the plot progresses, the government increasingly resorts to legislation by executive orders instead of laws debated in Congress—echoing the actual experience of the Roosevelt era, when Congress delegated enormous swathes of power to the president alone. And in a combination of Roosevelt's habit of relying on subordinates and Truman's Babbitt-like unintellectualism, the increasing tyranny depicted in the novel is imposed not by a single tyrant, but by a cadre of anti-individualist minions. The autocrat who oversees them is a characterless nonentity named simply "Mr. Thompson," who is driven by no particular ideology at all. As the creators continue to disappear and the economy worsens, America's political leaders begin to panic, invoking language that echoes Roosevelt's "capital strike" rhetoric. In the end, they try to force industrialists to create, and even torture John Galt in an attempt to make him accept the role of dictator.

But although Rand, Paterson, and Lane were all inspired to write novels about the New Deal, none opposed the Roosevelt administration out of mere partisanship. They were equally hostile, if not more so, to Republicans such as Hoover and Willkie. None defended business per se; they often saw business owners as timorous, and even as enemies of capitalism—and Rand especially condemned cheap commercialism in *The Fountainhead*. Their economic arguments were not based on mere tradition or hostility to modernity to which some conservative voices appealed, although they built on the work of classical economists and political thinkers from centuries before, such as Adam Smith and John Locke. In rejecting the ethics of self-sacrifice, they developed even older precedents, stretching back to the ancient Greeks. And far from being callous toward the plight of those who suffered during the Depression, they thought Roosevelt's policies worsened and prolonged the disaster, precisely to advance the interests of wealthy, politically connected "aristocrats of pull." They believed economic freedom would primarily benefit the less well-off—a view that was vindicated when postwar deregulation led to an economic boom. For all their differences, the value these three writers were most emphatic about—their commitment to individualism—was grounded in their own personal experiences: the transformation from frontier poverty to technological fortune that Paterson and Lane witnessed, and the despotism and misery of communist Russia that Rand escaped.

Thus none of the three could fairly be called conservatives. Only Rand was an atheist, but none of the "furies" considered herself a Christian, and on matters of race relations, freedom of speech, and sexual autonomy, they were decades ahead of their time in embracing views later classified as "liberal."[68] Paterson objected to "the impression, generally held, we daresay, that our views are what is sometimes called conservative." The reality was that "our views are so advanced nobody can believe it yet." All three rejected the conservative label, regarding themselves instead as politically radical, even revolutionary. They thought the collectivists supporting Roosevelt were the true reactionaries, since they advocated a return to the authoritarian, bureaucratized politics of the premodern era. "The most suitable material form for their writings," Paterson quipped, "would be hieroglyphics."[69]

Rand, Paterson, and Lane were beneficiaries of a radical cultural shift that resulted from a spirit of enterprise and opportunity unique to America at the dawn of the 20th century. That shift released a vast amount of human energy and created a world in which everything seemed possible—where the sky was no limit. It is significant that the engineering firm for which John Galt works in *Atlas Shrugged* is named the Twentieth Century Motor Company, and that his resignation precipitates its bankruptcy—Rand's metaphor for the way the century's unprecedented advances had been made possible by the political and economic liberty of the Airplane Generation, and the fact that by midcentury, humanity had experienced unprecedented horrors, thanks to the dogmas of statism and collectivism.

All three writers hoped to see a revival of individualism in their lifetimes, particularly in literature. "For years, nihilism has dominated American fiction," Lane wrote in 1950. "The acclaimed fiction writers have denied human aspirations, they have seen no victory of human effort, they have had no respect for the honesty, perseverance, self-discipline, indomitable courage, with which all men daily earn their daily bread, nor for the patience, kindness, sympathy, human co-operation that hold families, societies, economies, the whole human world in existence." But almost a decade after its publication, the only exception she could think of—the "solitary pioneer of important individualist novels"—was still "Ayn Rand's huge market-success, *The Fountainhead*."[70]

Lane did see some hopeful signs of an individualist revival in the works of writers such as Lionel Trilling and J. Saunders Redding. But as the postwar era unfolded, this hope was only imperfectly realized. The creativity, insight, and potential of the individual—and his value in contrast with that of the collective—served as an important theme in Cold War literature. Yet it was almost entirely confined to the genres of westerns and science fiction. When counterculture writers such as Ken Kesey or Tom Robbins appeared in the 1960s, their work featured no wealth-creating entrepreneurs or business owners, and Rand in particular viewed their anti-establishment attitudes as a counterfeit form of individualism. With only rare exceptions, such as the novels of Cameron Hawley, capitalists existed in postwar fiction mainly as villains, victims, or fools. More often, they were ignored. Meanwhile, the literature celebrated by cultural elites tended to denigrate the individual, or to view him as alienated or obsolete in a world of materialism, phoniness, and vulgarity. Popular audiences fell in love with the heroes of John Wayne films and Robert Heinlein novels, but it was works such as Arthur Miller's *Death of a Salesman* and William Faulkner's *Requiem for a Nun*, with their themes of the individual's overwhelming insignificance, that garnered the prizes.[71]

▰▲◣

After publication of *Atlas Shrugged*, Rand became an iconoclastic intellectual, even a pop culture celebrity. She was interviewed in *Playboy*, appeared on *The Tonight Show*, and was referenced in a 1966 Simon and Garfunkel song.[72] She began publishing nonfiction that called for a generation of "New Intellectuals" to defend the ideals of reason and liberty. She had accomplished much of her dream of challenging the philosophical status quo and promoting the cause of individualism. By the 1970s, she found herself in the position that her mentor had once occupied: now she was the veteran, passing along to admirers the ideas of an America that seemed increasingly under assault. The cultural clashes of the Vietnam era—the anti-capitalist, anti-industrial movement of the New Left, the ethnocentrism of racial activists, the advent of the Great Society, and the abandonment of the space race—echoed the social transformations of the 1930s. It seemed the remnants of individualism were being supplanted by institutions based on dependency, belligerence, and victimhood.

In a 1971 article titled "Don't Let It Go," she sought to articulate America's endangered "sense of life"—by which she meant the nation's mores; "actions and attitudes which people take for granted and believe to be self-evident, but which are produced by complex evaluations involving a fundamental view of man's nature."[73] This American sense of life consisted of admiration for achievement, a refusal to be bossed around, and a pervasive feeling of equality and personal independence. These attitudes had no equivalent among Europeans: "The emotional keynote of most Europeans is the feeling that man belongs to the State, as a property to be used and disposed of, in compliance with his natural, metaphysically determined fate."[74] Americans do not, in their heart of hearts, embrace the fatalism of an oppressed people—they do not truly believe evil is a significant factor in the universe.

To reinforce this point, Rand quoted a line from Badger Clark, a cowboy poet whose 1917 ode "The Westerner" expressed the spirit of frontier self-reliance that the New Deal's leaders had rejected and that was again under assault in the Great Society era. The poem is narrated by a son of pioneers who reveres his brave ancestors but refuses to base his self-assessment on their achievements alone.

> I lay proud claim to their blood and name,
> But I lean on no dead kin;
> My name is mine for the praise or scorn,
> And the world began when I was born
> And the world is mine to win.

The speaker does not ask for anyone to help him, and although he is willing to aid those in need, he has no interest in a society of dependence ("I dream no dreams of a nursemaid State / That will spoon me out my food") or any desire to rule over others ("I waste no thought on my neighbor's birth / Or the way he makes his prayer"). And he thinks solemnly of how he will make deserts bloom and create cities and railroads in what is now a wilderness:

> I'll build as they only dreamed.
> The smoke scarce dies where the trail camp lies,
> Till rails glint down the pass;
> The desert springs into fruit and wheat
> And I lay the stones of a solid street
> Over yesterday's untrod grass.[75]

The poem, Rand said, represented "what had once been the spirit of America . . . which we must now struggle to bring to a rebirth."[76]

Rose Wilder Lane knew the country Badger Clark wrote about. In her own career, she, too, strove to memorialize and perpetuate the individualistic spirit so central to her vision of America. She had tried to encapsulate it in *Let the Hurricane Roar* and *Free Land*. Both were bestsellers, but it was in the books for which she took no credit during her life—the *Little House* novels secretly coauthored with her mother—that she achieved that ambition most effectively.

Read together, the *Little House* series builds a case for rugged individualism—one that romanticizes the life of the pioneer generation, but balances that romanticism with a clear-eyed recognition of the hardship and pain endured by those who settled the West. The climax of that argument comes in *Little Town on the Prairie*, published in 1941, in a passage in which Laura attends the Independence Day celebration in the new village that has emerged from the "Long Winter" of the previous year. The townspeople listen to a reading of the Declaration of Independence and then begin singing "My Country 'Tis of Thee" (which served as the national anthem before the "Star Spangled Banner" was given that position in 1931). Hearing the lyrics, it occurs to Laura—now 15 and about to start work as a teacher—that "Americans won't obey any king on earth. Americans are free. That means they have to obey their own consciences. No king bosses Pa; he has to boss himself. . . . When I am a little older, Ma and Pa will stop telling me what to do, and there isn't anyone else who has a right to give me orders. I will have to make myself good."[77]

For Lane, freedom was a paradox: each individual's natural self-responsibility meant that the obligation to obey the moral law of human behavior is self-imposed. That law consisted not of a set of decrees from government rulers, but of the facts of the reality, woven by God into the nature of man as fully as the laws of physics are in the universe. One implication of that self-responsibility was that no person should be sacrificed to the interests of another, or feel obligated to sacrifice himself for, or subordinate himself to, anyone else. Another was that all human beings are connected in some subrational way to all others through the principle she called "human brotherhood"—one that drove people to help one another, not out of duty, but because it was in their own self-interest to do so. This paradox of autonomous individualism and what she referred to as "neighborliness" formed the core of the pioneer spirit.

In 1943, Lane was introduced to a 14-year-old boy named Roger Lea MacBride, whose father Burt was an editor at *Reader's Digest*. The *Digest* had just reprinted a section of *The Discovery of Freedom*, and Roger was intrigued when he read it. Lane took him under her wing, "adopting" him as she had Rexh Meta and others in decades gone by. He eventually became her closest confidant, and after her retirement from the *NECRB* in 1950, she came increasingly to rely on him. After her death, he ran for president on the Libertarian Party ticket and served as coproducer of the *Little House on the Prairie* television series, which introduced a new generation to the Ingalls family and the hard work and independence their lives now symbolized.

Not long after meeting MacBride, Lane also befriended Robert LeFevre, organizer of a Colorado-based educational institution called the Freedom School. The school convened seminars about free-market economics and the philosophy of liberty taught by such luminaries as Ludwig von Mises, Milton Friedman, and Henry Hazlitt. (Paterson was asked, but declined.) When the Freedom School suffered a shortfall of funds, Lane donated her entire bank account to prevent its closure.[78] She maintained, as usual, her garrulous correspondence with friends and allies across the nation, and continued her restless wanderings. In 1965, at the age of 79, she traveled to Vietnam to write a feature on the war for *Woman's Day* magazine.

Never satisfied with *The Discovery of Freedom*, she allowed a businessman named Henry Grady Weaver to publish an edition with his own extensive revisions in 1947, under the title *The Mainspring of Human Progress* (a synonym for both "fountainhead" and "god of the machine"). It sold remarkably well, and readers became so interested in Lane's original version that in the 1960s, she decided to try rewriting it. That manuscript, which she called *The Discovery of Liberty*, grew to unwieldy proportions and remained unfinished when she died at the age of 81 in 1968. Five years later, MacBride tried to assemble her drafts into the first 100 or so pages of what he believed she had in mind. As with the original, it detailed how freedom releases "human energy" in new and unprecedented ways and creates a culture—often taken for granted—unique in human history. *The Discovery of Liberty* was more religious than the original version, arguing that faith is the "basis" of all human action, and it clarified Lane's "brotherhood" theory.[79] Likening human beings to "shipwrecked survivors on a raft," she argued that "the safety and welfare of each depends on the safety and welfare of the others," a fact that made the principle of "love your neighbor" the prudentially sound, as well as morally correct, policy.[80] But because cooperating with others takes more human energy than working by oneself, each person must obtain a profit from interacting with others.

Human relationships, made possible by this profit, are a virtually infinite set of activities that together make up society. This society is not an entity, but a process—and that means it is dynamic, constantly shifting. Lane analogizes it to a dance—one so complicated that no central power can possibly coordinate it. This makes it senseless to speak of nations or other groups as having desires or imposing mandates on people. Instead, all government action consists of some people forcing others to do things. The idea of the nation or society being "somehow more than human, therefore more worthy of respect, allegiance, loyalty, even self-sacrifice and worship" is an illusion.[81] It is the great fallacy at the heart of all forms of collectivism: that the state is a real entity, separate and apart from the people who compose it. That erroneous belief fosters a mystique that encourages people to imagine that government, instead of enforcing law, actually *creates* law—that it stands outside of human interactions at some Archimedean point, as an authority capable of telling people how to live. That misconception founders on the fact that people are inescapably self-responsible. "In obedience to Law, water must flow, fire must burn, planets must circle suns . . . [and] a living person, endowed by his Creator with liberty, controls his own action."[82] More smoothly written, with a greater grasp of philosophical subtleties, *The Discovery of Liberty* was more promising than the original book had been. But it was never completed, and it remains unpublished.

◤ Epilogue ◥

Lane was always a controversial and outspoken personality, who earned enemies in her life and still does after death. In 2017, *Little House* scholar Caroline Fraser won the Pulitzer Prize for *Prairie Fires*, a biography of Laura Ingalls Wilder. The book's most notable feature, however, was not its profile of Wilder but its scathing assault on Lane, whom Fraser characterized as a virtual psychopath. In her telling, Lane's opposition to the New Deal was motivated by manic depression and coldness toward the less fortunate (notwithstanding Lane's lifelong habit of adopting needy people such as Rexh Meta and Roger MacBride, and paying out of her own pocket for her parents' care). Lane's habit of exaggerating anecdotes was transformed in Fraser's treatment into pathological lying, and her opposition to socialism was portrayed as dishonest on the grounds that frontiersmen resorted to socialism to get through hard times—a claim that can be justified only by defining "socialism" so broadly as to include virtually any form of private insurance. Thoroughly hostile to Lane's political views, Fraser even resorted to criticizing Lane's gravestone for "shouting," because the epitaph is written in all capital letters.[1] If nothing else, the intensity of Fraser's hatred for the writer—a half century after her passing—demonstrates how lasting an impression Lane's arguments for freedom left on defenders of the welfare state.

More balanced assessments recognize that for all of Lane's faults—including her tendency toward fabulism and a sometimes-poor grasp of philosophical nuances—she was nevertheless a pioneer in her own right: an early feminist and self-made woman who gave voice to a political cause dear to millions today. In a 2015 article in the *Journal of American History*, scholar Jennifer Burns—not sympathetic to Lane's political views—nevertheless classifies her alongside Paterson and Rand as an important feminist figure who has "fallen through the cracks of historical memory in part because of [her] politics."[2] As fierce individualists, all three would have objected to being considered representatives or mouthpieces for their sex, and Rand was especially vocal in her opposition to the 1960s feminist movement. Nevertheless, being women affected their views on individual liberty in intriguing and sometimes complicated ways.

For Paterson, that effect can be most clearly seen in her association of freedom with masculinity. In her novels, especially *The Golden Vanity* and *If It Prove Fair Weather*, she viewed the loss of freedom in the 1930s as a degeneration in the American character, especially among men. The bold, enterprising men of earlier days had been replaced by quislings, cowards, and fools, who sought to evade responsibility and to profit from political influence instead of creating new things or breaking through boundaries as the Wright brothers had done. "She grew up, as she once told me, in an age when men were men," recalled Whittaker Chambers.[3] She was astonished by the way the Depression and the expansion of government seemed to have rendered men uncertain. It punished those with ability and intelligence, and encouraged others to "grab dictatorships and start drilling for war as a means of aggrandizing their insufficient egos."[4] For the most part, men seemed unable to *decide* things anymore. "The Depression," writes historian Robert McElvaine, "can be seen as having effected a 'feminization' of American society," in which "the self-centered, aggressive, competitive, 'male' ethic of the 1920s was discredited."[5] Paterson would have agreed—and she did not approve.

For Rand, the relationship of individualism and femininity was more complicated. She tended to view femininity as inherently characterized by a desire to look up to masculine virtue. In 1969, she declared that she would never support a female candidate for president because no rational woman would *want* to be president. "It is not an issue of feminine 'inferiority,'" she explained; it was that "the essence of femininity is hero worship." Since the president is the highest authority, a woman would find the Oval Office "unbearable"—nobody would be above her.[6] Yet the main character of *Atlas Shrugged* is a woman who runs a vast railroad corporation, and Rand's sole comment on the subject in that novel is, "[Dagny] was fifteen when it occurred to her for the first time that women did not run railroads and that people might object. To hell with that, she thought—and never worried about it again."[7] Rand was emphatic about the rights of women—and particularly outspoken in defense of women's sexual freedom—but she viewed the essential quality of femaleness as appreciation and that of manhood as conquering nature. Thus she was amused to learn that Ludwig von Mises, after reading her work, had assumed she was a man.[8]

But it was Lane who explored the relationships between freedom and femininity in most detail. In *Old Home Town*, *Free Land*, and *Let the Hurricane Roar*—and, of course, the *Little House* series—her female characters bear the harshest burdens and enjoy the most meaningful benefits of liberty. For some, the hardships are almost too much to bear: Caroline's ordeal secluded in her cabin in *Hurricane* is shocking in its realism; Mary in *Free Land* despises the frontier; Ma in the *Little House* books would, if she could, quit moving and settle down. Yet it is through their endurance that the blessings of liberty are handed on to the next generation—that is, to their daughters Ernestine (in *Old Home Town*) and Helen (in *Diverging Roads*), who are free to pursue their lives as they choose thanks to their mothers' struggles.

Lane never imagined that freedom was a panacea for women. "My life has been arid and sterile at the core, because I have been a human being instead of a woman, a wife," she wrote in a 1936 article titled "A Woman's Place Is in the Home." "A self-centered self-reliance as protective and imprisoning armor is the effect of careers upon women."[9] She could never have survived the stifling of individuality that she saw as inextricable from marriage, but she was also frank about the costs of independence. She never resolved the tension between her dreams of creating lasting work as a journalist and author, and the maternal desires that drove her to adopt a half dozen young people throughout her life. Perhaps the best expression of that paradox is the fact that her clearest commentary on the relationship between femininity and freedom came in her 1963 *Woman's Day Book of American Needlework*, a beautifully illustrated overview of needlepoint from crochet to rug making, which included histories and instructions for dozens of projects.

Lane had admired and practiced needlework all her life, and the book gave her an opportunity to explore the nature of this distinctively female art form, which she saw as a kind of cultural barometer. American embroidery revealed the uniquely individualistic society of the New World—a melting pot where the cross-stich of Italy and Russia met the woven plaid of Scotland and the Aztec patterns of Mexico. "American women, children of all these lands, took all this and more and made it American in spirit," she wrote. Other societies imposed class-based restrictions on the designs women could use—with peasant work being plainly different from the formal patterns permitted to the upper classes. No such barriers existed in America, with the result that "this republic is the only country that has no peasant needlework."[10] Instead, American women, ignoring the old cultural rules dictating how fabrics and stitching were to be completed, fashioned their own designs by adapting and developing traditional patterns. In other words, needlepoint was a means by which women articulated "the spirit of our revolutionary country, the spirit of individual human beings in freedom."[11] In her classic 1982 study *The Subversive Stitch: Embroidery and the Making of the Feminine*, Rozsika Parker wrote, "To know the history of embroidery is to know the history of women."[12] Anticipating her by two decades, Lane argued that to know the history of American needlework was to know the lives of women who had experienced the "new and unique spirit" of a nation conceived in liberty.[13]

▰▲◣

It was often asked during their lifetimes why the cause of American individualism was being championed primarily by women. Isabel Paterson was repulsed when Herbert Hoover told her that it was because men were too busy. A better answer might have been that during the Depression, men had more to lose by challenging the prevailing trends of politics and culture. At a time when jobs were scarce and many were funded by the government, political dissent was likely to result in firing or blacklisting. Since men were still the primary breadwinners in that era, this may have made them reluctant to risk opposing the status quo. But that can only be part of the answer, for many men had opportunities to stand up for individualism—including the leaders of the American Liberty League and the National Association of Manufacturers, not to mention Wendell Willkie and other leading Republicans—and none did so with such lasting, persuasive, and thoroughly considered force as the "furies."

Today, polls show that women are less likely than men to endorse the principles of free markets and individual liberty that Paterson, Lane, and Rand espoused.[14] Some attribute this to women's tendency to think more empathetically than men, or to care more about social relationships when considering political questions.[15] Others point out that women tend to be less likely to take unorthodox ideological positions generally, especially on religious matters.[16] Yet religious and political causes outside the mainstream have also drawn extraordinary women throughout American history, including Anne Hutchinson, Emma Goldman, Madalyn Murray O'Hair, Alice Paul, Harriet Beecher Stowe, and the Grimké sisters. And women's contributions to the ideas of individualism have always been significant—including such figures as Abigail Adams, Mary Wollstonecraft, Germaine de Staël; and in the 20th century, Hannah Arendt, Joan Kennedy Taylor, Margaret Thatcher, Camille Paglia, Wendy McElroy, and Virginia Postrel.

A better explanation is that women in the early 20th century had experienced an unprecedented liberation. Lane and Paterson were both in their thirties when women were given the right to vote. They were conscious of the fact that theirs was the first generation to escape the drudgery of farm labor, and to have a genuine opportunity to define their own lives and participate in American democracy and the American economy. Their opportunities were still far from truly equal, but it was a bracing new freedom nonetheless, and it animated much of the Revolt from the Village. After all, it was a woman—Carol Kennicott—whom Sinclair Lewis used to articulate that revolt in *Main Street*.

Then came the horrific disasters of the 20th century—the Depression, the wars, the atomic arms race—and looming over it all was the haunting fear that that liberty might vanish within their lifetimes. As women, they knew all too well how freedom can be destroyed by those who claim they are only trying to "help," or who try to "protect" people from the obligations and rewards of living their own lives. They viewed the New Deal as precisely that kind of debilitating paternalism. And having witnessed the century's unimaginable scientific and technological transformations—Paterson set a world altitude record in a flimsy airplane in 1912; 57 years later, her protégée Rand attended the launch of Apollo 11—they understood how rare and fragile that progress really was. They feared that abandoning the legal and economic principles that created such progress would plunge humanity into a new Dark Age.

In her study of female conservatives of the 1930s, historian June Melby Benowitz argues that women who opposed the New Deal did so out of fear of social transformation. "They sensed that they were being left behind," she writes, and sought "to turn back the clock to what they considered better times."[17] But the opposite was true of the "furies." They saw themselves as genuinely modern, and they viewed fascism, communism, and the New Deal as reactionary movements that sought to turn back the clock, undoing the progress toward individualism they had experienced in their youths and reimposing the authoritarianism and philistinism so well pilloried in *Main Street*. None of the three thought of themselves as speaking for women, or even *as* women—they were individualists, addressing their arguments to the minds and hearts of all people, everywhere—but the fact that they did so at a time when women were still not considered social equals was a remarkable accomplishment. They "have shown the male world of this period how to think *fundamentally*," wrote the conservative editor Albert Jay Nock in 1943. "They make all of us male writers look like Confederate money."[18]

▛ Timeline ▜

1885

Sinclair Lewis born on February 7 in Sauk Centre, Minnesota.

1886

Isabel Paterson (née Mary Bowler) born on January 22 on Manitoulin Island, Canada. Rose Wilder Lane born on December 5 in De Smet, South Dakota.

1888

Edward Bellamy's socialist novel *Looking Backward* becomes a bestseller.

1893

Severe depression hits the United States. Dorothy Thompson born on July 9 in New York City.

1894

"Coxey's Army" protest marches to Washington, DC.

1903

Wright brothers fly first powered airplane at Kitty Hawk, North Carolina.

1905

Ayn Rand (née Alisa Rosenbaum) born in St. Petersburg, Russia.

1909

Lane marries journalist Claire Gillette Lane.

1910

Paterson marries, separates soon afterward.

1912

Paterson moves to New York.

1915

Lane gets a job writing for the *San Francisco Bulletin*.

1916

Paterson publishes her first novel, *The Shadow Riders*.

1917

United States enters World War I. Paterson's second novel, *The Magpie's Nest* is published; she moves to San Francisco. Lane, also living in San Francisco, publishes *Henry Ford's Own Story* and begins publishing a serial biography of Jack London. Bolshevik Revolution begins in Russia. Rand's family travels to Crimea for safety.

1918

Lane quits the *San Francisco Bulletin* and gets a job with the Red Cross Publicity Bureau.

1919

Lane publishes *Diverging Roads*. Sherwood Anderson publishes *Winesburg, Ohio*.

1920

Lane publishes *The Making of Herbert Hoover* and travels to Paris to report on Red Cross work in Europe. She meets Dorothy Thompson. Sinclair Lewis publishes *Main Street*. Paterson working for sculptor Gutzon Borglum in Connecticut. Prohibition adopted. Census Bureau reports that for the first time, more Americans live off farms than on them. Nineteenth Amendment ratified, giving women the right to vote.

1921

Lane visits Albania for the first time. In Soviet Union, "war communism" ends when Bolsheviks proclaim New Economic Policy. Rand enters Petrograd State University.

1922

Sinclair Lewis publishes *Babbitt*. Lane visits Armenia and Georgia, where she witnesses Soviet oppression. USSR officially proclaimed in December. Mussolini becomes dictator of Italy.

1923

Lane publishes *The Peaks of Shala*.

1924

Paterson's first "Turns with a Bookworm" column appears, September 21. Her novel *The Singing Season* is published. Lenin dies in USSR.

1925

For the first time, half of all American homes have electricity. Sinclair Lewis publishes *Arrowsmith*, for which he is awarded the Pulitzer Prize, and refuses it. Lane publishes *He Was a Man*, which Paterson mentions in "Turns." After traveling through Turkey, Egypt, and Iraq, Lane returns home to Missouri.

1926

Rand arrives in the United States in February. Six months later, travels to Hollywood and gets a job with Cecil B. DeMille. Lane buys a house in Albania, intending to live there permanently. Paterson publishes *The Fourth Queen*.

1927

Sinclair Lewis publishes *Elmer Gantry*. Charles and Mary Beard publish *The Rise of American Civilization*.

1928

Lane is summoned by her mother back to Missouri. Dorothy Thompson marries Sinclair Lewis. Herbert Hoover elected president. Rand begins work on *The Little Street*. Joseph Stalin becomes dictator of the Soviet Union.

1929

Rand marries Frank O'Connor. After repeated declines, the stock market crashes in October. Great Depression begins. Hoover administration responds to Depression with massive public works projects, restrictions on agricultural production, sharp limits on immigration.

1930

Sinclair Lewis receives the Nobel Prize. Laura Ingalls Wilder and Rose Wilder Lane begin working on manuscript that will eventually become the *Little House* series. Lane visits Dorothy Thompson and Sinclair Lewis and babysits for them while they travel to Europe to collect the Nobel. Congress adopts Smoot-Hawley Tariff. Paterson publishes *The Road of the Gods*.

1931

Swope Plan for government control of industry proposed.

1932

Charles Beard publishes "The Myth of Rugged Individualism." Rand sells *Red Pawn* to Universal, begins writing *Night of January 16th*. "Cox's Army" marches to Washington; shortly afterward, much larger "Bonus Army" marches on Washington. After months of camping on federal land, they are forcibly dispersed. Theodore Dreiser prepares manuscript called *A New Deal for America*. Stuart Chase publishes *A New Deal*. Both propose massive government takeovers of the economy. Hoover drastically expands federal welfare spending and establishes Reconstruction Finance Corporation. Franklin Roosevelt elected president. Laura Ingalls Wilder publishes *Little House in the Big Woods*. Stalin's Ukrainian genocide begins.

1933

Hitler becomes chancellor of Germany in January. Franklin Roosevelt inaugurated president on March 4. Declares "banking holiday" and suspends gold standard. Congress passes Glass-Steagall Act, Federal Economic Recovery Act, Agricultural Adjustment Act, National Industrial Recovery Act, Federal Communications Act, and creates the Public Works Administration. Paterson publishes *Never Ask the End*. Lane publishes *Let the Hurricane Roar*. Laura Ingalls Wilder publishes *Farmer Boy*. Lane travels through Midwest, reporting on drought and effects of federal agricultural policy on wheat farmers. H. L. Mencken leaves the *American Mercury*. Prohibition repealed December 3.

1934

Paterson moves from Manhattan to a house in Connecticut. Publishes *The Golden Vanity*. Dorothy Thompson expelled from Germany for reporting on Hitler.

1935

Laura Ingalls Wilder publishes *Little House on the Prairie*. Lane publishes *Old Home Town*. Begins working on a book about Missouri history. Congress creates Works Progress Administration, Federal Writers Project, Federal Theater Project, and passes Social Security Act, National Labor Relations Act. Dorothy Thompson publishes reports on New Deal for *Saturday Evening Post*. Huey Long assassinated in Louisiana. Sinclair Lewis publishes *It Can't Happen Here*. Supreme Court strikes down National Industrial Recovery Act. Rand begins planning *The Fountainhead*.

1936

Rand publishes *We the Living*, which Paterson mentions briefly in "Turns." *Gone with the Wind* published. Franklin Roosevelt reelected. Lane and Garet Garrett travel the Midwest investigating the Resettlement Administration. Lane publishes *Give Me Liberty*.

1937

Franklin Roosevelt takes the oath of office on January 20. Announces court-packing plan. Laura Ingalls Wilder publishes *On the Banks of Plum Creek*. In April, Roosevelt administration files antitrust lawsuit against ALCOA. "Memorial Day Massacre" at Republic Steel plant on May 30. "Depression within a Depression" begins in autumn; administration blames "capital strike."

1938

Lane publishes *Free Land*. Paterson begins writing political column "I Sometimes Think"; devotes many to opposing military conscription. *Kristallnacht* occurs in Germany. Frank Lloyd Wright's Fallingwater appears on the cover of *Time*.

1939

Laura Ingalls Wilder publishes *By the Shores of Silver Lake*. Dorothy Thompson gives a speech that offends Lane. Lane testifies in support of the Ludlow Amendment. Germany invades Poland in September, leading to war with Britain. Hatch Act passed, limiting president's ability to spend taxpayer money for political purposes.

1940

Laura Ingalls Wilder publishes *The Long Winter*. Paterson publishes *If It Prove Fair Weather*. Rand works for Wendell Willkie campaign. Franklin Roosevelt reelected.

1941

Franklin Roosevelt delivers "four freedoms" speech in January. Rand, trying to organize a group of individualist intellectuals, invites Paterson to join and meets her. Begins attending Paterson's weekly salons at the *New York Herald Tribune* offices. Laura Ingalls Wilder publishes *Little Town on the Prairie*. Antitrust case against ALCOA dismissed in October—government appeals. After Japan attacks Pearl Harbor, United States enters the war in December.

1943

Laura Ingalls Wilder publishes *These Happy Golden Years* in March. Lane publishes *The Discovery of Freedom* in April. Paterson's *The God of the Machine* published in May. Rand's *The Fountainhead* published in May. Bernard DeVoto denounces the Revolt from the Village, to which Sinclair Lewis publishes a bitter reply.

1944

Rand finishes screenplay for *The Fountainhead* film. Writes script for *Love Letters* and begins writing *The Moral Basis of Individualism*. Franklin Roosevelt reelected. F. A. Hayek publishes *The Road to Serfdom*. Ludwig von Mises publishes *Omnipotent Government*.

1945

In March, court of appeals reverses judgment in ALCOA antitrust case and rules for the government. Franklin Roosevelt dies in April, succeeded by Harry Truman. Germany surrenders May 8. Atomic bombs dropped on Japan in August; Japan surrenders. Rand begins working on *Top Secret*, a movie about the atomic bomb, and planning for *The Strike*. Lane begins editing the *NECRB* in August. Lane and Paterson quarrel, leading to the end of their friendship.

1946

Rand writes "Textbook of Americanism." Lane and Rand correspond about the nature of rights. Fundamentalist preacher Carl McIntire publishes *Author of Liberty*. Henry Hazlitt publishes *Economics in One Lesson*.

1947

Rand testifies before House Un-American Activities Committee. Meets Lane for the first time. Lane campaigns against Tarshis economics textbook. Pierre Lecomte du Noüy publishes *Human Destiny*.

1948

Rand, doing research for *Atlas Shrugged*, operates the Twentieth Century Limited, meets with Kaiser Steel executives. Paterson visits Rand in California. After a series of unpleasant confrontations, their friendship essentially ends.

1949

Paterson's last "Turns with a Bookworm" column published. *The Fountainhead* film released. Mises publishes *Human Action*. USSR detonates atomic bomb. China falls to communists.

1951

Sinclair Lewis dies January 10.

1956

H. L. Mencken dies January 29.

1957

Rand publishes *Atlas Shrugged*. Laura Ingalls Wilder dies.

1959

Paterson visits Rand to ask her thoughts on draft novel *Joyous Gard*.

1961

Isabel Paterson dies January 10. Dorothy Thompson dies January 30.

1962

Rand begins publishing the *Objectivist Newsletter*.

1968

Rose Wilder Lane dies October 30.

1974

Little House on the Prairie TV series begins.

1982

Ayn Rand dies March 6.

▶ Notes ◀

Abbreviations:

AR = Ayn Rand

DoF = Rose Wilder Lane, *The Discovery of Freedom* (San Francisco: Fox & Wilkes, 1993)

DT = Dorothy Thompson

FDR = Franklin Delano Roosevelt

GoM = Isabel Paterson, *The God of the Machine* (New Brunswick, NJ: Transaction Publishers, 2009)

HLM = H. L. Mencken

IMP = Isabel Paterson

NECRB = *National Economic Council Review of Books*

NYHT = *New York Herald Tribune*

RWL = Rose Wilder Lane

SL = Sinclair Lewis

TF = Ayn Rand, *The Fountainhead* (New York: Plume, 2005)

The Paterson and Lane papers are at the Hoover Presidential Library in Iowa. The correspondence between Lane and Paterson must have been extensive, but was destroyed or lost at some point. Lane told Rand once that she typically destroyed letters after answering them, but her extensive personal papers at the Hoover Library belie this. It is therefore impossible to determine whether the destruction of this correspondence was intentional. But Lane's letters to Rand are only to be found in the Ayn Rand Papers at the Ayn Rand Institute

413

in California (ARI Papers). Paterson's friend Muriel Hall, placed her letters to Rand in the Paterson Papers. Because she had the frustrating habit of not dating her letters (sometimes dating them only as "Wednesday," or "Thursday," but more often not at all), and the Hoover Library has scanned them into a single PDF document, my citations to her letters are to the pages of this single PDF file. Quotations from Rand's letters are drawn either from the published versions in Michael S. Berliner, ed., *Letters of Ayn Rand* (New York: Dutton, 1995), or from the recently unveiled website of Rand's correspondence that includes PDF scans of the originals.

Introduction

1. Winston Churchill, "Weight off Russia This Year," May 19, 1943, *Vital Speeches of the Day*, vol. 9, pp. 482–87.

2. John Chamberlain, *A Life with the Printed Word* (Chicago: Regnery Gateway, 1982), p. xii. None of the three embraced the term "libertarian," however. Paterson died before the term gained circulation. Rand overtly rejected the term, objecting to the presence within the libertarian movement of moral relativists. Lane used the term, but only late in life. She preferred to call herself an "American revolutionary."

Chapter 1

1. IMP, "Turns with a Bookworm," *NYHT*, September 21, 1924.

2. Burton Rascoe, *We Were Interrupted* (Garden City, NY: Doubleday, 1947), vol. 1, p. 141.

3. Rascoe, *We Were Interrupted*, vol. 1, p. 142.

4. William F. Buckley Jr., "RIP, Mrs. Paterson," *National Review*, January 28, 1961, p. 43.

5. Stephen Cox, *The Woman and the Dynamo: Isabel Paterson and the Idea of America* (New Brunswick, NJ: Transaction Publishers, 2004), p. 28.

6. Walter Lord, *The Good Years: From 1900 to the First World War* (New Brunswick, NJ: Transaction Publishers, 2011), p. xv.

7. James D. Doenecke, *Nothing Less Than War: A New History of America's Entry into World War I* (Lexington: University Press of Kentucky, 2011), p. 297; *Buck v. Bell*, 274 U.S. 200, 207 (1927).

8. Robert Nisbet, *The Present Age: Progress and Anarchy in Modern America* (New York: Harper & Row, 1988), pp. 44–45.

9. Hurst Kreek Majors, "American Rationing during the First World War" (master's thesis, Kansas State College of Agriculture and Applied Science, 2017), pp. 53–56.

10. H. C. Peterson and Gilbert C. Fite, *Opponents of War, 1917–1918* (Madison: University of Washington Press, 1957), p. 234.

11. *Schenck v. United States*, 249 U.S. 47, 52 (1919).

12. Nisbet, *The Present Age*, p. 47.

13. Geoff Dyer, *The Missing of the Somme* (New York: Random House, 1994), p. 5.

14. Cox, *Woman and the Dynamo*, p. 57.

15. Malcolm Cowley, *A Second Flowering: The Works and Days of the Lost Generation* (New York: Viking, 1973), chap. 1.

16. IMP, "Turns," May 13, 1934.

17. Nathan Miller, *New World Coming: The 1920s and the Making of Modern America* (New York: Scribner, 2003), p. 204.

18. IMP, "Turns," July 7, 1933.

19. IMP, "Turns," April 11, 1937.

20. IMP, "Turns," January 17, 1943.

21. IMP, "Turns," August 8, 1943.

22. IMP, *If It Prove Fair Weather* (New York: G. P. Putnam's Sons, 1940), p. 106.

23. IMP, "Turns," February 27, 1927.

24. Howard Shaff and Audrey Karl Shaff, *Six Wars at a Time: The Life and Times of Gutzon Borglum, Sculptor of Mount Rushmore* (Sioux Falls, SD: Center for Western Studies, 1985), pp. 214–15.

25. Biographers apparently dispute whether the incident actually occurred, but it was reported on the front page of the *New York Times*. "Sculptor Destroys His Cathedral Angels," *New York Times*, October 11, 1905. See also Shaff and Shaff, *Six Wars*, pp. 93–94.

26. Cox, *Woman and the Dynamo*, p. 59.

27. Richard Kluger, *The Paper: The Life and Death of the New York Herald Tribune* (New York: Knopf, 1986), p. 273.

28. IMP, "Turns," July 7, 1934. This book omits Paterson's ellipses in subsequent quotations from "Turns."

29. Cox, *Woman and the Dynamo*, p. 79.

30. IMP, "Turns," December 1, 1946.

31. Irene and Allen Cleaton, *Books and Battles: American Literature 1920–1930* (Boston: Houghton Mifflin, 1937), p. 130.

32. Basil Davenport, "The Apostle of Common Sense," *Saturday Review of Literature*, October 27, 1934, p. 237.

33. Cox, *Woman and the Dynamo*, p. 84.

34. Bruce Gould, *American Story: Memories and Reflections of Bruce Gould and Beatrice Blackmar Gould* (New York: Harper & Row, 1968), p. 92.

35. Jacob Zeitlin and Homer Woodbridge, *Life and Letters of Stuart P. Sherman* (New York: Farrar & Rinehart, 1929), vol. 2, p. 698.

36. John Chamberlain, *A Life with the Printed Word* (Chicago: Regnery Gateway, 1982), p. 35; Angna Enters, *Silly Girl: A Portrait of Personal Remembrance* (Cambridge, MA: Houghton Mifflin, 1944), p. 136; Gould, *American Story*, p. 92.

37. Undated letter from RWL to AR (143-LN3-012-002), ARI Papers.

38. IMP, "A Confession from the Lost Generation," *NYHT*, May 27, 1934.

39. Carl Van Doren, "The Revolt from the Village," *The Nation* (October 12, 1921), reprinted in Carl Van Doren, *The American Novel: 1789–1939*, rev. ed. (New York: MacMillan, 1940). See also Anthony Channell Hilfer, *The Revolt from the Village 1915–1930* (Chapel Hill: University of North Carolina Press, 1969).

40. IMP, "Turns," June 21, 1925.

41. HLM, "Something New under the Sun," in *Mencken's Smart Set Criticism*, ed. William H. Nolte (Washington: Regnery Gateway, 1987), p. 272.

42. Fred Hobson, *Mencken: A Life* (Baltimore: Johns Hopkins University Press, 1994), p. 228; Nolte, *Smart Set Criticism*, p. 280.

43. IMP, "Turns," November 16, 1930.

44. IMP, "Turns," December 1, 1935 (emphasis in original).

45. SL, *Main Street* (New York: Harcourt, Brace, & Howe, 1920), p. 173.

46. SL, *Main Street*, p. 266.

47. SL, *Main Street*, p. 361.

48. SL, *Main Street*, p. 374.

49. SL, *Main Street*, p. 343.

50. SL, *Main Street*, p. 422.

51. SL, *Main Street*, p. 450.

52. Richard Lingeman, *Sinclair Lewis: Rebel from Main Street* (New York: Random House, 2002), p. 162.

53. SL, *Main Street*, p. 172.

54. IMP, "Sinclair Lewis Writes in His Kindliest Mood," *NYHT*, January 28, 1934.

55. SL, *Main Street*, p. 265.

56. Mark Schorer, ed., *Lewis at Zenith* (New York: Harcourt, Brace & World, 1961), p. ix.

57. Studs Terkel, *Hard Times* (New York: New Press, 1986), p. 32.

58. IMP, "Turns," August 30, 1931.

59. SL, *Main Street*, p. 224.

60. SL, *Babbitt* (New York: Grosset & Dunlap, 1922), p. 234.

61. SL, *Babbitt*, p. 271.

62. SL, *Babbitt*, pp. 374, 391.

63. SL, *Babbitt*, p. 390.

64. IMP, "Turns," May 16, 1926.

65. Charles A. Fecher, ed., *The Diary of H. L. Mencken* (New York: Knopf, 1989), p. 5.

66. Mark Schorer, *Sinclair Lewis: An American Life* (New York: McGraw-Hill, 1961), p. 543.

67. Schorer, *Sinclair Lewis*, pp. 516–17 (emphasis added).

68. Alfred Kazin, *On Native Grounds: An Interpretation of Modern American Prose Literature* (Garden City, NY: Doubleday, 1956), p. 164.

69. In 1943, SL made the same point: "To the grandparents, if they are still alive—and they easily may be, aged somewhere over eighty—these modern children must seem selfish, idle, weak, and terrified of ghosts; armored in luxuries of which the old folks never heard, yet whimpering because some finicky sweetheart does not like the length of their noses. And to the grandchildren, the pioneers seem as hard and narrow as the steel rails that, on a prairie track, stretch bleakly out till they meet. And how wrong both generations are!" *Three Readers*, Clifton Fadiman et al., eds., (New York: The Readers Club, 1943), p. 174.

70. IMP, "Books and Other Things," *NYHT*, November 12, 1930, p. 17.

71. IMP, *The Golden Vanity* (New Brunswick: Transaction, 2017), pp. 131–32.

72. IMP, "Reading with Tears," *The Bookman*, October 1926, p. 64.

73. HLM, *My Life as Author and Editor* (New York: Knopf, 1993), p. 386.

74. IMP, "Turns," November 8, 1931.

75. Vincent Fitzpatrick, *H. L. Mencken* (New York: Continuum, 1989), p. x.

76. HLM, "H. L. Mencken, By Himself," in *A Second Mencken Chrestomathy*, ed. Terry Teachout (New York: Knopf, 1994), p. 471; HLM, "Liberty and Democracy," in *Second Mencken Chrestomathy*, p. 35; Terry Teachout, *The Skeptic: A Life of H. L. Mencken* (New York: Harper Collins, 2002), p. 124.

77. HLM, "William Jennings Bryan," in *The American Mercury Reader* (Philadelphia: Blakiston Co., 1944), p. 36.

78. IMP, "Turns," July 31, 1927.

79. IMP, "Turns," November 8, 1931.

80. IMP, "Turns," January 10, 1926.

81. IMP, "Turns," December 1, 1929.

82. Ronald J. Pestritto, *Woodrow Wilson and the Roots of Modern Liberalism* (Lanham, MD: Rowman & Littlefield, 2005); John Marini and Ken Masugi, eds., *The Progressive Revolution in Politics and Political Science* (Lanham, MD: Claremont Institute, 2005); Michael McGerr, *A Fierce Discontent: The Rise and Fall of the Progressive Movement in America* (New York: Free Press, 2003).

83. John Dewey, *Liberalism and Social Action* (New York: Capricorn Books, 1963), pp. 54–55.

84. McGerr, *Fierce Discontent*, p. 57.

85. Neal Gabler, *Walt Disney: The Triumph of American Imagination* (New York: Knopf, 2007), p. 19.

86. IMP, "Turns," March 13, 1932.

87. IMP, "Turns," September 1, 1940.

88. Lida Parce Robinson, "The Dangers of Exclusive Masculinism," *Socialist Woman*, July 1908, p. 3.

89. Donald Crichlow, *Socialism in the Heartland: The Midwestern Experience 1900–1925* (Notre Dame, IN: University of Notre Dame Press, 1986), p. 7.

90. Jeffrey Paul, "The Socialism of Herbert Spencer," *History of Political Thought* 3, no. 3 (1982): 499–514; Mark Pittenger, *American Socialists and Evolutionary Thought, 1870–1920* (Madison: University of Wisconsin Press, 1993), pp. 17–23.

91. Pittenger, *American Socialists*, p. 26.

92. Kevin Starr, *Americans and the California Dream* (New York: Oxford University Press, 1973), p. 215.

93. Jack London, *War of the Classes* (London: Mills & Boon, 1905), pp. 212–13.

94. Carolyn Johnston, *Jack London—An American Radical?* (Westport, CT: Greenwood Press, 1984), p. 68.

95. McGerr, *Fierce Discontent*, p. xiv.

96. Schorer, *Sinclair Lewis*, pp. 164–69, 186–87.

97. IMP, "Turns," July 17, 1938.

98. IMP, "Turns," September 28, 1947.

99. IMP, "Turns," March 21, 1926.

100. IMP, "Turns," May 24, 1925.

Chapter 2

1. RWL, *Old Home Town* (Lincoln: University of Nebraska Press, 1963), p. 24.

2. RWL, *The Peaks of Shala* (New York: Harper & Bros., 1923), p. 148.

3. Quoted in Christine Woodside, *Libertarians on the Prairie* (New York: Arcade Publishing, 2016), p. 21.

4. William Holtz, *The Ghost in the Little House* (Columbia: University of Missouri Press, 1995), p. 19.

5. Holtz, *Ghost*, p. 38.

6. "Who's Who—and Why: Rose Wilder Lane," *Saturday Evening Post*, July 6, 1935, p. 30.

7. *NECRB*, November 1948.

8. RWL Diary, April 10, 1933, Lane Papers, Hoover Library.

9. Holtz, *Ghost*, p. 33.

10. RWL Diary, February 3, 1933, Lane Papers, Hoover Library (emphasis in original).

11. RWL Diary, July 3, 1933, Lane Papers, Hoover Library.

12. RWL, *Old Home Town*, p. 148.

13. Holtz, *Ghost*, p. 50.

14. Holtz, *Ghost*, p. 52.

15. Holtz, *Ghost*, p. 51.

16. Holtz, *Ghost*, p. 61.

17. RWL, "I, Rose Wilder Lane, Am the Only Truly *Happy* Person I Know, and I Discovered the Secret of Happiness on the Day I Tried to Kill Myself," in *The Rediscovered Writings of Rose Wilder Lane*, ed. Amy Mattson Lauters (Columbia: University of Missouri Press, 2007), p. 94.

18. RWL, "I, Rose Wilder Lane," p. 96.

19. Julia C. Ehrhardt, *Writers of Conviction: The Personal Politics of Zona Gale, Dorothy Canfield Fisher, Rose Wilder Lane, and Josephine Herbst* (Columbia: University of Missouri Press, 2004), p. 93.

20. Virginia Woolf, *A Room of One's Own* (New York: Fall River Press, 2007), p. 56.

21. Ehrhardt, *Writers of Conviction*, p. 102 (emphasis in original).

22. Pamela Smith Hill, ed., *Pioneer Girl: The Annotated Autobiography* (Pierre: South Dakota Historical Society Press, 2014), p. xxxiii; Martha Banta, *Tailored Lives*, quoted in Donna M. Campbell, "Fictionalizing Jack London: Charmian London and Rose Wilder Lane as Biographers," *Studies in American Naturalism* 7, no. 2 (2012): 176–92.

23. Holtz, *Ghost*, p. 68.

24. Campbell, "Fictionalizing Jack London," p. 179.

25. Holtz, *Ghost*, pp. 69–70.

26. Joan Hoff Wilson, *Herbert Hoover: Forgotten Progressive*, ed. Oscar Handlin (Long Grove, IL: Waveland Press, 1975), p. 38.

27. Holtz, *Ghost*, p. 194.

28. Holtz, *Ghost*, p. 190.

29. RWL, *The Making of Herbert Hoover* (New York: Century, 1920), pp. 194, 223–26.

30. RWL, *Making of Herbert Hoover*, p. 190

31. RWL, *Making of Herbert Hoover*, p. 307.

32. RWL, *Making of Herbert Hoover*, pp. 261, 301.

33. RWL, *Diverging Roads* (New York: Century, 1919), pp. 240–43.

34. RWL, *Diverging Roads*, p. 268.

35. RWL, *Diverging Roads*, p. 318.

36. RWL, "Diverging Roads," *Sunset*, June 1919, p. 64.

37. RWL, *Diverging Roads*, p. 318.

38. RWL, *Diverging Roads*, p. 352.

39. RWL, *Diverging Roads*, p. 355.

40. Ehrhardt, *Writers of Conviction*, p. 104.

41. The book was made into an Oscar-winning film in 1928, but its most lasting impact came in the 1960s, when it inspired entrepreneur Joe Coulombe to use it as the basis for the branding of his new chain of grocery stores, called Trader Joe's. Jessica Tyler, "Trader Joe's Execs Reveal Why Employees Wear Hawaiian Shirts at Work," *Business Insider*, October 1, 2018.

42. Peter Kurth, *American Cassandra: The Life of Dorothy Thompson* (Boston: Little, Brown, 1991), pp. 50–51.

43. Marion K. Sanders, *Dorothy Thompson: A Legend in Her Time* (New York: Avon Books, 1974), p. 72.

44. Kurth, *American Cassandra*, p. 58.

45. Kurth, *American Cassandra*, pp. 190–92.

46. Holtz, *Ghost*, p. 183.

47. RWL, letter to DT, October 26, 1927, in William Holtz, ed., *Dorothy Thompson and Rose Wilder Lane: Forty Years of Friendship* (Columbia: University of Missouri Press, 1991), p. 62 (emphasis in original).

48. RWL, *Peaks of Shala*, p. 86.

49. Harriette Ashbrook, "Goes to Moslems for Feminine Freedom," *Brooklyn Daily Eagle*, April 4, 1926.

50. Ashbook, "Feminine Freedom"; IMP, "Turns with a Bookworm," *NYHT*, November 22, 1936.

51. RWL, *Peaks of Shala*, p. 159.

52. RWL, *Peaks of Shala*, pp. 106–19.

53. *DoF*, p. 8.

54. Roger Lea MacBride, ed., *The Lady and the Tycoon: The Best of Letters between Rose Wilder Lane and Jasper Crane* (Caldwell, ID: Caxton, 1973), p. 287.

55. RWL, *Peaks of Shala*, p. 160.

56. After World War II, Meta—who after graduating from Cambridge returned to Albania to work in the Finance Directorate—was arrested by agents of Albania's communist dictator, Enver Hoxha, and sentenced to death. That sentence was commuted, but he spent nearly three decades in Burrel Prison, before being released in the 1980s. Holtz, *Ghost*, p. 346.

57. Richard Pipes, *The Formation of the Soviet Union* (Cambridge, MA: Harvard University Press, revised edition 1964), pp. 229–41.

58. Holtz, *Ghost*, p. 128.

59. RWL, "Peasant and Priest in Armenia," *Asia*, July 1923, pp. 494–98.

60. RWL, "Peasant and Priest in Armenia," p. 498.

61. RWL, "Credo," *Saturday Evening Post*, March 7, 1936.

62. *NECRB*, September 1949.

63. Bruce Ramsey, *Unsanctioned Voice: Garet Garrett, Journalist of the Old Right* (Caldwell, ID: Caxton Press, 2009), p. 102.

64. Holtz, *Ghost*, p. 141.

65. Holtz, *Ghost*, p. 143.

66. Holtz, *Ghost*, p. 151.

67. Ehrhardt, *Writers of Conviction*, p. 110.

68. Caren Irr, *The Suburb of Dissent: Cultural Politics in the U.S. and Canada during the 1930s* (Durham, NC: Duke University Press, 1998), p. 102.

69. Holtz, *Ghost*, p. 159.

70. RWL, *He Was a Man*, pp. 113, 116.

71. RWL, *He Was a Man*, pp. 130–31.

72. RWL, *He Was a Man*, p. 131.

73. RWL, *He Was a Man*, p. 155.

74. RWL, *He Was a Man*, p. 359.

75. RWL, *He Was a Man*, pp. 169, 228, 238, 300.

76. Intriguingly, Blake finds "his greatest pleasure" comes from lying to farmers who give him meals along the way—telling them elaborate fictions about his life. He gets a thrill from "the stories he told, the different persons he was, never twice the same, and the play of his wits against the always different minds behind the doors" (p. 161). In fact, he enjoys it so much that he eventually finds himself starting to believe his own fabrications. This passage is suggestive in light of Lane's later habit of exaggerating her own life story, a trait that decades later would drive Isabel Paterson to call her a liar and refuse to have anything to do with her.

77. RWL, *He Was a Man*, p. 207.

78. RWL, *He Was a Man*, p. 208.

79. RWL, *He Was a Man*, p. 311 (emphasis in original).

80. RWL, *He Was a Man*, p. 373.

81. Jack London, *John Barleycorn, or, Alcoholic Memoirs* (London: Mills & Boon, 1914), pp. 140, 277.

82. Daniel Okrent, *Last Call: The Rise and Fall of Prohibition* (New York: Scribner, 2010), p. 63.

83. RWL, letter to *Harper's Monthly Magazine*, June 1924, p. 143.

84. Quoted in Campbell, "Fictionalizing Jack London," p. 187.

85. Floyd Dell, *Saturday Review of Literature*, March 28, 1925, p. 630.

86. Laurence Stallings, "The Latest Books," *Buffalo Sunday Courier Magazine*, March 29, 1925, p. 15.

87. Holtz, *Ghost*, p. 153.

88. Holtz, *Ghost*, p. 173 (emphasis in original).

89. Holtz, *Ghost*, p. 179 (emphasis removed).

90. RWL, letter to DT, February 16, 1927, in Holtz, *Thompson and Lane*, p. 42.

91. RWL, letter to DT, March 11, 1927, in Holtz, *Thompson and Lane*, pp. 51–52 (emphasis in original).

92. Mustafa Akyol, *Reopening Muslim Minds: A Return to Reason, Freedom, and Tolerance* (Washington: Cato Institute, 2021), p. 233.

93. Part of her fondness for Albania may have been rooted in a family legend that held that her father's name, Almanzo, had been handed down from a Crusades-era ancestor named Wilder whose life was spared by a Muslim fighter called El Manzoor. Henry Grady Weaver, *The Mainspring of Human Progress* (Irvington-on-Hudson, NY: Foundation for Economic Education, 1953), p. 122n.

94. MacBride, *Lady and the Tycoon*, p. 143.

95. *DoF*, p. 83 (emphasis in original).

96. *DoF*, p. 86.

97. *DoF*, p. 100.

98. *DoF*, pp. 110–11.

99. RWL, letter to DT, January 10, 1928, in Holtz, *Thompson and Lane*, p. 65 (italics added).

100. RWL, "How I Wrote 'Yarbwoman,'" in Lauters, *Rediscovered Writings of RWL*, p. 98.

101. Woodside, *Libertarians on the Prairie*, p. 43.

102. Woodside, *Libertarians on the Prairie*, p. 43.

103. Woodside, *Libertarians on the Prairie*, p. 38.

104. RWL, letter to DT, August 14, 1928, in Holtz, *Thompson and Lane*, p. 94 (emphasis in original).

105. RWL, letter to DT, August 14, 1928, in Holtz, *Thompson and Lane*, p. 93 (emphasis in original).

106. RWL, letter to DT, July 11, 1928, in Holtz, *Thompson and Lane*, p. 85.

107. RWL, letter to DT, July 13, 1928, in Holtz, *Thompson and Lane*, p. 88.

108. MacBride, *Lady and the Tycoon*, p. 98.

109. *NECRB*, July 1950.

110. IMP, "Turns," April 1, 1928.

111. Holtz, *Ghost*, p. 202.

Chapter 3

1. Murray Rothbard, *America's Great Depression*, 5th ed. (Auburn, AL: Mises Institute, 2000), p. 30.

2. Joan Hoff Wilson, *Herbert Hoover: Forgotten Progressive*, ed. Oscar Handlin (Long Grove, IL: Waveland Press, 1975), p. 84.

3. Garet Garrett, "Hoover of Iowa and California," *Saturday Evening Post*, June 2, 1928, p. 158.

4. Adam Smith, *An Inquiry into the Nature and Causes of the Wealth of Nations* (New York: P. F. Collier & Sons, 1912), vol. 1, p. 442.

5. Benjamin F. Alexander, *Coxey's Army: Popular Protest in the Gilded Age* (Baltimore: Johns Hopkins University Press, 2015), pp. 88–89, 108; Donald L. McMurry, *Coxey's Army: A Study of the Industrial Army Movement of 1894* (Seattle: University of Washington Press, 1968), pp. 243, 250.

6. Rothbard, *America's Great Depression*, p. 211.

7. Arthur M. Schlesinger Jr., *The Crisis of the Old Order: 1919–1933* (Boston: Houghton Mifflin, 1957), p. 73.

8. *GoM*, p. 231.

9. Rothbard, *America's Great Depression*, p. 213.

10. Amity Shlaes, *The Forgotten Man: A New History of the Great Depression*, rev. ed. (New York: Harper Perennial, 2008), p. 93.

11. Quoted in Rothbard, *America's Great Depression*, p. 333.

12. Herbert Hoover, *American Individualism* (Garden City, NY: Doubleday, Page & Co., 1923), pp. 10, 53.

13. Hoover, *American Individualism*, pp. 17, 11, 22.

14. Hoover, *American Individualism*, pp. 13, 29.

15. IMP to AR, November 30, 1943, Hoover Library, p. 11.

16. IMP, "Turns with a Bookworm," *NYHT*, March 15, 1936.

17. Ford Madox Ford, "Dedicatory Letter," *The Last Post* (New York: Literary Guild of America, 1928).

18. RWL, undated letter to AR (143-LN3-012-002), ARI papers.

19. Stephen Cox, *The Woman and the Dynamo: Isabel Paterson and the Idea of America* (New Brunswick, NJ: Transaction Publishers, 2004), pp. 114–15.

20. Cox, *Woman and the Dynamo*, p. 115.

21. IMP, "Turns," August 8, 1943.

22. IMP, *Never Ask the End* (New York: Literary Guild, 1933), p. 165.

23. IMP, *Never Ask*, p. 162.

24. IMP, *Never Ask*, p. 192.

25. IMP, *Never Ask*, p. 99 (emphasis in original).

26. IMP, *Never Ask*, p. 110.

27. IMP, *Never Ask*, p. 140 (emphasis added).

28. IMP, *Never Ask*, p. 313.

29. IMP, *Never Ask*, p. 327.

30. IMP, *Never Ask*, p. 328.

31. *Publisher's Weekly*, November 5, 1932, p. 1755.

32. Fanny Butcher, "An Intelligent Novel Praised as Rare Thing," *Chicago Tribune*, January 4, 1933.

33. Emily Clark, "The Beautiful, Unusual Novel of Isabel Paterson," *Philadelphia Inquirer*, January 7, 1933.

34. Julius Rowan Raper, ed., "Modern Tempo and American Spirit," *Ellen Glasgow's Reasonable Doubts: A Collection of Her Writings* (Baton Rouge: Louisiana State University Press, 1988), pp. 179–82. Paterson called Glasgow her idol in Ishbel Ross, *Ladies of the Press*, 5th ed. (New York: Harper & Bros., 1936), p. 406.

35. IMP, letter to Burton Rascoe, ca. December 1931, in *Culture and Liberty: Writings of Isabel Paterson*, ed. Stephen Cox (New York: Transaction Publishers, 2015), p. 152 (emphasis in original).

36. IMP, letter to Garreta Busey, February 1, 1933, in Cox, *Culture and Liberty*, p. 160.

37. IMP, "Turns," February 12, 1933.

38. *GoM*, p. 192.

39. RWL, *The Making of Herbert Hoover* (New York: Century, 1920), p. 344.

40. Rothbard, *America's Great Depression*, p. 231.

41. IMP, letter to Burton Rascoe, ca. December 1931, in Cox, *Culture and Liberty*, p. 155.

42. Proclamation No. 1872, March 22, 1929.

43. Shlaes, *Forgotten Man*, p. 96.

44. Rothbard, *America's Great Depression*, p. 241.

45. Deborah Kalb, Gerhard Peters, and John T. Woolley, eds., *State of the Union: Presidential Rhetoric from Woodrow Wilson to George W. Bush* (Washington: CQ Press, 2007), p. 204.

46. For example, although Hoover resisted outright rationing of flour in 1918, he did so only by implementing a mandate requiring consumers to buy a pound of wheat substitute for every pound of flour purchased. Hurst Kreek Majors, "American Rationing during the First World War" (master's thesis, Kansas State College of Agriculture and Applied Science, 2017), p. 63.

47. Ira Katznelson, *Fear Itself: The New Deal and the Origins of Our Time* (New York: Liveright, 2013), p. 12.

48. William Y. Elliott, "Mussolini, Prophet of the Pragmatic Era in Politics," *Political Science Quarterly* 41, no. 2 (1926): 161.

49. Schlesinger, *Crisis of the Old Order*, p. 149.

50. IMP, letter to Burton Rascoe, ca. December 1931, in Cox, *Culture and Liberty*, p. 152.

51. IMP, letter to Burton Rascoe, ca. December 1931, in Cox, *Culture and Liberty*, p. 155.

52. Shlaes, *Forgotten Man*, p. 111.

53. Rothbard, *America's Great Depression*, p. 268.

54. William Holtz, *The Ghost in the Little House* (Columbia: University of Missouri Press, 1995), p. 217.

55. Pamela Smith Hill, ed., *Pioneer Girl: The Annotated Autobiography* (Pierre: South Dakota Historical Society Press, 2014), p. xxii; Holtz, *Ghost*, p. 224.

56. Christine Woodside, *Libertarians on the Prairie* (New York: Arcade Publishing, 2016), p. 51.

57. Hill, *Pioneer Girl*, p. xlvii.

58. William Anderson, ed., *The Selected Letters of Laura Ingalls Wilder* (New York: Harper, 2016), p. 71.

59. Woodside, *Libertarians on the Prairie*, p. 57.

60. Woodside, *Libertarians on the Prairie*, p. 57 (emphasis in original).

61. RWL Diary, January 25, 1933, Lane Papers, Hoover Library.

62. Shlaes, *Forgotten Man*, pp. 137–39.

63. *Cong. Rec.*, January 11, 1932, p. 1742.

64. Joseph Schumpeter, *Capitalism, Socialism, and Democracy* (New York: Harper & Bros., 1942).

65. IMP, *The Shadow Riders* (New York: John Lane, 1916), p. 203 (emphasis in original).

66. Arthur Ekirch, *Ideologies and Utopias: The Impact of the New Deal on American Thought* (Chicago: Quadrangle Books, 1969), p. 50.

67. Butler Shaffer, *In Restraint of Trade: The Business Campaign against Competition 1918–1938* (Auburn, AL: Mises Institute, 2008), pp. 93–94.

68. Shaffer, *In Restraint of Trade*, p. 95.

69. Herbert Hoover, *Memoirs: The Great Depression 1929–1941* (New York: Macmillan, 1952), p. 420.

70. Charles Beard, "A Five-Year Plan for America," *Forum* 85 (1931): 5–6.

71. Matthew Josephson, *Infidel in the Temple: A Memoir of the Nineteen-Thirties* (New York: Knopf, 1967), p. 104.

72. Jerome Loving, *The Last Titan: A Life of Theodore Dreiser* (Berkeley: University of California Press, 2005), p. 363.

73. IMP, "Turns," July 26, 1931.

74. Stuart Chase, *A New Deal* (New York: Macmillan, 1933), pp. 162–63.

75. Chase, *A New Deal*, pp. 7, 11, 13, 17, 163 (quoting John Maynard Keynes).

76. Chase, *A New Deal*, pp. 164–65.

77. Chase, *A New Deal*, p. 252.

78. IMP, "Turns," February 26, 1933.

79. IMP, "Turns," January 29, 1933.

80. Holtz, *Ghost*, p. 222.

81. IMP, "Turns," November 16, 1930.

82. IMP, "Turns," February 12, 1933.

83. Rothbard, *America's Great Depression*, p. 301.

84. Rothbard, *America's Great Depression*, p. 305.

85. Jim Powell, *FDR's Folly: How Roosevelt and His New Deal Prolonged the Great Depression* (New York: Three Rivers Press, 2003), pp. 18–20.

86. IMP, "Turns," June 12, 1932.

87. IMP, "Turns," March 13, 1932.

88. IMP, "Turns," June 12, 1932.

89. IMP, "Turns," July 6, 1930.

90. IMP, "Turns," November 27, 1932.

91. IMP, "Turns," July 6, 1930.

92. IMP, "Turns," March 13, 1932.

93. Schlesinger, *Crisis of the Old Order*, p. 43.

94. Schlesinger, *Crisis of the Old Order*, p. 3.

95. IMP, "Turns," March 23, 1930.

96. Studs Terkel, *Hard Times* (New York: New Press, 2005), p. 423.

97. Elliott J. Gorn, *Dillinger's Wild Ride: The Year That Made America's Public Enemy Number One* (Oxford: Oxford University Press, 2009), pp. 170–71.

98. Terkel, *Hard Times*, p. 97.

99. Holtz, *Ghost*, p. 230.

100. Ekirch, *Ideologies and Utopias*, p. 31.

101. Pare Lorentz, "A Young Man Goes to Work," reprinted in *College Readings on Today and Its Problems*, ed. Dudley Chadwick Gordon and Vernon Rupert King (New York: Oxford University Press, 1934), pp. 69–76.

102. Shlaes, *Forgotten Man*, p. 122.

103. Zora Neale Hurston, "Mourner's Bench," in *You Don't Know Us Negroes and Other Essays*, ed. Genevieve West and Henry Louis Gates Jr. (New York: Amistad Books, 2022), p. 275.

104. Herbert Hoover, speech of November 2, 1932, *Public Papers of the Presidents: Herbert Hoover 1932–33* (Washington: Government Printing Office, 1977), pp. 766–67.

105. James Truslow Adams, *The Epic of America* (New Brunswick, NJ: Transaction Publishers, 2012), p. 31.

106. Terry Cooney, *Balancing Acts: American Thought and Culture in the 1930s* (New York: Twayne Publishers, 1995), pp. 44–50.

107. Charles A. Beard, "The Myth of Rugged American Individualism," *Harper's*, December 1931, pp. 13–22.

108. Ekirch, *Utopias and Ideologies*, pp. 55, 57.

109. Holtz, *Ghost*, p. 235.

110. RWL, *Let the Hurricane Roar* (New York: Longmans, Green, 1933), p. 83.

111. RWL, *Hurricane*, p. 129.

112. RWL Diary, April 29, 1933, Lane Papers, Hoover Library (emphasis in original).

113. Woodside, *Libertarians on the Prairie*, p. 66.

114. In 1976, the book was retitled *Young Pioneers*, and the names of the characters changed to Molly and David, in part to avoid confusion with the *Little House* novels, which by then had been adapted into the popular television series. *Young Pioneers* was itself made into a short-lived TV series.

115. Donald A. Ritchie, *Electing FDR: The New Deal Campaign of 1932* (Lawrence: University of Kansas Press, 2007), p. 11.

116. Martin L. Fausold, *The Presidency of Herbert Hoover* (Lawrence: University Press of Kansas, 1985), chap. 10.

117. Ritchie, *Electing FDR*, p. 137.

118. Fredrick Lewis Allen, *Only Yesterday: An Informal History of the Nineteen-Twenties* (New York: Harper & Row, 1931), p. 256.

119. Ritchie, *Electing FDR*, p. 98; Sean Beienburg, *Prohibition, the Constitution, and States' Rights* (Chicago: University of Chicago Press, 2019), pp. 217–18.

120. Marion Elizabeth Rodgers, ed., *The Impossible H. L. Mencken* (New York: Anchor Books, 1991), p. 314.

121. Rodgers, *Impossible H. L. Mencken*, pp. 327–28.

122. Malcolm Cowley, *The Dream of the Golden Mountains: Remembering the 1930s* (New York: Viking, 1980), p. 109.

123. FDR, Sioux City speech, September 29, 1932, *The Public Papers and Addresses of Franklin D. Roosevelt*, vol. 1 (New York: Random House, 1938), p. 761.

124. FDR, speech of March 2, 1930, *Public Papers and Addresses*, vol. 1, p. 571.

125. FDR, speech of October 19, 1932, *Public Papers and Addresses*, vol. 1, p. 808.

126. FDR, speech of October 19, 1932, *Public Papers and Addresses*, vol. 1, p. 798.

127. Marriner Eccles, *Beckoning Frontiers* (New York: Knopf, 1951), p. 95; James P. Warburg, *Hell Bent for Election* (Garden City, NY: Doubleday, 1935), p. 76.

128. FDR, radio address of April 7, 1932, in *Public Papers and Addresses*, vol. 1, p. 624.

129. IMP, "Turns," November 5, 1933; Shlaes, *Forgotten Man*, p. 12.

130. IMP, "Turns," February 20, 1944. Sumner's forgotten man, agreed Mencken, "was the hard-working, self-supporting fellow who pays his own way in the world and asks for no favors from anyone. Roosevelt converted him, by a curious perversion, into a mendicant beneficiary of the New Deal doles." HLM, *The American Language, Supplement One* (New York: Knopf, 1962), p. 303, n. 5.

131. Shlaes, *Forgotten Man*, p. 128.

132. Vincent Fitzpatrick, *H. L. Mencken* (New York: Continuum, 1989), p. 86; Cox, *Woman and the Dynamo*, p. 111.

Chapter 4

1. FDR, "First Inaugural Address," in *Great Speeches: Franklin Delano Roosevelt*, ed. John Grafton (Mineola, NY: Dover Publications, 1999), pp. 28–33.

2. Ira Katznelson, *Fear Itself: The New Deal and the Origins of Our Time* (New York: W. W. Norton, 2013), p. 105.

3. Wolfgang Schivelbusch, *Three New Deals: Reflections on Roosevelt's America, Mussolini's Italy, and Hitler's Germany, 1933–1939* (New York: Picador, 2006), p. 23.

4. Harvey Klehr, *The Heyday of Communism* (New York: Basic Books, 1984), p. 332.

5. B. J. Widick, *Detroit: City of Race and Class Violence* (Detroit: Wayne State University Press, 1989), pp. 49–53.

6. Blaise Picchi, *The Five Weeks of Giuseppe Zangara: The Man Who Would Assassinate FDR* (Chicago: Academy Chicago Publishers, 1998), p. 148.

7. FDR, press conference, May 31, 1935, https://www.presidency.ucsb.edu/documents/press-conference-23. Many sources have quoted Roosevelt as referring to the Supreme Court's decision in the *Schechter Poultry* case as adopting a "horse-and-buggy definition of interstate commerce," but Roosevelt did not claim that the court had changed its interpretation of the Constitution. Instead, he objected that it had *not* done so. He essentially agreed that the court had applied the original understanding of the Constitution. "The country was in the horse-and-buggy age when that clause was written," he said. "Since that time . . . we have developed an entirely different philosophy." The court's error, in his eyes, was that it had failed to embrace that "entirely different philosophy."

8. Jeff Shesol, *Supreme Power: Franklin Roosevelt versus the Supreme Court* (New York: W. W. Norton, 2010), p. 76. Rexford Tugwell likewise denounced the "unreasoning, almost hysterical, attachment of

certain Americans to the Constitution" for obstructing the "experimental attitude" necessary to permit government control over the economy. Rexford Tugwell and Howard Copeland Hill, *Our Economic Society and Its Problems* (New York: Harcourt, Brace, 1934), p. 542.

9. "A Center Report: Rewriting the Constitution," *Center Magazine*, March 1968, p. 18.

10. Benjamin L. Alpers, *Dictators, Democracy, and American Public Culture* (Chapel Hill: University of North Carolina Press, 2003), p. 26; Page Smith, *Redeeming the Time: A People's History of the 1920s and the New Deal* (New York: McGraw-Hill, 1987), p. 432; Anne O'Hare McCormick, "The Excitement of the Hundred Days," in *The New Deal and the American People*, ed. Frank Freidel (Englewood Cliffs, NJ: Prentice-Hall, 1964), p. 15.

11. Ben H. Procter, *William Randolph Hearst: The Final Edition 1911–1951* (New York: Oxford University Press, 2007), pp. 165, 177–78, 204.

12. Schivelbusch, *Three New Deals*, p. 18.

13. RWL Diary, March 5, 1933, Lane Papers, Hoover Library.

14. IMP, "Turns with a Bookworm," *NYHT*, March 5, 1933.

15. Gary Dean Best, *Peddling Panaceas: Popular Economists in the New Deal Era* (New York: Routledge, 2017), p. 252.

16. IMP, "Turns," April 23, 1933.

17. FDR, *Selected Speeches, Messages, Press Conferences, and Letters*, ed. Basil Rauch (New York: Rinehart, 1957), p. 72.

18. IMP, "Turns," April 23, 1933.

19. IMP, "Turns," September 25, 1932. This speculation is based on the fact that Paterson's references to Lane in "Turns" became more frequent and drew from in-person conversations after this point. Also, a year later, Paterson would include Lane as a minor character in *Never Ask the End*.

20. IMP, "Turns," August 11, 1940.

21. George Fitzhugh, "Oliver Goldsmith and Doctor Johnson," *DeBow's Review*, May 1860, p. 513 (emphasis in original).

22. Timothy Sandefur, *Frederick Douglass: Self-Made Man* (Washington: Cato Institute, 2018), p. 32.

23. FDR, Commonwealth Club address, September 23, 1932, in *Campaign Speeches of American Presidential Candidates, 1928–1972*, ed. Aaron Singer (New York: Ungar, 1976), p. 80.

24. Harold Laski, *Democracy in Crisis* (London: Allen & Unwin, 1933), p. 44.

25. *Congressional Record*, 73rd Cong. 1st sess., vol. 77, part 3, May 10, 1933, p. 3201.

26. "Revolution in America, 1933," *Kansas City Star*, May 14, 1933.

27. Jonathan Norton Leonard, *Men of Maracaibo* (New York: G. P. Putnam's Sons, 1933), p. 285.

28. Lawrence R. Samuel, *The American Way of Life: A Cultural History* (Madison, NJ: Farleigh Dickenson University Press, 2017), p. 3.

29. John Dewey, "The Future of Liberalism," in *John Dewey: The Later Works, 1925–1953*, ed. Jo Ann Boydston (Carbondale: Southern Illinois University Press, 2008), vol. 2, p. 291.

30. DT, "Let Us Be Thankful," *NYHT*, November 4, 1936.

31. Jim Powell, *FDR's Folly: How Roosevelt and His New Deal Prolonged the Great Depression* (New York: Three Rivers Press, 2003), p. 5.

32. IMP, "Turns," June 11, 1933.

33. IMP, "Turns," April 2, 1933.

34. IMP, "Turns," June 11, 1933 (emphasis added).

35. Walter Lippmann, "The Metaphysics of Gold," *NYHT*, January 26, 1934.

36. IMP, "Turns," February 4, 1934.

37. William E. Leuchtenburg, *Franklin D. Roosevelt and the New Deal: 1932–1940* (New York: Harper & Row, 1963), p. 79.

38. John Maynard Keynes, "From Keynes to Roosevelt: Our Recovery Plan Assayed," *New York Times*, December 31, 1933.

39. J. George Frederick, *A Primer of "New Deal" Economics* (New York: Business Bourse, 1932), p. 82.

40. Amity Shlaes, *The Forgotten Man: A New History of the Great Depression*, rev. ed. (New York: Harper Perennial, 2008), p. 168; D. A. FitzGerald, *Livestock under the AAA* (Washington: Brookings Institution, 1935), p. 79; Edwin Norse, Joseph S. Davis, and John D. Black, *Three Years of the Agricultural Adjustment Administration* (New York: Da Capo Press, 1971), pp. 86–87.

41. Powell, *FDR's Folly*, p. 131.

42. John Steinbeck, *The Grapes of Wrath* (New York: Penguin, 2002), pp. 348–49.

43. Ogden Nash, "One from One Leaves Two," *Saturday Evening Post*, June 23, 1934.

44. Shlaes, *The Forgotten Man*, p. 168.

45. Barry Cushman, *Rethinking the New Deal Court* (New York: Oxford University Press, 1998), p. 35; Rexford G. Tugwell, *The Stricken Land: The Story of Puerto Rico* (Garden City, NY: Doubleday, 1947), p. 24.

46. E. B. White, "One Man's Meat," *Harper's*, January 1941, pp. 217–18.

47. Frederick, *Primer of "New Deal" Economics*, p. 162.

48. Ellis Wayne Hawley, *The New Deal and the Problem of Monopoly* (Princeton, NJ: Princeton University Press, 1966), p. 484. Alongside the federal NIRA, states also established their own cartel systems, often through occupational licensing laws. J. A. C. Grant, "The Gild Returns to America," *Journal of Politics* 4, no. 3 (1942): 303–36 (part 1); *Journal of Politics* 4, no. 4 (1942): 458–77 (part 2).

49. Burton W. Folsom, *New Deal or Raw Deal?* (New York: Threshold Editions, 2008), p. 55.

50. Garet Garrett, "Plowing Up Freedom," *Saturday Evening Post*, November 16, 1935.

51. Folsom, *New Deal or Raw Deal?*, pp. 50–51.

52. Hadley Arkes, *The Return of George Sutherland* (Princeton, NJ: Princeton University Press, 1994), pp. 160–61.

53. Folsom, *New Deal or Raw Deal?*, p. 54.

54. Shesol, *Supreme Power*, p. 140.

55. Carol Gelderman, *Henry Ford: The Wayward Capitalist* (New York: Dial Press, 1981), p. 325.

56. Sidney Fine, *The Automobile under the Blue Eagle* (Ann Arbor: University of Michigan Press, 1963), pp. 80–81.

57. George Martin, *Madam Secretary: Frances Perkins* (Boston: Houghton Mifflin, 1976), p. 335.

58. John Kennedy Ohl, *Hugh S. Johnson and the New Deal* (DeKalb: Northern Illinois University Press, 1985), p. 106; Schivelbusch, *Three New Deals*, p. 203, n. 28.

59. Arthur M. Schlesinger, *The Coming of the New Deal* (Boston: Houghton Mifflin, 1988), p. 114.

60. "Johnson Urges Buying Drive," *Louisville Courier-Journal*, September 5, 1933.

61. Shlaes, *The Forgotten Man*, pp. 221–22.

62. Arkes, *Return of George Sutherland*, p. 85.

63. IMP, "Turns," April 2, 1933.

64. F. A. Hayek, "The Use of Knowledge in Society," *American Economic Review* 45, no. 4 (1945): 519–30.

65. IMP, letter to Burton Rascoe, ca. late 1933, in *Culture and Liberty: Writings of Isabel Paterson*, ed. Stephen Cox (New York: Transaction Publishers, 2015), p. 163.

66. IMP, "Turns," January 18, 1942.

67. IMP, "Turns," December 17, 1933.

68. Robert M. MacIver, "The Ambiguity of the New Deal," in *New Deal Thought*, ed. Howard Zinn (Indianapolis: Bobbs-Merrill, 1966), p. 60.

69. Fiorello LaGuardia, "Urban Support for the Farmer," in Zinn, *New Deal Thought*, p. 228.

70. Francis W. Coker, *Recent Political Thought* (New York: Appleton-Century-Crofts, 1934), p. 555.

71. IMP, "Turns," March 13, 1935.

72. David M. Kennedy, *Freedom from Fear* (New York: Oxford University Press, 2001), p. 209.

73. Howard Ball, *Hugo L. Black: Cold Steel Warrior* (New York: Oxford University Press, 1996), pp. 83–86; David T. Beito, "New Deal Mass Surveillance: The 'Black Inquisition Committee,' 1935–1936," *Journal of Policy History* 30, no. 2 (2018): 169–201.

74. *Hearst v. Black*, 87 F.2d 68, 70 (DC Cir. 1936).

75. Ball, *Hugo L. Black*, p. 85.

76. Senate Hearings, 75th Cong. 3rd sess., May 6, 1938, pp. 2188–89.

77. "Vallee Stockholder in 'Propaganda' Journal," *Honolulu Star-Bulletin*, May 6, 1938.

78. T. Harry Williams, *Huey Long* (New York: Knopf, 1969), pp. 795–98.

79. Frank Vazzano, "Harry Hopkins and Martin Davey: Federal Relief and Ohio Politics during the Great Depression," *Ohio History Journal* 96 (1987): 124–39; Christopher Ogden, *Legacy: A Biography of Moses and Walter Annenberg* (Boston: Little, Brown, 1999), chap. 13; David Beito, "FDR's War against the Press," *Reason*, May 2017; W. A. Swanberg, *Citizen Hearst* (New York: Bantam, 1963), p. 563; Robert Frederick Burk, *The Corporate State and the Broker State: The DuPonts and American National*

Politics, 1925–1940 (Cambridge, MA: Harvard University Press, 1990), p. 213; Shlaes, *The Forgotten Man*, pp. 189–96, 288–90.

80. Elliott Roosevelt and James Brough, *A Rendezvous with Destiny: The Roosevelts of the White House* (New York: Putnam, 1975), p. 102.

81. Shlaes, *The Forgotten Man*, p. 313; H. W. Brands, *A Traitor to His Class* (New York: Anchor Books, 2009), pp. 654–55; Jack Mitchell, *Executive Privilege* (New York: Hippocrene Books, 1992), pp. 169–82; Burton W. Folsom, "FDR and the IRS," Hillsdale College, Hillsdale, MI, 2006.

82. Ithiel de Sola Pool, *Technologies of Freedom* (Cambridge, MA: Harvard University Press, 1983), pp. 127–29.

83. Betty Houchin Winfield, *FDR and the News Media* (Urbana: University of Illinois Press, 1990), chap. 4. See also Gary Dean Best, *The Critical Press and the New Deal: The Press versus Presidential Power, 1933–1938* (Westport, CT: Praeger Press, 1993).

84. David Bradbury, *Armstrong* (London: Haus Publishing, 2003), p. 72; Guido van Rijn, *Roosevelt's Blues: African-American Blues and Gospel Songs on FDR* (Jackson: University of Mississippi Press, 1997), p. 89.

85. Schivelbusch, *Three New Deals*, p. 78 (quoting David Culbert) (emphasis in original); Winfield, *FDR and the News Media*, chap. 4.

86. Schivelbusch, *Three New Deals*, p. 99.

87. "Dr. Boyd Addresses Business Women's Club," *Nashville Banner*, September 29, 1933.

88. "Hubbs Speaks at Noon Meet at Valley Inn," *Daily News-Times* (Neenah, WI), September 25, 1935.

89. "The Community Spirit in Burlington: What it Means . . . What it Does!," *Daily Times-News* (Burlington, NC), July 31, 1933.

90. Gabrielle Esperdy, *Modernizing Main Street: Architecture and Consumer Culture in the New Deal* (Chicago: University of Chicago Press, 2008), p. 51.

91. Esperdy, *Modernizing Main Street*, p. 83.

92. Esperdy, *Modernizing Main Street*, p. 72.

93. Schlesinger, *Coming of the New Deal*, p. 115.

94. "Objectors to N.R.A. to Get Sock on Nose," *Daily Times-News* (Burlington, NC), July 29, 1933.

95. HLM, *A Carnival of Buncombe* (New York: Vintage Books, 1960), pp. 291–92.

96. HLM, *My Life as Author and Editor* (New York: Knopf, 1993), p. 386.

97. Terry Teachout, *The Skeptic: A Life of H. L. Mencken* (New York: Harper Collins, 2002), p. 7. Fred Hobson disputes the story, noting that the journalist actually took Roosevelt's teasing in good stride. But his articles thereafter certainly grew more personally bitter toward Roosevelt. Hobson, *Mencken*, pp. 383–84.

98. HLM, "Three Years of Dr. Roosevelt," *American Mercury*, March 1936.

99. "Rose Wilder Lane's Pioneers Face the West," *Kansas City Star*, February 25, 1933, p. 12; "When Courage Conquered," *Los Angeles Times*, March 5, 1933.

100. "Pioneering Problems Valiantly Attacked by Women in Ozarks," *Detroit Free Press*, February 8, 1933.

101. Clifton Fadiman, ed., *The Three Readers* (New York: Press of the Readers Club, 1943), p. 173. Publishers ultimately did not allow *Hurricane* to appear in *The Three Readers*. William Holtz, "Sinclair Lewis, Rose Wilder Lane, and the Midwestern Short Novel," *Studies in Short Fiction* 24, no. 1 (1987): 41–48.

102. RWL Diary, January 28, 1933, Lane Papers, Hoover Library. Lane's detractors, most notably historian Caroline Fraser, have seen evidence of treachery in this incident: that Lane had used her mother's *Pioneer Girl* material without permission. But that was not what Wilder objected to. She had no plans to use *Pioneer Girl* for an adult novel herself, and would have said so if she had. Rather, her objection was that Lane had fictionalized elements of the story—changing names, dates, and locales to suit the novel's demands—and fictionalizing was always a point of contention between the two women.

103. RWL Diary, June 2, 1933, Lane Papers, Hoover Library (emphasis in original).

104. RWL Diary, June 25, 1933, Lane Papers, Hoover Library (emphasis in original).

105. RWL Diary, May 26, 1933, Lane Papers, Hoover Library.

106. RWL, letter to DT, January 21, 1928, in *Dorothy Thompson and Rose Wilder Lane: Forty Years of Friendship*, ed. William Holtz (Columbia: University of Missouri Press, 1991), p. 69.

107. Richard O'Connor, *O. Henry: The Legendary Life of William S. Porter* (Garden City, NY: Doubleday, 1970), p. 232.

108. HLM, "Something New under the Sun," in *H. L. Mencken's Smart Set Criticism*, ed. William H. Nolte (Washington: Regnery Gateway, 1987), pp. 272–73.

109. Ray Lewis White, *Winesburg, Ohio: An Exploration* (Boston: Twayne Publishers, 1990), pp. 9–10, 88.

110. Sherwood Anderson, *A Story Teller's Story* (New York: Penguin, 1969), p. 119.

111. William Holtz, "Sherwood Anderson and Rose Wilder Lane," *Journal of Modern Literature* 12, no. 1 (1985): 142.

112. Holtz, "Anderson and Lane," p. 146. This was written in a letter to Anderson that Lane ended up not sending.

113. Holtz, "Anderson and Lane," p. 147.

114. Notably, Ernestine has the same surname that Lane gave to her previous fictional stand-in, Gordon Blake, in *He Was a Man*.

115. RWL, *Old Home Town*, p. 119.

116. RWL, *Old Home Town*, pp. 23–25.

117. RWL, *Old Home Town*, p. 286.

118. RWL, *Old Home Town*, p. 287.

119. William Holtz, "Rose Wilder Lane's *Old Home Town*," *Studies in Short Fiction* 26, no. 4 (1989): 486.

120. RWL, "Don't Send Your Son to College" (August 1938), in *The Rediscovered Writings of Rose Wilder Lane: Literary Journalist*, ed. Amy Mattson Lauters (Columbia: University of Missouri Press, 2007), pp. 106–7.

121. Lewis Gannett, "Books and Things," *NYHT*, January 3, 1936.

122. RWL, letter to DT, August 3, 1932, in Holtz, *Thompson and Lane*, p. 133 (emphasis in original).

123. IMP, "Turns," September 11, 1932.

124. This reevaluation of the small town in American popular culture is discussed in detail in Robert S. McElvaine, *The Great Depression* (New York: Times Books, 1993), especially chap. 9. McElvaine argues that films and novels of the era "reject[ed] the ethic of acquisitive individualism" in favor of "a society based more on cooperation" (p. 220). Lane's novels arguably fit this trend to some degree; however, Paterson's and Rand's clearly do not. More precisely, they viewed the New Deal itself as a manifestation of an even more cynical version of "acquisitiveness," and argued that the solution was an embrace of authentic individualism.

125. IMP, "Turns," March 18, 1934. Paterson herself had mixed feelings about *Little Women*, thinking that while it had "literary merits," it also "registered the emergence in the United States of the humanitarian philosophy which has plumb ruined the modern world. You can't help noticing that she saw no ethical values in any specifically productive effort—business, industry, or even farming—but only in endowed benevolences, spending an income to 'do good,' giving things away, or taking care of such fuzzy old incompetents as 'grandpa.' The rebellious independent youth was redeemed—heaven save us—by finally getting a bureaucratic government job." IMP, "Turns," May 5, 1946.

126. IMP, "Turns," April 1, 1928.

127. In a 1932 letter in *Harper's*, Lane observed that this agrarian ideal had been destroyed largely by taxes that had to be paid in cash. The farmer "must therefore turn one-fourth of his crop into money, or see his farm sold." RWL, "Editor's Easy Chair," *Harper's*, September 1932.

128. IMP, "Turns," June 11, 1933.

129. "Foolish Grasshoppers and Thrifty Ants," *Tampa Times*, June 8, 1934.

130. IMP, "Turns," May 21, 1933.

131. Fanny Butcher, "'Golden Vanity' Factual Story of Two Women," *Chicago Tribune*, November 17, 1934; "The Weekly Book Shelf," *Pittsburgh Post-Gazette*, November 3, 1934; IMP, *The Golden Vanity* (New Brunswick, NJ: Transaction Publishers, 2017), p. 219.

132. Raymond Moley, *The First New Deal* (New York: Harcourt, Brace & World, 1966), pp. 51–54; Frederick Vanderbilt Field, *From Right to Left: An Autobiography* (Westport, CT: L. Hill, 1983), p. 182. In "Turns," Paterson expressed her "mild wonder at Mr. Vincent Astor, publisher of *Today*, supporting an Administration which proposes to 'redistribute wealth.' We don't see why he should call upon the government to redistribute his wealth." IMP, "Turns," December 31, 1933.

133. IMP, *Golden Vanity*, pp. 85–86.

134. IMP, *Golden Vanity*, p. 175.

135. IMP, *Golden Vanity*, p. 176.

136. John Tauranac, *Empire State Building: The Making of a Landmark* (New York: St. Martin's Griffin, 1995), p. 267; Okrent, *Great Fortune*, p. 276.

137. IMP, *Golden Vanity*, pp. 229–30.

138. IMP, *Golden Vanity*, p. 233.

139. IMP, *Golden Vanity*, p. 189.

140. IMP, *Golden Vanity*, p. 262.

Chapter 5

1. Jerre Mangione, *The Dream and the Deal: The Federal Writers' Project, 1935–1943* (Boston: Little, Brown, 1972), p. 42.

2. Mangione, *The Dream and the Deal*, p. 43.

3. Mangione, *The Dream and the Deal*, p. 105.

4. Mangione, *The Dream and the Deal*, p. 177.

5. Zachary Leader, *The Life of Saul Bellow*, vol. 1, *To Fame and Fortune, 1915–1964* (New York: Knopf, 2015), p. 220.

6. Valerie Boyd, *Wrapped in Rainbows: The Life of Zora Neale Hurston* (New York: Scribner, 2003), p. 319.

7. Mangione, *The Dream and the Deal*, p. 99.

8. Daniel Aaron, *Writers on the Left: Episodes in American Literary Communism* (New York: Harcourt, Brace & World, 1961), p. 206.

9. Edwin Seaver, "The Proletarian Novel," in *American Writers' Congress*, ed. Henry Hart (New York: International Publishers, 1935), p. 215.

10. *Publishers Weekly*, September 3, 1932, p. 757; "Books: Bankster's Moll," *Time*, October 30, 1933; SL, "More about Neglected Books," *New Republic*, May 23, 1934; Herschel Brickell, "Tragedy in the Machine Age," *NYHT*, October 9, 1932.

11. IMP, "Turns with a Bookworm," *NYHT*, August 14, 1935.

12. IMP, *The Golden Vanity* (New Brunswick: Transaction Publishers, 2017), p. 110.

13. IMP, "Turns," May 27, 1934.

14. Andrew Nagorski, *Hitlerland: American Eyewitnesses to the Nazis Rise to Power* (New York: Simon & Schuster, 2012), p. 85.

15. DT, "Chromos over Germany," *NYHT*, August 9, 1937.

16. Nagorski, *Hitlerland*, p. 168.

17. Robert O. Paxton, *The Anatomy of Fascism* (New York: Vintage Books, 2004), pp. 142, 219.

18. DT, "Our Ghostly Commonwealth," *Saturday Evening Post*, July 27, 1935.

19. Peter Kurth, *American Cassandra: The Life of Dorothy Thompson* (Boston: Little, Brown, 1991), p. 208.

20. DT, "Are They Self Evident?," *NYHT*, June 27, 1936.

21. DT, "The President's Speech," *NYHT*, November. 2, 1936.

22. Kurth, *American Cassandra*, p. 207.

23. Harnett Thomas Kane, *Huey Long's Louisiana Hayride* (New York: Pelican, 1971), pp. 105–8.

24. Arthur M. Schlesinger Jr., *The Age of Roosevelt: The Politics of Upheaval* (New York: Houghton Mifflin, 1960), chap. 4.

25. DT, "Our Ghostly Commonwealth," *Saturday Evening Post*, July 27, 1935.

26. SL, *It Can't Happen Here* (Garden City, NY: Dial Press, 1935), p. 75.

27. Journalist Mark Sullivan devoted a column to the similarities between Windrip and Roosevelt. "Lewis's Book 'It Can't Happen Here' Seen as Warning That It Can—With Roosevelt Politics Paving the Way," *Lancaster (PA) New Era*, October 23, 1935. Other reviewers detected in Windrip echoes of Georgia governor Eugene Talmadge, the Daughters of the American Revolution, the American Federation of Labor, the American Legion, Warren Harding, and to such New Dealers as Rexford Tugwell and Harry Hopkins. Elmer Davis, "Ode to Liberty," *Saturday Review*, October 19, 1935, p. 5; Herschell Brickell, book review, *North American Review*, August 1935, pp. 543–45; "Farley Doesn't Miss a Thing," *Detroit Free Press*, October 30, 1936.

28. Mark Shorer, *Sinclair Lewis: An American Life* (New York: McGraw-Hill, 1961), p. 611 (emphasis in original).

29. IMP, "Turns," December 1, 1935.

30. Kay Halle, ed., *Winston Churchill on America and Britain* (New York: Walker, 1970), p. 286.

31. "Nazis, Fascists Pleased at Ban by Hays on Film of Lewis' Book," *Montreal Gazette*, February 17, 1936.

32. Ben Urwand, *The Collaboration: Hollywood's Pact with Hitler* (Cambridge, MA: Harvard University Press, 2013), pp. 175–76.

33. IMP, "Turns," November 8, 1936 (emphasis in original).

34. Richard Lingeman, *Sinclair Lewis: Rebel from Main Street* (New York: Random House, 2002), p. 411; Martin Light, *The Quixotic Vision of Sinclair Lewis* (West Lafayette, IN: Purdue University Press, 1975), p. 137.

35. Terry Teachout, "Cradle of Lies," *Commentary*, February 2000.

36. Caroline Fraser, *Prairie Fires: The American Dreams of Laura Ingalls Wilder* (New York: Metropolitan Books, 2017), p. 415.

37. Charles Higham, *Orson Welles: The Rise and Fall of an American Genius* (New York: St. Martin's Press, 1985), p. 99.

38. Malcolm Goldstein, *The Political Stage: American Drama and Theater of the Great Depression* (New York: Oxford University Press, 1974), pp. 53–54, 274–76.

39. No reference to this trend, for instance, is to be found in Peter Conn's *The American 1930s: A Literary History* (Cambridge: Cambridge University Press, 2009), Terry Cooney's *Balancing Acts: American Thought and Culture in the 1930s* (New York: Twayne Publishers, 1995), or Morris Dickstein's *Dancing in the Dark: A Cultural History of the Great Depression* (New York: W. W. Norton, 2009), none of which mention Lane, Laura Ingalls Wilder, Ellen Glasgow, Pearl Buck, Bess Streeter Aldrich, Marion Strobel, Jessica Nelson North, John Faulkner, or other individualistic or anti–New Deal writers. The sole exception is Dickstein's

discussion of Zora Neale Hurston in *Dancing in the Dark*, which nevertheless ignores her opposition to the New Deal. One good source on the subject is Jamie Hammack Smith, *A Criticism of Village Life as Seen in Novels and Tales of the Mid-West* (master's thesis, Boston University, 1939), but it antedates much of the relevant material.

40. Caroline Fraser, ed., *The Little House Books* (New York: Library of America, 2012), vol. 1, p. 297.

41. Hamlin Garland, *Main-Travelled Roads* (New York: Harper & Row, 1899), p. vi.

42. *Little House on the Prairie* has become controversial in recent years for its depiction of Native Americans. Wilder herself was sympathetic to the plight of Natives who had been chased off their land, and expressed that sympathy in her books. On one occasion, when a young reader objected that Wilder had written that there were no "people" on the prairie—thus subtly implying that Indians were not people—Wilder apologized immediately for the error and had it changed in future printings. Although in the novels, Wilder and Lane consistently depict Ma as fearing and hating Natives—a detail drawn from real life—they portray Pa as far less prejudiced. In any event, the novel was not intended as history, and important as the Osage characters are, the novel is not about the competing claims of Native or settler rights. Notwithstanding certain exaggerated claims to the contrary, the worst that can be said of the *Little House* novels is that they were written in an age before it would have occurred to Wilder and Lane to devote more attention to addressing such matters. Scholar John Miller claims that Wilder was "more enlightened in her thinking" than Lane regarding racial questions, but the reality is that Lane was quite advanced and outspoken in her hostility to any form of racism. Miller cites as proof of his claim the fact that Lane referred to Indians "as 'barbarians' who lived a 'communist' lifestyle," but at the time the term "barbarism" was used more as a synonym for primordialism than as a pejorative or an epithet (see, for instance, Charles and Mary Beard, *The Rise of American Civilization* [New York: Macmillan, 1927], vol. 1, p. 17). Even today, many writers claim that Natives lived a communist lifestyle. See, for example, Howard Zinn, *A People's History of the United States* (New York: Harper Perennial, 1999), chap. 1. On Lane and race, see David T. Beito and Linda Royster Beito, "Isabel Paterson, Rose Wilder Lane, and Zora Neale Hurston on War, Race, the State, and Liberty," *Independent Review* 12, no. 4 (2008): 553–73; RWL, letter to the editor, *American Mercury*, December 1938.

43. Bess Streeter Aldrich, *The Rim of the Prairie* (Lincoln: University of Nebraska Press, 1966), pp. 351–52.

44. IMP, "Turns," May 31, 1936.

45. IMP, "Turns," May 31, 1936.

46. AR, "The Inexplicable Personal Alchemy," in *The Return of the Primitive*, ed. Peter Schwartz (New York: Meridian, 1999), p. 122 (emphasis in original).

47. Friedrich Nietzsche, *Thus Spoke Zarathustra*, trans. Walter Kaufmann (New York: Viking, 1966), pp. 42–44.

48. AR, *Atlas Shrugged* (New York: Dutton, 1992), p. 1069.

49. Anne C. Heller, *Ayn Rand and the World She Made* (New York: Nan A. Talese/Doubleday, 2009), p. 35.

50. Heller, *Ayn Rand*, p. 38.

51. Vladimir Gsovski and Kazimierz Grzybowski, eds., *Government, Law and Courts in the Soviet Union and Eastern Europe* (London: Stevens, 1960), vol. 1, p. 212.

52. Timothy W. Luke, *Ideology and Soviet Industrialization* (Westport, CT: Greenwood Press, 1985), p. 115.

53. John Humphrey Noyes, *History of American Socialisms* (New York: Lippincott, 1870), p. 194.

54. IMP, "Turns," February 16, 1936.

55. Richard Pipes, *Russia under the Bolshevik Regime* (New York: Vintage Books, 1994), pp. 370–71.

56. Pipes, *Bolshevik Regime*, p. 419.

57. Pipes, *Bolshevik Regime*, pp. 394–96; Martin Malia, *The Soviet Tragedy* (New York: Free Press, 1994), chap. 5.

58. Sheila Fitzpatrick, *The Russian Revolution 1917–1932* (Oxford: Oxford University Press, 1984), pp. 103, 120.

59. Malia, *Soviet Tragedy*, pp. 168–69.

60. Heller, *Ayn Rand*, p. 42.

61. AR, "The Age of Envy," in *The Return of the Primitive*, ed. Peter Schwartz (New York: Meridian, 1999), p. 130.

62. Rick Davis, *Ibsen: Four Major Plays*, trans. Brian Johnson (Lyme, NH: Smith & Kraus, 1995), pp. 184–85.

63. Davis, *Ibsen*, p. 60.

64. Marlene Podritske and Peter Schwartz, *Objectively Speaking: Ayn Rand Interviewed* (Lanham, MD: Lexington Books, 2009), pp. 101–7.

65. Podritske and Schwartz, *Objectively Speaking*, p. 105.

66. Michael Meyer, *Ibsen: A Biography* (Garden City, NY: Doubleday, 1971), pp. 600–601; Leo Tolstoy, "What Is Religion?," in *The Complete Works of Leo Tolstoy*, ed. Leo Weiner (Boston: Dana Estes & Co., 1904), vol. 24, pp. 109–10.

67. DT, *The New Russia* (New York: Holt, 1928), pp. 218–19 (emphasis in original).

68. Heath Pearson, "Economics and Altruism at the *Fin de Siècle*," in *Worlds of Political Economy*, ed. Martin J. Daunton and Frank Trentmann (Basingstoke, UK: Palgrave Macmillan, 2004); Stefan Collini, *Public Moralists: Political Thought and Intellectual Life in Britain, 1850–1930* (Oxford: Clarendon Press, 1991); Thomas Dixon, *The Invention of Altruism: Making Moral Meanings in Victorian Britain* (Oxford: Oxford University Press, 2008); Katharina Metz, *The Language of Altruism in Late Nineteenth-Century America* (PhD diss., Free University of Berlin Graduate School of North American Studies, 2017); Richard Hofstadter, *The Age of Reform* (New York: Vintage, 1955), pp. 260,

281; John D. Buenker, John C. Burnham, and Robert M. Crunden, eds., *Progressivism* (Cambridge: Schenckman, 1977), pp. 17, 23.

69. Heller, *Ayn Rand*, p. 45.

70. AR, *We the Living* (New York: Signet, 1995), p. 201 (emphasis in original).

71. AR, "Inexplicable Personal Alchemy," p. 122.

72. IMP, "Turns," June 29, 1941.

73. Heller, *Ayn Rand*, p. 54.

74. Heller, *Ayn Rand*, p. 53.

75. David Harriman, ed., *Journals of Ayn Rand* (New York: Dutton, 1999), p. 8.

76. IMP, "Turns," May 31, 1936.

77. Tore Boeckmann, "*The Fountainhead* as a Romantic Novel," in *Essays on Ayn Rand's* The Fountainhead, ed. Robert Mayhew (Lanham, MD: Lexington Books, 2007), p. 130; Robert Mayhew, "Humor in *The Fountainhead*," in Mayhew, *Essays*, pp. 219–20; Shoshana Milgram, "Looking Up to Sinclair Lewis: Ayn Rand's Admiration for *It Can't Happen Here*" (Presentation, Objectivist Summer Conference, Newport Beach, CA, June 28, 2008).

78. AR, *The Art of Fiction* (New York: Plume, 2000), p. 18.

79. Podritske and Schwartz, *Objectively Speaking*, p. 105.

80. Stephen L. Tanner, "Sinclair Lewis and Fascism," *Studies in the Novel* 22, no. 1 (1990): 57–66.

81. Milgram, "Looking Up to Sinclair Lewis"; undated (1936) letter to SL, https://letters.aynrandarchives.org/document/105051 (emphasis in original). An edited version of this letter was published in Michael Berliner, "Thirteen Previously Unpublished Letters of Ayn Rand," *Objective Standard* 12, no. 4 (2017/18): 15. It is not known whether Rand ever sent this letter to Lewis.

82. SL, *It Can't Happen Here* (Garden City, NY: Doubleday, 1935), pp. 229–31 (emphasis added); Milgram, "Looking Up to Sinclair Lewis."

83. AR, undated letter to SL, https://letters.aynrandarchives.org/document/56734.

84. Harriman, ed., *Journals*, pp. 23–24 (emphasis in original).

85. Harriman, ed., *Journals*, p. 46.

86. Harriman, ed., *Journals*, p. 25 (emphasis in original). In recent years, critics have seized on Rand's notes to claim that she had an "erotic investment in death and destruction" (Lisa Duggan, *Mean Girl: Ayn Rand and the Culture of Greed* [Oakland: University of California Press, 2019], p. 4), or that she, and by implication her admirers, were or are psychopaths (Johann Hari, "How Ayn Rand Became an American Icon," *Slate*, November 2, 2009, https://slate.com/culture/2009/11/two-biographies-of-ayn-rand.html). Of course, Rand was not glorifying the actual murderer who inspired the idea for the story. Robert Tracinski, "Anti-Ideal: A Critic of Ayn Rand's 'Lost' Novel Proves Her Point," *The Federalist*, July 22, 2015. Writers of all persuasions have used murderers as characters for any number of reasons. This includes Hugo and Dostoyevsky, two of Rand's favorites. During the

Depression, particularly, gangsters and murderers were common literary devices. Dickstein, *Dancing in the Dark*, p. 313. Theodore Dreiser's *An American Tragedy* in 1925, John Steinbeck's *Of Mice and Men* in 1937, Richard Wright's *Native Son* in 1940, and any number of other novels employed similar motifs during the period. Lisa Duggan, the author of *Mean Girls*, even published an entire book exploring the way murder stories have played a role in transcending the "cultural narrative" and "engag[ing] a more thoroughgoing critical examination of the material institutions and cultural inequalities" within society. Lisa Duggan, *Sapphic Slashers: Sex, Violence, and American Modernity* (Durham, NC: Duke University Press, 2000), pp. 4–5. Both the unwritten *Little Street* and *TF* make a particularly fruitful contrast with *Native Son*. In both, the character commits a crime as a form of rebellion against society, only to be tried in a highly publicized trial that climaxes in a long, philosophical speech. In Wright's novel, being a proletarian novel, the reader is led to the conclusion that the murderer, Bigger Thomas, killed as a consequence of social circumstances over which he had no control. Rand's novel takes the opposite position—regarding the individual as responsible for his own acts—and as having a right to that responsibility.

87. AR, letter to Jean Wick, August 20, 1934, in *Letters of Ayn Rand*, ed. Michael S. Berliner (New York: Dutton, 1995), p. 15.

88. Frank Partnoy, *The Match King: Ivar Kreuger, the Financial Genius behind a Century of Wall Street Scandals* (New York: PublicAffairs, 2009), p. 225; Håkan Lindgren, "The Kreuger Crash of 1932: In Memory of a Financial Genius, or Was He a Simple Swindler?," *Scandinavian Economic History Review* 30, no. 3 (2011): 189–206.

89. IMP, "Turns," October 30, 1032 (emphasis in original).

90. AR, *Night of January 16th* (New York: Penguin, 1971), p. 10.

91. Trevor Allen, *Ivar Kreuger: Match King, Croesus, and Crook* (London: J. Long, 1932), pp. 90, 141.

92. William Archer, ed., *The Collected Works of Henrik Ibsen* (New York: Charles Scribner's Sons, 1907), vol. 11, p. 318.

93. SL, *Main Street*, p. 374.

94. AR, *Ideal* (New York: New American Library, 2015), pp. 40–41.

95. AR, *Night of January 16th*, p. 120.

96. AR, *Night of January 16th*, p. 120.

97. *TF*, p. xi.

98. AR, *Night of January 16th*, p. 8.

99. AR, letter to Jean Wick, October 27, 1934, in Berliner, *Letters*, p. 19.

100. AR, letter to Jean Wick, March 23, 1934, in Berliner, *Letters*, p. 4 (emphasis in original).

101. AR, *Philosophy: Who Needs It*, p. 9.

102. DT, *The New Russia*, pp. 32–36, 40.

103. E. E. Cummings, *Eimi* (New York: Liveright, 2007), p. 129.

104. AR, *We the Living*, p. 373.

105. Such passports, or *propiski*, were not documents for international travel, but were "labor books," used as all-purpose licensing books, and were required for everything from obtaining a job to finding a residence. See Timothy Sandefur, *The Permission Society* (New York: Encounter Books, 2016), pp. 42–45.

106. AR, *We the Living*, pp. 43–45. The passage makes a striking parallel with two others: one in which Andrei's funeral is similarly contrasted with the details of his individual personality, and another in which Rand provides a backstory for the guard who shoots Kira—thus highlighting the novel's theme of individualism as opposed to the anonymity and uniformity imposed by collectivism.

107. AR, *We the Living*, p. 297.

108. AR, *We the Living*, pp. 136–37.

109. AR, *We the Living*, p. 440.

110. AR, letter to John Temple Graves, July 5, 1934, in Berliner, *Letters*, p. 33.

111. AR, *We the Living*, p. 89 (emphasis in original).

112. AR, *We the Living*, p. 404.

113. Robert Mayhew, "*We the Living*, '36 and '59," in Mayhew, *Essays*, p. 209.

114. AR, letter to Archibald Ogden, August 16, 1943, in Berliner, *Letters*, p. 10.

115. AR, letters to HLM, July 28, 1934, and August 8, 1934, in Berliner, *Letters*, pp. 13–14.

116. AR, letter to Gouverneur Morris, April 14, 1936, in Berliner, *Letters*, p. 27; Harold Strauss, "Soviet Triangle," *New York Times Book Review*, April 19, 1936, p. 7; Ben Bellitt, "The Red and the White," *The Nation*, April 22, 1936, pp. 522–24.

117. Ruth M. Allaben, "Books," *Binghamton (NY) Press*, May 23, 1936. Another review commented: "Miss Rand writes like a man. . . . Miss Rand is proud of that. She makes no secret of her belief that too often the creative offspring of women are afflicted with inherent sentimentality." Jack Stinnett, "As a New Yorker Sees Things," *Rochester Democrat and Chronicle*, May 21, 1936; Mayhew, *Essays*, pp. 139–43.

118. IMP, "Turns," May 31, 1936.

119. IMP, "Turns," April 26, 1936.

120. Kent Blaser, "*The Rise of American Civilization* and the Contemporary Crisis in American Historiography," *The History Teacher* 26, no. 1 (1992): 71–90.

121. Beard and Beard, *Rise*, vol. 1, p. 126.

122. American Historical Association, *Conclusions and Recommendations of the Commission on the Social Studies* (New York: Charles Scribner's Sons, 1934), p. 16.

123. Louis Hacker, "The Anticapitalist Bias of American Historians," in *Capitalism and the Historians*, ed. F. A. Hayek (Chicago: University of Chicago Press, 1954), p. 79.

124. Jack P. Greene, ed. *The Reinterpretation of the American Revolution, 1763–1789* (New York: Harper & Row, 1968); Richard Hofstadter, "Beard and the Constitution: The History of an Idea," *American Quarterly* 2 (1950): 195–212; Douglas Adair, "The Tenth Federalist Revisited," *William &*

Mary Quarterly 8 (1951): 48–67; Forrest McDonald, *We the People: The Economic Origins of the Constitution* (Chicago: University of Chicago Press, 1958).

125. Beard and Beard, *Rise*, vol. 1, pp. 291, 295.

126. Beard and Beard, *Rise*, vol. 2, p. 800.

127. Beard and Beard, *Rise*, vol. 1, p. 535.

128. *NECRB*, July 1948.

129. William Holtz, *The Ghost in the Little House* (Columbia: University of Missouri Press, 1995), p. 259.

130. IMP, "Turns," July 10, 1932.

131. RWL Diary, May 28, 1933, Lane Papers, Hoover Library.

132. RWL Diary, June 28, 1933, Lane Papers, Hoover Library.

133. "Wheat and the Great American Desert," *Saturday Evening Post*, September 23, 1933.

134. Wolfgang Schivelbusch, *Three New Deals: Reflections on Roosevelt's America, Mussolini's Italy, and Hitler's Germany*, 1933–1939 (New York: Picador, 2006), chap. 4.

135. Paul Conkin, *Tomorrow a New World* (Ithaca, NY: American Historical Association, 1957), p. 6.

136. Folsom, *New Deal or Raw Deal?*, p. 70.

137. *Township Franklin v. Tugwell*, 85 F.2d 208, 222 (DC Cir. 1936).

138. Roger Lea MacBride, ed., *The Lady and the Tycoon: The Best of Letters between Rose Wilder Lane and Jasper Crane* (Caldwell, ID: Caxton Printers, 1973), p. 168.

139. MacBride, *Lady and the Tycoon*, p. 169 (emphasis in original).

140. Garet Garett, "Plowing up Freedom," *Saturday Evening Post*, November 16, 1935.

141. Bruce Ramsey, *Unsanctioned Voice: Garet Garrett, Journalist of the Old Right* (Caldwell, ID: Caxton Press, 2009), p. 185.

142. MacBride, *Lady and the Tycoon*, p. 125. A persistent legend, recounted by Justin Raimondo in *Reclaiming the American Right: The Lost Legacy of the Conservative Movement* (Burlingame, CA: Center for Libertarian Studies, 1993), tells that Rand's *Atlas Shrugged* borrowed heavily from a novel Garrett published in 1922 called *The Driver*. Although there are some similarities, most notably the fact that the heroes of both novels have the last name Galt, the two books are so different as to belie much if any relationship, as Garrett's biographer notes. Ramsey, *Unsanctioned Voice*, pp. 115–17.

143. Frederick Jackson Turner, *The Frontier in American History* (New York: Henry Holt & Co., 1940), pp. 37–38.

144. *Public Papers of the Presidents: Franklin Roosevelt* (New York: Random House, 1940), p. 752.

145. FDR, *Looking Forward* (New York: John Day, 1933), pp. 49–50.

146. Fraser, *Prairie Fires*, p. 374.

147. "Johnson Urges Buying Drive," *Louisville (KY) Courier-Journal*, September 5, 1933.

148. Beard and Beard, *Rise*, vol. 1, pp. 648, 751–52.

149. Beard and Beard, *Rise*, vol. 2, pp. 247–53.

150. Garet Garrett, *The American Omen* (New York: Dutton, 1928), p. 192.

151. *NECRB*, November 1945.

152. RWL, "Keeping Posted," *Saturday Evening Post*, March 5, 1938.

153. Fraser, *Little House Books*, vol. 2, p. 138.

154. RWL, "Credo," *Saturday Evening Post*, March 7, 1936.

155. RWL, *Give Me Liberty* (New York: Longman's, 1936), p. 14.

156. RWL, *Give Me Liberty*, p. 13.

157. RWL, *Give Me Liberty*, p. 25.

158. RWL, *Give Me Liberty*, pp. 25–26.

159. RWL, *Give Me Liberty*, pp. 32–33.

160. RWL, *Give Me Liberty*, pp. 41–45 (emphasis added).

161. RWL, *Give Me Liberty*, p. 47.

Chapter 6

1. IMP, "Turns with a Bookworm," *NYHT*, June 7, 1936.

2. Thomas Fleming, *The New Dealers' War* (New York: Basic Books, 2002), p. 58.

3. Lester Vernon Chandler, *America's Greatest Depression, 1929–1941* (New York: Harper & Row, 1970), pp. 129, 137.

4. Chandler, *America's Greatest Depression*, p. 129; U.S. Department of Commerce, *National Income and Product of the United States, 1929–1950* (Washington: Government Printing Office, 1951), p. 146.

5. Amity Shlaes, *The Forgotten Man: A New History of the Great Depression* (New York: Harper Perennial, 2008), p. 266.

6. DT, "Let Us Be Thankful!," *NYHT*, November 4, 1936. Thompson wrote this column before the election, although it was published after.

7. Donald R. McCoy, *Landon of Kansas* (Lincoln: University of Nebraska Press, 1966), p. 319.

8. McCoy, *Landon of Kansas*, pp. 343–44.

9. HLM, *A Carnival of Buncombe* (New York: Vintage Books, 1960), p. 329.

10. McCoy, *Landon of Kansas*, pp. 342–43.

11. William Holtz, *The Ghost in the Little House* (Columbia: University of Missouri Press, 1995), p. 271.

12. Fleming, *New Dealers' War*, p. 58.

13. DT, "President at Crossroads," *NYHT*, November 6, 1936.

14. *Nebbia v. New York*, 291 U.S. 502 (1934); *Home Building and Loan v. Blaisdell*, 209 U.S. 398 (1934).

15. Elliott Roosevelt, ed., *FDR: His Personal Letters 1928–1945* (New York: Duell, Sloan & Pearce, 1947), vol.1, pp. 456–60.

16. *Norman v. Baltimore & Ohio Railroad Co.*, 294 U.S. 240 (1935); *Nortz v. United States*, 294 U.S. 317 (1935); *Perry v. United States*, 294 U.S. 330 (1935).

17. *A.L.A. Schechter Poultry Corp. v. United States*, 295 U.S. 495 (1935).

18. *United States v. Butler*, 297 U.S. 1 (1936).

19. Ira Katznelson, *Fear Itself: The New Deal and the Origins of Our Time* (New York: Liveright, 2013), pp. 178–79.

20. Ellis Wayne Hawley, *The New Deal and the Problem of Monopoly* (Princeton, NJ: Princeton University Press, 1966), p. 130.

21. IMP, "Turns," December 6, 1936.

22. IMP, "Security Act Apologist Asked How Deficit Can Be Investment," *NYHT*, August 29, 1938.

23. Stephen Cox, *The Woman and the Dynamo: Isabel Paterson and the Idea of America* (New Brunswick, NJ: Transaction Publishers, 2004), p. 325. In recent years, it has become fashionable to criticize Rand for accepting Social Security payments in old age, on the grounds that this represented hypocrisy on her part. Rand, however, addressed the question in a 1966 essay called "The Question of Scholarships" (*Objectivist Newsletter*, June 1966). In her view, it was legitimate to accept payments from government programs because "Whenever the welfare-state laws offer them some small restitution, *the victims should take it*." To do otherwise would only constitute "self-inflicted martyrdom" that would "let the looters profit doubly, by letting them distribute the money exclusively to the parasites who clamored for it."

24. James Holt, "The New Deal and the American Anti-Statist Tradition," in *The New Deal*, ed. Robert H. Bremner and David Brody (Columbus: Ohio State University Press, 1975), vol. 1, pp. 27–49.

25. David M. Kennedy, *Freedom from Fear* (New York: Oxford University Press, 2001), p. xiv.

26. IMP, "Turns," May 28, 1933.

27. Alan Brinkley, *The End of Reform: New Deal Liberalism in Recession and War* (New York: Knopf, 1995), pp. 131–36.

28. Howard Zinn, ed., *New Deal Thought* (Indianapolis: Bobbs-Merrill, 1966), p. 10.

29. Zinn, *New Deal Thought*, p. 60.

30. Joseph P. Kennedy, *I'm for Roosevelt* (New York: Reynal & Hitchcock, 1936), p. 110.

31. Kennedy, *I'm for Roosevelt*, p. 14.

32. Caroline Fraser, ed., *The Little House Books* (New York: Library of America, 2012), vol. 1, pp. 583–84.

33. Jeffrey Lockwood, *Locust* (New York: Basic Books), p. 21.

34. Pamela Smith Hill, ed., *Pioneer Girl: The Annotated Autobiography* (Pierre: South Dakota Historical Society Press, 2014), p. 81.

35. Annette Atkins, *Harvest of Grief: Grasshopper Plagues and Public Assistance in Minnesota, 1873–1878* (St. Paul: Minnesota Historical Society Press, 1984), chap. 5.

36. William Anderson, ed., *The Selected Letters of Laura Ingalls Wilder* (New York: Harper, 2016), p. 120.

37. Holtz, *Ghost*, p. 270.

38. Holtz, *Ghost*, p. 268.

39. Holtz, *Ghost*, p. 268.

40. RWL Diary, April 7 and April 16, 1937, Lane Papers, Hoover Library.

41. Robert S. McElvaine, *The Great Depression: America 1929–1941* (New York: Three Rivers Press, 2009), p. 298.

42. Brinkley, *End of Reform*, p. 30.

43. Amity Shlaes, *The Forgotten Man*, rev. ed. (New York: Harper Perennial, 2008), p. 395.

44. *NLRB v. Jones & Laughlin Steel Corp.*, 301 U.S. 1 (1937).

45. Folsom, *New Deal or Raw Deal?*, pp. 120–21.

46. Robert H. Zieger, *American Workers, American Unions, 1920–1985* (Baltimore: Johns Hopkins University Press, 1986), pp. 48–49.

47. Thomas R. Brooks, *Picket Lines and Bargaining Tables: Organized Labor Comes of Age, 1933–1955* (New York: Grosset & Dunlap, 1968), p. 107; Robert Shogan, *Backlash: The Killing of the New Deal* (Chicago: Ivan R. Dee, 2006), pp. 193–94. A subsequent investigation by a labor-friendly Senate committee, chaired by the far-left senator Robert La Follette Jr., laid the blame on the Chicago police.

48. Gene Smiley, *Rethinking the Great Depression* (Chicago: Ivan R. Dee, 2002), p. 122.

49. Richard Vedder and Lowell Gallaway, *Out of Work, Unemployment and Government in Twentieth-Century America* (New York: New York University Press, 1997), p. 141.

50. IMP, "Politics Called Only Sure Gainer with Any Sort of Wagner Act," *NYHT*, June 8, 1938.

51. IMP, "Take Two Chairs," *NYHT*, January 20, 1937.

52. A court later ruled the administration's acts unlawful, but that decision was reversed on appeal. In the interim, the government's actions proved so politically unpopular that the administration backed down and allowed Avery to resume his post. Richard Polenberg, *War and Society: The United States 1941–1945* (New York: Lippincott, 1972), pp. 171–76.

53. IMP, "Politics Called Only Sure Gainer."

54. IMP, "Turns," July 23, 1939.

55. IMP, "Turns," September 17, 1939.

56. Jim Powell, *FDR's Folly: How Roosevelt and His New Deal Prolonged the Great Depression* (New York: Three Rivers Press, 2003), p. 80.

57. Powell, *FDR's Folly*, pp. ix–x.

58. Benjamin M. Anderson, *Economics and the Public Welfare: Financial and Economic History of the United States, 1914–1946* (Princeton, NJ: Van Nostrand, 1949), p. 374.

59. Kennth D. Roose, *The Economics of Recession and Revival: An Interpretation of 1937–38* (New Haven, CT: Yale University Press, 1969), p. 228.

60. Brinkley, *End of Reform*, pp. 56–58.

61. James A. Farley, *Jim Farley's Story: The Roosevelt Years* (New York: McGraw-Hill, 1948), p. 101.

62. Farley, *Jim Farley's Story*, pp. 106–7.

63. "Big Business Seeks U.S. Control in Capital Strike, Says Atty. General Aide," *Hartford (CT) Sentinel*, December 29, 1937; "Capital on Strike, Jackson Charges," *New York Daily News*, December 30, 1937.

64. "Ickes Lashes at Big Business," *Boston Globe*, December 31, 1937.

65. FDR, address at the Jackson Day Dinner, January 8, 1938, *Public Papers of the Presidents: Franklin D. Roosevelt* (New York: Macmillan, 1941), vol. 7, pp. 44–45.

66. Brinkley, *End of Reform*, pp. 56–58.

67. McElvaine, *The Great Depression*, pp. 298–99.

68. Michael Janeway, *The Fall of the House of Roosevelt: Brokers of Ideas and Power from FDR to LBJ* (New York: Columbia University Press, 2004), p. 93.

69. Paul K. Conkin, *The New Deal* (New York: Crowell, 1967), pp. 96–97.

70. Rexford Tugwell, *The Industrial Discipline and the Governmental Arts* (New York: Columbia University Press, 1933), p. 202; Arthur Feiler, "Conscription of Capital," *Social Research* 8, no. 1 (1941): 1–23.

71. Arthur O. Dahlberg, *When Capital Goes on Strike: How to Speed Up Spending* (New York: Harper & Bros. 1938), p. 190.

72. IMP, "Turns," September 17, 1939.

73. "Mrs. Roosevelt Favors Forcing Youth to Train," *NYHT*, June 4, 1940; Britt Haas, *Fighting Authoritarianism: American Youth Activism in the 1930s* (New York: Fordham University Press, 2018), p. 228; Blanche Wiesen Cook, *Eleanor Roosevelt*, vol. 3, *The War Years and After, 1939–1962* (New York: Viking, 2016), pp. 54–55.

74. "First Lady Denies Fascism in Compulsory Work Camps if Established by Congress," *Cincinnati Enquirer*, December 29, 1940.

75. Nicola Pizzolato, "State Sanctioned Coercion and Agricultural Contract Labor," in *On Coerced Labor: Work and Compulsion after Chattel Slavery*, ed. Marcel van der Linden and Magaly Rodríguez García (Lieden: Brill, 2016), p. 212; Evelyn Nakano Glenn, *Unequal Freedom: How Race and Gender Shaped American Citizenship and Labor* (Cambridge, MA: Harvard University Press, 2002).

76. Elaine Elinson, *Wherever There's a Fight* (Berkeley, CA: Heyday Books, 2009), p. 400.

77. U.S. National Youth Administration, *Final Report of the National Youth Administration: Fiscal Years 1936–1943* (Washington: Government Printing Office, 1944), pp. 2–8.

78. Jim Warren and Kathleen Carlisle, *On the Side of the People: A History of Labour in Saskatchewan* (Regina: Coteau Books, 2005), pp. 95–96.

79. "CCC Likened to Austria's Work Camps," *Hartford (CT) Courant*, June 20, 1937.

80. DT, "A Job for Youth," *Ladies' Home Journal*, February 1940, p. 2. Then again, during negotiations with her employers for a raise, DT was quick to assert that "nobody can be held to compulsory labor." Peter Kurth, *American Cassandra: The Life of Dorothy Thompson* (Boston: Little, Brown, 1990), p. 252.

81. IMP, "Turns," February 18, 1940.

82. David Lynch, *The Concentration of Economic Power* (New York: Columbia University Press, 1946), p. 337.

83. This incident is detailed in Kim McQuaid, *Big Business and Presidential Power: From FDR to Reagan* (New York: Morrow, 1982).

84. IMP, "Key Sought to New Deal Riddle of Steel, Stocks, Wages, Prices," *NYHT*, June 29, 1938.

85. IMP, "Capital Is on Strike," *NYHT*, May 25, 1938.

86. Marc Levinson, *The Great A&P and the Struggle for Small Business in America* (New York: Will & Wang, 2011), pp. 110–71.

87. Gabrielle Esperdy, *Modernizing Main Street: Architecture and Consumer Culture in the New Deal* (Chicago: University of Chicago Press, 2008), p. 28.

88. "Chain Store Fight Opened by Congressman Halleck in Two Addresses Here," *Indiana (PA) Weekly Messenger*, April 30, 1936.

89. DT, "The Cracker-Barrel Bill," *NYHT*, May 5, 1936. Mussolini's government had imposed strikingly similar restrictions a decade earlier. Jonathan Morris, "Retailers, Fascism, and the Origins of the Social Protection of Shopkeepers in Italy," *Contemporary European History* 5, no. 3 (1996): 285–318.

90. Thurman Arnold, *Symbols of Government* (New Haven, CT: Yale University Press, 1935), pp. 232–33; Thurman Arnold, *The Folklore of Capitalism* (New Haven, CT: Yale University Press, 1937), p. 115.

91. Arnold, *Folklore*, p. 170.

92. Arnold, *Folklore*, p. 23 (emphasis in original).

93. Arnold, *Folklore*, p. 188.

94. Arnold, *Folklore*, p. 189.

95. Arnold, *Folklore*, pp. 391–92.

96. Arnold, *Folklore*, p. 153.

97. IMP, "Turns," February 13, 1938.

98. IMP, "Turns," March 20, 1938.

99. McQuaid, *Big Business*, pp. 11–16.

100. Stephen B. Adams, *Mr. Kaiser Goes to Washington: The Rise of a Government Entrepreneur* (Chapel Hill: University of North Carolina Press, 1997), pp. 101–2.

101. IMP, "Monopolies with Competition New Wrinkle in Changing Law," *NYHT*, June 1, 1938.

102. IMP, "Turns," May 28, 1933.

103. IMP, "Turns," May 28, 1933.

104. IMP, "Turns," November 17, 1935.

105. Earl Reeves et al., *Truth about the New Deal* (New York: Longmans, Green, 1936), p. 80.

106. Stewart Utley, *The American System: Shall We Destroy It?* (Detroit: Speaker-Hines Press, 1936), p. 282.

107. IMP, "Turns," November 17, 1935.

108. IMP, "Turns," November 17, 1935.

109. "On Hands and Knees," *Sioux City (IA) Journal*, June 12, 1938.

110. IMP, "Notes on President's Vocabulary, Particularly anent Opposition," *NYHT*, June 6, 1938.

111. B. C. Forbes, "Courage Is Need of Businessmen," *Philadelphia Inquirer*, May 26, 1938.

112. Wendell Willkie, "Brace Up, America!," *Atlantic Monthly*, June 1939, pp. 749–56.

113. "Morgenthau Tells Business to Abandon 'What's-the-Use' Attitude," *Vancouver Sun*, February 23, 1939.

114. W. Anderson, *Selected Letters*, pp. 114–15. Not everyone saw individualism in retreat, however. Paterson, Lane, Rand, and Wilder would likely have been amused at the dismay with which leftist social planners Robert and Helen Lynd reported that in "Middletown," both the working class and the business class appeared as devoted to individualism as ever. "These people were convincing themselves, with the aid of such things as the *Saturday Evening Post*'s articles . . . that they would already have been on the march long since toward the businessman's New Jerusalem, thanks to 'natural forces' had it not been for the meddling Roosevelt administration which seeks to 'ruin the country.'" Robert Lynd and Helen Merrell Lynd, *Middletown in Transition* (New York: Harvest, 1937), p. 473.

115. Nasaw, *The Chief*, p. 181.

116. Nasaw, *The Chief*, p. 500.

117. Nasaw, *The Chief*, p. 502.

118. Nasaw, *The Chief*, p. 507.

119. Nasaw, *The Chief*, p. 512.

120. Nasaw, *The Chief*, p. 506; W. A. Swanberg, *Citizen Hearst: A Biography of William Randolph Hearst* (New York: Collier, 1961), p. 565.

121. Nasaw, *The Chief*, p. 548.

122. Ben H. Procter, *William Randolph Hearst: The Later Years, 1911–1951* (New York: Oxford University Press 2007), p. 204; Elliott Roosevelt and James Brough, *A Rendezvous with Destiny: The Roosevelts of the White House* (New York: Putnam, 1975), p. 102.

123. Procter, *William Randolph Hearst: The Later Years*, pp. 206–16.

124. IMP, letter to Burton Rascoe, ca. late 1933, in *Culture and Liberty: Writings of Isabel Paterson*, ed. Stephen Cox (New York: Transaction Publishers, 2015), p. 164 (emphasis in original).

125. Kurth, *American Cassandra*, p. 215.

126. Mirra Komarovsky, *The Unemployed Man and His Family* (New York: Dryden, 1940); Winona Morgan, *The Family Meets the Depression* (Minneapolis: University of Minnesota Press, 1939). Other prairie novelists, notably Bess Streeter Aldrich, used their stories to explore the meaning of masculinity. Nicholas J. Karolides, *The Pioneer in the American Novel, 1900–1950* (Norman: University of Oklahoma Press, 1967), pp. 96–97.

127. RWL, *Free Land* (Lincoln: University of Nebraska Press, 1984), p. 7.

128. RWL, *Free Land*, p. 135.

129. RWL, *Free Land*, p. 146.

130. RWL, *Free Land*, p. 267.

131. RWL, *Free Land*, pp. 92–93.

132. RWL, *Free Land*, p. 281.

133. RWL, *Free Land*, pp. 176–77.

134. RWL, *Free Land*, p. 328.

135. RWL, *Free Land*, p. 300.

136. RWL, *Free Land*, p. 332.

137. RWL, *Free Land*, p. 331.

138. Julia C. Ehrhardt, *Writers of Conviction: The Personal Politics of Zona Gale, Dorothy Canfield Fisher, Rose Wilder Lane, and Josephine Herbst* (Columbia: University of Missouri Press, 2004), p. 133.

139. RWL, "Don't Send Your Son to College," in *The Rediscovered Writings of Rose Wilder Lane*, ed. Amy Mattson Lauters (Columbia: University of Missouri Press, 2007), p. 107.

140. Caroline Fraser, *Prairie Fires* (New York: Henry Holt & Co. 2010), p. 402.

141. Fraser, *Prairie Fires*, p. 163.

142. Thomas J. Schoenberg and Lawrence J. Trudeau, eds., *Twentieth-Century Literary Criticism* (Farmington Hills, MI: Cengage Gale, 2006), vol. 177, p. 265.

143. Lane herself responded to *New York Times* critic Fred T. Marsh, who pointed to the Wilder family's failure as evidence that *Free Land* was false history. "Is he perhaps too young to know what optimism is? I would like to remind him of the lines that someone—[Walter] Pater?—says were discovered on a forgotten gravestone on one of the Greek islands: 'A ship-wrecked sailor, buried on this coast / Bids you set sail. / Full many a gallant ship when we were lost / Weathered the gale.'" *New York Times Book Review*, June 5, 1938, p. 24.

144. Fraser, *Prairie Fires*, p. 163.

145. RWL, "American Revolution 1939," *Saturday Evening Post*, January 7, 1939.

146. RWL, *Give Me Liberty* (New York: Longman's, 1936), p. 26; Christine Woodside, *Libertarians on the Prairie* (New York: Arcade Publishing, 2016), p. 119.

147. Fraser, *Prairie Fires*, p. 402.

148. RWL, *Free Land*, p. 9.

149. RWL, *Free Land*, p. 39.

150. IMP, letter to AR, ca. March 7, 1944, IMP Papers, Hoover Library, p. 43.

151. IMP, letter to AR, ca. February 17, 1944, IMP Papers, Hoover Library, p. 37; IMP, letter to AR, ca. March 7, 1944, Hoover Library, p. 43.

152. IMP, *Never Ask the End* (New York: Literary Guild, 1933), p. 242.

153. RWL, undated letter to AR (143-LN3-012-002), ARI Papers.

154. IMP, "Turns," May 22, 1938.

155. "Thumbnail Reviews," *Pittsburgh Press*, May 22, 1938; "The True Salt of Our Nation," *Philadelphia Inquirer*, May 14, 1938; "Stirring Reality Given to Story of Pioneers," *Chicago Tribune*, May 7, 1938; Ralph Thompson, "Books of the Times," *New York Times*, May 4, 1938.

156. IMP, "Turns," June 19, 1938 (emphasis added).

157. Emma Bugbee, "Rose Wilder Lane Settles Down on Connecticut Farm—For a While," *NYHT*, June 6, 1938.

158. Holtz, *Ghost*, p. 286.

159. IMP, "Turns," September 8, 1940.

160. IMP, "Turns," March 7, 1937.

161. IMP, "Turns," July 24, 1938.

162. IMP, *The Golden Vanity* (New Brunswick, NJ: Transaction Publishers, 2017), p. 219.

163. IMP, *If It Prove Fair Weather* (New York: G. P. Putnam's Sons, 1940), p. 275.

164. IMP, *Fair Weather*, p. 276.

165. IMP, *Fair Weather*, p. 58.

166. Naomi Bender, "Love under the Microscope," *Miami Herald*, September 1, 1940.

167. Fred G. Hyde, "Love Affair, Analyzed," *Philadelphia Inquirer*, September 4, 1940.

168. "Intelligent Woman's Book Disappoints," *Hartford (CT) Courant*, September 1, 1940.

169. IMP, "As the Author Sees It," *Saturday Review*, September 7, 1940, p. 10.

170. The reference to "twenty years ago" was likely an allusion to the case of Bertrand Russell, who only months before Paterson's novel was published was declared "morally unfit" to teach at the City University of New York in a trial that filled headlines in New York City. The accusation originated partly from Russell's widely published views regarding sexual freedom, as well as his 1921 divorce. Ray Monk, *Bertrand Russell: The Ghost of Madness, 1921–1970* (New York: Free Press, 2001), p. 237. But other scandalous examples in the twenties may have also been on her mind: in 1919, William Randolph Hearst separated from his wife and lived openly with his mistress Marion Davies. In 1922, Frank Lloyd Wright was finally granted a divorce, years after he abandoned his family to carry on an affair with a client's wife.

171. IMP, "As the Author Sees It," p. 10.

172. IMP, *Fair Weather*, p. 284.

173. IMP, *Fair Weather*, p. 284.

174. IMP, "Turns," July 16, 939 (quoting Colum's "The Deer of Ireland").

175. Deirdre McCloskey, "Bourgeois Virtues," *American Scholar* 63, no. 2 (1994): 177–91.

176. IMP, "Turns," July 16, 1939.

177. RWL, "American Revolution 1939," *Saturday Evening Post*, January 7, 1939.

178. RWL, letter to DT, October 15, 1938, in *Dorothy Thompson and Rose Wilder Lane: Forty Years of Friendship*, ed. William Holtz (Columbia: University of Missouri Press, 1991), p. 147.

179. RWL, letter to DT, October 15, 1938, in Holtz, *Thompson and Lane*, p. 147.

180. Arthur Ekirch, *Ideologies and Utopias: The Impact of the New Deal on American Thought* (Chicago: Quadrangle Books, 1969), pp. 225–28.

181. Sean McMeekin, *Stalin's War* (New York: Basic Books, 2021), pp. 349–51.

182. IMP, "Turns," August 2, 1942. See also "Turns," December 20, 1942 ("When any nation whatever has to borrow from the intellectual resources of another, or ask to be rescued or defended by another, it is in that respect acknowledging that the other is superior.")

183. DT, "'Peace'—And the Crisis Begins!," *NYHT*, October 1, 1938; Kurth, *American Cassandra*, p. 281.

184. Kurth, *American Cassandra*, pp. 284–85.

185. DT, "Toward a Showdown," *NYHT*, September 1, 1936.

186. Kurth, *American Cassandra*, p. 313.

187. DT, "What Is the New Deal?", *NYHT*, October 23, 1936.

188. DT, "The President's Speech," *NYHT*, November 2, 1936; DT, "Let Science Manage Society," *NYHT*, September 20, 1936.

189. IMP, "Turns," February 14, 1943.

190. IMP, "Turns," April 4, 1943 (emphasis added).

191. DT, "A 'Loyal Opposition,'" *NYHT*, November 11, 1940; IMP, "Turns," November 24, 1940.

192. RWL, letter to DT, June 1, 1939, in Holtz, *Thompson and Lane*, p. 157. Krivitsky's revelations were widely publicized and he testified before Congress before being found dead in a Washington, DC, hotel room in February 1941. Whether he committed suicide or was murdered by Soviet Intelligence has never been conclusively proved. Thompson also later revealed that one of her research assistants, Herman Budzislawski, had in fact been a Soviet agent, feeding propaganda into her columns. Kruth, *American Cassandra*, p. 390.

193. *Munitions Industry: Preliminary Report on Wartime Taxation and Price Control by the Special Committee on Investigation of the Munitions Industry*, 74th Cong. 1st sess. Report No. 944, part 2 (Washington: Government Printing Office 1935), p. 47. This was a reference to the House-Grey agreement. See Charles E. Neu, *Colonel House: A Biography of Woodrow Wilson's Silent Partner* (New York: Oxford University Press, 2015), chap. 18; James D. Doenecke, *Nothing Less than War: A New History of America's Entry into World War I* (Lexington: University Press of Kentucky, 2011), pp. 143–46, 302.

194. Ernest C. Bolt Jr., *Ballots before Bullets* (Charlottesville: University Press of Virginia, 1977), chap. 8; Charles Chatfield, *For Peace and Justice: Pacifism in America, 1914–1941* (Knoxville: University of Tennessee Press, 1971), pp. 283–84.

195. W. Anderson, *Selected Letters*, p. 179.

196. Fraser, *Prairie Fires*, p. 422.

197. RWL, "Why I Am for the People's Vote on War," *Liberty*, April 1, 1939, pp. 11–12.

198. Eleanor Roosevelt, "Why I Am against the People's Vote on War," *Liberty*, April 8, 1939, pp. 7–8.

199. W. Anderson, *Selected Letters*, p. 197.

200. In *GoM*, pp. 133–34, Paterson similarly argued that reliance on a militia instead of a standing army indicated that the Constitution's Framers expected individual citizens' refusal to participate in war to operate as a check on war making by politicians. This had some historical precedent: during the War

of 1812, many state militia members refused to cross into Canada, thereby helping thwart a planned invasion. Samuel J. Newland, "The National Guard: Whose Guard Anyway?," *Parameters* 28, no. 2 (1988): 43.

201. *War Referendum: Hearings before a Subcommittee of the Senate Judiciary Committee* on S.J. Res. 84 (1939), pp. 21–23.

202. RWL, "American Revolution 1939," *Saturday Evening Post*, January 7, 1939.

203. RWL Diary, September 1, 1939, Lane Papers, Hoover Library.

Chapter 7

1. B. D. Zevin, ed., *Nothing to Fear: The Selected Addresses of Franklin Delano Roosevelt 1932–1945* (Freeport, NY: Books for Libraries Press, 1970), p. 181.

2. FDR, "Second Inaugural Address," in *Great Speeches of Franklin Delano Roosevelt*, ed. John Grafton (Mineola, NY: Dover Publications, 1999), p. 61.

3. IMP, "Turns with a Bookworm," *NYHT*, July 5, 1936.

4. IMP, "Turns," November 22, 1936.

5. Kenneth Davis, *FDR: Into the Storm, 1937–1940* (New York: Random House, 1993), pp. 593–601.

6. RWL Diary, May 10, 1940, Lane Papers, Hoover Library (emphasis in original). Lane's reference to "three times" was an allusion to Luke 22:61.

7. RWL, letter to the editor, *American Mercury*, December 1938.

8. RWL Diary, May 11, 1940, Lane Papers, Hoover Library.

9. DT, "The Presidency," *NYHT*, October 9, 1940.

10. IMP, "Turns," May 18, 1941 (emphasis added). Paterson was quoting DT's remarks at a dinner in her honor earlier that month. "3,000 Hear Dorothy Thompson Ask U.S. Be Put on War Footing," *NYHT*, May 7, 1941.

11. RWL Diary, May 10, 1940, Lane Papers, Hoover Library (emphasis in original).

12. RWL Diary, June 15, 1940, Lane Papers, Hoover Library.

13. RWL Diary, June 17, 1940, Lane Papers, Hoover Library.

14. RWL Diary, June 18, 1940, Lane Papers, Hoover Library.

15. RWL Diary, May 23, 1940, Lane Papers, Hoover Library.

16. "Book Notes," *Davenport (IA) Daily Times*, August 24, 1940. It never ran, although the publisher used it for advertising, given her gushing praise that it was a masterpiece and that "witches were burned for doing less than this."

17. RWL Diary, September 17, 1940, Lane Papers, Hoover Library.

18. Caroline Fraser, ed., *The Little House Books* (New York: Library of America, 2012), vol. 2, p. 179 (emphasis in original).

19. *DoF*, p. 149.

20. Fraser, ed., *Little House Books*, vol. 2, p. 267.

21. In 1974, Ayn Rand would use the same metaphor in one of her most effective lectures on economics. AR, "Egalitarianism and Inflation," in *Philosophy: Who Needs It* (New York: Signet, 1982), pp. 170–73.

22. Fraser, ed., *Little House Books*, vol. 2, p. 321.

23. John E. Miller, *Laura Ingalls Wilder and Rose Wilder Lane: Authorship, Place, Time, and Culture* (Columbia: University of Missouri Press, 2008), pp. 204–5.

24. Richard Lingeman, *Sinclair Lewis: Rebel from Main Street* (New York: Random House, 2002), p. 145.

25. Ellsworth Barnard, *Wendell Willkie: Fighter for Freedom* (Marquette: Northern Michigan University Press, 1966), p. 229.

26. Steve Neal, *Dark Horse: A Biography of Wendell Willkie* (Garden City, NY: Doubleday, 1984), p. 146.

27. Wendell Willkie, "Evening Star of the Great Day of the Whigs: A Lively Portrait of Lusty Lord Melbourne and His Caroline," *NYHT*, August 27, 1939; Wendell Willkie, "British Defender of American Liberty: William Pitt, the Great Commoner Courageous and Liberal," *NYHT*, May 12, 1940.

28. Neal, *Dark Horse*, chap. 7; David Levering Lewis, *The Improbable Wendell Willkie* (New York: Liveright, 2018), p. 114.

29. Neal, *Dark Horse*, p. 75.

30. Wendell Willkie, "Brace Up, America!," *Atlantic Monthly*, June 1939, pp. 749–56. An excerpt of the article appeared in the *NYHT*, May 20, 1939.

31. RWL, undated letter to AR (143-LN3-012-001), ARI Papers.

32. AR, *Ideal*, p. 118.

33. David Harriman, ed., *Journals of Ayn Rand* (New York: Dutton, 1999), p. 221.

34. Harriman, ed., *Journals*, p. 80 (emphasis in original).

35. Harriman, ed., *Journals*, pp. 80–81 (emphasis in original).

36. Isabel Paterson, "Reading with Tears," *The Bookman*, October 1926, p. 64.

37. Robert Hughes, *American Visions* (New York: Knopf, 1997), p. 405.

38. Meryle Secrest, *Frank Lloyd Wright: A Biography* (Chicago: University of Chicago Press, 1992), pp. 388, 391.

39. Franklin Toker, *Fallingwater Rising: Frank Lloyd Wright, E. J. Kaufmann, and America's Most Extraordinary House* (New York: Knopf, 2005), p. 293. MOMA hosted several displays of Wright's works during the period when Rand was writing *TF*. The Fallingwater exhibit, held between January and March 1938, was a small display of 20 photos. The February 1939 exhibit, "Three Centuries of American Architecture," showcased work by many architects, including Wright. They were presented at Rockefeller Center because MOMA's main gallery on 53rd Street was still under construction. A solo show, "Frank Lloyd Wright, American Architect," opened at that gallery on November 13, 1940, a week after the Roosevelt-Willkie election.

40. Robert C. Twombly, *Frank Lloyd Wright: An Interpretive Biography* (New York: Harper & Rowe, 1973), pp. 206–7.

41. Toker, *Fallingwater Rising*, p. 293. Toker speculates that Rand adopted the title *Fountainhead* because of its resemblance to the name Fallingwater. Actually, Rand chose the name from a thesaurus when it was pointed out that *Second-Hand Lives* was too negative. But the house's visual metaphor would certainly have struck her as aptly suited to her title. At a time when socialists, fascists, and New Dealers were concentrating on the *redistribution* of wealth, Rand, Paterson, and Lane were all concerned with understanding the *source* of wealth and the origin of innovation, creativity, and meaning. The word "fountainhead" means the source of a flow of life-giving water, and the house Fallingwater is designed in such a way that it appears perched atop the waterfalls, as though this manmade artifact is generating the stream. Thus the metaphor of the architect as master of nature, and mankind as the creator of values, was implicit in the house's structure. Indeed, the name *Fountainhead* is roughly synonymous with "god of the machine": both refer to the element of vitality that cannot be controlled or planned by authorities or made part of a merely mechanical process. For Rand, that source was the principle of individual creativity that her main character embodied.

42. Originally published in 1932, Wright's autobiography was republished in 1933, in 1938, and, with revisions, in 1943, after *TF* appeared.

43. Daniel Okrent, *Great Fortune: The Epic of Rockefeller Center* (New York: Viking, 2003), p. 181.

44. Okrent, *Great Fortune*, pp. 300–323.

45. Shoshana Milgram Knapp, "'Seven Shows a Day': Ayn Rand's Howard Roark, Individualism, and the Presidential Election of 1940" (Presentation at the Social Science History Association Annual Conference, Boston, November 11, 2021).

46. Neal, *Dark Horse*, pp. 153–54.

47. Willkie, "Brace Up, America!"

48. Barnard, *Wendell Willkie*, p. 248.

49. Ben H. Procter, *William Randolph Hearst: Final Edition, 1911–1951* (Oxford: Oxford University Press, 2007), p. 229.

50. Thomas Fleming, *The New Dealers' War* (New York: Basic Books, 2001), p. 2.

51. IMP, "Turns," October 6, 1940. Willkie's 1943 book *One World* would become one of the best-selling books in American history—yet Paterson studiously ignored it.

52. Charles A. Fecher, ed., *The Diary of H. L. Mencken* (New York: Knopf, 1989), p. 360.

53. HLM, "Coroner's Inquest" (November 10, 1940), in Marion Elizabeth Rodgers, ed., *The Impossible H. L. Mencken* (New York: Anchor Books, 1991), p. 375.

54. AR, letter to Earle Balch, November 28, 1943, in *Letters of Ayn Rand*, ed. Michael Berliner (New York: Dutton, 1995), p. 102.

55. AR, letter to Gerald Loeb, August 5, 1944, in Berliner, *Letters*, p. 155.

56. Lane and Paterson were not alone in believing this. In *Nineteen Eighty-Four,* published almost a decade later, George Orwell would give expression to similar fears. And in 1942, the Jewish writer Stefan Zweig, in despair about what he called "this endless war," committed suicide in Brazil.

57. IMP, "Turns," November 6, 1940; RWL Diary, November 6, 1940, Lane Papers, Hoover Library.

58. Arthur Vandenberg, "The New Deal Must Be Salvaged," *American Mercury,* January 1940, pp. 1–10.

59. AR, letter to Channing Pollock, May 27, 1941, https://letters.aynrandarchives.org/exhibits/show/letters-of-ayn-rand/item/76800.

60. Jennifer Burns, *Goddess of the Market: Ayn Rand and the American Right* (New York: Oxford University Press, 2009), p. 49. The letter was not published.

61. Harriman, *Journals,* pp. 349–51 (emphasis in original).

62. George Wolfskill, *The Revolt of the Conservatives: A History of the American Liberty League, 1934–1940* (Westport, CT: Greenwood Press, 1962), pp. 260–63.

63. Harriman, *Journals,* pp. 353–54 (emphasis in original).

64. Channing Pollock, *Harvest of My Years: An Autobiography* (Indianapolis: Bobbs-Merrill, 1943), p. 271.

65. Pollock, *Harvest,* p. 202.

66. Pollock, *Harvest,* pp. 369–70; William Grange, "Channing Pollock: The American Theater's Forgotten Polemicist," *Zeitschrift für Anglistik un Amerikanistik* 35, no. 2 (1987): 158–63; Channing Pollock, "Apology for Success," *American Mercury,* November 1938; Channing Pollock, "I Am a Reactionary," *American Mercury,* March 1939; Channing Pollock, "Two Thirds of a Nation," *American Mercury,* July 1938.

67. IMP, "Turns," May 18, 1941.

68. IMP, "Turns," April 9, 1939.

69. IMP, "Turns," November 23, 1947, September 23, 1945.

70. AR, letter to Linda Lynneberg, February 21, 1948, https://courses.aynrand.org/works/previously-unpublished-ayn-rand-letters-4/.

71. This trope was common in Russian folktales, but also in American literature. It appeared, among other places, in Willa Cather's *My Àntonia,* a book Paterson considered "one of the most beautiful novels ever written." IMP, "Turns," August 1, 1926.

72. IMP, "Turns," August 9, 1942.

73. Stephen Cox, *Woman and the Dynamo: Isabel Paterson and the Idea of America* (New Brunswick, NJ: Transactions Publishers, 2004), p. 221.

74. Scott McConnell, ed., *100 Voices: An Oral History of Ayn Rand* (New York: New American Library, 2010), p. 358.

75. AR, letter to IMP, April 3, 1948, in Berliner, *Letters,* p. 202.

76. *TF,* p. 569.

77. Michel de Montaigne, "On Affectionate Relationships" (*De l'amitié*), M. A. Screech, trans., *Montaigne: The Complete Essays* (London: Penguin, 2003), p. 230. Screech translates Montaigne's original wording (*"parce que c'était lui, parce que c'était moi"*) a little differently. See also Adam Sutcliffe, "Friendship in the European Enlightenment: The Rationalization of Intimacy?," in *Conceptualizing Friendship in Time and Place*, ed. Carla Risseeuw and Marlein van Raalte (Leiden: Brill-Rodopi, 2017), p. 152. Paterson's book inscribed to Rand is in the possession of a private collector.

78. Cox, *Woman and the Dynamo*, p. 221.

79. AR, letter to Leonard Read, May 18, 1946, in Berliner, *Letters*, p. 276.

80. IMP, letter to AR, October 13, 1943, Hoover Library, p. 4 (emphasis in original). Although Rand, Paterson, and Lane were unaware of it, a similar revival of Aristotelian virtue ethics was starting in Great Britain at the time—remarkably enough, also under the leadership of a group of female friends. Benjamin Lipscomb, *The Women Are up to Something* (Oxford: Oxford University Press, 2021).

81. AR, "Introducing Objectivism," in *The Voice of Reason: Essays in Objectivist Thought*, ed. Leonard Peikoff (New York: New American Library, 1990), p. 3.

82. Julia Annas, *The Morality of Happiness* (New York: Oxford University Press, 1993), p. 223.

83. Anne C. Heller, *Ayn Rand and the World She Made* (New York: Nan A. Talese/Doubleday, 2009), p. 275.

84. IMP, "Turns," September 1, 1946.

85. IMP, "Turns," May 7, 1944.

86. IMP, "Turns," May 7, 1944; "Turns," November 19, 1933.

87. *GoM*, p. 253.

88. *GoM*, pp. 91–92.

89. Heller, *Ayn Rand*, p. 136.

90. IMP, letter to AR, ca. June 1948, Hoover Library, p. 104 (emphasis in original).

91. Nor can that conversation have been of much significance in Rand's view. The specific example they had discussed was apparently inspired by an exchange related in Boswell's *Life of Johnson*, in which Boswell asked Dr. Johnson a hypothetical question: suppose he found himself trapped in a castle with a newborn baby not his own—would he care for the child? Rand generally disapproved of efforts to do moral philosophy through hypotheticals, and particularly what she called "lifeboat" hypotheticals of this sort. In her view, ethics was properly focused on how human beings should live in the real world, under normal circumstances. Emergency situations or bizarre hypotheticals were of little use in leading to the discovery of moral truth. AR, "The Ethics of Emergencies," in *The Virtue of Selfishness* (New York: Signet, 1964), pp. 39–45.

92. IMP, letter to AR, ca. December 15, 1943, IMP Papers, Hoover Library, p. 17 (emphasis in original).

93. *TF*, p. 711.

94. Harriman, *Journals*, p. 247.

95. IMP, "Turns," January 17, 1943. Paterson was not exaggerating. In 1938, Congress had established the Civil Aeronautics Board and charged it with the job of restricting competition in the airline industry.

96. IMP, "Turns," May 16, 1943 and May 23, 1943; see also March 21, 1943.

97. IMP, "Turns," August 8, 1943.

98. Orville Wright denied it, as well. Katherine "was a loyal sister who had great confidence in her brothers, and [when] we said we would fly she believed we would," he wrote. "But she never contributed anything either in money or mathematics." William Hazelgrove, *Wright Brothers, Wrong Story: How Wilbur Wright Solved the Problem of Manned Flight* (New York: Prometheus Books, 2018), p. 98.

99. IMP, "Turns," June 20, 1943.

100. IMP, "Turns," June 9, 1935.

101. AR, letter to IMP, February 7, 1948, in Berliner, *Letters*, p. 188.

102. IMP, *Never Ask the End* (New York: Literary Guild, 1933), p. 69.

103. AR, *Atlas Shrugged* (New York: Dutton, 1992), pp. 153–54.

104. AR, *Atlas Shrugged*, p. 1058.

105. Significantly, Rand located the refuge to which the world's geniuses flee not in the east, but in Colorado.

106. IMP, "Turns," September 16, 1934; see also September 2, 1934 ("We know the world actually is pretty grim and tragic, that terrible things happen, and they aren't a bit comic. But any vision of the world that we can encompass has comedy in it, not only superficially but in the nature of things. Whatever destiny attends the human race may hold a sanguinary sword in her right hand, but in her left hand, concealed under her apron, she carries a banana peel, and every once in a while, delaying the fatal stroke, she slips around in front of her victim and catches him right at the top of a moving staircase, or making a speech on some solemn occasion.")

107. *TF*, p. 237.

108. Harriman, *Journals*, p. 193.

109. IMP, *The Golden Vanity* (New Brunswick, NJ: Transaction Publishers, 2017), p. 102. A number of intellectuals at the time claimed to have discovered profound philosophical and political significance in cartoon characters. Diego Rivera, for example, curated an art exhibit on Mickey Mouse in 1931, for which he published an essay celebrating the character's cartoons as having "the greatest efficacy as social products" and enabling "the masses" to "rest" after their toils. Diego Rivera, "Mickey Mouse and American Art," in *A Mickey Mouse Reader*, ed. Garry Apgar (Jackson: University Press of Mississippi, 2014), p. 53. Paterson took note of Rivera's essay in "Turns," February 14, 1932. German philosopher Walter Benjamin argued throughout the 1930s that Mickey Mouse was an emblem of the breakdown of individuality in modern culture. "The ancient truth expressed by Heraclitus, that those who are awake have a world in common while each sleeper has a world of his own, has been invalidated by film," he wrote, "less by depicting the dream world itself than by creating figures of collective dream, such as the globe-encircling Mickey Mouse." Howard Eiland and Michael W. Jennings, eds.,

Walter Benjamin: Selected Writings (Cambridge, MA: Harvard University Press, 2002), p. 118. In her notes for *TF*, Rand also expressed concern about the recently released Disney cartoon *Ferdinand the Bull*, which was based on a controversial 1936 children's novel, viewed by many as communist propaganda in light of the ongoing Spanish Civil War. In the story, a seemingly fierce bull refuses to fight when prodded by spectators because he prefers to lie in the sun and smell flowers. Because Toohey's "greatest enemy" is "independence of spirit," Rand wrote, he would seek to "discredit great achievement" by "set[ting] up standards which are easy for the phonies," including "Walt Disney, and *Ferdinand the Bull*." Harriman, *Journals*, pp. 209–10.

110. John Chamberlain, *A Life with the Printed Word* (Chicago: Regnery Gateway, 1982), pp. 136–37.

111. AR, "America's Persecuted Minority: Big Business," in *Capitalism: The Unknown Ideal* (New York: Signet, 1968), p. 61.

112. AR, "The Sanction of the Victims," in Peikoff, *Voice of Reason*, pp. 153–54.

113. *GoM*, p. 250.

114. *GoM*, p. 162.

Chapter 8

1. AR, "The Roots of War," in *Capitalism: The Unknown Ideal* (New York: Signet, 1968), p. 30.

2. *GoM*, p. 288.

3. IMP, "Turns with a Bookworm," *NYHT*, January 18, 1942.

4. Martin Malia, *The Soviet Tragedy* (New York: Free Press, 1995), p. 211 ("The Soviet system was always a militarized political economy, both in its organizational structure and in its products.") See also Ludwig von Mises, *Omnipotent Government* (New Rochelle, NY: Arlington House, 1969), pp. 107–10.

5. IMP, "Turns," May 28, 1933.

6. Pete Seeger, Rob Rosenthal, and Sam Rosenthal, *Pete Seeger: His Life in His Own Words* (New York: Routledge, 2012), p. 18; Ronald D. Cohen and Dave Samuelson, *Songs for Political Action* (Battle Ground, IN: Bear Family, 1996), p. 85. The lyrics were inspired by a speech by Senator Burton K. Wheeler, who in January 1941 characterized Roosevelt's Lend-Lease plan as "the New Deal's triple-A foreign policy; it will plow under every fourth American boy." Lynne Olson, *Those Angry Days: Roosevelt, Lindbergh, and America's Fight over World War II* (New York: Random House, 2013), p. 276.

7. Wolfgang Schivelbusch, *Three New Deals: Reflections on Roosevelt's America, Mussolini's Italy, and Hitler's Germany*, 1933–1939 (New York: Picador, 2006), p. 136.

8. See, for example, "Turns," September 10, 1939; "Books and Things," *NYHT*, July 4, 1939.

9. *GoM*, pp. 79–80.

10. IMP, "Turns," December 15, 1940.

11. Carolyn C. Jones, "Mass-Based Income Taxation: Creating a Taxpaying Culture, 1940–1942," in *Funding the Modern American State, 1941–1995*, ed. W. Elliott Brownlee (Washington: Woodrow Wilson Center Press, 1996), pp. 107–47.

12. IMP, "Turns," July 7, 1946. The phrase "politics and pull" was a common locution for cronyism in the era. See "The Docile Democrats," *New York Tribune*, June 3, 1900; "People's Column," *Buffalo (NY) Enquirer*, July 19, 1917; "'Politics and Pull' Blamed for City Crime," *New York Tribune*, March 17, 1919; and "Distracted Mother," *New York Daily News*, February 27, 1935. Rand would employ the phrase "aristocracy of pull" to refer to cronyism resulting from political control over business. See Marlene Podritske and Peter Schwartz, *Objectively Speaking: Ayn Rand Interviewed* (Lanham, MD: Lexington Books, 2009), p. 78; and AR, *Atlas Shrugged* (New York: Dutton, 1992), p. 404.

13. Thomas Fleming, *The New Dealers' War* (New York: Basic Books, 2002), pp. 124–25.

14. IMP, "Turns," February 20, 1944.

15. IMP, "Turns," August 8, 1943.

16. IMP, "Turns," July 19, 1942.

17. RWL, "Notions of Freedom of Most Modern 'Thinkers' Is a Delusion," *Pittsburgh Courier*, January 20, 1945.

18. *GoM*, p. 157n.

19. IMP, "Turns," February 18, 1940.

20. IMP, "Turns," March 3, 1940.

21. IMP, "Turns," December 22, 1940.

22. Henry Steele Commager, *Majority Rule and Minority Rights* (New York: Oxford University Press, 1943), pp. 13–14.

23. IMP, "Turns," April 28, 1940.

24. IMP, "Turns," February 14, 1943. Note the similar dialogue in *Atlas Shrugged*, p. 141.

25. DT, *Dorothy Thompson's Political Guide* (New York: Stackpole, 1938), p. 77.

26. DT, *Political Guide*, p. 80.

27. IMP, "Turns," February 14, 1943.

28. IMP, "'Liberalism' Is Seen as a Shield for 'Every Form of Coercion,'" *NYHT*, August 12, 1938.

29. IMP, "Turns," May 13, 1945.

30. IMP, "Individual Declared Final Judge on Taxes and Military Service," *NYHT*, July 6, 1938.

31. IMP, "Military Conscription Declared Negation of American Principle," *NYHT*, July 1, 1938.

32. Geoffrey R. Stone, *Perilous Times: Free Speech in Wartime* (New York: W. W. Norton, 2004), p. 245.

33. Stone, *Perilous Times*, p. 249; Ira Katznelson, *Fear Itself: The New Deal and the Origins of Our Time* (New York: W. W. Norton, 2013), pp. 322–23; Richard W. Steele, *Free Speech in the Good War* (New York: St. Martin's Press, 1999), pp. 28–29.

34. Herbert Mitgang, *Dangerous Dossiers: Exposing the Secret War against America's Greatest Authors* (New York: Ballantine Books, 1989), pp. 37, 171; Herbert Mitgang, "Policing America," *New Yorker*, September 28, 1987; Meryle Secrest, *Frank Lloyd Wright: A Biography* (Chicago: University of Chicago Press, 1998), p. 490.

35. Phillip W. Magness, "How E. C. Harwood Stood Firm against FDR's Attempts to Censor AIER," American Institute for Economic Research, Great Barrington, MA, September 13, 2018.

36. IMP, "Turns," May 19, 1940.

37. John E. Moser, *Right Turn: John T. Flynn and the Transformation of American Liberalism* (New York: New York University Press, 2005), p. 104.

38. "'I Am the Law,' Mayor Hague Tells 1,000 in Speech on Jersey City Government," *New York Times*, November 11, 1937; "'It Has Happened Here,' Lewis Tells Audience in New York," *New Brunswick (NJ) Daily Home News*, November 11, 1937.

39. "Hague Suggests Alaskan Camp for U.S. 'Reds,'" *NYHT*, June 15, 1938.

40. IMP, "Found: A Common Denominator for Hague and Some of His Foes," *NYHT*, June 22, 1938 (emphasis added).

41. Peter Kurth, *American Cassandra: The Life of Dorothy Thompson* (Boston: Little, Brown, 1991), p. 240. Hague was eventually forced to back down. "Jersey City to Hear a Critic of Hague," *New York Times*, January 25, 1938.

42. IMP, "Turns," November 19, 1939.

43. IMP, "A Tip to Representative Dies: Real Danger Is Closer to Home," *NYHT*, August 26, 1938. Lane, by contrast, when asked in 1940 whether she believed the Dies Committee should continue its work, answered yes. "The Gallup Poll of Authors," *Saturday Review*, January 13, 1940, p. 12.

44. IMP, "Turns," March 15, 1936. See also June 7, 1936.

45. Fleming, *New Dealers' War*, pp. 112–15.

46. Valerie Boyd, *Wrapped in Rainbows: The Life of Zora Neale Hurston* (New York: Scribner, 2004), pp. 360–61.

47. IMP, letter to AR, ca. February. 2, 1944, IMP Papers, Hoover Library, p. 29.

48. Alan Theoharis, *Abuse of Power: How Cold War Surveillance and Secrecy Policy Shaped the Response to 9/11* (Philadelphia: Temple University Press, 2011), pp. 130–33; Jonathan Turley, "Art and the Constitution: The Supreme Court and the Rise of the Impressionist School of Constitutional Interpretation," in *Cato Supreme Court Review: 2003–2004*, ed. Mark Moller (Washington, Cato Institute, 2004), pp. 69–117.

49. IMP, "What Do They Do All Day?," in *Culture and Liberty: Writings of Isabel Paterson*, ed. Stephen Cox (New York: Transaction Publishers, 2015), p. 84.

50. *GoM*, p. 62.

51. *GoM*, p. 228.

52. *GoM*, p. 194.

53. *GoM*, p. 228.

54. *GoM*, p. 153.

55. *GoM*, p. 155. Popper would call this "the arrested state." Karl Popper, *The Open Society and Its Enemies*, vol. 1, *The Spell of Plato*, 5th ed. (Princeton, NJ: Princeton University Press, 1971), p. 21.

56. *GoM*, p. 89.

57. *GoM*, p. 152 (emphasis in original). Paterson frequently used the perpetual motion metaphor. In his 1937 book *The Good Society*—written as a response to Harold Laski's *Democracy in Crisis*—Paterson's *Herald Tribune* colleague Walter Lippmann used the same metaphor to attack the idea of a planned economy. "I have come finally to see that such a social order is not even theoretically conceivable," Lippmann wrote. To suppose one could "find planners and managers who were wise and disinterested enough" to organize an economy was "as complete a delusion as perpetual motion." Walter Lippmann, *The Good Society* (New Brunswick, NJ: Transaction Publishers, 2005), p. xlvi. It is impossible to know whether Lippmann borrowed the image from Paterson.

58. *GoM*, p. 238 (emphasis in original).

59. *GoM*, p. 239.

60. *GoM*, p. 241 (emphasis in original).

61. *GoM*, p. 249 (emphasis in original).

62. AR, letter to Earle Balch, November 28, 1943, https://letters.aynrandarchives.org/document/76404.

63. *GoM*, p. 253, quoting Lafcadio Hearn, *Japan: An Introduction* (New York: Macmillan, 1894).

64. *GoM*, p. 258.

65. AR, "The Comprachicos," in *The Return of the Primitive: The Anti-Industrial Revolution*, ed. Peter Schwartz (New York: Meridian, 1999), pp. 51–95. Rand called this one of her favorite essays in an article in *The Objectivist*, September 1971.

66. *GoM*, pp. 69–70.

67. AR, letter to IMP, August 4, 1945, in *Letters of Ayn Rand*, ed. Michael Berliner (New York: Dutton, 1995), p. 184.

68. AR, "Man's Rights," in *Capitalism: The Unknown Ideal*, p. 370.

69. Stephen Jay Gould, *Dinosaur in a Haystack* (New York: Three Rivers Press, 1995), p. 25.

70. AR, letter to IMP, August 4, 1945, in Berliner, *Letters*, p. 184.

71. Scott George, "Well-Argued Thesis," *Nashville (TN) Banner*, September 29, 1943; "What Generates Society's Energy?," *Baltimore Evening Sun*, June 12, 1943.

72. As F. A. Hayek was later to put it, the market is a cosmos rather than a taxis. F. A. Hayek, *Law, Legislation and Liberty*, vol. 1, *Rules and Order* (Chicago: University of Chicago Press, 1973), chap. 2.

73. Paterson referred to Ludwig von Mises's *Omnipotent Government* in one "Turns" column (May 21, 1944), but not to Hayek or other Austrian economists.

74. Janek Wasserman, *The Marginal Revolutionaries* (New Haven, CT: Yale University Press, 2019); Ludwig von Mises, *Economic Calculation in the Socialist Commonwealth* (Auburn, AL: Mises Institute, 1990).

75. *GoM*, p. 232. Paterson's "explosion" language is counterintuitive in one way. Whereas Rand contends, particularly in *Anthem*, that government oppression will sap and ultimately kill economic activity,

Paterson is suggesting that government controls will cause a "leakage" of excess productivity, which will result in an uncontrolled *release* of economic energy. In other words, rather than the government being too powerful for the economy, the economy is too powerful for the government, and economic disruptions caused by repression in one economic area are liable to result in social forces that lead to violence—riots, wars, and so on.

76. "Walter Winchell in New York," *Tucson (AZ) Daily Citizen*, June 22, 1943.

77. Paul Jordan-Smith, "Machine Expresses America's Free Will," *Los Angeles Times*, May 30, 1943; John Storck, "The Dynamics of Our Society," *New York Times Book Review*, May 23, 1943, p. 29.

78. *NECRB*, February 1946.

79. AR, letter to John C. Gall, July 4, 1943, https://letters.aynrandarchives.org/document/1329.

80. AR, letter to Earle Balch, November 28, 1943, https://letters.aynrandarchives.org/document/76404.

81. IMP, letter to AR, November 30, 1943, Paterson Papers, Hoover Library, p. 11.

82. IMP, letter to AR, November 30, 1943, Paterson Papers, Hoover Library, p. 13.

83. *DoF*, p. xi.

84. *DoF*, pp. xi–xii.

85. *DoF*, p. 78.

86. *DoF*, p. 79.

87. *DoF*, p. 80.

88. *DoF*, p. 83 (emphasis in original).

89. *DoF*, p. 86.

90. *DoF*, p. 26.

91. *DoF*, p. 114.

92. *DoF*, p. 179.

93. Brian Doherty, *Radicals for Capitalism: A Freewheeling History of the Modern American Libertarian Movement* (New York: Public Affairs, 2007), pp. 130–31.

94. *DoF*, p. 159.

95. *DoF*, p. xiii.

96. "She's for Freedom," *Baltimore Sun*, January 23, 1943; Arno L. Bader, "Fiction Writer Turns to Field of Nonfiction," *Chicago Sunday Tribune*, January 17, 1943.

97. David T. Beito and Linda Royster Beito, "Selling Laissez-Faire Antiracism to the Black Masses: Rose Wilder Lane and the *Pittsburgh Courier*," *Independent Review* 15, no. 2 (2010): 279–94.

98. *DoF*, p. 182.

99. RWL, letter to Robert LeFevre, July 24, 1957, Lane Papers, Hoover Library.

100. *NECRB*, December 1947.

101. Roger Lea MacBride, ed., *The Lady and the Tycoon: The Best of Letters between Rose Wilder Lane and Jasper Crane* (Caldwell, ID: Caxton, 1973), p. 321 (emphasis in original).

102. *DoF*, p. 110.

103. *DoF*, p. 110.

104. RWL, letter to DT, August 3, 1932, in William Holtz, ed., *Dorothy Thompson and Rose Wilder Lane: Forty Years of Friendship* (Columbia: University of Missouri Press, 1991), p. 135.

105. *DoF*, p. xii.

106. RWL, letter to Robert LeFevre, August 2, 1957, Lane Papers, Hoover Library.

107. RWL, letter to AR, August 6, 1946 (142-LN1-005-001), ARI Papers.

108. IMP, "Turns," January 3, 1943 and August 8, 1943. Rand appears to have taken even less interest. There is no evidence she ever read it. She did read Lane's *Give Me Liberty*, when it was reprinted in 1945. She disapproved, repeatedly marking up the margins with the comment "good god!" This copy is in a private collection. Although Rand owned a copy of *DoF*, it contained no such markings. My thanks to Jeff Britting of the Ayn Rand Institute for looking into this.

109. IMP, letter to AR, ca. October 7, 1943, Hoover Library, p. 21 (emphasis in original).

110. IMP, letter to AR, ca. January, 19, 1944, Hoover Library, p. 26.

111. MacBride, *Lady and the Tycoon*, p. 46.

112. William Anderson, ed., *The Selected Letters of Laura Ingalls Wilder* (New York: Harper Perennial, 2017), p. 242.

113. Lorenzo O'Rourke, trans., *Victor Hugo's Intellectual Autobiography* (New York: Funk & Wagnalls, 1907), p. 121.

114. *TF*, p. 653.

115. *TF*, pp. 584, 656.

116. *TF*, p. 716.

117. *TF*, p. 716.

118. *TF*, p. 725.

119. *GoM*, p. 241.

120. *NECRB*, October 1948.

121. *TF*, p. 717.

122. Anne C. Heller, *Ayn Rand and the World She Made* (New York: Nan A. Talese/Doubleday, 2009), p. 120.

123. Friedrich Nietzsche, *Ecce Homo*, in *On the Genealogy of Morals and Ecce Homo*, ed. Walter Kaufmann (New York: Vintage Books, 1989), p. 224; Friedrich Nietzsche, *Beyond Good and Evil*, sec. 247, in *Basic Writings of Nietzsche*, ed. Walter Kaufmann (New York: Modern Library, 2000), p. 419; Aristotle, *Nichomachean Ethics*, 1124b, in *The Basic Works of Aristotle*, ed. Richard McKeon (New York: Random House, 1941), p. 993. As Shoshana Milgram Knapp observes, Roark in the finished novel differs from Nietzsche's ideal in part because, among other things, he finds fulfillment in his work, does not view the world as an enemy, and actively seeks friendship with like-minded individuals—elements not found in Nietzsche's conception of the

Übermensch. Shoshana Milgram Knapp, "*The Fountainhead* from Notebook to Novel," in *Essays on Ayn Rand's* The Fountainhead, ed. Robert Mayhew (Lanham, MD: Lexington Books, 2007), pp. 28–29.

124. IMP, letter to AR, ca. October 14, 1943, Hoover Library, p. 6.

125. Bruce Brooks Pfeiffer, ed., *Frank Lloyd Wright: Collected Writings 1894–1930* (New York: Random House, 1992), vol. 1, p. 141; quoted in David Harriman, ed., *Journals of Ayn Rand* (New York: Dutton, 1999), p. 145.

126. This quotation appeared in a statement Wright had printed for publication in his 1930 book *Modern Architecture*, which he sent to Kahn. Rand copied it into her journals. Harriman, *Journals*, p. 144.

127. Harriman, *Journals*, p. 156.

128. IMP, letter to AR, ca. April 6, 1944, Hoover Library, p. 52.

129. Robert Mayhew, ed., *Ayn Rand Answers* (New York: New American Library, 2005), p. 190. Wright sent Rand an elevation for a hillside house based on his 1930 design for the Elizabeth Noble Terrace Apartments in Los Angeles. Neither was ever built.

130. N. L. Rothman ("Howard Roark, Architect," *Saturday Review of Literature*, May 29, 1943, p. 30) was one exception. He noted that *TF* was "comparable in ideals and in satiric attack" with SL's *Arrowsmith*. Robert Mayhew and Shoshana Milgram Knapp discuss SL's influence in depth. Mayhew, "Humor in *The Fountainhead*," in *Essays*; Knapp, "Looking Up to Sinclair Lewis: Ayn Rand's Admiration for *It Can't Happen Here*" (Presentation, Objectivist Summer Conference, Newport Beach, CA, June 28, 2008).

131. Alex Madsen, *Stanwyck* (New York: Harper Collins, 1994), p. 226.

132. *TF*, p. 141.

133. Harriman, *Journals*, p. 79.

134. *TF*, p. 101; HLM, "The New Architecture," in *A Mencken Chrestomathy* (New York: Vintage Books, 1982), pp. 557–59.

135. *TF*, p. 226.

136. IMP, letter to Burton Rascoe, ca. December 1931, in Cox, *Culture and Liberty*, p. 153.

137. Richard R. Lingeman, *Sinclair Lewis: Rebel from Main Street* (New York: Random House, 2002), pp. 425, 473.

138. AR, "Art and Sense of Life," in *The Romantic Manifesto*, rev. ed. (New York: Signet, 975).

139. *TF*, p. 724.

140. Tara Smith, "Unborrowed Vision: Independence and Egoism in *The Fountainhead*," in Mayhew, *Essays*, pp. 289–91.

141. *TF*, p. 609.

142. John Updike, "No Brakes," *New Yorker*, February 4, 2002.

143. AR, *We the Living*, p. 335.

144. Harriman, *Journals*, p. 154.

145. Leonard Peikoff, ed., *The Early Ayn Rand*, rev. ed. (New York: Signet, 2005), p. 471.

146. *TF*, p. 328.

147. IMP, "Turns," June 30, 1943.

148. Michael S. Berliner, "*The Fountainhead* Reviews," in Mayhew, *Essays*, chap. 4.

149. Lorine Pruette, "Battle against Evil," *New York Times Book Review*, May 16, 1943, p. 7.

150. Frank Lloyd Wright, letter to Ayn Rand, April 23, 1944 (emphasis in original), https://letters.aynrandarchives.org/document/57278.

151. Albert Guerard, "Novel on Architectural Genius: Superman versus the Rabble of Second-Handers Is Its Theme," *NYHT*, May 30, 1943.

152. Aside from Mike Donnigan, the electrician, Roark is also "helped" by the jury that acquits him, and is made up largely of laborers.

153. Andrew Bernstein, "Understanding the Rape Scene in *The Fountainhead*," in Mayhew, *Essays*, p. 201. Rape was a common literary device at the time, seen also in such works as Margaret Mitchell's *Gone with the Wind* (1936) and Zora Neale Hurston's *Seraph on the Suwanee* (1948).

154. *NECRB*, October 1945.

155. IMP, "Turns," June 9, 1935.

Chapter 9

1. Philip Gleason, "Americans All: World War II and the Shaping of American Identity," *Review of Politics* 43, no. 4 (1981): 501–2.

2. Thomas Fleming, *The New Dealers' War* (New York: Basic Books, 2002), p. 158.

3. *W. Virginia State Bd. of Educ. v. Barnette*, 319 U.S. 624, 642 (1943).

4. Alistair Cooke, *The Home Front* (New York: Grove Press, 2006), p. 310.

5. Marcia Noe, *Susan Glaspell: Voice from the Heartland* (Macomb: Western Illinois University Press, 1983).

6. IMP, "Turns with a Bookworm," *NYHT*, September 27, 1936; April 4, 1937; Gilbert Seldes, *Mainland* (New York: Scribner's, 1936), p. 13.

7. Seldes, *Mainland*, p. 421.

8. Archibald MacLeish, *The Irresponsibles: A Declaration* (New York: Duell, Sloan & Pearce, 1940), pp. 17, 21.

9. Bernard DeVoto *The Literary Fallacy* (Boston: Little, Brown, 1944), p. 167.

10. DeVoto, *Literary Fallacy*, pp. 135, 166–67.

11. DeVoto, *Literary Fallacy*, p. 101.

12. Bernard DeVoto, "They Turned Their Backs on America," *Saturday Review*, April 8, 1944, pp. 5–7; SL, "Fools, Liars, and Mr. DeVoto," *Saturday Review*, April 15, 1944, pp. 9–12.

13. IMP, "Turns," September 8, 1940.

14. IMP, "Lewis Writes in His Kindliest Mood," *NYHT*, January 28, 1934.

15. IMP, "Turns," April 18, 1943.

16. IMP, "Turns," April 2, 1944.

17. Bernard DeVoto, "An Exciting Batch of Assorted Prejudices," *NYHT*, March 14, 1943 (emphasis added).

18. Letter to the FBI, dated March 15, 1943, in Lane's FBI file.

19. William Holtz, *The Ghost in the Little House* (Columbia: University of Missouri Press, 1995), pp. 317–18 (emphasis in original); David T. Beito and Linda Royster Beito, "Isabel Paterson, Rose Wilder Lane, and Zora Neale Hurston on War, Race, the State, and Liberty," *Independent Review* 12, no. 4 (2008): 565–66; RWL, letter to Roger Baldwin, September 9, 1943, FBI file.

20. "Forced to Quiz Author: FBI Explains Investigation of Rose Wilder Lane," *Kansas City Times*, August 10, 1943.

21. RWL, letter to J. Edgar Hoover, September 9, 1943, FBI file. This did not end the bureau's surveillance of Lane, however. A year later, the bureau's field office in New Haven reported to Hoover that Lane had given an "extremely seditious" speech to the local Lions Club—a matter Hoover passed on to Assistant Attorney General Tom Clark. Roger Gleason, memorandum to J. Edgar Hoover, April 22, 1944; Hoover, memorandum to Tom Clark, May 16, 1944, FBI file.

22. RWL, letter to DT, May 20, 1943, in *Dorothy Thompson and Rose Wilder Lane: Forty Years of Friendship*, ed. William Holtz (Columbia: University of Missouri Press, 1991), p. 176.

23. RWL, letter to DT, May 20, 1943, in Holtz, *Thompson and Lane*, pp. 168, 178.

24. Axel Madsen, *Stanwyck* (New York: Harper Collins, 1994), p. 226.

25. Anne C. Heller, *Ayn Rand and the World She Made* (New York: Nan A. Talese/Doubleday, 2009), p. 157; Finis Farr, *Margaret Mitchell of Atlanta* (New York: Avon, 1974), p. 173.

26. IMP, letter to AR, ca. December 30, 1943, Hoover Library, p. 26.

27. IMP, letter to AR, ca. February 2, 1944, Hoover Library, p. 29.

28. IMP, letter to AR, ca. December 30, 1943, Hoover Library, p. 26 (emphasis in original).

29. AR, letter to IMP, October 10, 1943, in Berliner, *Letters*, pp. 173–74.

30. IMP, letter to AR, ca. December 30, 1943, Hoover Library, p. 26.

31. IMP, letter to AR, ca. February 2, 1944, Hoover Library, p. 32.

32. Jeff Britting, "Adapting *The Fountainhead* to Film," in *Essays on Ayn Rand's* The Fountainhead, ed. Robert Mayhew (Lanham, MD: Lexington Books, 2007), p. 91.

33. AR, letter to IMP, July 26, 1945, in Berliner, *Letters*, p. 178.

34. Scott McConnell, ed., *100 Voices: An Oral History of Ayn Rand* (New York: New American Library, 2010), p. 91.

35. AR, letter to IMP, July 26, 1945, in Berliner, *Letters*, p. 177.

36. AR, letter to IMP, July 26, 1945, in Berliner, *Letters*, p. 179.

37. AR, "The Only Path to Tomorrow," *Reader's Digest*, January 1944 (emphasis in original).

38. AR, "Only Path to Tomorrow."

39. IMP, letter to AR, July 30, 1945, Hoover Library, p. 69.

40. AR, letter to IMP, July 26, 1945, in Berliner, *Letters*, p. 179.

41. IMP, letter to AR, July 30, 1945, Hoover Library, p. 70.

42. IMP, letter to AR, July 30, 1945, Hoover Library, p. 71.

43. AR, letter to IMP, August 4, 1945, in Berliner, *Letters*, pp. 180–81.

44. AR, letter to IMP, August 4, 1945, in Berliner, *Letters*, p. 184.

45. Paterson appears to have read Gilson only after completing *GoM*. She referred to him twice in "Turns" (October 10, 1943, and June 18, 1944).

46. Robert Mayhew, ed., *Ayn Rand's Marginalia: Her Critical Comments on the Writings of over 20 Authors* (New Milford, CT: Second Renaissance Books, 1995), p. 38.

47. AR, letter to IMP, August 4, 1945, Berliner, *Letters*, p. 184.

48. Paterson also continued to insist that Rand had indeed once argued that new things were necessarily better—a position that was plainly wrong, since, for example, radio was inferior to print. Part of her reasoning was that radio by nature had to be regulated by the government—given that absent such regulation, radio station broadcasts would interfere with one another—whereas nothing about newspapers or books required such regulation. IMP, letter to AR, August 9, 1945, Hoover Library, p. 72. Twenty years later, Rand would reject this premise, arguing that nothing about radio required government licensing. "The Property Status of Airwaves," *Objectivist Newsletter*, April 1964.

49. IMP, letter to AR, ca. August 9, 1945, Hoover Library, p. 75.

50. IMP, letter to AR, ca. August 9, 1945, Hoover Library, p. 78.

51. IMP, letter to AR, ca. August 31, 1945, Hoover Library, p. 82.

52. Brian Doherty, *Radicals for Capitalism: A Freewheeling History of the Modern American Libertarian Movement* (New York: PublicAffairs, 2007), pp. 150–51.

53. IMP, letter to Robert Henry, ca. January 1944, in *Culture and Liberty: Writings of Isabel Paterson*, ed. Stephen Cox (New York: Transaction Publishers, 2015), p. 196. Paterson first met Read in December 1943 or January 1944.

54. AR, letter to Leonard Read, November 12, 1944, in Berliner, *Letters*, p. 169.

55. AR, letter to Leonard Read, November 12, 1944, in Berliner, *Letters*, p. 171.

56. RWL, letter to AR, June 7, 1945 (142-LN1-001-001), ARI Papers.

57. Kim Phillips-Fein, *Invisible Hands: The Making of the Conservative Movement from the New Deal to Reagan* (New York: W. W. Norton, 2009), p. xi. See also Lawrence Glickman, *Free Enterprise: An American History* (New Haven, CT: Yale University Press, 2019).

58. IMP, letter to AR, November 1944, Hoover Library, p. 59.

59. "Rose Lane Says," *Pittsburgh Courier*, December 23, 1944, p. 6 (emphasis in original). The Smith-Connally Act, also called the War Labor Disputes Act, was adopted in June 1943. It allows the government to seize industries threatened by labor disputes when necessary for war production.

60. No definitive evidence indicates that Rand obtained *Boot Straps* from Paterson, but Paterson commented in "Turns" (September 19, 1943) that she had read the advance copy, and it seems likely she shared it with Rand, who told Girdler she had received it from a friend. Months afterward, Rand met Girdler and reported to Paterson that Girdler had read and praised *TF* and *GoM*. Berliner, *Letters*, pp. 81, 175.

61. Rand was not in principle opposed to unions; on the contrary, in a 1972 interview she called them "the only decent group today, ideologically," and "the ones who will save this country and save capitalism, if anybody can." But she believed business owners had a right to refuse to negotiate with them. It was laws like the National Labor Relations Act, by which "labor unions are government-enforced and thus become a monopoly," that violated business owners' rights and cause unemployment. Marlene Podritske and Peter Schwartz, eds., *Objectively Speaking: Ayn Rand Interviewed* (Lanham, MD: Lexington Books, 2009), p. 215.

62. IMP, "Turns," September 19, 1943.

63. Tom Girdler, *Boot Straps* (New York: Scribner's, 1943), p. 363.

64. Girdler, *Boot Straps*, pp. 357–58.

65. AR, letter to Tom Girdler, July 12, 1943, in Berliner, *Letters*, pp. 81–85. Girdler replied politely, but made clear in *Boot Straps* that "I don't think of hope of reward as selfishness. . . . Most of the people I have known in my life have been constantly trying to get a fatter pay envelope, not for themselves, but for those they love." *Boot Straps*, p. 458.

66. F. A. Hayek, *The Road to Serfdom* (Chicago: University of Chicago Press, 1944), pp. 145–46 (emphasis added). Rand and Lane were not the only writers to note the equivocal nature of Hayek's defense of freedom. John Maynard Keynes wrote to Hayek after reading the book in 1944: "You admit here and there that it is a question of knowing where to draw the line [between freedom and restriction]. You agree that the line has to be drawn somewhere. . . . But you give us no guidance whatever as to where to draw it. In a sense this is shirking the practical issue." Quoted in Scott Scheall, *F. A. Hayek and the Epistemology of Politics* (London: Routledge, 2020), p. 171.

67. Hayek, *Road to Serfdom*, pp. 145–46.

68. Hayek, *Road to Serfdom*, p. 17.

69. Mayhew, *Ayn Rand's Marginalia*, pp. 146–47 (emphasis in original).

70. Hayek, *Road to Serfdom*, p. 121.

71. AR, letter to Leonard Read, August 1, 1946, in Berliner, *Letters*, p. 299; AR, letter to RWL, August 21, 1946, in Berliner, *Letters*, p. 308.

72. *NECRB*, January 1946; *NECRB*, October 1948.

73. *NECRB*, September 1946.

74. George Peck, "Was Hitler's Face Red?", *Fort Lauderdale News*, July 31, 1946.

75. AR, letter to George Peck, August 30, 1946, in Berliner, *Letters*, p. 313.

76. RWL, letter to AR, August 6, 1946 (142-LN1-005-001), ARI Papers (emphasis in original).

77. AR, letter to William Mullendore, Sepember 20, 1946, in Berliner, *Letters*, p. 321–22 (emphasis in original).

78. Milton and Rose Friedman, *Two Lucky People: Memoirs* (Chicago: University of Chicago Press, 1998), pp. 149–50.

79. RWL, letter to AR, October 11, 1946 (142-LN1-009-001, 142-LN1-009-002), ARI Papers (emphasis in original).

80. Henry Hazlitt, *Economics in One Lesson* (New York: Harper & Brothers, 1946), p. 5.

81. RWL, letter to AR, August 24, 1946 (142-LN1-007-003), ARI Papers.

82. *NECRB*, September 1946 (emphasis in original).

83. RWL, letter to AR, August 24, 1946 (142-LN1-007-003), ARI Papers.

84. AR, letter to RWL, October 9, 1946, in Berliner, *Letters*, p. 331; Hazlitt, *Economics in One Lesson*, p. 192.

85. Rand addressed this point in detail in her discussion of "socially objective values" in her 1965 article, "What Is Capitalism?," in AR, *Capitalism: The Unknown Ideal* (New York: Signet, 1968), pp. 24–26. See also F. A. Hayek, "Competition as a Discovery Procedure," *Quarterly Journal of Austrian Economics* 5, no. 3 (2002): 9–23.

86. AR, letter to RWL, October 9, 1946, Berliner, *Letters*, p. 331.

87. RWL, letter to AR, January 21, 1948 (143-LN3-004-001), ARI Papers (emphasis in original).

88. IMP, letter to AR, ca. February 2, 1944, Hoover Library, p. 29.

89. IMP, letter to AR, ca. August 9, 1945, Hoover Library, p. 78. The whole idea of atomic weaponry sickened Paterson. To the "recurrent suggestion that one must at least admire the concoction of the atom bomb as a marvelous technological achievement," she wrote in "Turns" that it might have been an admirable achievement if it were done by baboons, but for human beings to devote their talents to creating a bigger, more horrific bomb was nothing to admire. IMP, "Turns," August 1, 1948. As for the newsreels of Nazi death camps, Paterson made no public comments on them because she, like Lane and Rand, viewed them as the inevitable consequences of collectivism, whether of the Nazi or Soviet varieties. Indeed, Paterson had made that point as far back as 1940, when she expressed puzzlement at leftist intellectuals who were surprised at the "wholesale murder, brutal deportation, planned starvation, and imprisonment of hundreds of thousands of people in horrible labor concentration camps," which were the necessary consequences of their "dream of a conscript, planned, expropriated world." IMP, "Turns," June 23, 1940.

90. Harriman, *Journals*, p. 312 (emphasis in original). It would be hard to deny Rand's prescience on this point. The 1983 television movie *The Day After*—reputed to be among the most widely viewed shows in TV history—proved to have a significant impact on Cold War politics and the ongoing nuclear arms race.

91. Harriman, *Journals*, p. 315 (emphasis in original).

92. Harriman, *Journals*, p. 316.

93. Harriman, *Journals*, p. 324 (emphasis in original).

94. John R. Baker, *Science and the Planned State* (London: Allen & Unwin, 1945), p. 109.

95. Baker, *Science and the Planned State*, p. 44.

96. Valery Soyfer, *Lysenko and the Tragedy of Soviet Science* (New Brunswick, NJ: Rutgers University Press, 1994).

97. Baker, *Science and the Planned State*, p. 20. Baker and Michael Polanyi founded the Society for Freedom in Science. John R. Baker, "Michael Polanyi's Contributions to the Cause of Freedom in Science," *Minerva* 16, no. 3 (1978): 382–96.

98. IMP, "Turns," September 30, 1945; *NECRB*, January 1946.

99. Harriman, *Journals*, p. 320 (emphasis in original).

100. Harriman, *Journals*, p. 330.

101. Harriman, *Journals*, p. 342.

102. Harriman, *Journals*, p. 325.

103. Robert H. Jackson, *That Man: An Insider's Portrait of Franklin D. Roosevelt* (Oxford: Oxford University Press, 2003), p. 120.

104. *GoM*, pp. 172–73.

105. IMP, "New Deal Likened to Small Boy Always Stalking the Jam Jar," *NYHT*, June 24, 1938.

106. Raymond Clapper, "Ideas on Monopoly Likely to Be Revised," *Pittsburgh Press*, June 16, 1938.

107. "Americans can destroy the whole automotive industry tomorrow, simply by buying planes," wrote Lane in *DoF* (p. 245), "just as, simply by buying cars, they destroyed yesterday that looming monster, that Shame of the Cities, the Street Car Monopoly."

108. Ellis Wayne Hawley, *The New Deal and the Problem of Monopoly* (Princeton, NJ: Princeton University Press, 1966), pp. 481–84.

109. IMP, "Small Boy Always Stalking the Jam Jar."

110. Dominick T. Armentano, *Antitrust and Monopoly: Anatomy of a Policy Failure*, 2nd ed. (Oakland, CA: Independent Institute, 1990), pp. 100–112; *United States v. Aluminum Co. of America*, 44 F. Supp. 97, 309 (S.D.N.Y. 1941).

111. *United States v. Aluminum Co. of America*, 148 F.2d 416, 431 (2d Cir. 1945).

112. AR, "America's Persecuted Minority: Big Business," in *Capitalism: The Unknown Ideal*, p. 56. Lane condemned the ALCOA decision in *NECRB*, June 1948.

113. Stephen B. Adams, *Mr. Kaiser Goes to Washington: The Rise of a Government Entrepreneur* (Chapel Hill: University of North Carolina Press, 1997), p. 178.

114. Edward Gibbon, *The Decline and Fall of the Roman Empire*, ed. R. Hutchins (Chicago: Encyclopedia Britannica, 1923), vol. 1, pp. 188, 597.

115. IMP, "Books and Things," *NYHT*, January 11, 1938.

116. IMP, "Turns," August 30, 1931.

117. IMP, letter to AR, ca. December 30, 1943, Hoover Library, p. 2. The quotation is from Gilson's, *Reason and Revelation in the Middle Ages* (New York: Scribner's, 1939), p. 49. Paterson had recommended that book in "Turns" alongside *TF.* IMP, "Turns," October 10, 1943.

118. AR, letter to IMP, October 10, 1943, in Berliner, *Letters*, p. 174. As Rand later told the story, *Atlas Shrugged* was inspired by a phone call in which an unnamed friend—evidently Paterson—told her she had a "duty" to publish a nonfiction book about her philosophy, to which Rand responded by angrily suggesting she would go "on strike." It seems likely that this conversation concerned *The Moral Basis of Individualism*, which Rand never completed. The most plausible explanation is that Rand and Paterson discussed the idea of a "strike" novel for some time before that call.

119. Harriman, *Journals*, p. 392.

120. Harriman, *Journals*, p. 264 (emphasis in original).

121. IMP, letter to AR, ca. November 1944, Hoover Library, p. 63.

122. IMP, "Turns," August 25, 1946.

Chapter 10

1. Jonathan Hoenig, ed., *A New Textbook of Americanism: The Politics of Ayn Rand* (Chicago: Capitalist Pig Publications, 2018), p. 4.

2. *NECRB*, September 1946.

3. RWL, letter to AR, August 24, 1946 (142-LN-007-001), ARI Papers.

4. In the language of metaphysics, Lane appears to have thought that rights exist in the form of becoming rather than being. See Aristotle, *Metaphysics*, Book VII.

5. AR, letter to RWL, August 21, 1946, in Michael S. Berliner, ed., *Letters of Ayn Rand* (New York: Dutton, 1995), p. 308.

6. RWL, letter to AR, August 24, 1946 (142-LN1-007-001–142-LN1-007-002), ARI Papers (emphasis in original).

7. AR, "Man's Rights," in *Capitalism: The Unknown Ideal* (New York: Signet, 1968), p. 321.

8. Fred D. Miller Jr. and Adam Mossoff, "Ayn Rand's Theory of Rights: An Exposition and Response to Critics," in *Foundations of a Free Society: Reflections on Ayn Rand's Political Philosophy*, ed. Gregory Salmieri and Robert Mayhew (Pittsburgh: University of Pittsburgh Press, 2019), p. 120.

9. *NECRB*, September 1946 (emphasis in original).

10. AR, letter to RWL, October 9, 1946, in Berliner, *Letters*, p. 331 (emphasis in original).

11. RWL, letter to AR, October 11, 1946 (142-LN1-009-004), ARI Papers (emphasis in original).

12. AR, letter to RWL, November 3, 1946, in Berliner, *Letters*, pp. 344–46 (emphasis in original).

13. *TF*, p. 320 (emphasis in original).

14. AR, letter to RWL, November 3, 1946, in Berliner, *Letters*, p. 346.

15. RWL, letter to AR, November 6, 1946 (142-LN2-002-002–142-LN2-002-005), ARI Papers (emphasis in original). There is no evidence that Rand read the *Little House* books.

16. RWL, letter to AR, November 22, 1946 (142-LN2-003-002–142-LN2-003-005), ARI Papers (emphasis in original).

17. This tension between the classical liberal argument for individual autonomy and the need for solidarity among individuals to defend each other's rights is a longstanding one in classical liberal theory. For example, Harry Jaffa argued that Thomas Jefferson's mythos of the agrarian farmer represented an "*ad hoc* remedy" for this paradox. Harry V. Jaffa, *Crisis of the House Divided* (New York: Doubleday, 1959), pp. 323–27. For Rand, the solution was self-esteem; in a speech to West Point cadets, she praised soldiers for defending the country, not as an act of self-sacrifice but because "in my morality, the defense of one's country means that a man is personally unwilling to live as the conquered slave of any enemy, foreign or domestic." AR, *Philosophy: Who Needs It* (New York: Signet, 1982), p. 14. To the degree that a mythos was necessary to support this principle, it was expressed in her fiction.

18. For more on McIntire, see Markku Ruotsila, *Fighting Fundamentalist: Carl McIntire and the Politicization of American Fundamentalism* (New York: Oxford University Press, 2016). William Holtz—*The Ghost in the Little House* (Columbia: University of Missouri Press, 1995), p. 333—believes Lane did not take McIntire seriously, and only saw what she called "tactical value" in his work. But her repeated praise for his books and use of his arguments suggests a stronger affinity than that. Alexander McPhee-Browne, "Evangelists for Freedom: Libertarian Populism and the Intellectual Origins of Modern Conservatism, 1930–1950" (master's thesis, University of Melbourne, April 2018), https://minerva-access.unimelb.edu.au/bitstream/handle/11343/213890/Masters%20Thesis%20%28326632%29.pdf?sequence=2&isAllowed=y.

19. Roger Lea MacBride, ed., *The Lady and Tycoon: The Best of Letters between Rose Wilder Lane and Jasper Crane* (Caldwell, ID: Caxton Press, 1973), p. 231 (emphasis in original).

20. MacBride, *Lady and the Tycoon*, p. 44.

21. AR, letter to RWL, December 1946, in Berliner *Letters*, p. 354.

22. AR, letter to RWL, December 1946, in Berliner, *Letters*, p.355.

23. AR, letter to RWL, December 1946, in Berliner, *Letters*, p. 356.

24. RWL, letter to AR, dated "Sunday, the day after" (142-LN2-005-001), ARI Papers. See also RWL, letter to Robert LeFevre, August 2, 1957, Lane Papers, Hoover Library.

25. IMP, letter to AR, ca. January 19, 1944, Hoover Library, p. 26.

26. *DoF*, pp. 9–10.

27. Felix Morley, *For the Record* (South Bend, IN: Regnery Gateway, 1979), p. 428.

28. In both cases, it is possible that some version of the story is true. Stalin traveled in the Caucasian countries around the time Lane was there, and she may have attended some of the meetings Reed attended in New York in 1920. Holtz, *Ghost*, pp. 87, 340.

29. IMP, letter to Jasper Crane, January 9, 1946 (145-PA5-005-001), ARI Papers. See also RWL, letter to AR, dated "Sunday, the day after" (145-PA5-005-001), ARI Papers.

30. IMP, letter to AR, ca. August 30, 1945, Hoover Library, p. 81.

31. AR, letter to Leonard Read, May 18, 1946, in Berliner, *Letters*, pp. 275–76. The letter from Paterson to Read appears to have been lost.

32. RWL, fragmentary undated letter to AR (143_LN3_012_001), ARI Papers.

33. IMP, letter to AR, ca. October 7, 1943, Hoover Library, p. 21.

34. IMP, letter to AR, November 1944, Hoover Library, p. 60 (emphasis in original).

35. Wes D. Gehring, *Will Cuppy, American Satirist: A Biography* (Jefferson, NC: McFarland & Company, 2013), p. 143.

36. David Harriman, ed., *The Journals of Ayn Rand* (New York: Dutton, 1997), p. 392.

37. Harriman, *Journals*, p. 412.

38. AR, letter to IMP, February 7, 1948, in Berliner, *Letters*, pp. 190–91.

39. AR, letter to IMP, February 7, 1948, in Berliner, *Letters*, pp. 191–92.

40. IMP, letter to AR, ca. February 14, 1948, Hoover Library, p. 86.

41. IMP, letter to AR, ca. February 14, 1948, Hoover Library, p. 83.

42. AR, letter to IMP, February 7, 1948, in Berliner, *Letters*, p. 188; AR, *Atlas Shrugged* (New York: Dutton, 1992), pp. 239–40.

43. Caroline Fraser, ed., *The Little House Books* (New York: Library of America, 2012), vol. 2, p. 63.

44. Fraser, *Little House Books*, vol. 2, p. 64.

45. AR, *Atlas Shrugged*, p. 910.

46. IMP, *Never Ask*, p. 284. Paterson likely assisted Rand in researching the history of railroads. In a 1959 essay on the subject, Rand cited books by Oscar Lewis and Stewart Holbrook that Paterson had praised in "Turns with a Bookworm," (*NYHT*, July 24, 1938; August 14, 1938; August 28, 1938; October 12, 1947). In return, Paterson enjoyed the fruits of Rand's own research, even sharing the letter about the Twentieth Century Limited with her friend Ralph Henry, an important member of the American Association of Railroads who had helped her with research on *The God of the Machine*.

47. AR, *Atlas Shrugged*, p. 66.

48. AR, letter to IMP, March 13, 1948, in Berliner, *Letters*, pp. 199–200 (emphasis in original).

49. IMP, letter to AR, ca. March 24, 1948, Hoover Library, p. 93 (emphasis in original).

50. AR, letter to IMP, March 13, 1948, in Berliner, *Letters*, p. 201.

51. IMP, letter to AR, ca. April 15, 1948, Hoover Library, pp. 98–99 (emphasis in original).

52. Some scholars have detected a growing tension in their correspondence at this time, but in fact they remained affectionate. However, Rand did sometimes have difficulty detecting Paterson's sarcastic sense of humor. When Paterson claimed that she was the only person who had ever understood capitalism, Rand replied, "Does it seem to you that I have not been born yet . . .? It was from my theory of ethics that

you learned why the morality of altruism and sacrifice is evil and improper." AR, letter to IMP, May 8, 1948, in Berliner, *Letters*, p. 211. Paterson tried to soothe her. "I was not (in the ironic sentence you quote) suggesting that you do not know how capitalism works," she answered, but "you drive me to say that in fact I think I was the very first person to . . . see and describe the whole working connections of the economic system." IMP, letter to AR, ca. June, 1948, Hoover Library, p. 105. She did not mean that previous economists had failed to describe the phenomenon of trade, but that her insight into what would later be called "spontaneous order" was original. That, Rand conceded, was "most certainly" true. "I learned *from you* the historical and economic aspects of Capitalism, which I knew before only in a general way." AR, letter to IMP, May 17, 1948, in Berliner, *Letters*, p. 215 (emphasis in original).

53. IMP, letter to AR, ca. April 29, 1948, Hoover Library, p. 103 (emphasis in original).

54. AR, letter to IMP, May 8, 1948, in Berliner, *Letters*, p. 212.

55. AR, letter to IMP, May 8, 1948, in Berliner, *Letters*, p. 214.

56. IMP, letter to AR, ca. June 1948, Hoover Library, p. 107.

57. Robert Mayhew, *Ayn Rand and "Song of Russia": Communism and Anti-Communism in 1940s Hollywood* (Lanham, MD: Scarecrow Press, 2005), p. 64.

58. Harriman, *Journals*, p. 377.

59. Mayhew, *Song of Russia*, p. 146.

60. Harriman, *Journals*, p. 374.

61. Harriman, *Journals*, p. 380. Rand's statement that the victims of Soviet tyranny did not smile was ridiculed by communists at the time, and by Rand's detractors since, but it was true. Mayhew, *Song of Russia*, p. 167. Soviet official propaganda even characterized American smiling as a symptom of capitalist exploitation. Michael Bohm, "Why Russians Don't Smile," *Moscow Times*, April 28, 2011. Recent research supports the thesis that the American habit of smiling is a consequence of its freer and more diverse culture. Olga Khazan, "Why Some Cultures Frown on Smiling," *The Atlantic*, May 27, 2016. Soviet humor tended to be dark. Novelist Martin Amis even made the question of laughter and Stalin's rule the focus of his devastating book *Koba the Dread* (New York: Hyperion, 2002), in which he describes the uniquely dark quality of Soviet laughter. "There has never been a regime quite like [the USSR]," he wrote. "To have its subjects simultaneously quaking with terror, with hypothermia, with hunger—and with laughter" (p. 191).

62. RWL, letter to Jasper Crane, March 13, 1963, Lane Papers, Hoover Library.

63. *NECRB*, April 1947.

64. Pierre Lecomte du Noüy, *Human Destiny* (New York: David McKay, 1947), p. 217.

65. Orthogenesis has no scientific basis. See Stephen Jay Gould, *The Structure of Evolutionary Theory* (Cambridge, MA: Beklnap Press, 2002), chap. 5. For a thorough discussion of du Noüy, see Wallace Matson, *The Existence of God* (Ithaca, NY: Cornell University Press, 1965), pp. 102–31; George N. Schuster and Ralph E. Thorson, eds., *Evolution in Perspective: Commentaries in Honor of Pierre Lecomte du Noüy* (Notre Dame, IN: Notre Dame Press, 1970), p. xi.

66. Du Noüy, *Human Destiny*, p. 62.

67. Du Noüy, *Human Destiny*, pp. 237–38.

68. Du Noüy, *Human Destiny*, p. 238.

69. Paterson first mentioned him in 1937, when discussing his book *Biological Time*. IMP, "Turns," July 11, 1937. She discussed *Human Destiny* in "Turns," April 7, 1946; March 30, 1947; July 6, 1947; and December 26, 1948. See also Mary Lecomte du Noüy, *The Road to "Human Destiny": A Life of Pierre Lecomte du Noüy* (New York: Longmans, Green, 1955), p. 261.

70. IMP, "A Man of Destiny," in *Culture and Liberty: Writings of Isabel Paterson*, ed. Stephen Cox (New York: Transaction Publishers, 2015), p. 128 (emphasis in original). At the time Paterson was writing, it was still plausible to object that "the variations" in evolution "are not accounted for"; this issue was resolved only with the formulation of the "Darwinian synthesis" in the late 1950s. Peter J. Bowler, "Variation from Darwin to the Modern Synthesis," in *Variation: A Central Concept in Biology*, ed. Benedict Hallgrímsson and Brian K. Hall (Amsterdam: Elsevier, 2005). It is unclear why Paterson thought human exploitation of the environment proves human uniqueness, given that birds, apes, and other animals do the same thing.

71. IMP, "Turns," March 30, 1947.

72. RWL, letter to Robert LeFevre, December 26, 1957, Lane Papers, Hoover Library (emphasis in original).

73. In this, Lane differed slightly from Paterson. She thought the only thing du Noüy got wrong was his belief that God stands outside the physical realm.

74. See Wallace Matson, *Grand Theories and Everyday Beliefs* (Oxford: Oxford University Press, 2011), pp. 68–72. As for an "anti-chance" force preventing matter from losing its coherence, no such force exists. On the contrary, entropy dictates the opposite; matter does decohere eventually, and if one could wait long enough before putting one's foot down on the floor, the floor would indeed have withered away into dust. Unlike matter, living beings can stave off this process temporarily by taking in energy in the form of food, but they, too, eventually succumb. The "anti-chance" argument appears to assume that entropy is incompatible with stages of stability, which is false. See J. Bronowski, "New Concepts in the Evolution of Complexity: Stratified Stability and Unbounded Plans," *Synthese* 21, no. 2 (1970): 228–46.

75. Robert Mayhew, ed., *Ayn Rand's Marginalia* (Marina del Rey, CA: Ayn Rand Institute Press, 1998), p. 37.

76. For one thing, the argument raises again the question Rand posed to Lane: does God continually create every atom of His own being? See also Matson, *Existence of God*, pp. 93–96.

77. RWL, letter to AR, dated "Sunday, the day after" (LN- 143-LN3-005-006), ARI Papers.

78. *GoM*, p. 119. Rand, meanwhile, thought free will is a self-evident fact of the universe, just as life itself is, and that its origin was relatively unimportant. AR, "The Metaphysical and Man-Made," in *Philosophy: Who Needs It*, p. 26. Rand believed the idea of proving the *absence* of free will was

inherently self-contradictory. Although philosophers might debate precisely *how* volition works, she thought the existence of free will as not legitimately subject to debate. Leonard Peikoff, *Objectivism: The Philosophy of Ayn Rand* (New York: Meridian, 1993), pp. 69–70.

79. George Smith, "Atheism and Objectivism," *Reason*, November 1973.

80. Tobin Grant, "Why 1940s America Wasn't as Religious as You Think—The Rise and Fall of American Religion," Religion News Service, December 11, 2014; Benjamin E. Zeller, "American Postwar 'Big Religion': Reconceptualizing Twentieth-Century American Religion Using Big Science as a Model," *Church History* 80, no. 2 (2011): 321–51.

81. AR was repelled by Sheen's book because of its "blatant hatred for capitalism." AR, letter to IMP, April 11, 1948, in Berliner, *Letters*, p. 205; IMP agreed, telling AR she "did not think it worth reading." IMP, letter to AR, ca. April 1948, Hoover Library, p. 95.

82. RWL, letter to Robert LeFevre, December 26, 1957, Lane Papers, Hoover Library.

83. MacBride, *Lady and the Tycoon*, p. 174. As late as 1957, however, Lane insisted she was not a Christian. RWL, letter to Robert LeFevre, August 2, 1957, Lane Papers, Hoover Library.

84. RWL, letter to Robert LeFevre, December 26, 1957; RWL, letter to Jasper Crane, March 13, 1963, Lane Papers, Hoover Library.

Chapter 11

1. Thomas Fleming, *The New Dealers' War* (New York: Basic Books, 2002), pp. 477–82.

2. Joshua Muravchik, *Heaven on Earth: The Rise and Fall of Socialism* (New York: Encounter Books, 2002), p. 5.

3. Robert Higgs, *Depression, War, and Cold War: Studies in Political Economy* (Oxford: Oxford University Press, 2006), chap. 5.

4. George Gilder, *War and Poverty: A New Edition for the Twenty-First Century* (Washington: Regnery, 2012), pp. 375–76.

5. Robert H. Ferrell, *Harry S. Truman: A Life* (Columbia: University of Missouri Press, 2013), p. 91; Merle Miller, *Plain Speaking: An Oral Biography of Harry S. Truman* (New York: Berkley Books, 1980), p. 388; Donald Aida DiPace, *Citizen Soldier: A Life of Harry S. Truman* (New York: Basic Books, 2012), p. 71; David McCullough, *Truman* (New York: Simon & Schuster, 1992), p. 406.

6. McCullough, *Truman*, p. 470.

7. McCullough, *Truman*, pp. 468, 473–74.

8. David Henderson, "The U.S. Postwar Miracle," Mercatus Center Working Paper No. 10-67, Mercatus Center at George Masion University, November 2010; Cecil Bohanon, "Economic Recovery: Lessons from the Post-World War II Period," policy brief, Mercatus Center, August 2012.

9. Walter MacDougall, *The Heavens and the Earth: A Political History of the Space Age* (New York: Basic Books, 1985), chap. 10.

10. For more on cargo cults, see Glynn Cochrane, *Big Men and Cargo Cults* (Oxford: Clarendon Press, 1970); Richard Feynman, "Cargo Cult Science," in *The Pleasure of Finding Things Out* (Cambridge, MA: Helix Books, 1999), pp. 205–17.

11. Henry Hazlitt, *The Failure of the "New Economics"* (Auburn, AL: Mises Institute, 2007).

12. Peter Boettke and Patrick Newman, "The Consequences of Keynes," *Journal of Markets and Morality* 20, no. 1 (2017): 158.

13. IMP, "Turns with a Bookworm," *NYHT*, June 8, 1941.

14. *NECRB*, August 1950.

15. Ludwig von Mises, *Human Action* (Auburn, AL: Mises Institute, 1998), p. 737.

16. *NECRB*, October 1949; Robert Hessen, review of *Human Action*, *Objectivist Newsletter*, September 1963.

17. Ludwig von Mises, *Theory and History* (Auburn, AL: Mises Institute, 2007), p. 14; Jörg Guido Hülsmann, *Mises: The Last Knight of Liberalism* (Auburn, AL: Mises Institute, 2007), p. 959.

18. Ludwig von Mises, *Liberalism: The Classical Tradition* (Irvington-on-Hudson, NY: Foundation for Economic Education, 1996), p. 34.

19. *NECRB*, November 1945.

20. Ludwig von Mises, *Omnipotent Government* (New Haven, CT: Yale University Press 1944), p. 120.

21. *NECRB*, November 1945.

22. AR, letter to RWL, August 21, 1946, in Michael Berliner, ed., *Letters of Ayn Rand* (New York: Dutton, 1995), p. 308.

23. David M. Levy, Sandra J. Peart, and Margaret Albert, "Economic Liberals as Quasi-Public Intellectuals: The Democratic Dimension," in *Documents on Government and the Economy: Research in the History of Economic Thought and Methodology*, ed. Marianne Johnson (Bingley, UK: Emerald Publishing, 2012), vol. 30-B, pp. 47–48.

24. Lorie Tarshis, *The Elements of Economics: An Introduction to the Theory of Price and Employment* (Cambridge, MA: Riverside Press, 1947), pp. 53, 346, 686.

25. Tarshis, *Elements*, chap. 20.

26. Tarshis, *Elements*, p. 421.

27. Tarshis, *Elements*, p. 3.

28. Tarshis, *Elements*, p. 491.

29. Tarshis, *Elements*, p. 438.

30. William F. Buckley Jr., *God and Man at Yale*, rev. ed. (Chicago: Regnery, 1986), p. 81 (emphasis in original).

31. Tarshis, *Elements*, p. 54.

32. Tarshis, *Elements*, p. 686.

33. Sar A. Levitan, review, *Political Science Quarterly* 63, no. 2 (1948): 302.

34. *NECRB*, September 1947.

35. IMP, letter to AR, ca. February 14, 1948, Hoover Library, p. 85; IMP, letter to AR, ca. February 1948, Hoover Library, p. 87.

36. IMP, letter to AR, ca. February 1948, Hoover Library, pp. 87–88 (emphasis in original).

37. "Screen Guide for Americans" (November 1947), in *Plain Talk: An Anthology from the Leading Anti-Communist Magazine of the 40s*, ed. Isaac Don Levine (New Rochelle, NY: Arlington House, 1951), pp. 387–88.

38. IMP, letter to AR, March 8, 1948, Hoover Library, p. 92.

39. AR, letter to IMP, May 17, 1948, in Berliner, ed., *Letters*, 217.

40. John Cogley, *Report on Blacklisting*, vol. 1, *Movies* (New York: Fund for the Republic, 1956), pp. 76–77.

41. Anne Heller, *Ayn Rand and the World She Made* (New York: Anchor Books, 2010), p. 214.

42. Heller, *Ayn Rand*, pp. 214–15 (emphasis in original).

43. Michael S. Berliner, "*The Fountainhead* Reviews," in *Essays on Ayn Rand's* The Fountainhead, ed. Robert Mayhew (Lanham, MD: Lexington Books, 2007), p. 79.

44. IMP, letter to AR, July 30, 1945, Hoover Library, p. 66.

45. Stephen Cox, *The Woman and the Dynamo: Isabel Paterson and the Idea of America* (New Brunswick, NJ: Transaction Publishers, 2004), p. 314.

46. The studio did not even bother telling Stanwyck she had been rejected. Rand herself broke the news. Stephen Michael Shearer, *Patricia Neal: An Unquiet Life* (Lexington: University Press of Kentucky, 2006), p. 60.

47. Harold Heffernan, "Gary Cooper at Last Becomes Glib," *St. Louis Post-Dispatch*, September 30, 1948.

48. Richard Kluger, *The Paper: The Life and Death of the New York Herald Tribune* (New York: Knopf, 1986), pp. 475–76.

49. Cox, *Woman and the Dynamo*, pp. 317–23.

50. IMP, letter to Edward Hall, February 24, 1959, in *Culture and Liberty: Writings of Isabel Paterson*, ed. Stephen Cox (New York: Transaction Publishers, 2015), p. 244 (emphasis in original).

51. Cox, *Woman and the Dynamo*, p. 358.

52. IMP, letter to Edward Hall, February 24, 1959, in Cox, *Culture and Liberty*, p. 244.

53. IMP, "Turns," August 25, 1946.

54. IMP, letter to Muriel Hall, November 1957, in Cox, *Culture and Liberty*, p. 237.

55. John Chamberlain, "Ayn Rand's Political Parable and Thundering Melodrama," *NYHT*, October 6, 1957.

56. Michael S. Berliner, "The *Atlas Shrugged* Reviews," in *Essays on Ayn Rand's* Atlas Shrugged, ed. Robert Mayhew (Lanham, MD: Lexington Books: 2009), pp. 133–43.

57. A good account of Buckley's war against Rand is Carl T. Bogus, *Buckley: William F. Buckley Jr. and the Rise of American Conservatism* (New York: Bloomsbury Press, 2011), pp. 199–218.

58. Buckley claimed that upon first meeting Rand, her "very first words" to him were "You are too intelligent to believe in God." William F. Buckley, *Right Reason* (New York: Knopf Doubleday, 1985), p. 410; John B. Judis, *William F. Buckley Jr.: Patron Saint of the Conservatives* (New York: Touchstone, 1988), p. 160. Although something like this may have happened, we only have Buckley's version of the story, and it seems unlikely that it happened in the way described. For one thing, the sentence is a quotation from Rand's favorite poet, Alexander Blok, who once told Maxim Gorky, "We have become too intelligent to believe in God, yet not strong enough to believe only in ourselves." Maxim Gorky, *Foma Gordeyev* (New York: Delta, 1962), p. 6. For another, it would have been out of character for Rand to begin a conversation that way, particularly with anyone she considered intelligent. Rand did not consider belief in God a matter of intelligence per se, nor did she refuse to befriend people who believed in God. Finally, it was Buckley, not Rand, who appears to have enjoyed trying to provoke based on religion. Buckley boasted that he "used to send her postcards in liturgical Latin." Buckley, *Right Reason*, p. 410. In fact, in his reply to Paterson's letter objecting to the Chambers review of *Atlas Shrugged*, he chuckled that he had just sent her such a postcard. Whatever the real circumstances may have been, Buckley's animosity toward Rand likely obscured his memory of the actual incident. My thanks to Robert Hessen for insights on this question.

59. "Isabel M. Paterson Dies," *NYHT*, January 11, 1961.

60. AR, review of *GoM*, *Objectivist Newsletter*, October 1964.

61. Paterson's biographer Stephen Cox suggests that Rand sought to distance herself from Paterson's engineering terminology because it "led directly to . . . the God of the universe and theism." The truth is more likely the reverse: the reason Rand refused to characterize Paterson's language as merely metaphorical was because she admired its purely mechanistic frame of reference—which in Rand's view clashed with Paterson's appeal to religion. Had she viewed Paterson's argument as leading logically to a belief in theism, she would have been *more* inclined to characterize it as merely metaphorical. Stephen Cox, "Merely Metaphorical? Ayn Rand, Isabel Paterson, and the Language of Theory," *Journal of Ayn Rand Studies* 8, no. 2 (2007): 257.

62. Henry Adams, *The Education of Henry Adams* (Boston: Houghton Mifflin, 1918), p. 388.

63. *GoM*, p. 156.

64. *GoM*, p. 156.

65. HLM, letter to SL, October 15, 1945, in *Letters of H. L. Mencken*, ed. Guy J. Forgue (New York: Knopf, 1961), p. 491.

66. Notwithstanding her objections to SL, Lane praised *Kingsblood Royal* in the *NECRB* as "shrewd" and "essential" reading. *NECRB*, May 1947.

67. Harriman, *Journals*, p. 405; Eubank proposes a plan to limit the sales of books as a form of wealth redistribution (AR, *Atlas Shrugged* [New York: Dutton, 1992], p. 134), paralleling Cain's 1946 proposal to create an "American Authors Authority"—a compulsory union of writers that would own the copyrights to writers' works, and control their licensing. When Cain's idea gained traction, Rand, Lane, and other writers organized the American Writers Association, which campaigned against and ultimately defeated

the proposal. Roy Hoopes, *Cain: The Biography of James M. Cain* (New York: Holt, Rinehart & Winston, 1982), chap. 16. Emma Chalmers's fondness for community farming (*Atlas Shrugged*, p. 937) satirizes Eleanor Roosevelt's enthusiasm for similar endeavors, such as the Subsistence Homesteads project's Arthurdale and Jersey Homesteads experiments. Nancy Hoffman, *Eleanor Roosevelt and the Arthurdale Experiment* (North Haven, CT: Linnet Books, 2001); Paul Conkin, *Tomorrow a New World: The New Deal Community Program* (Ithaca, NY: Cornell University Press, 1959), chap. 10 and 11.

68. Rand, Paterson, and Lane all spoke out against segregation and other forms of racial oppression. Paterson excoriated racism and the Ku Klux Klan in her column (calling such ideas "bunk" [IMP, "Adventures in Biology and Bunk," in Cox, *Culture and Liberty*, p. 95] and "a relapse into a primitive social method of action" [IMP, "Turns," May 4, 1947; see also February 5, 1939]). Lane went further, writing a column in a black newspaper for years, and attacking racism in the *NECRB* (e.g., May 1947, June 1947, and July 1950). Rand, too, condemned racism and its variations as "primitive" forms of collectivism. AR, "Racism," in *Objectivist Newsletter*, September 1963; "Global Balkanization," in *The Voice of Reason: Essays in Objectivist Thought*, ed. Leonard Peikoff (New York: New American Library, 1990), p. 115. The three also championed other causes now labeled "liberal." Rand was an outspoken advocate of abortion rights, for instance. Paterson prided herself on being among the first journalists ever to publish an article calling for the legalization of prostitution. Cox, *Woman and the Dynamo*, p. 108.

69. IMP, "Turns," October 12, 1947.

70. *NECRB*, July 1950.

71. This phenomenon has been studied in detail by several scholars, beginning with John Chamberlain, whose November 1948 *Fortune* article "The Businessman in Fiction" drew attention to the virtual absence of admirable business owners as characters in contemporary literature. Others followed suit. Howard R. Smith, "The American Businessman in the American Novel," *Southern Economic Journal* 25, no. 3 (1959): 265–302; Henry Nash Smith, "The Search for a Capitalist Hero: Businessmen in American Fiction," in *The Business Establishment*, ed. Earl F. Cheit (New York: Wiley, 1964); Emily Stipes Watts, *The Businessman in American Literature* (Athens: University of Georgia Press, 1982). Films in which entrepreneurs and business owners are presented as heroes remain exceptionally rare.

72. Paul Simon and Art Garfunkel, "A Simple Desultory Philippic," Track 9 on *Parsley, Sage, Rosemary and Thyme*, Columbia Records, 1966.

73. AR, "Don't Let It Go" (1971), in *Philosophy: Who Needs It*, p. 280.

74. AR, "Don't Let It Go," p. 282.

75. Badger Clark, *Sun and Saddle Leather* (Boston: Gorham Press, 1919), pp. 86–88.

76. AR, "Global Balkanization," in Peikoff, *Voice of Reason*, p. 129. It is tempting to imagine that Rand was introduced to the poem either by Paterson (who was prone to quoting poetry) or by Lane, who, like Clark, was from South Dakota, and who had published articles alongside Clark's poems in the 1910s. But no evidence of such a connection appears to exist. The copy of the poem in Rand's papers is clipped from a magazine dating to the 1960s, and neither Lane nor Paterson is known to have ever referred to Clark in their writings. I thank Shoshana Knapp for helping look into this.

77. Caroline Fraser, ed., *The Little House Books* (New York: Library of America, 2012), vol. 2, p. 412.

78. William Holtz, *The Ghost in the Little House* (Columbia: University of Missouri Press, 1995), p. 347.

79. RWL, *Discovery of Liberty*, manuscript 41, Lane Papers, Hoover Library.

80. RWL, *Discovery of Liberty*, manuscript 52, Lane Papers, Hoover Library.

81. RWL, *Discovery of Liberty*, manuscript 69, Lane Papers, Hoover Library.

82. RWL, *Discovery of Liberty*, manuscript 102, Lane Papers, Hoover Library.

Epilogue

1. Caroline Fraser, *Prairie Fires: The American Dreams of Laura Ingalls Wilder* (New York: Metropolitan Books, 2017), pp. 498–99.

2. Jennifer Burns, "The Three 'Furies' of Libertarianism: Rose Wilder Lane, Isabel Paterson, and Ayn Rand," *Journal of American History* 102, no. 3 (2015): 774.

3. Whittaker Chambers, *Odyssey of a Friend: Whittaker Chambers' Letters to William F. Buckley, Jr.* (New York: Putnam, 1970), p. 94.

4. IMP, "Turns," March 7, 1937.

5. Robert S. McElvaine, *The Great Depression* (New York: Times Books, 1993), p. 340.

6. AR, "About a Woman President," in *The Voice of Reason: Essays in Objectivist Thought*, ed. Leonard Peikoff (New York: New American Library, 1990), p. 269.

7. AR, *Atlas Shrugged* (New York: Dutton, 1992), p. 51.

8. Anne C. Heller, *Ayn Rand and the World She Made* (New York: Anchor Books, 2010), p. 249.

9. *Ladies' Home Journal*, October 1936.

10. RWL, *The Woman's Day Book of American Needlework* (New York: Simon & Schuster, 1963), p. 10.

11. RWL, *American Needlework*, p. 205.

12. Rozsika Parker, foreword to *The Subversive Stitch: Embroidery and the Making of the Feminine* (London: Women's Press, 1984).

13. RWL, *American Needlework*, p. 10.

14. Nora Caplan-Bricker, "Why Aren't There More Female Libertarians?," *New Republic*, October 30, 2013.

15. Melissa Deckman, "Melissa Deckman on the Limits of Libertarianism for Women," Public Religion Research Institute, November 22, 2013, https://www.prri.org/spotlight/melissa-deckman-on-the-limits-of-libertarianism-for-women/.

16. "The Gender Gap in Religion around the World," Pew Research Center, March 22, 2016.

17. June Melby Benowitz, *Days of Discontent: American Women and Right-Wing Politics, 1933–1945* (Dekalb: Illinois University Press, 2002), 174–75.

18. Albert Jay Nock, *Letters from Albert Jay Nock, 1924–1945* (Caldwell, ID: Caxton Printers, 1949), p. 183 (emphasis in original).

▼ Index ◤

Note: Within page numbers, information in figures is indicated by *f*; n designates a numbered note.

◤ About the Author ◥

Timothy Sandefur is vice president for legal affairs at the Goldwater Institute, where he also holds the Clarence J. & Katherine P. Duncan Chair in Constitutional Government. He has litigated important cases involving economic liberty, private property, and other individual rights. Sandefur is the author of seven books—*Some Notes on the Silence* (2022), *The Ascent of Jacob Bronowski* (2019), *Frederick Douglass: Self-Made Man* (2018), *Cornerstone of Liberty: Property Rights in 21st Century America* (second edition, coauthored with Christina Sandefur, 2016), *The Permission Society* (2016), *The Conscience of the Constitution* (2014), and *The Right to Earn a Living: Economic Freedom and the Law* (2010)—as well as scholarly articles on subjects ranging from eminent domain and economic liberty to antitrust, Indian law, copyright, evolution and creationism, slavery and the Civil War, and legal issues in Shakespeare, ancient Greek drama, and *Star Trek*.

◤ About the Cato Institute ◥

Founded in 1977, the Cato Institute is a public policy research foundation dedicated to broadening the parameters of policy debate to allow consideration of more options that are consistent with the principles of limited government, individual liberty, and peace. To that end, the Institute strives to achieve greater involvement of the intelligent, concerned lay public in questions of policy and the proper role of government.

The Institute is named for *Cato's Letters*, libertarian pamphlets that were widely read in the American Colonies in the early 18th century and played a major role in laying the philosophical foundation for the American Revolution.

Despite the achievement of the nation's Founders, today virtually no aspect of life is free from government encroachment. A pervasive intolerance for individual rights is shown by government's arbitrary intrusions into private economic transactions and its disregard for civil liberties. And while freedom around the globe has notably increased in the past several decades, many countries have moved in the opposite direction, and most governments still do not respect or safeguard the wide range of civil and economic liberties.

To address those issues, the Cato Institute undertakes an extensive publications program on the complete spectrum of policy issues. Books, monographs, and shorter studies are commissioned to examine the federal budget, Social Security, regulation, military spending, international trade, and myriad other issues.

In order to maintain its independence, the Cato Institute accepts no government funding. Contributions are received from foundations, corporations, and individuals, and other revenue is generated from the sale of publications. The Institute is a nonprofit, tax-exempt, educational foundation under Section 501(c)3 of the Internal Revenue Code.

CATO INSTITUTE
1000 Massachusetts Ave. NW
Washington, DC 20001
www.cato.org

Libertarianism.org

Liberty. It's a simple idea and the linchpin of a complex system of values and practices: justice, prosperity, responsibility, toleration, cooperation, and peace. Many people believe that liberty is the core political value of modern civilization itself, the one that gives substance and form to all the other values of social life. They're called libertarians.

Libertarianism.org is the Cato Institute's treasury of resources about the theory and history of liberty. The book you're holding is a small part of what Libertarianism.org has to offer. In addition to hosting classic texts by historical libertarian figures and original articles from modern-day thinkers, Libertarianism.org publishes podcasts, videos, online introductory courses, and books on a variety of topics within the libertarian tradition.